Adobe® Photoshop® 7.0

User Guide

Adobe

Contents

Chapter 2   **Getting Images into Photoshop and ImageReady**

Chapter 3   **Working with Color**

Chapter 17

Introduction

Welcome to Adobe® Photoshop® 7.0, the professional image-editing standard. With its integrated Web tool application, Adobe ImageReady®, Photoshop delivers a comprehensive environment for professional designers and graphics producers to create sophisticated images for print, the Web, wireless devices, and other media. Moreover, Photoshop provides a consistent work environment with other Adobe applications including Adobe Illustrator®, Adobe InDesign®, Adobe GoLive®, Adobe LiveMotion™, Adobe After Effects®, and Adobe Premiere®.

Registration

Adobe is confident you will find that its software greatly increases your productivity. So that Adobe can continue to provide you with the highest quality software, offer technical support, and inform you about new Photoshop software developments, please register your application.

When you first start Photoshop or ImageReady, you're prompted to register online. You can choose to submit the form directly or fax a printed copy. You can also register by filling out and returning the registration card included with your software package.

Installing Adobe Photoshop and ImageReady

You must install Photoshop and ImageReady from the Adobe Photoshop CD onto your hard drive; you cannot run the program from the CD.

Follow the on-screen installation instructions. For more detailed information, see the *HowToInstall* file on the CD. The single installer installs both Photoshop and ImageReady.

Getting started

Adobe provides a variety of options for you to learn Photoshop, including printed guides, online Help, and tool tips. Using the Adobe Online feature, you can easily access a host of continually updated Web resources for learning Photoshop, from tips and tutorials to tech support information. Getting up to speed depends on your experience with previous versions of Photoshop and ImageReady.

If you are new to Photoshop:

• See "An Overview of Adobe Photoshop" on page 9 to get an introduction to the software.

• Explore the Toolbox Overviews in online Help to get familiar with the basic tools and their functions. See "Using online Help" on page 3.

- Use the tool tips feature to help identify tools, buttons, and palette controls as you work in Photoshop and ImageReady. See "Using tool tips" on page 4.

- Go to the Adobe.com Web site and work through some of the Photoshop tutorials for hands-on lessons. See "Using Web resources" on page 4.

If you are an experienced Photoshop user:

- See "What's New in Photoshop 7.0" on page 15.

- Scan through "Using the File Browser (Photoshop)" on page 68 to learn how to view, sort, and organize images without opening the files.

- See "Working with brushes" on page 172 to explore the powerful new paint engine.

- See "About optimization" on page 333 and "Using the Rollovers palette" on page 315 to see new Web features such as transparency and simplified authoring.

If you want to focus on Web features:

- See "Create compelling Web designs" on page 12 for an introduction to the powerful Web tools.

- See "Creating and viewing slices" on page 288 to explore layer-based, user-defined, and automatic slices.

- See "About optimization" on page 333 to learn how to fine-tune your Web designs by applying transparency, dithered transparency, or weighted optimization.

- See "Using the Rollovers palette" on page 315 to see how easy it is to manage slices, rollovers, image maps, and animations.

- See "Creating and editing animations" on page 321 to learn how to create instant GIF animations from layered Photoshop and Illustrator files.

If you want to concentrate on photo editing and retouching:

- See "Edit images with ease" on page 10 for an introduction to the Photoshop image-editing features.

- See "Using the File Browser (Photoshop)" on page 68 to find out how to quickly inspect files before opening them in Photoshop.

- See "Using the healing brush tool (Photoshop)" on page 135 to learn how to remove flaws effortlessly while preserving tonality and texture.

- See "Creating multiple-image layouts (Photoshop)" on page 376 to find out how to quickly create contact sheets and customized photo pages.

- For more information on how to fine-tune the color and tonality in your photographs, see "Making color adjustments" in online Help.

If you want to focus on productivity features:

- See "Automate repetitive tasks" on page 13 for an overview of the Photoshop and ImageReady productivity tools.

- See "Using the File Browser (Photoshop)" on page 68 to learn how to locate and organize images easily, and how to manage files and folders.

- See "About data-driven graphics" on page 415 to learn how to produce variable designs such as Web banners or catalog pages automatically.

- See "Using the Rollovers palette" on page 315 to see how easy it is to get instant access to all document states.

- See "Managing files with WebDAV (Photoshop)" on page 72 to learn about the asset management features in Photoshop.

Using the printed documentation

In addition to the printed documents included with the application, you will find many PDF documents on the Photoshop CD; Adobe Acrobat® Reader® software, included on the Photoshop CD, lets you view PDF files.

Two printed documents are included with Photoshop 7.0:

Adobe Photoshop 7.0 User Guide   Contains essential information on using Photoshop and ImageReady commands and features. Complete information on all topics is available in online Help. The printed guide and help also indicate when a topic, procedure, or command pertains specifically to Photoshop or ImageReady, e.g., "Choose View > Actual Pixels (Photoshop) or View > Actual Size (ImageReady)."

Adobe Photoshop Quick Reference Card
Contains basic information about the Adobe Photoshop and ImageReady tools and palettes, and shortcuts for using them. Shortcuts are also included in the online Help.

Using online Help

Adobe Photoshop and ImageReady include complete documentation in an HTML-based help system. The help system includes all of the information in the *Adobe Photoshop 7.0 User Guide* plus information on additional features, keyboard shortcuts, and full-color illustrations.

Online Help provides three ways of locating information. The Contents and Index tabs let you find general information, and the Search tab lets you look up specific words or phrases.

For more detailed information about using online Help, click the Help button next to the Content, Index, and Search tabs.

To properly view online Help topics, you need Netscape Communicator 4.0 (or later) or Microsoft® Internet Explorer 4.0 (or later). You must also have JavaScript active.

To start online Help:

Do one of the following:

- Choose Help > Photoshop Help (Photoshop) or Help > ImageReady Help (ImageReady).

- Press F1 (Windows).

Using tool tips

The tool tips feature lets you display the name of tools, or buttons and controls in palettes.

To identify a tool or control:

Position the pointer over a tool or control and pause. A tool tip appears showing the name and keyboard shortcut (if any) for the item.

If tool tips don't appear, the preference for displaying them may be turned off.

To display tool tips:

1 Choose Edit > Preferences > General (Windows and Mac OS 9) or Photoshop > Preferences > General (Mac OS X).

2 Select Show Tool Tips, and click OK.

Note: Tool tips are not available in most dialog boxes.

Using Web resources

If you have an Internet connection, you can use the Adobe Online feature to access additional resources for learning Photoshop and ImageReady located on the Adobe.com Web site. From the Adobe.com home page, select Products. Then choose Photoshop and go to Training & Events.

These resources are continually updated and include the following:

Tutorials and Techniques Provide step-by-step instructions on using Photoshop or help on performing advanced techniques. These tutorials can help you go beyond the reference information contained in the user guide and show you how to use Photoshop with other applications.

How Tos and Backgrounders Provide access to procedures for performing tasks in Photoshop and to detailed reference information on a variety of topics. This information provides help on everything from common processes to the complex inter-application tasks necessary to prepare graphics for the Web.

Troubleshooting Provides access to solutions to problems you may encounter using Photoshop. You should check out troubleshooting information available through Adobe Online and the Adobe Web site before you call customer support.

To access the Adobe home page for your region:

1 Open the Adobe U.S. home page at www.adobe.com.

2 From the Adobe Worldwide menu, choose your geographical region. Adobe's home page is customized for 20 different geographical regions.

About Adobe Online

Adobe Online provides access to the latest tutorials, quicktips, and other Web content for Photoshop and other Adobe products. Using Adobe Online, you can also download and view the current version of the Photoshop Top Issues document containing the latest Photoshop technical support solutions. Bookmarks are also included to take you quickly to noteworthy Adobe- and Photoshop-related sites.

Using Adobe Online

Adobe Online is constantly changing, so you should refresh before you use it. Refreshing through Adobe Online updates bookmarks and buttons so you can quickly access the most current content available. You can use preferences to automatically refresh Adobe Online.

When you set up an Internet connection to Adobe Online, Adobe can either notify you whenever new information is available through the Updates feature or automatically download that information to your hard disk. If you choose not to use the automatic download feature, you can still view and download new files whenever they are available using the Updates command in the Help menu.

To use Adobe Online:

1 In Photoshop or ImageReady, choose Help > Adobe Online, or click the icon at the top of the toolbox.

Adobe Online icon

Note: *You must have an Internet connection to access Adobe Online. Adobe Online will launch your browser using your default Internet configuration.*

2 If prompted, do any of the following:

- Click Updates to access updated files.

- Click Preferences to set up your operating system to enable automatic updates.

Note: *You can set Adobe Online preferences by choosing Edit > Preferences > Adobe Online (Windows and Mac OS 9) or Photoshop > Preferences > Adobe Online (Mac OS X).*

- Click Go Online to access the Adobe Web site.

- Click Cancel (Windows and Mac OS 9) or Close (Mac OS X) to return to Photoshop or ImageReady.

Accessing Adobe Online through the Help menu

The Help menu includes options to view and download information from the Adobe Web site.

To view updated articles or documents:

Click Help and choose the topic you want to view.

To view and download information from the Adobe Web site using the Help menu:

1 In Photoshop or ImageReady, choose Edit > Preferences > Adobe Online (Windows and Mac OS 9) or Photoshop > Preferences > Adobe Online (Mac OS X).

Choose an item from the Check for Updates pop-up menu to determine how often Photoshop launches an automatic update.

2 Choose Help > Updates.

3 Select a View Option:

• Select New Updates to view only the files that are new since the last time you viewed downloadable files or were notified of them.

• Select All Updates to view all the files on Adobe's Web site that are currently available.

4 To see a description of a file, click on a filename and view its description in the Item Description section.

5 To see the location where a file will be installed if downloaded, select a file and view its location in the Download Location section. To change the location, click Choose.

6 To download a file, click the check box and then click Download.

7 To close the Adobe Product Updates dialog box, click Close.

Other learning resources

Other Adobe learning resources are available but are not included with your application.

Adobe Press Offers a library of books that provide in-depth training in Adobe software, including the acclaimed Classroom in a Book series developed by experts at Adobe. For information on purchasing Adobe Press titles, visit the Adobe Web site at www.adobe.com, or contact your local book distributor.

The Adobe Certification program Offers users, instructors, and training centers the opportunity to demonstrate their product proficiency and promote their software skills as Adobe Certified Experts or Adobe Certified Training Providers. Certification is available worldwide. Visit the Partnering with Adobe Web site at www.partners.adobe.com to learn how you can become certified.

Customer support

When you register your product, you may be entitled to technical support. Terms may vary depending on the country of residence. For more information, refer to the technical support card provided with the Photoshop documentation.

Customer support on Adobe Online

Adobe Online provides access to the Photoshop Knowledgebase, where you can find answers to technical questions.

Additional customer support resources

Adobe Systems provides several forms of automated technical support:

- See the ReadMe and ReadMe First! files installed with the program for information that became available after this guide went to press.

- Explore the extensive customer support information on Adobe's World Wide Web site (www.adobe.com). To access the Adobe Web site from Photoshop, choose Help > Adobe Online or click the icon at the top of the toolbox. See "Using Web resources" on page 4.

- Read the Top Issues PDF that is available from the Help menu.

An Overview of Adobe Photoshop

This overview introduces you to the key features in Adobe Photoshop, the professional image-editing standard. Photoshop provides a comprehensive toolset, unmatched precision, and powerful creative options to help you create professional-quality images for Web, print, and emerging media such as wireless devices. And when you use Photoshop in tandem with other Adobe software, you can take advantage of superior Adobe technologies such as cross-product color management tools, Smart Object technology, and transparency.

Explore state-of-the-art tools

With its comprehensive set of retouching, painting, drawing, and Web tools, Photoshop helps you complete any image-editing task efficiently. And with features like the History palette and editable layer effects, you can experiment freely without sacrificing efficiency.

Work more efficiently

From file management to workspace controls to editing multiple steps at one time—Photoshop gives you the tools you need to keep the work on track and bring it in on deadline.

File Browser Quickly inspect images before opening them in Photoshop. The easy-to-view File Browser displays thumbnails and metadata such as date modified, dimensions, and EXIF information from your digital camera. You can also use the File Browser to sort files and manage folders. See "Using the File Browser (Photoshop)" on page 68.

Layers With layers, you can work on one element without disturbing others. To rearrange elements, simply shift the order in the Layers palette. You can lock layers to prevent accidental changes, hide them to get a clear view of the element you're working on, and link layers to move them as a group. The Layers palette also makes it easy to apply instant, editable effects including blending modes, adjustment layers, and layer effects. See "Using the Layers palette" on page 229.

Options bar The tool options bar gives you instant access to different settings for the tool you're using. You can also customize any tool and save the customized version to use again. See "Using the tool options bar" on page 21 and "Using tool presets (Photoshop)" on page 22.

History palette Undo or redo multiple steps with the History palette. Or store a snapshot—a temporary copy of the image—in the palette, and continue experimenting. If you don't like the results, simply return to the snapshot. You can also create multiple snapshots, capturing different effects, to compare them easily. See "Using the History palette" on page 33 and "Making a snapshot of an image (Photoshop)" on page 35.

Customizable workspace Personalize your Photoshop desktop by arranging a layout of palettes and saving the arrangement as a workspace. Or create task-specific workspaces—one to provide easy access to painting tools, for example, and another for photo retouching. See "Customizing your workspace" on page 24.

Context-sensitive menus Get instant access to commands relevant to the active tool, palette, or selection by right-clicking (Windows) or Control-clicking (Mac OS). See "Using context menus" on page 28.

Edit images with ease

Photoshop delivers high-powered image editing, photo retouching, and compositing tools to help you get professional-quality results.

Color correction Photoshop offers two basic methods for adjusting color in an image. Use the options in the Image > Adjustments menu—including the Auto Color command, which analyzes the image to make instant and reliable color corrections—to change the image permanently. Or use an adjustment layer to apply editable color and tonal corrections. See "About adjustment layers and fill layers" on page 257. For more information, see "Making color adjustments" and "Using the Auto Color command (Photoshop)" in online Help.

Healing brush Effortlessly remove dust, scratches, blemishes, and other flaws with a single tool. The healing brush automatically preserves the shading, lighting, and texture of the original photo. See "Using the healing brush tool (Photoshop)" on page 135.

Selection tools From the click-and-drag marquee tools, to magnetic selection tools that snap to the edges of an element, to the pen tool that lets you define a shape precisely, Photoshop offers a range of shape-selection options. You can also select by color, using the magic wand or the Color Range command. And the Extract command provides a sophisticated way to isolate a foreground object from the background. See "About selections" on page 103.

Precision masking Masks let you hide part of an image, or protect and preserve one section while you apply color changes, filters, or other effects to the rest of the artwork. You can also use masks to save complex selection borders for reuse. See "Masking layers" on page 259 and "About masks (Photoshop)" on page 223.

Clipping paths Use a clipping path to cut a foreground element away from the background—without actually altering the original image. See "Using image clipping paths to create transparency" on page 377.

Sharpening controls Photoshop's sharpening tools include the powerful Unsharp Mask filter, based on traditional film compositing techniques. Use Unsharp Mask after scaling, rotating, color correcting—any process that affects the pixel structure of an image—to bring the artwork into crisp focus. For more information, see "Sharpening images" in online Help.

Edge smoothing Use the anti-aliasing option to smooth the jagged edges of a selection, or apply feathering to create soft edges. See "Softening the edges of a selection" on page 111.

Contact sheet generation Export an entire folder of images on a single page to allow easy cataloging, previewing, and printing. Or use the Picture Package feature to print photos of different sizes on the same page. See "Creating multiple-image layouts (Photoshop)" on page 376.

Web photo display Showcase your work online by posting a Web photo gallery. You'll find a collection of ready-made templates on the Photoshop CD to make the job quick and easy—and you can stamp each image with copyright text to help protect against illegal downloads. See "Creating Web photo galleries (Photoshop)" on page 309.

Enjoy unlimited creative options

With innovative special-effect options and powerful painting and drawing tools, there's no limit to the results you can achieve with Photoshop.

Painting tools The powerful Photoshop paint engine lets you simulate traditional painting techniques, including charcoal, pastel, and wet or dry brush effects. Choose from the many preset brush styles on the Photoshop CD, or use the Brushes palette to create your own unique effects. See "Working with brushes" on page 172 and "Selecting preset brushes" on page 173.

Drawing tools Draw resolution-independent vector shapes instantly with the line, rectangle, ellipse, polygon, and custom shape tools. Or use the pen tool to draw just as you would in Adobe Illustrator. Because they're vector shapes, you can edit them easily. See "Drawing shapes and paths" on page 147.

Layer effects Shadows, glows, bevels, embossed effects, and more—with the Layer Styles dialog box, adding three-dimensional effects to a layer is quick and easy. You can apply any combination of layer effects, then save the combination as a style and apply it to other layers instantly. To edit or delete the effect, simply open the Layer Styles dialog box and change the settings. See "Using layer effects and styles" on page 246.

Color effects Choose solid colors from swatch libraries, define your own colors in Color palette, or use the gradient tools to create a gradual blend between multiple colors. Use the Layers palette to change the opacity of an image or to apply a blending mode that affects the way the color in one layer interacts with the layers below. See "Using the gradient tool (Photoshop)" on page 188 and "Setting opacity and blending options" on page 240.

Filters Photoshop includes more than 95 special effect filters—from fine-art effects, to motion blurs, to lighting effects and distortions. For more information, see "Previewing and applying filters" in online Help.

Pattern Maker Create seamless patterns automatically. Simply make a selection and apply the Pattern Maker plug-in to generate textures and background patterns. See "Generating patterns" on page 198.

Transformation tools Scale, rotate, distort, or skew images easily. Apply the 3D Transform filter to simulate three-dimensional effects such as jar labels and boxes. Use the Liquify command to interactively push, pull, pucker, or bloat an image. See "Transforming objects in two dimensions" on page 127, "Transforming objects in three dimensions" on page 132, and "Using the Liquify command" on page 140.

Create compelling Web designs

Produce exceptional imagery for the Web and wireless devices with Photoshop and ImageReady, which ships with Photoshop.

Slicing Use the slice tool to create slices by hand, or generate layer-based slices automatically. Apply slice-by-slice formatting and optimization to keep file size small and image quality high. See "Creating and viewing slices" on page 288.

Optimization tools The Photoshop Save for Web dialog box and the ImageReady Optimization palette display a side-by-side comparison of format and compression options and let you apply weighted optimization to keep vector edges— type and logos, for example—crisp and clean. See "Optimizing images" on page 333 and "Using weighted optimization" on page 345.

Rollovers palette Use one convenient palette to view the entire set of rollovers, slices, image maps, and animations in a document, making authoring and navigation easier. See "Using the Rollovers palette" on page 315.

Transparency Apply instant transparency to Web page elements by knocking out one or more colors. Or apply dithered transparency to create edges that blend into any Web background. See "About optimization" on page 333.

Quick GIF animations Start with a layered Photoshop file, and use the Animation palette in ImageReady to convert individual layers into frames. Then apply the Tween command to generate additional frames and smooth out the action. See "Creating and editing animations" on page 321.

Link generation To create a URL link, simply select an Image slice—a slice with image data or a rollover state—and enter a URL in the Photoshop Slice Options dialog box or the ImageReady Slice palette. See "Assigning a URL to an Image slice" on page 299.

Enjoy precise typographic control

Photoshop delivers professional-quality type controls to help you create imagery that communicates with precision and style.

Editable text Text retains its crisp vector edges— and its editability—unless you rasterize it (by applying a filter, for example, or flattening the layers). You can distort it, warp it, and apply layer effects and still use the type tool to retype the text. See "Working with type layers" on page 270.

Formatting Use the Character and Paragraph palettes for precise control over individual letters and paragraph formatting. See "Formatting characters" on page 274 and "Formatting paragraphs" on page 283.

Spelling checker Avoid misspelled words with the built-in spelling checker, which includes search-and-replace functionality. You can even check spelling in multiple languages within the same file—to help you create buttons for multilingual Web sites, for example. See "Checking for spelling errors (Photoshop)" on page 281.

Convert to Shapes Use the Convert to Shapes command to turn type into an instant vector mask. See "Converting type to shapes (Photoshop)" on page 274.

Stay ahead of deadlines

Photoshop helps you streamline your workflow and meet any production challenge with tools like the File Browser that lets you manage files and folders conveniently.

Automate repetitive tasks

Streamline and simplify the production process by turning time-consuming jobs into automated operations.

Data-driven graphics Automate the production of repetitive artwork—such as business cards or Web banners—with the Variables feature. Design a template in Photoshop, set elements in the template as variables, and then generate an unlimited number of unique variations quickly by using scripts to replace the variable elements. See "About data-driven graphics" on page 415.

File browser Use the File Browser to quickly organize and retrieve images from your hard drive, external drives, CDs, and disks directly. Rotate images before opening them, batch rename, sort files, and manage image folders—all within the File Browser. The File Browser also displays image metatada, such as date created, date modified, and Exchangeable Image File (EXIF) information from digital cameras. See "Using the File Browser (Photoshop)" on page 68.

Actions Automate routine tasks such as batch processing by recording the steps as an action. Then simply click a button in the Actions palette to apply the action to other projects. For everyday jobs, turn the action into a droplet. Save the droplet on your desktop so that you can simply drag-and-drop to apply the action to individual files or folders of images. See "About actions" on page 397 and "Using droplets" on page 410.

Metadata support Repurpose, archive, or automate files in a workflow using XMP (Extensible Metadata Platform) format to embed metadata into a document. You can also ensure that image information—such as caption, credits, and copyright—travel with the file. See "Adding file information (Photoshop)" on page 374.

Develop a reliable workflow

Keep files moving efficiently from the beginning of the process to the end.

Cross-platform compatibility Complete cross-platform support ensures a smooth workflow between Windows and Mac OS systems.

WebDAV support Connect Photoshop to a WebDAV server, and enjoy the benefits of workgroup management. You can streamline collaboration by making sure the entire team has access to the files they need—with no fear that anyone will overwrite updates. See "Managing files with WebDAV (Photoshop)" on page 72.

Annotation tools Attach non-printing review comments or production notes to your Photoshop file with the notes tool, or use the audio annotation tool to record a voice message. See "Annotating images (Photoshop)" on page 44.

PDF security Protect your images by assigning passwords to your Photoshop PDF files. Use passwords to keep unauthorized people from opening a document or to disable printing and editing. See "Saving files in Photoshop PDF format (Photoshop)" on page 370.

Tight integration The familiar Adobe interface makes it easy to use Photoshop in tandem with other Adobe software. See "Take advantage of tighter-than-ever integration" on page 18.

Maintain color precisely

Keep color consistent across different devices and count on reliable output to any media.

Color management Photoshop simplifies color management by gathering the controls into the Color Settings dialog box and providing predefined settings for the most common workflows. See "Setting up color management" on page 90, "Using predefined color management settings" on page 90, and "Soft-proofing colors" on page 97.

Color options Whether you're creating artwork for print or Web, Photoshop lets you choose the color mode that's best for the job. When you're creating imagery for four-color printing, you can work more efficiently—and use a wider range of filters—by creating the art in RGB mode. Use the Gamut Warning command to identify colors that can't be reproduced in CYMK so you won't be disappointed with the results when you convert the finished, flattened file to CMYK. See "About color modes and models (Photoshop)" on page 77. For more information, see "Identifying out-of-gamut colors (Photoshop)" in online Help.

Precision print controls Photoshop gives you precise controls for printing full-color images, spot colors, duotones, or grayscale and black-and-white art. For high-end prepress workflows, there are even controls for dot gain, black-plate generation, and more. See "Printing images" on page 381, "Adding spot colors (Photoshop)" on page 217, "Printing duotones" on page 390, and "Setting output options" on page 384.

What's New in Photoshop 7.0

Adobe Photoshop 7.0 delivers innovative creativity tools, powerful efficiency features, and superior image-editing capability to help you maintain your competitive edge in today's challenging business environment. With Photoshop 7.0, it's easier than ever to produce exceptional imagery for print, the Web, wireless devices, and other media.

Meet every challenge

Photoshop 7.0 rounds out its comprehensive toolset with new capabilities that help you meet every creative challenge, master every production demand, and handle any image-editing task efficiently.

File Browser Search for images visually and intuitively rather than just by filename. With the easy-to-view thumbnails in the File Browser window, you can quickly organize and retrieve images from your hard drive, external drives, CDs, and disks directly within Photoshop. The File Browser also displays image metatada, such as date created, date modified, and Exchangeable Image File (EXIF) information from digital cameras. Rotate images, batch rename, sort files, and manage image folders—all within the File Browser. See "Using the File Browser (Photoshop)" on page 68.

Healing brush Effortlessly remove dust, scratches, blemishes, and wrinkles from your photographs, using only one tool. Unlike other cloning tools, the healing brush preserves the original shading, tonality, and texture in the retouched area. Use the related patch tool to work with selections. See "Using the healing brush tool (Photoshop)" on page 135.

Web transparency Make Web page elements transparent in Photoshop and ImageReady by simply clicking on the color you want to knock out. And with the new dithered transparency option, you can apply partial transparency to blend Web graphics seamlessly into any background—even patterns—without having to select a matte color first. If you need to edit the transparent effects later, you can remap more than one color at a time and easily restore colors to their original settings. See "About optimization" on page 333.

Enhanced Web output Keep vector art and text looking crisp by letting Photoshop or ImageReady automatically assign a higher priority to those areas when you optimize an image for the Web. See "Using weighted optimization" on page 345.

WBMP support Preview and save for Web in WBMP format, commonly used for displaying images on PDAs and wireless devices. See "Optimization options for WBMP format" on page 342.

Rollovers palette Use one convenient palette to create, view, and set rollover states. Add a layer-based rollover to a Web page by simply clicking a button, and use the Selected state option in the Rollovers palette to add sophisticated interactivity, with no need for Java scripting. For example, you can create navigation bars that trigger different rollover effects simultaneously. The Rollovers palette also displays all the slices, rollovers, image maps, and animations in a file, making it easy to get a quick overview of all the document states. See "Using the Rollovers palette" on page 315.

Workspaces Customize your Photoshop working environment by creating a palette layout and then saving the layout as a workspace. If you share a computer, saving a workspace lets you instantly access your personalized Photoshop desktop each time you sit down to work. You can also create workspaces for specific tasks—one for painting and another for photo retouching or Web work, for example. See "Customizing your workspace" on page 24.

Tool presets Customize any tool and save your settings as a new, unique tool. Access your presets instantly from the options bar or the new tool Presets palette, which lets you view presets for all your tools in one convenient place. See "Using tool presets (Photoshop)" on page 22.

Auto Color command With the new Auto Color command, color correction has never been easier—and Auto Color provides more reliable results than Auto Levels or Auto Contrast. For more information, see "Using the Auto Color command (Photoshop)" in online Help.

Data-driven graphics Whether you're creating corporate business cards, an online catalog with hundreds of photos and descriptions, or a direct-mail piece with customized data, the new data-driven graphics features in ImageReady let you combine visual sophistication with automated production. Design a template and use the Layers palette to designate key elements as variables. Then use scripts, a Web production tool such as GoLive, or an image server such as Adobe AlterCast® to replace the variables with text or images pulled from an ODBC-compliant database. See "About data-driven graphics" on page 415.

Stay competitive

Photoshop 7.0 delivers new and enhanced tools to help you achieve your creative best. Experiment with sophisticated painting effects and patterns to turn your ideas into images that stand out.

New paint engine Create and save custom brushes with a powerful new paint engine that lets you adjust dozens of different brush settings—including size, shape, tilt, spacing, scatter, and jitter—to get precisely the effect you want. You can even simulate different canvas and paper textures. See "Working with brushes" on page 172 and "About brush dynamics (Photoshop)" on page 176.

Art studio brushes In addition to the brushes you create yourself, you can use the preset brushes included on the Photoshop CD to simulate traditional wet and dry brush painting techniques to duplicate the fine-art effects such as charcoal or pastel. There are also special brushes for effects such as grass and leaves. See "Selecting preset brushes" on page 173.

Pattern Maker Simply make a selection and apply the Pattern Maker plug-in to generate abstract patterns or realistic textures such as sand or rocks. The plug-in performs a sophisticated analysis of your selection to avoid repetition and seamlessly tile the image. Use the patterns to create compelling Web backgrounds, enhance printed or on-screen artwork, or produce unique new imagery in combination with the painting engine. See "Generating patterns" on page 198.

Liquify enhancements The enhanced Liquify plug-in gives you greater control over image warping with zoom, pan, and multiple undo. You can also save your meshes, which lets you return to an image after experimenting with the Liquify tools and start where you left off. Or apply the same mesh to different images; experiment on a low-resolution image, for example, and then apply the mesh to a high-resolution version. Create effects such as smoke or fire with the new Turbulence brush. Use the new backdrop option to view individual layers or a flattened version of the file so that you can see your distortions in context as you create them. See "Using the Liquify command" on page 140.

Work with confidence

Photoshop 7.0 provides new controls and security settings for superior images, precise output, and worry-free file sharing.

PDF security Photoshop 7.0 offers complete support for Adobe Acrobat 5.0 security settings, allowing you to add tighter security to your Photoshop PDF files before sharing them with others online or adding them to an Adobe PDF workflow. You can set password protection to keep users who don't know the password from opening the file. Or set one password to open the file and another to allow printing or editing. See "Saving files in Photoshop PDF format (Photoshop)" on page 370.

Picture Package enhancements Save time and money when printing by using Picture Package to print multiple images on one page. Enhancements to Photoshop 7.0 let you print to different page sizes, add labels or text to each image, print more than one image per page, and output images as one flattened document or to separate layers. See "Creating multiple-image layouts (Photoshop)" on page 376.

Web photo gallery enhancements Showcase your work online quickly and easily by posting a gallery of images. Photoshop 7.0 offers sophisticated new templates to give you more design flexibility, and a new security option lets you enter text or embed the filename, caption, or copyright information on the image as a watermark. See "Creating Web photo galleries (Photoshop)" on page 309.

XMP support XMP (Extensible Metadata Platform) format lets you embed metadata into a document so that you can easily repurpose, archive, or automate files in a workflow. You can also ensure that image information—such as caption, credits, and copyright—travel with the file. See "Adding file information (Photoshop)" on page 374.

Multilingual spelling checker Search and replace text, check spelling in multiple languages within the same file, and correct spelling on one text layer or across all text layers in the same document. See "Checking for spelling errors (Photoshop)" on page 281.

Take advantage of tighter-than-ever integration

Work more efficiently, thanks to tight integration between Photoshop and the latest releases in Adobe's family of professional graphics software.

Illustrator Move files freely between Photoshop and Adobe Illustrator—layers, masks, transparency, and compound shapes are preserved. Maintain rollovers and animation information when you import Photoshop files into Illustrator, and export Illustrator HTML tables with CSS layers to Photoshop.

InDesign Paste or drop native Photoshop files into Adobe InDesign—even layered images. Paths, masks, and alpha channels in the Photoshop file can be used to remove image backgrounds or to create text wraps in the InDesign document.

GoLive Design and slice your Web page in Photoshop and then bring the sliced file directly into GoLive. Use the GoLive Smart Objects feature to generate variable designs automatically from Photoshop templates.

LiveMotion Drag and drop layered Photoshop files into a LiveMotion composition and quickly convert them into animation-ready independent objects, groups, or sequences. Photoshop blending modes, layer masks, and effects are preserved, and the Photoshop artwork stays editable as you animate and code.

Acrobat Include transparency information in PDF files saved out of Photoshop, add password protection to secure your Photoshop PDF files, and use the Include Vector Data option to preserve text and vector graphics as resolution-independent objects.

AlterCast When you want to automate the production of dynamic data-driven graphics, Adobe AlterCast is the perfect tool. This new image server software (available only in English) automatically replaces the variables—both text and graphics—in your Photoshop templates.

Chapter 1: Looking at the Work Area

Welcome to Adobe Photoshop and Adobe ImageReady. Photoshop and ImageReady give you an efficient work area and user interface to create and edit images for both print and the Web.

Getting familiar with the work area

The Photoshop and ImageReady work area is arranged to help you focus on creating and editing images.

About the work area

The work area consists of the following components:

Menu bar The menu bar contains menus for performing tasks. The menus are organized by topic. For example, the Layers menu contains commands for working with layers.

Options bar The options bar provides options for using a tool. (See "Using the tool options bar" on page 21.)

Toolbox The toolbox holds tools for creating and editing images. (See "Using the tools" on page 19.)

Palette well (Photoshop) The palette well helps you organize the palettes in your work area. (See "Using the palette well (Photoshop)" on page 22.)

Palettes Palettes help you monitor and modify images. (See "Using palettes" on page 23.)

Using the toolbox

The first time you start the application, the toolbox appears on the left side of the screen. Some tools in the toolbox have options that appear in the context-sensitive tool options bar. (See "Using the tool options bar" on page 21.) These include the tools that let you use type, select, paint, draw, sample, edit, move, annotate, and view images. Other tools in the toolbox allow you to change foreground/background colors, go to Adobe Online, work in different modes, and jump between Photoshop and ImageReady applications.

For more information on the foreground and background color controls, see "Choosing foreground and background colors" on page 201.

 For an overview of each tool, see the "Toolbox overview" topics in online Help.

Using the tools

You select a tool by clicking its icon in the toolbox. A small triangle at the lower right of a tool icon indicates hidden tools. Positioning the pointer over a tool displays a tool tip with the tool's name and keyboard shortcut.

To show or hide the toolbox:

Choose Window > Tools. A check mark indicates the item is showing.

To move the toolbox:

Drag the toolbox by its title bar.

To select a tool:

Do one of the following:

- Click its icon or press its keyboard shortcut. If the icon has a small triangle at its lower right corner, hold down the mouse button to view the hidden tools. Then, click the tool you want to select.

- Press the tool's keyboard shortcut. The keyboard shortcut is displayed in its tool tip.

To cycle through hidden tools:

Hold down Shift and press the tool's shortcut key.

To enable or disable cycling through a set of hidden tools (Photoshop):

1 Do one of the following:

- In Windows or Mac OS 9.x, choose Edit > Preferences > General.

- In Mac OS X, choose Photoshop > Preferences > General.

2 Select or deselect Use Shift Key for Tool Switch.

To display or hide tool tips:

1 Do one of the following:

- In Windows or Mac OS 9.x, choose Edit > Preferences > General.

- (Photoshop) In Mac OS X, choose Photoshop > Preferences > General.

- (ImageReady) In Mac OS X, choose ImageReady > Preferences > General.

2 Select or deselect Show Tool Tips.

Using the tool pointers

When you select most tools, the mouse pointer matches the tool's icon. The marquee pointer appears by default as cross hairs, the text tool pointer as an I-beam, and painting tools default to the Brush Size icon.

Each default pointer has a different *hotspot*, where an effect or action in the image begins. With all tools except the move tool, annotation tools, and the type tool, you can switch to precise cursors, which appear as cross hairs centered around the hotspot.

To set the tool pointer appearance:

1 Do one of the following:

- (Photoshop) In Windows or Mac OS 9.x, choose Edit > Preferences > Display & Cursors.

- (Photoshop) In Mac OS X, choose Photoshop > Preferences > Display & Cursors.

- (ImageReady) In Windows or Mac OS 9.x, choose Edit > Preferences > Cursors.

- (ImageReady) In Mac OS X, choose ImageReady > Preferences > Cursors.

2 Choose a tool pointer setting:

- Click Standard under Painting Cursors, Other Cursors, or both to display pointers as tool icons.

- Click Precise under Painting Cursors, Other Cursors, or both to display pointers as cross hairs.

- Click Brush Size under Painting Cursors to display the painting tool cursors as brush shapes representing the size of the current brush. Brush Size cursors may not display for very large brushes.

3 Click OK.

The Painting Cursors options control the pointers for the following tools:

- (Photoshop) Eraser, pencil, paintbrush, healing brush, rubber stamp, pattern stamp, smudge, blur, sharpen, dodge, burn, and sponge tools.

- (ImageReady) Paintbrush, pencil, and eraser tools.

The Other Cursors options control the pointers for the following tools:

- (Photoshop) Marquee, lasso, polygon lasso, magic wand, crop, slice, patch, eyedropper, pen, gradient, line, paint bucket, magnetic lasso, magnetic pen, measure, and color sampler tools.

- (ImageReady) Marquee, lasso, magic wand, eyedropper, paint bucket, and slice tools.

 To toggle between standard and precise cursors in some tool pointers, press Caps Lock. Press Caps Lock again to return to your original setting.

Using the tool options bar

Most tools have options that are displayed in the tool options bar. The options bar is context sensitive and changes as different tools are selected. Some settings in the options bar are common to several tools (such as painting modes and opacity), and some are specific to one tool (such as the Auto Erase setting for the pencil tool).

You can move the options bar anywhere in the work area, and dock it at the top or bottom of the screen.

To display the tool options bar:

Do one of the following:

- Choose Window > Options.

- Click a tool in the toolbox.

Lasso options bar

To return a tool or all tools to the default settings:

Do one of the following:

- Click the tool icon on the options bar, then choose Reset Tool or Reset All Tools from the context menu.

- (ImageReady) In Windows or Mac OS 9.x, choose Edit > Preferences > General, then click Reset All Tools.

- (ImageReady) In Mac OS X, choose ImageReady > Preferences > General, then click Reset All Tools.

To move the options bar:

Drag the options bar by the gripper bar at its left edge.

Using the palette well (Photoshop)

The Photoshop options bar includes a palette well that helps you organize and manage palettes. The palette well is only available when using a screen resolution greater than 800 pixels x 600 pixels (a setting of at least 1024 x 768 is recommended).

Palettes are considered hidden when stored in the palette well. The Window menu item associated with a stored palette will say Show when it is stored. Clicking on the title of a palette stored in the well shows the palette until you click outside the palette.

To store palettes in the palette well:

Drag the palette's tab into the palette well so that the palette well is highlighted.

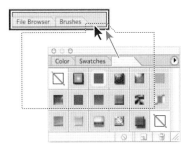

Docking a palette in the tool options bar

To use a palette in the palette well:

Click the palette's tab. The palette remains open until you click outside it or click in the palette's tab.

Using tool presets (Photoshop)

Tool presets let you save and reuse tool settings. You can load, edit, and create libraries of tool presets using the Tool Preset picker in the options bar, the Tool Presets palette, and the Preset Manager.

Tool Presets palette with All option selected

Tool Preset picker in the options bar

To create a tool preset:

1 Choose a tool, and set the options you want in the options bar.

2 Click the Tool Preset button on the left side of the options bar, or choose Window > Tool Presets to display the Tool Presets palette.

3 Do one of the following:

• Click the Create New Tool Preset button ⬚ .

• Choose New Tool Preset from the palette menu.

4 Enter a name for the tool preset, and click Save.

To choose a tool preset:

Do one of the following:

- Click the Tool Preset button in the options bar, and select a preset from the pop-up palette.
- Choose Window > Tool Presets, and select a preset.

To change the list of presets in the Tool Preset pop-up palette:

Do one of the following:

- To show all loaded presets, choose Show All Tool Presets from the palette menu.
- To sort the presets by tool, choose Sort By Tool from the palette menu.
- To show only the loaded presets for the active tool, choose Show Current Tool Presets from the palette menu, or click the Current Tool Only button.
- To create, load, and manage libraries of tool presets, see "Using pop-up palettes" on page 25 and "Managing libraries with the Preset Manager (Photoshop)" on page 49.
- To change the display of presets in the pop-up palette, choose Text Only, Small Text, or Large Text from the palette menu.

Using palettes

Palettes help you monitor and modify images. By default, palettes appear stacked together in groups.

To display one palette:

Choose the palette name in the Window menu.

To show or hide multiple palettes:

Do one of the following:

- To show or hide all open palettes, the options bar, and the toolbox, press Tab.
- To show or hide all palettes, press Shift+Tab.

Changing the palette display

You can rearrange your palettes to make better use of your work area by using the following techniques:

- To make a palette appear at the front of its group, click the palette's tab, or choose the palette name from the Window menu.
- To move an entire palette group, drag its title bar.
- To rearrange or separate a palette group, drag a palette's tab. Dragging a palette outside of an existing group creates a new group.
- To move a palette to another group, drag the palette's tab to that group.
- To display a palette menu, position the pointer on the triangle ⊙ in the upper right corner of the palette, and press the mouse button.

- To change the size of a palette, drag any corner of the palette (Windows) or drag the size box at its lower right corner (Mac OS). Not all palettes can be resized.

- To collapse a group to palette titles only, click the Minimize/Maximize box (Windows) or the Zoom box (Mac OS), or double-click a palette's tab. You can still access the menu of a collapsed palette.

Click to collapse or expand palette.
A. *Windows* **B.** *Mac OS X*

- (ImageReady) To show or hide options for palettes that include hidden options (the Optimize, Color, Type, Layer Options, and Slice palettes), click the Show Options button ⬍ on the palette tab to cycle through palette displays, or choose Show Options or Hide Options from the palette menu.

Docking palettes together

Docking palettes together lets you view multiple palettes at the same time and move them as a group. Entire palette groups cannot be docked together at once, but you can dock the palettes from one group to another, one at a time.

In Photoshop, docked palettes and their locations are saved when you save a workspace.

💡 *In Photoshop, you can also store palettes in the palette well of the tool options bar. (See "Using the tool options bar" on page 21.)*

To dock palettes together:

Drag a palette's tab to the bottom of another palette so that the bottom of the target palette is highlighted.

To move an entire docked group, drag its title bar.

Customizing your workspace

The positions of all open palettes and movable dialog boxes are saved when you exit the application. Alternatively, you can always start with default palette positions or restore default positions at any time.

In addition to saving the positions of palettes and dialog boxes when you exit the application, you can save multiple layouts as different workspaces.

To save the current workspace layout:

1 Choose Window > Workspace > Save Workspace.

2 Enter a name for the workspace, and click OK.

To choose a workspace:

Choose Window > Workspace, and choose a workspace from the submenu.

To delete a workspace:

1 Choose Window > Workspace > Delete Workspace.

2 Select the workspace you want to delete, and click Delete.

To reset palettes to the default positions:

Do one of the following:

- In Windows or Mac OS 9.x, choose Edit > Preferences > General, then select Save Palette Locations.

- (Photoshop) In Mac OS X, choose Photoshop > Preferences > General, then select Save Palette Locations.

- (ImageReady) In Mac OS X, choose ImageReady > Preferences > General, then select Save Palette Locations.

- Choose Window > Workspace > Reset Palette Locations.

To always start with the default palette and dialog box positions:

1 Do one of the following:

- In Windows or Mac OS 9.x, choose Edit > Preferences > General.

- (Photoshop) In Mac OS X, choose Photoshop > Preferences > General.

- (ImageReady) In Mac OS X, choose ImageReady > Preferences > General.

2 Deselect Save Palette Locations. The change takes effect the next time you start the application.

Using pop-up sliders

A number of palettes and dialog boxes contain settings that use pop-up sliders (for example, the Opacity option in the Layers palette).

To use a pop-up slider:

Do one of the following:

- Position the pointer over the triangle next to the setting, hold down the mouse, and drag the slider or angle radius to the desired value.

- Click the triangle next to the setting to open the pop-up slider box, and drag the slider or angle radius to the desired value. Click outside the slider box or press Enter or Return to close the slider box. To cancel changes, press the Escape key (Esc).

To increase or decrease values in 10% increments when the pop-up slider box is open, hold down Shift and press the Up or Down arrow key.

Using pop-up palettes

Pop-up palettes provide easy access to libraries of brushes, swatches, gradients, styles, patterns, contours, and shapes. You can customize pop-up palettes by renaming and deleting items and by loading, saving, and replacing libraries. You can also change the display of a pop-up palette to view items by their names, as thumbnail icons, or with both names and icons.

The Brush pop-up palette in the options bar

To select an item in a pop-up palette:

1 Click the thumbnail image in the options bar.

2 Click an item in the pop-up palette.

To rename an item in a pop-up palette:

Select an item, click the triangle ⊙ in the upper right corner of the pop-up palette, and choose the Rename command from the palette menu. Enter a new name.

To delete an item in a pop-up palette:

Do one of the following:

• Select an item, click the triangle ⊙ in the upper right corner of the pop-up palette, and choose the Delete command from the palette menu.

• Hold down Alt (Windows) or Option (Mac OS) and click an item.

To customize the list of items in a pop-up palette:

1 Click the triangle ⊙ in the upper right corner of the pop-up palette to view the palette menu.

2 To return to the default library, choose the Reset command. You can either replace the current list or append the default library to the current list.

3 To load a different library, do one of the following:

• Choose the Load command to add a library to the current list. Then select the library file you want to use, and click Load.

• Choose the Replace command to replace the current list with a different library. Then select the library file you want to use, and click Load.

• Choose a library file (displayed at the bottom of the palette menu). Then click OK to replace the current list, or click Append to append the current list.

4 To save the current list as a library for later use, choose the Save command. Then enter a name for the library file, and click Save.

(Mac OS) You can specify that a file extension is always appended to a library file by setting Append File Extension to Always in the File Handling Preferences. You should put the extension on a library filename so that you can easily share the libraries across operating systems.

To change the display of items in a pop-up palette:

1 Click the triangle ⊙ in the upper right corner of the pop-up palette to view the palette menu.

2 Select a view option: Text Only, Small Thumbnail, Large Thumbnail, Small List, and Large List.

Using the Info palette (Photoshop)

The Info palette displays information about the color values beneath the pointer and, depending on the tool in use, other useful measurements.

To display the Info palette:

Choose Window > Info.

The Info palette displays the following information:

- When displaying CMYK values, the Info palette displays an exclamation point next to the CMYK values if the color beneath the pointer or color sampler is out of the printable CMYK color gamut.

  For more information, see "Identifying out-of-gamut colors (Photoshop) in online Help.

- When you use the marquee tool, the Info palette displays the x- and y-coordinates of the pointer position and the width (W) and height (H) of the marquee as you drag.

- When you use the crop tool or zoom tool, the Info palette displays the width (W) and height (H) of the marquee as you drag. The palette also shows the angle of rotation of the crop marquee.

- When you use the line tool, pen tool, or gradient tool or when you move a selection, the Info palette displays the x- and y-coordinates of your starting position, the change in X (DX), the change in Y (DY), the angle (A), and the distance (D) as you drag.

- When you use a two-dimensional transformation command, the Info palette displays the percentage change in width (W) and height (H), the angle of rotation (A), and the angle of horizontal skew (H) or vertical skew (V).

- When you use any color adjustment dialog box (for example, Curves), the Info palette displays the before and after color values of the pixels beneath the pointer and beneath color samplers.

  For more information, see "Seeing the color values of pixels (Photoshop)" in online Help.

(ImageReady) The Info palette displays the following information:

- The RGB numeric values for the color beneath the pointer.

- The Opacity value for the pixels beneath the pointer.

- The hexadecimal value for the color beneath the pointer.

- The index color table position for the color beneath the pointer.

- The x- and y-coordinates of the pointer.

- The x- and y-coordinates of your starting position (before you click in the image) and your ending position (as you drag in the image) when you use the marquee tool, the shape tools, the crop tool, and the slice tool.

- The width (W) and height (H) of the selection as you drag when you use the crop tool, the shape tools, the slice tool, or the zoom tool.

- The percentage change in width (W) and height (H), the angle of rotation (A), and the angle of horizontal skew (H) or vertical skew (V) when you use a Transform or Free Transform command.

To change the Info palette options:

1 Choose Palette Options from the Info palette menu.

2 For First Color Readout, choose one of the following display options:

- Actual Color to display values in the current color mode of the image.

- Total Ink to display the total percentage of all CMYK ink at the pointer's current location, based on the values set in the CMYK Setup dialog box.

- Opacity to display the opacity of the current layer. This option does not apply to the background.

- Any other option to display the color values in that color mode.

3 For Second Color Readout, choose a display option listed in step 2.

4 For Ruler Units, choose a unit of measurement.

5 Click OK.

To change measurement units, click the cross-hair icon in the Info palette for a menu of options. To change color readout modes, click the eyedropper icon.

Using context menus

In addition to the menus at the top of your screen, context-sensitive menus display commands relevant to the active tool, selection, or palette.

To display context menus:

1 Position the pointer over an image or palette item.

2 Click with the right mouse button (Windows) or hold down Control and press the mouse button (Mac OS).

Viewing images

The hand tool, the zoom tools, the Zoom commands, and the Navigator palette let you view different areas of an image at different magnifications. You can open additional windows to display several views at once (such as different magnifications) of an image. You can also change the screen display mode to change the appearance of the Photoshop or ImageReady work area.

Changing the screen display mode

The window controls let you change the screen display mode, including menu bar, title bar, and scroll bar options.

To change the screen display mode:

Click a screen mode button in the toolbox:

- The left button ▣ displays the default window with a menu bar at the top and scroll bars on the sides.

- The center button ▭ displays a full-screen window with a menu bar and a 50% gray background, but no title bar or scroll bars.

- The right button ▭ displays a full-screen window with a black background, but no title bar, menu bar, or scroll bars.

Using the document window

The document window is where your image appears. Depending on the screen display mode (see "Changing the screen display mode" on page 28), the document window may include a title bar and scroll bar.

In ImageReady, the document window allows you to switch easily between original and optimized views of an image using tabs, and to view the original image and multiple versions of an optimized image simultaneously. For information on changing the view in the document window, see "Viewing optimized images (ImageReady)" on page 336.

You can open multiple windows to display different views of the same file. A list of open windows appears in the Window menu. Available memory may limit the number of windows per image.

To open multiple views of the same image:

Do one of the following:

- Choose Window > Documents > New Window.

- (ImageReady) Drag any tab away from the document window.

To arrange multiple windows:

Do one of the following:

- Choose Window > Images > Cascade (Photoshop) or Window > Documents > Cascade (ImageReady) to display windows stacked and cascading from the upper left to the lower right of the screen.

- Choose Window > Images > Tile (Photoshop) or Window > Documents > Tile (ImageReady) to display windows edge to edge.

To close windows:

Choose a command:

- Choose File > Close to close the active window.

- (Mac OS) Choose File > Close All to close all windows.

- (Windows) Choose Window > Documents > Close All to close all windows.

Navigating the view area

If the entire image is not visible in the document window, you can navigate to bring another area of the image into view.

In Photoshop, you can also use the Navigator palette to quickly change the view of an image.

To view another area of an image:

Do one of the following:

- Use the window scroll bars.

- Select the hand tool ✋ and drag to pan over the image.

To use the hand tool while another tool is selected, hold down the spacebar as you drag in the image.

To move the view of an image using the Navigator palette (Photoshop):

1 Choose Window > Navigator.

2 Do one of the following:

- Drag the view box in the thumbnail of the image, which represents the boundaries of the image window.

- Click in the thumbnail of the image. The new view includes the area you click.

To change the color of the Navigator palette view box (Photoshop):

1 Choose Palette Options from the Navigator palette menu.

2 Choose a color:

- To use a preset color, choose an option for Color.

- To specify a different color, click the color box, and choose a color. For more information on choosing colors, see "Using the Adobe Color Picker" on page 205.

Magnifying and reducing the view

You can magnify or reduce your view using various methods. The window's title bar displays the zoom percentage (unless the window is too small for the display to fit), as does the status bar at the bottom of the window.

Note: The 100% view of an image displays an image as it will appear in a browser (based on the monitor resolution and the image resolution). (See "About image size and resolution" on page 54.)

To zoom in:

Do one of the following:

- Select the zoom tool 🔍 . The pointer becomes a magnifying glass with a plus sign in its center 🔍 . Click the area you want to magnify. Each click magnifies the image to the next preset percentage, centering the display around the point you click. When the image has reached its maximum magnification level of 1600%, the magnifying glass appears empty.

- Click the Zoom In button 🔍 in the options bar to magnify to the next preset percentage. When the image has reached its maximum magnification level, the command is dimmed.

- Choose View > Zoom In to magnify to the next preset percentage. When the image has reached its maximum magnification level, the command is dimmed.

- (Photoshop) Enter a magnification level in the Zoom text box at the lower left of the window.

- (ImageReady) Click on the Zoom Level pop-up menu at the bottom left of the document window, and choose a zoom level.

To zoom out:

Do one of the following:

- Select the zoom tool. Hold down Alt (Windows) or Option (Mac OS) to activate the zoom-out tool. The pointer becomes a magnifying glass with a minus sign in its center ⊖ . Click the center of the area of the image you want to reduce. Each click reduces the view to the previous preset percentage. When the file has reached its maximum reduction level, the magnifying glass appears empty.

- Click the Zoom out button ⊖ in the options bar to reduce to the previous preset percentage. When the image has reached its maximum reduction level, the command is dimmed.

- Choose View > Zoom Out to reduce to the previous preset percentage. When the image reaches its maximum reduction level, the command is dimmed.

- (Photoshop) Enter a reduction level in the Zoom text box at the lower left of the window.

- (ImageReady) Click on the Zoom Level pop-up menu at the lower left of the document window, and choose a zoom level.

To magnify by dragging:

1 Select the zoom tool.

2 Drag over the part of the image you want to magnify.

The area inside the zoom marquee is displayed at the highest possible magnification. To move the marquee around the artwork in Photoshop, begin dragging a marquee and then hold down the spacebar while dragging the marquee to a new location.

To display an image at 100%:

Do one of the following:

- Double-click the zoom tool.

- Choose View > Actual Pixels (Photoshop) or View > Actual Size (ImageReady).

To change the view to fit the screen:

Do one of the following:

- Double-click the hand tool.

- Choose View > Fit on Screen.

These options scale both the zoom level and the window size to fit the available screen space.

To automatically resize the window when magnifying or reducing the view:

With the Zoom tool active, select Resize Windows to Fit in the options bar. The window resizes when you magnify or reduce the view of the image.

When Resize Windows to Fit is deselected (the default), the window maintains a constant size regardless of the image's magnification. This can be helpful when using smaller monitors or working with tiled views.

To automatically resize the window when zooming in or out using keyboard shortcuts (Photoshop):

1 Do one of the following:

- In Windows or Mac OS 9.x, choose Edit > Preferences > General.

- In Mac OS X, choose Photoshop > Preferences > General.

2 Select Keyboard Zoom Resizes Windows.

Correcting mistakes

Most operations can be undone if you make a mistake. Alternatively, you can restore all or part of an image to its last saved version. But available memory may limit your ability to use these options.

For information on how to restore your image to how it looked at any point in the current work session, see "Reverting to a previous version of an image" on page 33.

To undo the last operation:

Choose Edit > Undo.

If an operation can't be undone, the command is dimmed and changes to Can't Undo.

To redo the last operation:

Choose Edit > Redo.

You can set the Redo keystroke preference to be the same for Photoshop and ImageReady. In the General section of the Preferences dialog box, select a preference for the Redo key. You can also set the key to toggle between Undo and Redo.

To free memory used by the Undo command, the History palette, or the Clipboard (Photoshop):

Choose Edit > Purge, and choose the item type or buffer you want to clear. If already empty, the item type or buffer is dimmed.

***Important:** The Purge command permanently clears from memory the operation stored by the command or buffer; it cannot be undone. For example, choosing Edit > Purge > Histories deletes all history states from the History palette. Use the Purge command when the amount of information held in memory is so large that Photoshop's performance is noticeably diminished.*

To revert to the last saved version:

Choose File > Revert.

***Note:** Revert is added as a history state in the History palette and can be undone.*

To restore part of an image to its previously saved version (Photoshop):

Do one of the following:

- Use the history brush tool to paint with the selected state or snapshot on the History palette.

For more information, see "Painting with a state or snapshot of an image (Photoshop)" in online Help.

- Use the eraser tool with the Erase to History option selected. (See "Using the eraser tool" on page 168.)

- Select the area you want to restore, and choose Edit > Fill. For Use, choose History, and click OK. (See "Filling and stroking selections and layers" on page 194.)

Note: To restore the image with a snapshot of the initial state of the document, choose History Options from the Palette menu and make sure that the Automatically Create First Snapshot option is on.

Reverting to a previous version of an image

The History palette lets you jump to any recent state of the image created during the current working session. Each time you apply a change to an image, the new state of that image is added to the palette.

For example, if you select, paint, and rotate part of an image, each of those states is listed separately in the palette. You can then select any of the states, and the image will revert to how it looked when that change was first applied. You can then work from that state.

About the History palette

Note the following guidelines when using the History palette:

- Program-wide changes, such as changes to palettes, color settings, actions, and preferences, are not changes to a particular image and so are not added to the History palette.

- By default, the History palette lists the previous 20 states. Older states are automatically deleted to free more memory for Photoshop. To keep a particular state throughout your work session, make a snapshot of the state. For more information, see "Making a snapshot of an image (Photoshop)" on page 35.

- Once you close and reopen the document, all states and snapshots from the last working session are cleared from the palette.

- By default, a snapshot of the initial state of the document is displayed at the top of the palette.

- States are added from the top down. That is, the oldest state is at the top of the list, the most recent one at the bottom.

- Each state is listed with the name of the tool or command used to change the image.

- By default, selecting a state dims those below. This way you can easily see which changes will be discarded if you continue working from the selected state. For information on customizing the history options, see "Setting history options (Photoshop)" on page 35.

- By default, selecting a state and then changing the image eliminates all states that come after.

- If you select a state and then change the image, eliminating the states that came after, you can use the Undo command to undo the last change and restore the eliminated states.

- By default, deleting a state deletes that state and those that came after it. If you choose the Allow Non-Linear History option, deleting a state deletes just that state. For more information, see "Setting history options (Photoshop)" on page 35.

Using the History palette

You can use the History palette to revert to a previous state of an image, to delete an image's states, and in Photoshop, to create a document from a state or snapshot.

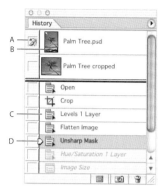

Photoshop History palette
A. Sets the source for the history brush **B.** *Thumbnail of a snapshot* **C.** *History state* **D.** *History state slider*

To display the History palette:

Choose Window > History, or click the History palette tab.

To revert to a previous state of an image:

Do any of the following:

- Click the name of the state.

- Drag the slider ▷ at the left of the state up or down to a different state.

- (Photoshop) Choose Step Forward or Step Backward from the palette menu or the Edit menu to move to the next or previous state.

To delete one or more states of the image (Photoshop):

Do one of the following:

- Click the name of the state, and choose Delete from the History palette menu to delete that change and those that came after it.

- Drag the state to the Trash button 🗑 to delete that change and those that came after it.

- Choose Clear History from the palette menu to delete the list of states from the History palette, without changing the image. This option doesn't reduce the amount of memory used by Photoshop.

- Hold down Alt (Windows) or Option (Mac OS), and choose Clear History from the palette menu to purge the list of states from the History palette without changing the image. If you get a message that Photoshop is low on memory, purging states is useful, since the command deletes the states from the Undo buffer and frees up memory.

Important: *This action cannot be undone.*

- Choose Edit > Purge > Histories to purge the list of states from the History palette for all open documents.

Important: *This action cannot be undone.*

To delete all of an image's states (ImageReady):

Choose Clear Undo/Redo History from the History palette menu.

Important: *This action cannot be undone.*

To create a new document from the selected state or snapshot of the image (Photoshop):

Do one of the following:

- Drag a state or snapshot onto the New Document button 🖿 .

- Select a state or snapshot, and click the New Document button.

- Select a state or snapshot, and choose New Document from the History palette menu.

The history list for the newly created document will be empty.

💡 *To save one or more snapshots or image states for use in a later editing session, create a new file for each state you save, and save each in a separate file. When you reopen your original file, plan to open the other saved files also. You can drag each file's initial snapshot to the original image and thus access the snapshots again from the original image's History palette.*

To replace an existing document with a selected state (Photoshop):

Drag the state onto the document.

Setting history options (Photoshop)

You can specify the maximum number of items to include in the History palette and set other options that customize the way you work with the palette.

To set history options:

1 Choose History Options from the History palette menu.

2 Select an option:

- Automatically Create First Snapshot to automatically create a snapshot of the initial state of the image when the document is opened.

- Automatically Create New Snapshot When Saving to generate a snapshot every time you save.

- Allow Non-Linear History to make changes to a selected state without deleting the states that come after. Normally, when you select a state and change the image, all states that come after the selected one are deleted. This enables the History palette to display a list of the editing steps in the order you made them. By recording states in a nonlinear way, you can select a state, make a change to the image, and delete just that state. The change will be appended at the end of the list.

- Show New Snapshot Dialog By Default to force Photoshop to prompt you for snapshot names even when using the buttons on the palette.

Making a snapshot of an image (Photoshop)

The Snapshot command lets you make a temporary copy (or *snapshot*) of any state of the image. The new snapshot is added to the list of snapshots at the top of the History palette. Selecting a snapshot lets you work from that version of the image.

Snapshots are similar to the states listed in the History palette, but they offer additional advantages:

- You can name a snapshot to make it easy to identify.

- Snapshots can be stored for an entire work session.

- You can compare effects easily. For example, you can take a snapshot before and after applying a filter. Then select the first snapshot, and try the same filter with different settings. Switch between the snapshots to find the settings you like best.

- With snapshots, you can recover your work easily. When you experiment with a complex technique or apply an action, take a snapshot first. If you're not satisfied with the results, you can select the snapshot to undo all the steps.

Important: Snapshots are not saved with the image—closing an image deletes its snapshots. Also, unless you select the Allow Non-Linear History option, selecting a snapshot and changing the image deletes all of the states currently listed in the History palette.

To create a snapshot:

1 Select a state.

2 To automatically create a snapshot, click the New Snapshot button on the History palette, or if Automatically Create New Snapshot When Saving is selected in the history options, choose New Snapshot from the History palette menu.

3 To set options when creating a snapshot, choose New Snapshot from the History palette menu, or Alt-click (Windows) or Option-click (Mac OS) the New Snapshot button.

4 Enter the name of the Snapshot in the Name text box.

5 For From, select the snapshot contents:

- Full Document to make a snapshot of all layers in the image at that state.

- Merged Layers to make a snapshot that merges all layers in the image at that state.

- Current Layer to make a snapshot of only the currently selected layer at that state.

To select a snapshot:

Do any of the following:

- Click the name of the snapshot.

- Drag the slider at the left of the snapshot up or down to a different snapshot.

To rename a snapshot:

Double-click the snapshot and enter a name.

To delete a snapshot:

Do one of the following:

- Select the snapshot, and choose Delete from the palette menu.

- Select the snapshot, and click the Trash button .

- Drag the snapshot to the Trash button.

For more information, see "Painting with a state or snapshot of an image (Photoshop)" in online Help.

Duplicating images

You can duplicate an entire image (including all layers, layer masks, and channels) into available memory without saving to disk. In ImageReady, you can also duplicate optimized versions of an image.

Using duplicates in ImageReady lets you experiment and then compare several versions of the optimized image to the original.

To duplicate an image (Photoshop):

1 Open the image you want to duplicate.

2 Choose Image > Duplicate.

3 Enter a name for the duplicated image.

4 To duplicate the image without layers, select Duplicate Merged Layers Only.

5 Click OK.

To duplicate an image in Photoshop and automatically append the name "copy" to its filename, hold down Alt (Windows) or Option (Mac OS) when you choose Image > Duplicate.

To duplicate an original image (ImageReady):

1 Open the image you want to duplicate.

2 Select the Original tab at the top of the image window.

3 Hold down Alt (Windows) or Option (Mac OS), and drag the Original tab from the image window, or choose Image > Duplicate.

4 Name the duplicate, specify whether to flatten the layers, and click OK.

To duplicate an optimized image (ImageReady):

1 Open the image you want to duplicate.

2 Select the Optimized tab at the top of the image window.

3 Hold down Alt (Windows) or Option (Mac OS), and drag the Optimized tab from the image window, or choose Image > Duplicate Optimized.

4 Name the duplicate, and click OK.

Note: When you duplicate an image in Optimized, 2-Up, or 4-Up view, the duplicate image appears in the Original view in the duplicate image window. If you want a duplicate optimized image to appear in the Optimized, 2-Up, or 4-Up view, duplicate the original image, and then select the Optimized, 2-Up, or 4-Up tab in the duplicate image window.

Using rulers, columns, the measure tool, guides, and the grid

Rulers, columns, the measure tool, guides, and the grid help you position images or elements precisely across the width or length of an image.

Note: You can also align and distribute parts of an image using the Layers palette. (See "Repositioning the contents of layers" on page 234.)

Using rulers

When visible, rulers appear along the top and left side of the active window. Markers in the ruler display the pointer's position when you move it. Changing the ruler origin (the (0, 0) mark on the top and left rulers) lets you measure from a specific point on the image. The ruler origin also determines the grid's point of origin.

To display or hide rulers:

Choose View > Rulers.

To change the rulers' zero origin:

1 To snap the ruler origin to guides, slices, or Document bounds, choose View > Snap To, then choose any combination of options from the submenu. (See "Using the Snap command" on page 117.)

(Photoshop) You can also snap to a grid in addition to guides, slices, and Document bounds.

2 Position the pointer over the intersection of the rulers in the upper left corner of the window, and drag diagonally down onto the image. A set of cross hairs appears, marking the new origin on the rulers.

To make the ruler origin snap to the ruler ticks (Photoshop), hold down Shift as you drag.

Note: To reset the ruler origin to its default value, double-click the upper left corner of the rulers.

To change the rulers' settings (Photoshop):

1 Do one of the following:

- Double-click a ruler.
- In Windows or Mac OS 9.x, choose Edit > Preferences > Units & Rulers.
- In Mac OS X, choose Photoshop > Preferences > Units & Rulers.

2 For Rulers, choose a unit of measurement.

Note: Changing the units on the Info palette automatically changes the units on the rulers.

3 For Point/Pica Size, choose from the following options:

- PostScript (72 points per inch) if you are printing to a PostScript device.
- Traditional to use printer's 72.27 points per inch.

4 Click OK.

Using columns (Photoshop)

The New, Image Size, and Canvas Size commands let you specify image width in terms of columns. Using columns is convenient when you plan to import an image into a page layout program, such as Adobe InDesign, and you want the image to fit exactly within a certain number of columns.

To specify columns for an image:

1 Do one of the following:

- In Windows and Mac OS 9.x, choose Edit > Preferences > Units & Rulers.
- In Mac OS X, choose Photoshop > Preferences > Units & Rulers.

2 Enter values for Width and Gutter.

Using the measure tool (Photoshop)

The measure tool calculates the distance between any two points in the work area. When you measure from one point to another, a nonprinting line is drawn and the options bar and Info palette show the following information:

- The starting location (X and Y).

- The horizontal (W) and vertical (H) distances traveled from the *x*- and *y*-axes.

- The angle measured relative to the axis (A).

- The total distance traveled (D1).

- When using a protractor, you can view two distances traveled (D1 and D2).

All measurements except the angle are calculated in the unit of measure currently set in the Units & Rulers preference dialog box. For information on setting the unit of measure, see "Using rulers" on page 37.

To display an existing measuring line:

Select the measure tool ✐ .

To measure between two points:

1 Select the measure tool ✐ .

2 Drag from the starting point to the ending point. Hold down the Shift key to constrain the tool to multiples of 45°.

3 To create a protractor from an existing measuring line, Alt-drag (Windows) or Option-drag (Mac OS) at an angle from one end of the measuring line, or double-click the line and drag. Hold down the Shift key to constrain the tool to multiples of 45°.

To edit a measuring line or protractor:

1 Select the measure tool ✐ .

2 Do one of the following:

- To resize the line, drag one end of an existing measuring line.

- To move the line, place the pointer on the line away from either endpoint, and drag the line.

- To remove the line, place the pointer on the line away from either endpoint, and drag the line out of the image.

Note: *You can drag out a measure line on an image feature that should be horizontal or vertical, then choose Image > Rotate Canvas > Arbitrary and the correct angle of rotation required to straighten the image will already be entered into the Rotate Canvas dialog box.*

Using guides and the grid

Guides appear as lines that float over the entire image and do not print. You can move, remove, or lock a guide to avoid accidentally moving it.

In Photoshop, a grid appears by default as nonprinting lines but can also be displayed as dots. The grid is useful for laying out elements symmetrically.

Guides and grids behave in similar ways:

- Selections, selection borders, and tools snap to a guide or the grid when dragged within 8 screen (not image) pixels. Guides also snap to the grid when moved. You can turn this feature on and off.

- Guide spacing, along with guide and grid visibility and snapping, is specific to an image.

- Grid spacing, along with guide and grid color and style, is the same for all images.

To show or hide a grid or guides:

Do one of the following:

- (Photoshop) Choose View > Show > Grid.

- Choose View > Show > Guides.

- Choose View > Extras. This command also shows or hides: (Photoshop) selection edges, target path, slices, and notes, or (ImageReady) selection edges, slices, image maps, text bounds, text baseline, and text selection. (See "Working with Extras" on page 41.)

To place a guide:

1 If the rulers are not visible, choose View > Rulers.

Note: For the most accurate readings, view the image at 100% magnification or use the Info palette.

2 Create a guide:

- (Photoshop) Choose View > New Guide. In the dialog box, select Horizontal or Vertical orientation, enter a position, and click OK.

- (ImageReady) Choose View > Create Guides. In the dialog box, specify guide options and click OK.

- Drag from the horizontal ruler to create a horizontal guide.

- Hold down Alt (Windows) or Option (Mac OS), and drag from the vertical ruler to create a horizontal guide.

- Drag from the vertical ruler to create a vertical guide.

- Hold down Alt (Windows) or Option (Mac OS), and drag from the horizontal ruler to create a vertical guide.

- (Photoshop) Hold down Shift and drag from the horizontal or vertical ruler to create a guide that snaps to the ruler ticks.

The pointer changes to a double-headed arrow when you drag a guide.

To move a guide:

1 Select the move tool , or hold down Ctrl (Windows) or Command (Mac OS) to activate the move tool. (This option does not work with the hand or slice tools.)

2 Position the pointer over the guide (the pointer turns into a double-headed arrow).

3 Move the guide:

- Drag the guide to move it.

- Change the guide from horizontal to vertical, or vice versa, by holding down Alt (Windows) or Option (Mac OS) as you click or drag the guide.

- (Photoshop) Align the guide with the ruler ticks by holding down Shift as you drag the guide. The guide will snap to the grid if the grid is visible and View > Snap To > Grid is selected.

To lock all guides:

Choose View > Lock Guides.

To remove guides from the image:

Do one of the following:

- To remove a single guide, drag the guide outside the image window.

- To remove all guides, choose View > Clear Guides.

To turn snapping to guides on or off:

Choose View > Snap To > Guides. (See "Using the Snap command" on page 117.)

To turn snapping to the grid on or off (Photoshop):

Choose View > Snap To > Grid. (See "Using the Snap command" on page 117.)

To set guide and grid preferences (Photoshop):

1 Do one of the following:

- In Windows or Mac OS 9.x, choose Edit > Preferences > Guides, Grid, & Slices.

- In Mac OS X, choose Photoshop > Preferences > Guides, Grid, & Slices.

2 For Color, choose a color for the guides, the grid, or both. If you choose Custom, click the color box, choose a color, and click OK. (See "Using the Color palette" on page 203.)

3 For Style, choose a display option for guides or the grid, or both.

4 For Gridline Every, enter a value for the grid spacing. For Subdivisions, enter a value to subdivide the grid.

If desired, change the units for this option. The Percent option creates a grid that divides the image into even sections. For example, choosing 25 for the Percent option creates an evenly divided 4-by-4 grid.

5 Click OK.

Working with Extras

Guides, grid, target paths, selection edges, slices, image maps, text bounds, text baselines, text selections, and annotations are nonprinting *Extras* that help you select, move, or edit images and objects. You can turn on or off an Extra or any combination of Extras without affecting the image. You can also show or hide Extras by choosing the Extras command in the View menu.

For a description of using specific Extras, see "Using guides and the grid" on page 39; "Annotating images (Photoshop)" on page 44; "Making pixel selections" on page 103; "Using the marquee tools" on page 104; "Selecting paths (Photoshop)" on page 158; "Entering paragraph type" on page 268; "Formatting characters" on page 274; "Creating and viewing slices" on page 288; and "Creating and viewing image maps (ImageReady)" on page 303.

To show Extras:

Choose View > Extras. A check mark appears next to all shown Extras in the Show submenu.

Note: *Choosing Extras also shows color samplers, even though color samplers are not an option in the Show submenu.*

To hide Extras:

With Extras showing, choose View > Extras. A dot (Windows) or a dash (Mac OS) appears next to all hidden Extras in the Show submenu.

Note: Hiding only suppresses the display of Extras. It does not turn off these options.

To show one Extra from a list of hidden Extras:

Choose View > Show and choose an Extra from the submenu. Choosing one of the hidden Extras will cause it to show, and turn off all other Extras.

To turn on and off a group of Extras:

Choose View > Show > All to turn on and show all available Extras. Choose View > Show > None to turn off all Extras.

Displaying status information (Photoshop)

The status bar at the bottom of the window displays useful information—such as the current magnification and file size of the active image, and brief instructions for using the active tool.

To show or hide the status bar (Windows only):

Choose Window > Status Bar. A check mark indicates the item is showing.

Displaying file and image information

Information about the current file size and other features of the image is displayed at the bottom of the application window (Windows) or document window (Mac OS).

Note: In ImageReady, if the document window is wide enough, two image information boxes appear, enabling you to view two different information options for the image at the same time. For more information about original and optimized images, see "Viewing optimized images (ImageReady)" on page 336.

You can also view copyright and authorship information that has been added to the file. This information includes standard file information and Digimarc® watermarks. Photoshop automatically scans opened images for watermarks using the Digimarc Detect Watermark plug-in. If a watermark is detected, Photoshop displays a copyright symbol in the image window's title bar and updates the Copyright & URL section of the File Info dialog box.

To display file information in the document window (Photoshop):

1 Click the triangle in the bottom border of the application window (Windows) or document window (Mac OS).

Illustration of file information view options in Photoshop

2 Select a view option:

- Document Size to display information on the amount of data in the image. The number on the left represents the printing size of the image—approximately the size of the saved, flattened file in Adobe Photoshop format. The number on the right indicates the file's approximate size including layers and channels.

- Document Profile to display the name of the color profile used by the image.

- Document Dimensions to display the dimensions of the image.

- Scratch Sizes to display information on the amount of RAM and scratch disk used to process the image. The number on the left represents the amount of memory that is currently being used by the program to display all open images. The number on the right represents the total amount of RAM available for processing images.

- Efficiency to display the percentage of time actually doing an operation instead of reading or writing the scratch disk. If the value is below 100%, Photoshop is using the scratch disk and, therefore, is operating more slowly.

- Timing to display the amount of time it took to complete the last operation.

- Current Tool to view the name of the active tool.

To display image information in the document window (ImageReady):

1 Click an image information box at the bottom of the document window.

2 Select a view option:

- Original/Optimized File Size to view the original and optimized file size images. The first value indicates the original image file size. The second value (present if the original image has been optimized) indicates the optimized image file size and file format based on the current settings in the Optimize palette.

- Optimized Information to view the file format, file size, number of colors, and dither percentage for the optimized image.

- Image Dimensions to view the image's pixel dimensions.

- Watermark Strength to view the strength of the Digimarc digital watermark in the optimized image, if present.

For more information on using digital watermarks, see "Adding digital copyright information" in online Help.

- Undo/Redo Status to view the number of undos and redos that are available for the image.

- Original in Bytes to view the size of the original, flattened image expressed in bytes.

- Optimized in Bytes to view the size of the optimized image expressed in bytes.

- Optimized Savings to view the percentage of the optimized image file size reduction, followed by the difference in bytes between the original and optimized sizes.

- Size/Download Time to view the file size for the optimized image and estimated download time using the selected modem speed.

Note: Download times may vary based on Internet traffic and modem compression schemes. The value displayed is an approximation.

To view additional file information:

Choose File > File Info.

To read a Digimarc watermark:

1 Choose Filter > Digimarc > Read Watermark. If the filter finds a watermark, a dialog box displays the Creator ID, copyright year (if present), and image attributes.

2 Click OK, or for more information, choose from the following:

- If you have a Web browser installed, click Web Lookup to get more information about the owner of the image. This option launches the browser and displays the Digimarc Web site, where contact details appear for the given Creator ID.

- Call the phone number listed in the Watermark Information dialog box to get information faxed back to you.

For more information on adding digital watermarks to an image, see "Adding digital copyright information with the Digimarc filter" in online Help.

Annotating images (Photoshop)

You can attach note annotations (notes) and audio annotations to an image in Photoshop. This is useful for associating review comments, production notes, or other information with the image. Because Photoshop annotations are compatible with Adobe Acrobat, you can use them to exchange information with Acrobat users as well as Photoshop users.

To circulate a Photoshop document for review in Acrobat, save the document in Portable Document Format (PDF) and ask reviewers to use Acrobat to add notes or audio annotations. Then import the annotations into Photoshop.

Notes and audio annotations appear as small nonprintable icons on the image. They are associated with a location on the image rather than with a layer. You can hide and show annotations, open notes to view or edit their contents, and play audio annotations. You can also add audio annotations to actions, and set them to play during an action or during a pause in an action. (See "Setting playback options (Photoshop)" on page 404.)

Adding notes and audio annotations

You can add notes and audio annotations anywhere on a Photoshop image canvas. When you create a note, a resizable window appears for entering text. When you record an audio annotation, you must have a microphone plugged into the audio-in port of your computer.

You can import both kinds of annotations from Photoshop documents saved in PDF or from Acrobat documents saved in PDF or Form Data Format (FDF).

To create a note:

1 Select the notes tool 📝 .

2 Set options as needed:

• Enter an author name. The name appears in the title bar of the notes window.

• Choose a font and size for the note text.

• Select a color for the note icon and the title bar of note windows.

3 Click where you want to place the note, or drag to create a custom-sized window.

4 Click inside the window, and type the text. If you type more text than fits in the note window, the scroll bar becomes active.

Edit the text as needed:

• You can use the standard editing commands for your system (Undo, Cut, Copy, Paste, and Select All). In Windows, right-click in the text area and choose the commands from the context menu. In Mac OS, choose the commands from the Edit and Select menus. You can also use standard keyboard shortcuts for these editing commands.

• If you have the required software for different script systems (for example, Roman, Japanese, or Cyrillic) installed on your computer, you can switch between the script systems. Right-click (Windows) or Control-click (Mac OS) to display the context menu, and then choose a script system.

5 To close the note to an icon, click the close box.

To create an audio annotation:

1 Select the audio annotation tool 🔊 .

2 Set options as needed:

• Enter an author name.

• Select a color for the audio annotation icon.

3 Click where you want to place the annotation icon.

4 Click Start and then speak into the microphone. When you're finished, click Stop.

To import annotations:

1 Choose File > Import > Annotations.

2 Select a PDF or FDF file that contains annotations, and then click Load. The annotations appear in the locations where they were saved in the source document.

Opening and editing annotations

A note or audio annotation icon marks the location of an annotation on an image. When you move the pointer over an annotation icon and pause, a message displays the author name. You use the icons to open notes or play audio annotations. You can show, hide, or move the icons, and edit the contents of notes.

Note: Resizing an image does not resize the annotation icons and note windows. The icons and note windows keep their locations relative to the image. Cropping an image removes any annotations in the cropped area; you can recover the annotations by undoing the Crop command.

To open a note or play an audio annotation:

Double-click the icon:

- If you are opening a note, a window appears, displaying the note text.

- If you are playing an audio annotation and have a sound card installed, the audio file begins to play.

To show or hide annotation icons:

Do one of the following:

- Choose View > Show > Annotations.

- Choose View > Extras. This command also shows or hides grids, guides, selection edges, target paths, and slices.

To edit annotations:

Do any of the following:

- To move an annotation icon, move the pointer over the icon until it turns into an arrow, and then drag the icon. You can do this with any tool selected. Moving a note icon does not move its note window.

- To move a note window, drag it by the title bar.

- To delete a selected annotation, press Delete.

- To edit the contents of a note, open the note, change any options, and add, delete, or change the text. You can use the same editing commands that you use when creating a note. (See "Adding notes and audio annotations" on page 45.)

- To delete all annotations, right-click (Windows) or Control-click (Mac OS) an annotation icon to display the context menu, and choose Delete All Annotations. You can also delete all annotations by clicking Clear All in the options bar for notes or audio annotations.

Jumping between applications

You can jump between Photoshop and ImageReady to transfer an image between the two applications for editing without closing or exiting the originating application. In addition, you can jump from ImageReady to other graphics editing applications and HTML editing applications installed on your system.

Jumping to an application saves you from having to close the file in one application and reopen it in another application.

Jumping between Photoshop and ImageReady

You can easily jump between Photoshop and ImageReady to use features in both applications when preparing graphics for the Web or other purposes. Jumping between the applications allows you to use the full feature sets of both applications while maintaining a streamlined workflow. Files and documents updated in one application can be automatically updated in the other application.

To jump between Photoshop and ImageReady:

Do one of the following:

• Click the Jump To button [icon] in the toolbox.

• Choose File > Jump To > Photoshop or File > Jump To > ImageReady.

When jumping between Photoshop and ImageReady, the applications use a temp file for transferring changes.

Jumping to other applications (ImageReady)

In addition to jumping to current versions of Photoshop, you can jump to other graphics-editing applications and HTML-editing applications from within ImageReady.

When you install ImageReady, Adobe graphics-editing and HTML-editing applications currently on your system are added to the Jump To submenu. You can add more applications, including non-Adobe applications, to the Jump To submenu.

When you jump to a graphics-editing application, the original file is opened in the destination application. When you jump to an HTML editor, the optimized file and the HTML file are saved and opened in the destination application. If the image contains slices, all files for the full image are included. A preference enables files updated in another application to be automatically updated in ImageReady, when jumping back to ImageReady.

To jump to another application from ImageReady:

1 Do one of the following:

• Choose File > Jump To, and choose the desired application from the submenu.

• If the desired application doesn't appear in the Jump To submenu, choose Other Graphics Editor or Other HTML Editor to specify the application.

2 If the file has been modified since the last save, choose an option in ImageReady for saving the file:

• Click Save, and save the file with its current name and location.

• Click Save As, and save the file with a new name, a new location, or both.

To add an application to the Jump To submenu:

1 Create a shortcut (Windows) or an alias (Mac OS) for the application you want to add to the menu.

2 Drag the icon for the shortcut or alias into the Jump To Graphics Editor or the Jump To HTML Editor folder in the Helpers folder in the Photoshop program folder.

3 Restart ImageReady to view the application in the Jump To submenu.

To automatically update a file when jumping back to ImageReady from another application:

1 Do one of the following:

• In Windows and Mac OS 9.x, choose Edit > Preferences > General.

• In Mac OS X, choose ImageReady > Preferences > General.

2 Select Auto-Update Files.

Previewing an image in a browser

You can open a browser and preview an optimized image. You can preview the image in any browser installed on your system. The browser displays the image with a caption listing the image's file type, pixel dimensions, file size, and compression specifications in the first paragraph, and filename and other HTML information in the second paragraph.

When you install Photoshop and ImageReady, the first Netscape and Internet Explorer browsers found on your system are added to the Preview In menu. You can add additional browsers to the menu, and specify which browser will be launched when using a keyboard shortcut.

To preview an optimized image in a browser:

Do one of the following:

• (Photoshop) Choose File > Save for Web, then select a browser from the Select Browser Menu at the bottom of the Save for Web window.

• (ImageReady) Choose File > Preview In, then choose an option from the submenu. (Choose Other to select a browser not listed in the submenu.)

• (ImageReady) Select a browser from the Preview in Browser tool in the toolbox.

To add a browser to the Preview In menu:

1 Create a shortcut (Windows) or an alias (Mac OS) for the browser you want to add to the menu.

2 Drag the icon for the shortcut or alias into the Preview In folder, located in the Helpers folder in the Photoshop program folder.

3 Restart Photoshop and ImageReady to view the browser in the Preview In menu.

(ImageReady) To specify a browser to be launched by the Preview In keyboard shortcut:

Do one of the following:

• Choose File > Preview In, then choose an option from the submenu.

• Select a browser from the Preview in Default Browser tool in the toolbox.

The shortcut specification takes effect immediately and will persist the next time you launch ImageReady.

Managing libraries with the Preset Manager (Photoshop)

The Preset Manager centralizes management of brushes, swatches, gradients, styles, patterns, contours, custom shapes, and preset tools. You can use the Preset Manager to change the current set of preset items and create new libraries. Once you load a library in the Preset Manager, you can access the library's items in all locations that the type of preset is available, such as the options bar, Styles palette, Gradient Editor dialog box, and so on.

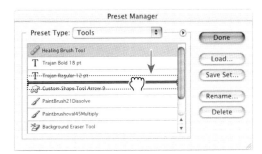

Illustration of rearranging tool presets in the Preset Manager

To display the Preset Manager:

Choose Edit > Preset Manager.

To switch between preset types:

Choose an option from the Preset Type pop-up menu.

To change how items are displayed:

Choose a display option palette menu:

- Text Only to display the name of each preset item.

- Small Thumbnail or Large Thumbnail to display a thumbnail of each preset item. (These options are not available for tool presets.)

- Small List or Large List to display the name and thumbnail of each preset item. (These options are not available for swatch presets.)

- Stroke Thumbnail to display a sample brush stroke and brush thumbnail of each brush preset. (This option is available for brush presets only.)

To load a library of preset items:

Do one of the following:

- Choose a library file from the bottom of the palette menu. Click OK to replace the current list, or click Append to append the current list.

- To add a library to the current list, click Load, select the library file you want to add, and click Load.

- To replace the current list with a different library, choose Replace *Preset Type* from the palette menu. Select the library file you want to use, and click Load.

Note: *Each type of library has its own file extension and default folder in the Presets folder in the Photoshop program folder.*

To rename presets items:

1 Select a preset item. Shift-click to select multiple items:

2 Do one of the following:

- Click Rename, then enter a new name for the brush, swatch, and so on.

- If the Preset Manager is set to display presets as thumbnails, double-click a preset, enter a new name, and click OK.

- If the Preset Manager is set to display presets as a list or text only, double-click a preset, enter a new name inline, and press Enter (Windows) or Return (Mac OS).

To rearrange preset items:

Drag an item up or down in the list.

To delete preset items:

Do one of the following:

- Select a preset item, and click Delete.

- Alt-click (Windows) or Options-click (Mac OS) the items you want to delete.

To create a new library of presets:

1 Do one of the following:

- To save all the presets in the list as a library, make sure that no items are selected.

- To save a subset of the current list as a library, hold down Shift, and select the items you want to save.

2 Click Save Set, choose a location for the library, enter a filename, and click Save.

You can save the library anywhere. However, if you place the library file in the appropriate Presets folder inside the Photoshop program folder, the library name will appear at the bottom of the palette menu after you restart Photoshop.

To return to the default library of preset items:

Choose Reset *Preset Type* from the palette menu. You can either replace the current list or append the default library to the current list.

Setting preferences

Numerous program settings are stored in Adobe Photoshop 7.0 Prefs file. Among the settings stored in this file are general display options, file-saving options, cursor options, transparency options, and options for plug-ins and scratch disks. Most of these options are set in the Preferences dialog box. Preference settings are saved each time you exit the application.

Note: *The default location of the Adobe Photoshop 7.0 Prefs file varies by operating system; use your operating system's Find command to locate this file.*

Unexpected behavior may indicate damaged preferences. By removing damaged preferences, you can restore preferences to their default settings.

To open a preferences dialog box:

1 Do one of the following:

• In Windows or Mac OS 9.x, choose Edit > Preferences and choose the desired preference set from the submenu.

• (Photoshop) In Mac OS X, choose Photoshop > Preferences and choose the desired preference set from the submenu.

• (ImageReady) In Mac OS X, choose ImageReady > Preferences and choose the desired preference set from the submenu.

2 To switch to a different preference set, do one of the following:

• Choose the preference set from the menu at the top of the dialog box.

• Click Next to display the next preference set in the menu list; click Prev to display the previous preference set.

For information on a specific preference option, see the Index.

To restore all preferences to their default settings:

Do one of the following:

• Press and hold Alt+Control+Shift (Windows) or Option+Command+Shift (Mac OS) immediately after launching Photoshop or ImageReady. You will be prompted to delete the current settings.

• In Mac OS, open the Preferences folder in the System Folder (Mac OS 9.x) or Library folder (Mac OS X), and drag the Adobe Photoshop 7.0 Settings folder to the Trash.

New Preferences files will be created the next time you start Photoshop or ImageReady.

Resetting all warning dialogs

Sometimes messages containing warnings or prompts regarding certain situations are displayed. You can disable the display of these messages by selecting the Don't Show Again option in the message. You can also globally reset the display of all messages that have been disabled.

To reset the display of all warning messages (Photoshop):

1 Do one of the following:

• In Windows or Mac OS 9.x, choose Edit > Preferences > General.

• In Mac OS X, choose Photoshop > Preferences > General.

2 Click Reset All Warning Dialogs, and click OK.

To turn on or off warning messages (ImageReady):

1 Do one of the following:

• In Windows or Mac OS 9.x, choose Edit > Preferences > General.

• In Mac OS X, choose Photoshop > Preferences > General.

2 Deselect or select Disable Warnings, and click OK.

Monitoring operations

A progress bar indicates that an operation is in process. You can interrupt the process or have the program notify you when it has finished.

To cancel operations:

Hold down Esc until the operation in progress has stopped. In Mac OS, you can also press Command+period.

To set notification for completion of operations:

1 Do one of the following:

• In Windows or Mac OS 9.x, choose Edit > Preferences > General.

• (Photoshop) In Mac OS X, choose Photoshop > Preferences > General.

• (Photoshop) In Mac OS X, choose ImageReady > Preferences > General.

2 Do one of the following:

• (Photoshop) Select Beep When Done.

• (ImageReady) Select Notify When Done and choose (Mac OS only): System Alert to use your system alert for notification or Text to Speech to use a spoken notification.

3 Click OK.

Closing files and quitting

To close a file:

1 Choose File > Close (Windows and Mac OS) or File > Close All (Mac OS).

2 Choose whether or not to save the file:

• Click Yes (Windows) or Save (Mac OS) to save the file.

• Click No (Windows) or Don't Save (Mac OS) to close the file without saving it.

To exit Photoshop or ImageReady:

1 Choose File > Exit (Windows) or File > Quit (Mac OS).

2 Choose whether or not to save any open files:

• Click Yes (Windows) or Save (Mac OS) for each open file to save the file.

• Click No (Windows) or Don't Save (Mac OS) for each open file to close the file without saving it.

For information on using Adobe and third-party plug-in modules, see "Using plug-in modules" in online Help.

Chapter 2: Getting Images into Photoshop and ImageReady

You can get digital images from a variety of sources—you can create new images, import them from another graphics application, or capture them using a digital camera. Often you will begin by scanning a photograph, a slide, or an image. To create effective artwork, you must understand some basic concepts about how to work with digital images, how to produce high-quality scans, how to work with a variety of file formats, and how to adjust the resolution and size of images.

About bitmap images and vector graphics

Computer graphics fall into two main categories—*bitmap* and *vector*. You can work with both types of graphics in Photoshop and ImageReady; moreover, a Photoshop file can contain both bitmap and vector data. Understanding the difference between the two categories helps as you create, edit, and import artwork.

Bitmap images Bitmap images—technically called *raster images*—use a grid of colors known as pixels to represent images. Each pixel is assigned a specific location and color value. For example, a bicycle tire in a bitmap image is made up of a mosaic of pixels in that location. When working with bitmap images, you edit pixels rather than objects or shapes.

Bitmap images are the most common electronic medium for continuous-tone images, such as photographs or digital paintings, because they can represent subtle gradations of shades and color. Bitmap images are resolution-dependent—that is, they contain a fixed number of pixels. As a result, they can lose detail and appear jagged if they are scaled on-screen or if they are printed at a lower resolution than they were created for.

3:1

24:1

Example of a bitmap image at different levels of magnification

Vector graphics Vector graphics are made up of lines and curves defined by mathematical objects called *vectors*. Vectors describe an image according to its geometric characteristics. For example, a bicycle tire in a vector graphic is made up of a mathematical definition of a circle drawn with a certain radius, set at a specific location, and filled with a specific color. You can move, resize, or change the color of the tire without losing the quality of the graphic.

Vector graphics are resolution-independent—that is, they can be scaled to any size and printed at any resolution without losing detail or clarity. As a result, vector graphics are the best choice for representing bold graphics that must retain crisp lines when scaled to various sizes—for example, logos.

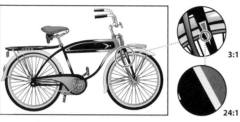

Example of a vector graphic at different levels of magnification

Because computer monitors represent images by displaying them on a grid, both vector and bitmap data is displayed as pixels on-screen.

About image size and resolution

In order to produce high-quality images, it is important to understand how the pixel data of images is measured and displayed.

Pixel dimensions   The number of pixels along the height and width of a bitmap image. The display size of an image on-screen is determined by the pixel dimensions of the image plus the size and setting of the monitor.

For example, a 15-inch monitor typically displays 800 pixels horizontally and 600 vertically. An image with dimensions of 800 pixels by 600 pixels would fill this small screen. On a larger monitor with an 800-by-600-pixel setting, the same image (with 800-by-600-pixel dimensions) would still fill the screen, but each pixel would appear larger. Changing the setting of this larger monitor to 1024-by-768 pixels would display the image at a smaller size, occupying only part of the screen.

When preparing an image for online display (for example, a Web page that will be viewed on a variety of monitors), pixel dimensions become especially important. Because your image may be viewed on a 15-inch monitor, you may want to limit the size of your image to 800-by-600 pixels to allow room for the Web browser window controls.

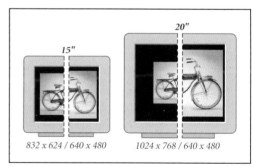

Example of an image displayed on monitors of various sizes and resolutions

Image resolution The number of pixels displayed per unit of printed length in an image, usually measured in pixels per inch (ppi). In Photoshop, you can change the resolution of an image; in ImageReady, the resolution of an image is always 72 ppi. This is because the ImageReady application is tailored to creating images for online media, not print media.

In Photoshop, image resolution and pixel dimensions are interdependent. The amount of detail in an image depends on its pixel dimensions, while the image resolution controls how much space the pixels are printed over. For example, you can modify an image's resolution without changing the actual pixel data in the image—all you change is the printed size of the image. However, if you want to maintain the same output dimensions, changing the image's resolution requires a change in the total number of pixels.

Example of an image at 72-ppi and 300-ppi

When printed, an image with a high resolution contains more, and therefore smaller, pixels than an image with a low resolution. For example, a 1-by-1-inch image with a resolution of 72 ppi contains a total of 5184 pixels (72 pixels wide x 72 pixels high = 5184). The same 1-by-1-inch image with a resolution of 300 ppi contains a total of 90,000 pixels. Higher-resolution images usually reproduce more detail and subtler color transitions than lower-resolution images. However, increasing the resolution of a low-resolution image only spreads the original pixel information across a greater number of pixels; it rarely improves image quality.

Using too low a resolution for a printed image results in *pixelation*—output with large, coarse-looking pixels. Using too high a resolution (pixels smaller than the output device can produce) increases the file size and slows the printing of the image; furthermore, the device will be unable to reproduce the extra detail provided by the higher resolution image.

Monitor resolution The number of pixels or dots displayed per unit of length on the monitor, usually measured in dots per inch (dpi). Monitor resolution depends on the size of the monitor plus its pixel setting. Most new monitors have a resolution of about 96 dpi, while older Mac OS monitors have a resolution of 72 dpi.

Understanding monitor resolution helps explain why the display size of an image on-screen often differs from its printed size. Image pixels are translated directly into monitor pixels. This means that when the image resolution is higher than the monitor resolution, the image appears larger on-screen than its specified print dimensions.

For example, when you display a 1-by-1 inch, 144-ppi image on a 72-dpi monitor, it appears in a 2-by-2 inch area on-screen. Because the monitor can display only 72 pixels per inch, it needs 2 inches to display the 144 pixels that make up one edge of the image.

Printer resolution The number of ink dots per inch (dpi) produced by all laser printers, including imagesetters. Most desktop laser printers have a resolution of 600 dpi, and imagesetters have a resolution of 1200 dpi or higher. To determine the appropriate resolution for your image when printing to any laser printer, but especially to imagesetters, see "screen frequency."

Ink jet printers produce a microscopic spray of ink, not actual dots; however, most ink jet printers have an approximate resolution of 300 to 720 dpi. To determine your printer's optimal resolution, check your printer documentation.

Screen frequency The number of printer dots or halftone cells per inch used to print grayscale images or color separations. Also known as screen ruling or line screen, screen frequency is measured in lines per inch (lpi)—or lines of cells per inch in a halftone screen.

The relationship between image resolution and screen frequency determines the quality of detail in the printed image. To produce a halftone image of the highest quality, you generally use an image resolution that is from 1.5 to at most 2 times the screen frequency. But with some images and output devices, a lower resolution can produce good results. To determine your printer's screen frequency, check your printer documentation or consult your service provider.

Note: Some imagesetters and 600-dpi laser printers use screening technologies other than halftoning. If you are printing an image on a nonhalftone printer, consult your service provider or your printer documentation for the recommended image resolutions.

Screen frequency examples:
A. 65 lpi: Coarse screen typically used to print newsletters and grocery coupons B. 85 lpi: Average screen typically used to print newspapers C. 133 lpi: High-quality screen typically used to print four-color magazines D. 177 lpi: Very fine screen typically used for annual reports and images in art books

File size The digital size of an image, measured in kilobytes (K), megabytes (MB), or gigabytes (GB). File size is proportional to the pixel dimensions of the image. Images with more pixels may produce more detail at a given printed size, but they require more disk space to store and may be slower to edit and print. For instance, a 1-by-1-inch, 200-ppi image contains four times as many pixels as a 1-by-1-inch, 100-ppi image and so has four times the file size. Image resolution thus becomes a compromise between image quality (capturing all the data you need) and file size.

Another factor that affects file size is file format—due to varying compression methods used by GIF, JPEG, and PNG file formats, file sizes can vary considerably for the same pixel dimensions. Similarly, color bit-depth and the number of layers and channels in an image affect file size.

Photoshop supports a maximum file size of 2 GB and maximum pixel dimensions of 30,000 by 30,000 pixels per image. This restriction places limits on the print size and resolution available to an image.

Changing image size and resolution

Once you have scanned or imported an image, you may want to adjust its size. In Photoshop, the Image Size command lets you adjust the pixel dimensions, print dimensions, and resolution of an image; in ImageReady, you can only adjust the pixel dimensions of an image.

For assistance with resizing and resampling images in Photoshop, choose Help > Resize Image. This interactive wizard helps you scale your images for print or online media.

Keep in mind that bitmap and vector data can produce different results when you resize an image. Bitmap data is resolution-dependent; therefore, changing the pixel dimensions of a bitmap image can cause a loss in image quality and sharpness. In contrast, vector data is resolution-independent; you can resize it without losing its crisp edges.

Displaying image size information

You can display information about the current image size using the information box at the bottom of the application window (Windows) or the document window (Mac OS). (See "Displaying file and image information" on page 42.)

To display the current image size:

Do one of the following:

• (Photoshop) Press Alt (Windows) or Option (Mac OS), position the pointer over the file information box, and hold down the mouse button. The box displays the width and height of the image (both in pixels and in the unit of measurement currently selected for the rulers), the number of channels, and the image resolution.

• (ImageReady) Click an image information box, and select Image Dimensions from the pop-up menu. The box displays the width and height of the image in pixels.

About resampling

Resampling refers to changing the pixel dimensions (and therefore display size) of an image. When you *downsample* (or decrease the number of pixels), information is deleted from the image. When you *resample up* (or increase the number of pixels), new pixels are added based on color values of existing pixels. You specify an *interpolation* method to determine how pixels are added or deleted. (See "Choosing an interpolation method" on page 58.)

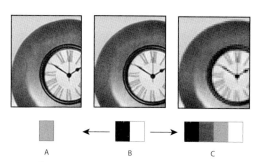

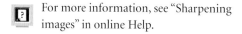

Resampling examples:
A. *Downsampled* **B.** *Original* **C.** *Resampled up*
(Selected pixels displayed for each image)

Keep in mind that resampling can result in poorer image quality. For example, when you resample an image to larger pixel dimensions, the image will lose some detail and sharpness. Applying the Unsharp Mask filter to a resampled image can help refocus the image's details.

For more information, see "Sharpening images" in online Help.

You can avoid the need for resampling by scanning or creating the image at a high enough resolution. If you want to preview the effects of changing pixel dimensions on-screen or print proofs at different resolutions, resample a duplicate of your file.

Choosing an interpolation method

When an image is resampled, an *interpolation method* is used to assign color values to any new pixels it creates, based on the color values of existing pixels in the image. The more sophisticated the method, the more quality and detail from the original image are preserved.

The General Preferences dialog box lets you specify a default interpolation method to use whenever images are resampled with the Image Size or transformation commands. The Image Size command also lets you specify an interpolation method other than the default.

To specify the default interpolation method:

1 Do one of the following:

- In Windows or Mac OS 9.x, choose Edit > Preferences > General.

- (Photoshop) In Mac OS X, choose Photoshop > Preferences > General.

- (ImageReady) In Mac OS X, choose ImageReady > Preferences > General.

2 For Interpolation, choose one of the following options:

- Nearest Neighbor (Jagged) for the fast but less precise method. This method is recommended for use with illustrations containing non-anti-aliased edges, to preserve hard edges and produce a smaller file. However, this method can result in jagged effects, which become apparent when distorting or scaling an image or performing multiple manipulations on a selection.

- (Photoshop) Bilinear for a medium-quality method.

- Bicubic (Smooth) for the slow but more precise method, resulting in the smoothest tonal gradations.

Changing the pixel dimensions of an image

When preparing images for online distribution, it's useful to specify image size in terms of the pixel dimensions. Keep in mind that changing pixel dimensions affects not only the size of an image on-screen but also its image quality and its printed characteristics—either its printed dimensions or its image resolution. (See "About image size and resolution" on page 54.)

To change the pixel dimensions of an image (Photoshop):

1 Choose Image > Image Size.

2 Make sure that Resample Image is selected, and choose an interpolation method. (See "Choosing an interpolation method" on page 58.)

3 To maintain the current proportions of pixel width to pixel height, select Constrain Proportions. This option automatically updates the width as you change the height, and vice versa.

4 Under Pixel Dimensions, enter values for Width and Height. To enter values as percentages of the current dimensions, choose Percent as the unit of measurement.

The new file size for the image appears at the top of the Image Size dialog box, with the old file size in parentheses.

For best results in producing a smaller image, downsample and apply the Unsharp Mask filter. To produce a larger image, rescan the image at a higher resolution.

To change the pixel dimensions of an image (ImageReady):

1 Choose Image > Image Size.

2 To maintain the current proportions of pixel width to pixel height, select Constrain Proportions.

3 Under New Size, enter values for Width, Height, or Percent. The New Size text field displays the new file size for the image.

4 Select a resampling method from the Quality pop-up menu.

For information on setting action options, see "Recording image size options (ImageReady)" on page 402.

Changing the print dimensions and resolution of an image (Photoshop)

When creating an image for print media, it's useful to specify image size in terms of the printed dimensions and the image resolution. These two measurements, referred to as the *document size*, determine the total pixel count and therefore the file size of the image; document size also determines the base size at which an image is placed into another application. You can further manipulate the scale of the printed image using the Print with Preview command; however, changes you make using the Print with Preview command affect only the printed image, not the document size of the image file. (See "Positioning and scaling images" on page 383.)

If you turn on resampling for the image, you can change print dimensions and resolution independently (and change the total number of pixels in the image). If you turn resampling off, you can change either the dimensions or the resolution—Photoshop adjusts the other value automatically to preserve the total pixel count. For the highest print quality, it's generally best to change the dimensions and resolution first without resampling. Then resample only as necessary.

To change the print dimensions and resolution of an image:

1 Choose Image > Image Size.

2 Change the print dimensions, image resolution, or both:

- To change only the print dimensions or only the resolution and adjust the total number of pixels in the image proportionately, make sure that Resample Image is selected. Then choose an interpolation method. (See "Choosing an interpolation method" on page 58.)

- To change the print dimensions and resolution without changing the total number of pixels in the image, deselect Resample Image.

3 To maintain the current proportions of image width to image height, select Constrain Proportions. This option automatically updates the width as you change the height, and vice versa.

4 Under Document Size, enter new values for the height and width. If desired, choose a new unit of measurement. Note that for Width, the Columns option uses the width and gutter sizes specified in the Units & Rulers preferences. For more information, see "Using columns (Photoshop)" on page 38.

5 For Resolution, enter a new value. If desired, choose a new unit of measurement.

To return to the original values displayed in the Image Size dialog box, hold down Alt (Windows) or Option (Mac OS), and click Reset.

To view the print size on-screen:

Do one of the following:

- Choose View > Print Size.

- Select the hand tool or zoom tool, and click Print Size in the options bar.

The magnification of the image is adjusted to display its approximate printed size, as specified in the Document Size section of the Image Size dialog box. Keep in mind that the size and resolution of your monitor affect the on-screen print size.

Determining a recommended resolution for an image (Photoshop)

If you plan to print your image using a halftone screen, the range of suitable image resolutions depends on the screen frequency of your output device. You can have Photoshop determine a recommended resolution for your image based on your device's screen frequency. (See "About image size and resolution" on page 54.)

Note: If your image resolution is more than 2.5 times the screen ruling, an alert message appears when you try to print the image. This means that the image resolution is higher than necessary for the printer. Save a copy of the file, and then reduce the resolution.

To determine a suggested resolution for an image:

1 Choose Image > Image Size.

2 Click Auto.

3 For Screen, enter the screen frequency for the output device. If desired, choose a new unit of measurement. Note that the screen value is used only to calculate the image resolution, not to set the screen for printing.

Important: To specify the halftone screen ruling for printing, you must use the Halftone Screens dialog box, accessible through the Print with Preview command. (See "Selecting halftone screen attributes" on page 386.)

4 For Quality, select an option:

• Draft to produce a resolution the same as the screen frequency (no lower than 72 pixels per inch).

• Good to produce a resolution 1.5 times the screen frequency.

• Best to produce a resolution 2 times the screen frequency.

Scanning images

Before you scan an image, make sure that the software necessary for your scanner has been installed. To ensure a high-quality scan, you should predetermine the scanning resolution and dynamic range your image requires. These preparatory steps can also prevent unwanted color casts from being introduced by your scanner.

Scanner drivers are provided and supported by the manufacturers of the scanners, not Adobe Systems Incorporated. If you have problems with scanning, make sure that you are using the latest version of the appropriate scanner driver.

Importing scanned images

You can import scanned images directly from any scanner that has an Adobe Photoshop-compatible plug-in module or that supports the TWAIN interface. To import the scan using a plug-in module, choose the scanner name from the File > Import submenu. See your scanner documentation for instructions on installing the scanner plug-in.

  For more information, see "Using plug-in modules" in online Help.

If your scanner does not have an Adobe Photoshop-compatible scanner driver, import the scan using the TWAIN interface. (See "Importing an image using the TWAIN interface" on page 62.)

If you can't import the scan using the TWAIN interface, use the scanner manufacturer's software to scan your images, and save the images as TIFF, PICT, or BMP files. Then open the files in Photoshop or ImageReady.

Importing an image using the TWAIN interface

TWAIN is a cross-platform interface for acquiring images captured by certain scanners, digital cameras, and frame grabbers. The manufacturer of the TWAIN device must provide a Source Manager and TWAIN Data source for your device to work with Photoshop and ImageReady.

You must install the TWAIN device and its software, and restart your computer, before you can use it to import images into Photoshop and ImageReady. See the documentation provided by your device manufacturer for installation information.

To import an image using the TWAIN interface (Photoshop):

Choose File > Import, and choose the device you want to use from the submenu.

To import an image using the TWAIN interface (ImageReady):

1 If you're using the TWAIN device for the first time with ImageReady, choose File > Import > TWAIN Select. Then select the device you want to use. You do not need to repeat this step for subsequent use of the TWAIN module.

If more than one TWAIN device is installed in your system and you want to switch devices, use the TWAIN Select command.

2 To import the image, choose File > Import > TWAIN Acquire.

For more information about scanning, see "Scanning using the resolution setting (Photoshop)," "Scanning using the file size setting (Photoshop)," "Optimizing the dynamic range of the scan (Photoshop)," and "Eliminating unwanted color casts (Photoshop)" in online Help.

Importing images using WIA (Windows Image Acquisition) Support

Certain digital cameras and scanners can be used to import images using WIA Support. When you use WIA Support, Photoshop works with Windows and your digital camera or scanner software to import images directly into Photoshop.

Note: WIA Support is only available if you are using WindowsME or Windows XP.

To import images from a digital camera using WIA Support:

1 Choose File > Import > WIA Support.

2 Choose a destination on your computer for saving your image files.

3 Make sure Open Acquired Images in Photoshop is checked. If you have a large number of images to import, or if you want to edit the images at a later time, deselect it.

4 Make sure Unique Subfolder is selected if you want to save the imported images directly into a folder named with the current date.

5 Click Start.

6 Select the digital camera that you want to import images from.

Note: If the name of your camera does not appear in the submenu, verify that the software and drivers were properly installed and that the camera is connected.

7 Choose the image or images you want to import:

- Click the image from the list of thumbnails to import the image.

- Hold down Shift and click on multiple images to import them at the same time.

- Click Select All to import all available images.

8 Click Get Picture to import the image.

To import images from a scanner using WIA Support:

1 Choose File > Import > WIA Support.

2 Choose a destination on your computer to save image files to.

3 Click Start.

4 Make sure Open Acquired Images in Photoshop is checked. If you have a large number of images to import, or if you want to edit the images at a later time, deselect it.

5 Make sure Unique Subfolder is selected if you want to save the imported images directly into a folder named with the current date.

6 Select the scanner that you want to use.

Note: If the name of your scanner does not appear in the submenu, verify that the software and drivers were properly installed and that the scanner is connected.

7 Choose the kind of image you want to scan:

- Color picture to use the default settings for scanning color images.

- Grayscale picture to use the default settings for scanning grayscale images.

- Black and White picture or Text to use the default settings.

- Click Adjust the Quality of the Scanned Picture to use custom settings.

8 Click preview to view the scan. Crop the scan if needed by pulling the rectangle so it surrounds the image.

9 Click Scan.

10 The scanned image will be saved in the .bmp file format.

Creating new images

The New command lets you create a blank image.

To create a new image:

1 Do one of the following:

- To base the image dimensions and resolution (Photoshop) on the Clipboard contents, choose File > New. If the Clipboard does not contain image data, the image dimensions and resolution are based on the last image you created.

- (Photoshop) To base the image size on the default dimensions and resolution or the last entered settings, hold down Alt (Windows) or Option (Mac OS) when you choose File > New.

2 If desired, type a name for the image, and set the width and height.

 (Photoshop) To match the width and height of the new image to that of any open image, choose a filename from the bottom section of the Windows menu.

3 (Photoshop) Set the resolution and mode. For more information, see "About image size and resolution" on page 54 and "About color modes and models (Photoshop)" on page 77.

4 Select an option for the contents of the background layer (Photoshop) or first layer (ImageReady) of the image:

- White to fill the background or first layer with white, the default background color.

- Background Color to fill the background or first layer with the current background color. (See "Choosing foreground and background colors" on page 201.)

- Transparent to make the first layer transparent, with no color values. The resulting document will have a single, transparent layer as its contents.

Opening and importing images

You can open and import images in various file formats. The available formats appear in the File Browser, the Open dialog box, the Open As dialog box (Windows), or the Import submenu.

 For more information, see "About file formats" in online Help.

Note: Photoshop and ImageReady use plug-in modules to open and import many file formats. If a file format does not appear in the Open dialog box or in the File > Import submenu, you may need to install the format's plug-in module.

For more information, see "Using plug-in modules" in online Help.

Opening files

You can open files using the Open command and Open Recent command. In Photoshop, you can also open files using the File Browser. For more information, see "Using the File Browser (Photoshop)" on page 68.

There may be instances when Photoshop cannot determine the correct format for a file. For example, transferring a file between Mac OS and Windows can cause the format to be mislabeled. In such cases, you must specify the correct format in which to open the file.

To open a file using the Open command:

1 Choose File > Open.

2 Select the name of the file you want to open. If the file does not appear, select the option for showing all files from the Files of Type (Windows) or Show (Mac OS) pop-up menu.

3 (Mac OS) Click Show Preview to preview the selected file. This option requires the Apple QuickTime extension.

Note: Previews display faster if they are saved with the file. In Photoshop, select Always Save for Image Previews in the Saving Files preferences to always save a preview; select Ask When Saving to save previews on a file-per-file basis.

4 Click Open. In some cases, a dialog box appears, letting you set format-specific options. (See "Opening and importing PDF files" on page 65 and "Opening PostScript artwork" on page 67.)

Note: If a color profile warning message appears, specify whether to convert the pixels based on the file's color profile. (See "Specifying color management policies" on page 94.)

 For information on opening files, see "Opening Photo CD files," "Opening Raw files (Photoshop)," "Importing anti-aliased PICT files (Mac OS)," and "Importing PICT Resources (Mac OS)" in online Help.

To open a recently used file:

Choose File > Open Recent, and select a file from the submenu.

To specify the number of files that are available in the Open Recent submenu:

1 Do one of the following:

- (Photoshop) In Windows or Mac OS 9.x, choose Edit > Preferences > File Handling.

- (Photoshop) In Mac OS X, choose Photoshop > Preferences > File Handling.

- (ImageReady) In Windows or Mac OS 9.x, choose Edit > Preferences > General.

- (ImageReady) In Mac OS X, choose ImageReady > Preferences > General.

2 Do one of the following:

- (Photoshop) Enter a number in the Recent File List Contains text box.

- (ImageReady) Enter a number in the Recent Files text box.

To specify the file format in which to open a file (Photoshop):

Do one of the following:

- (Windows) Choose File > Open As, and select the file you want to open. Then choose the desired format from the Open As pop-up menu, and click Open.

- (Mac OS) Choose File > Open, and choose All Documents from the Show pop-up menu. Then select the file you want to open, choose the desired file format from the Format pop-up menu, and click Open.

Important: If the file does not open, then the chosen format may not match the file's true format, or the file may be damaged.

Opening and importing PDF files

Portable Document Format (PDF) is a versatile file format that can represent both vector and bitmap data and can contain electronic document search and navigation features. PDF is the primary format for Adobe Illustrator and Adobe Acrobat.

 For more information, see "PDF" in online Help.

Some PDF files contain a single image. Other PDF files (called Generic PDF files) may contain multiple pages and images. When you open a Generic PDF file, you can choose which page to open and specify rasterization options. If you want to open an image (versus a page) from a PDF file, you can use the File > Import > PDF Image command.

You can also bring PDF data into Photoshop or ImageReady using the Place command, the Paste command, and the drag-and-drop feature. (See "Placing files" on page 71, "Using drag and drop to copy between applications" on page 116, and "Using the Clipboard to copy between applications" on page 116.)

To open a PDF file:

1 Choose File > Open.

2 Select the name of the file, and click Open. You can change which types of files show by selecting an option from the Files of Type (Windows) or Show (Mac OS) pop-up menu.

3 If you are opening a Generic PDF file, do the following:

• If the file contains multiple pages, select the page you want to open.

• Indicate the desired dimensions, resolution, and mode. If the file has an embedded ICC profile and Preserve Embedded Profiles is selected for Color Management Policies in the Color Settings dialog box, you can choose the profile from the mode pop-up menu.

• Select Constrain Proportions to maintain the same height-to-width ratio.

• Select Anti-aliased to minimize the jagged appearance of the artwork's edges as it is rasterized.

To import images from a PDF file:

1 Choose File > Import > PDF Image, select the file you want to import images from, and click Open.

2 Select the image you want to open:

• To open a specific image, select it and click OK. You can use the arrows to scroll through the images, or click Go to Image to enter an image number.

• To open each image as a separate file, click Import All Images.

> Press Esc to cancel the import operation before all images are imported.

To create a new Photoshop file for each page of a multiple-page PDF file (Photoshop):

1 Choose File > Automate > Multi-Page PDF to PSD.

2 Under Source PDF, click the Choose button, and select the file you want to import images from.

3 Under Page Range, specify a range of pages to import.

4 Under Output Options, specify a resolution, choose a color mode, and set the Anti-alias option for rasterizing each page of the PDF file. (To blend edge pixels during rasterization, select the Anti-alias option. To produce a hard-edged transition between edge pixels during rasterization, deselect the Anti-alias option.)

5 Under Destination, enter a base name for the generated files. (When Photoshop creates the new files, the base name is appended with a number that corresponds to the page number of the PDF file.) Then click the Choose button, and select the location where you want to save the generated files.

Opening PostScript artwork

Encapsulated PostScript® (EPS) can represent both vector and bitmap data and is supported by virtually all graphic, illustration, and page-layout programs. Adobe applications that produce PostScript artwork include Adobe Illustrator, Adobe Dimensions, and Adobe Streamline. When you open an EPS file containing vector art, it is *rasterized*—the mathematically defined lines and curves of the vector artwork are converted into the pixels or bits of a bitmap image.

You can also bring PostScript artwork into Photoshop or ImageReady using the Place command, the Paste command, and the drag-and-drop feature. (See "Placing files" on page 71, "Using drag and drop to copy between applications" on page 116, and "Using the Clipboard to copy between applications" on page 116.)

To open an EPS file:

1 Choose File > Open.

2 Select the file you want to open, and click Open.

3 Indicate the desired dimensions, resolution, and mode. To maintain the same height-to-width ratio, select Constrain Proportions.

4 Select Anti-aliased to minimize the jagged appearance of the artwork's edges as it is rasterized.

Turning off anti-aliasing for PDF and EPS files (ImageReady)

The Anti-alias PostScript option removes jagged edges from a pasted or placed selection by making a subtle transition between the edges of the selection and its surrounding pixels. Turning off this option produces a hard-edged transition between pixels—and therefore the appearance of jagged edges—when vector artwork is rasterized.

Note: In Photoshop, you can deselect the Anti-alias option when you open or place a PDF or EPS file.

To turn off the Anti-alias PostScript option:

1 Do one of the following:

• In Windows or Mac OS 9.x, choose Edit > Preferences > General.

• In Mac OS X, choose ImageReady > Preferences > General.

2 Deselect Anti-alias PostScript. Clearing this option can decrease the time it takes to import the file.

Using the File Browser (Photoshop)

File Browser lets you view, sort, and process image files. You can use the File Browser to perform tasks such as creating new folders; renaming, moving, and deleting files; and rotating images. You can also view individual file information and data imported from your digital camera.

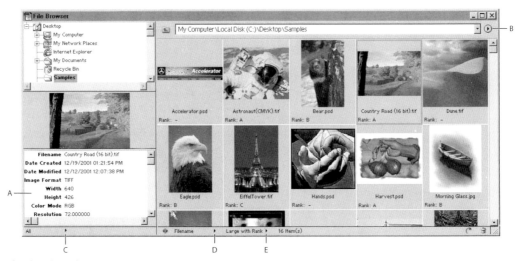

The Photoshop File Browser:
A. File information B. File Browser palette menu C. File information pop-up menu D. Sort By pop-up menu
E. View By pop-up menu

Displaying the File Browser Choose File > Browse or Window > File Browser. By default, the File Browser is displayed in the palette well. To display the File Browser in a separate window, choose Show in Separate Window from the palette menu. For more information on using palettes in the palette well, see "Using the palette well (Photoshop)" on page 22.

Using the File Browser palette menu Click the triangle ⊙ in the upper right corner of the palette to access commands for working with layers. If the palette is docked in the palette well, click the triangle on the palette tab.

Navigating in the File Browser Double-click a folder to view its contents. To show or hide folders on the right side of the palette, choose the Show Folders from the palette menu. A check mark indicates that folders are showing.

Changing the display of files Choose a thumbnail display option from the palette menu, or click the View By pop-up menu at the bottom of the File Browser and choose a display option.

Sorting files Click the Sort By pop-up menu at the bottom of the File Browser, and choose a sorting option.

Ranking files Ranking lets you manually control the sort order of files. To specify a rank, choose the Large Thumbnail with Rank display option, click in the Rank field, type a letter, and press Enter (Windows) or Return (Mac OS). Alternately, right click (Windows) or Control-click (Mac OS) a thumbnail and choose a rank from the context menu.

Note: To rank multiple files, select multiple thumbnails and then choose a rank from the context menu.

Displaying file information Click the File Information pop-up menu at the bottom of the File Browser, and select one of the following: All to view all image information for a file; or EXIF to view image information imported from your digital camera. For more information, see "Adding file information (Photoshop)" on page 374.

Selecting and deselecting files On the right side of the palette, click a thumbnail to select the file, or Shift-click to select multiple files. To select all files in the current folder, choose Select All from the palette menu. To deselect all files, choose Deselect All from the palette menu.

Opening files Select the file or files you want to open, and do one of the following: select a file and press Enter (Windows) or Return (Mac OS); double-click a selected file; drag the selected file or files out of the File Browser; or choose Open from the palette menu.

When the File Browser is docked in the palette well, double-clicking a file or selecting a file and pressing Enter (Windows) or Return (Mac OS) opens the image and closes the File Browser. To keep the File Browser open, hold down Alt (Windows) or Option (Mac OS) when you double-click the file, press Enter (Windows), or press Return (Mac OS).

Renaming files and folders On the right side of the palette, click a filename or folder name, or select a file or folder and choose Rename from the palette menu. Then type a new name, and press Enter (Windows) or Return (Mac OS).

Note: To move to the next filename, press Tab. To move to the previous filename, press Shift+Tab.

Renaming files in batches To rename all the files in a folder, make sure that no files are selected. To rename a subset of files in a folder, select the files you want to rename. Then choose Batch Rename from the palette menu, and set the following options:

• For Destination Folder, select where you want to place the renamed files: in the same folder or in a different folder. If you select Move to New Folder, click Browse to select a different folder.

• For File Naming, choose elements from the pop-up menus or enter text into the fields. The specified elements and text will be combined to create the new filename.

• For Compatibility, select the operating systems with which you want renamed files to be compatible. The current operating system is selected by default, and you cannot deselect it.

Deleting files Select the file or files you want to delete, and do one of the following: click the Trash button, drag the files to the Trash button 🗑, press the Delete key, or choose Delete from the palette menu.

Creating new folders Choose New Folder from the palette menu, type a name, and press Enter (Windows) or Return (Mac OS).

Moving and copying files To move a file, drag it to a different folder; to copy a file, Alt-drag (Windows) or Option-drag (Mac OS) it to a different folder.

Rotating images Select one or more files, and do one of the following: choose a rotation option from the palette menu; click the Rotate button ↻ to rotate the images clockwise by 90 degrees; or Alt-click (Windows) or Option-click (Mac OS) the Rotate button ↻ to rotate the images counter-clockwise by 90 degrees.

Refreshing the view When you rename a file, the order of files in the File Browser is not automatically updated. To refresh the view, choose Refresh Desktop View from the palette menu. Closing and reopening the File Browser also refreshes the view.

Displaying files in the Windows Explorer or Mac OS Finder Choose Reveal Location in Explorer (Windows) or Reveal Location in Finder (Mac OS) from the palette menu.

Purging the cache The cache stores thumbnail and file information to make loading times quicker when you return to a previously viewed folder. To purge the cache and free disk space, choose Purge Cache from the palette menu.

Note: Purging the cache deletes ranking and thumbnail information.

Exporting the cache Exporting the cache allows you to burn a CD without having to generate thumbnails. To export the cache, choose Export Cache from the palette menu. The cache is exported to the current folder in the File Browser.

Placing files

You can use the File > Place command to place artwork into a new layer in an image. In Photoshop, you can place PDF, Adobe Illustrator, and EPS files; in ImageReady, you can place files in any supported format, with the exception of Photoshop (PSD) files containing CMYK images.

When you place a PDF, Adobe Illustrator, or EPS file, it is rasterized; you cannot edit text or vector data in placed artwork. Keep in mind that artwork is rasterized at the resolution of the file into which it is placed.

To place a PDF, Adobe Illustrator, or EPS file (Photoshop):

1 Open the Photoshop image into which you want to place the artwork.

2 Choose File > Place, select the file you want to place, and click Place.

3 If you are placing a PDF file that contains multiple pages, select the page you want to place in the provided dialog box, and click OK.

The placed artwork appears inside a bounding box at the center of the Photoshop image. The artwork maintains its original aspect ratio; however, if the artwork is larger than the Photoshop image, it is resized to fit.

4 If desired, reposition the placed artwork by doing one or more of the following:

• Position the pointer inside the bounding box of the placed artwork, and drag.

• In the options bar, enter a value for X to specify the distance between the center point of the placed artwork and the left edge of the image. Enter a value for Y to specify the distance between the center point of the placed artwork and the top edge of the image.

• To adjust the center point of the placed artwork, drag the center point to a new location, or click a handle on the center point icon 🖽 in the options bar.

5 If desired, scale the placed artwork by doing one or more of the following:

• Drag one of the handles at the corners or sides of the bounding box. Hold down Shift as you drag a corner handle to constrain the proportions.

• In the options bar, enter values for W and H to specify the width and height of the artwork. By default, these options represent scale as a percentage; however, you can enter another unit of measurement. To constrain the proportions of the artwork, click the Constrain Proportions icon 🔓 ; the option is on when the icon has a white background.

6 If desired, rotate the placed artwork by doing one or more of the following:

• Position the pointer outside the bounding box of the placed artwork (the pointer turns into a curved arrow), and drag.

• In the options bar, enter a value (in degrees) for the Rotation option ⌂ .

The artwork rotates around the center point of the placed artwork. To adjust the center point, drag it to a new location, or click a handle on the Center Point icon ⊞ in the options bar.

7 If desired, skew the placed artwork by holding down Ctrl (Windows) or Command (Mac OS), and dragging a side handle of the bounding box.

8 Set the Anti-alias option in the options bar as desired. To blend edge pixels during rasterization, select the Anti-alias option. To produce a hard-edged transition between edge pixels during rasterization, deselect the Anti-alias option.

9 To commit the placed artwork to a new layer, do one of the following:

- Click the OK button ✔ in the options bar.

- Press Enter or Return.

To cancel the placement, click the Cancel button ⃠ in the options bar, or press Esc.

To place a file (ImageReady):

1 Open the ImageReady image into which you want to place the file.

2 Choose File > Place, select the file you want to place, and click Open.

3 Select offset options:

- From the Horizontal pop-up menu, choose an option for placing the file horizontally with respect to the image. In the Pixels text box, enter the number of pixels to offset the placed image horizontally.

- From the Vertical pop-up menu, choose an option for placing the file vertically with respect to the image. In the Pixels text box, enter the number of pixels to offset the placed image vertically.

Note: To enter a negative number (and offset the placed file to the left or below the image), type a hyphen (-) before the number.

4 Click OK.

5 If you are placing a PDF file that contains multiple pages, select the page you want to place, and click OK.

6 If you are placing a PDF or EPS file, select Rasterize options, and click OK:

- Enter Width and Height values for Image Size.

- Select Anti-aliased to minimize the jagged appearance of the artwork's edges as it is rasterized.

- Select Constrain Proportions to maintain the same height-to-width ratio.

Managing files with WebDAV (Photoshop)

Photoshop supports the Web Distributed Authoring and Versioning (WebDAV) server technology. Using this technology, you can connect to a WebDAV server, download and upload files, lock files so others cannot work on them at the same time as you, and add additional files (called *assets*) to the server. Use a WebDAV server to work in a collaborative environment without fear that files will be accidentally overwritten or updates lost.

About workgroup management

When working in a collaborative environment, users must share files. The process of passing files from one collaborator to another involves working with a *workgroup*. Controlling the hand-off—so that only one person can edit a file at any given time—is called *workgroup management*.

A WebDAV server provides workgroup management via the Web. When a file is managed by a WebDAV server, multiple users can download copies of the file, but only one user at a time can *check out* the file. The user who checks out the file can share his or her work with other users by updating the file on the server; however, other users can't make changes to the managed file until it is checked in. This check out/check in system allows multiple users to access the same file but prevents users from overwriting each other's work.

Getting started with workgroup management

To use the workgroup management features in Photoshop, you must be able to connect to a WebDAV server. You can find detailed information and the latest news about WebDAV at www.webdav.org.

Important: Firewall software can interfere with the process of connecting to a WebDAV server. Check with your system administrator or refer to your firewall software documentation for information about setting options to access outside servers.

You can also set preferences to determine whether or not the Workgroup pop-up menu 🗔 appears and the default behavior for checking out and updating files.

To set up a server for use with Photoshop:

1 Choose File > Workgroup > Workgroup Servers.

2 Specify a folder in which you want to store local copies of managed files. To change the default location, click Choose, and specify a different folder. Click Show to locate a folder in the Windows Explorer or the Mac OS Finder.

Note: The path you choose here is used for all servers you want to add. Changing this path does not change the location of files on existing servers.

3 Select the WebDAV server you want to use, or do one of the following:

• To add a new server to the list, click New Server, specify a unique server nickname and URL, and click OK.

• To edit a server in the list, click Edit Server. To view the folder where local copies of managed files are stored, click Advanced Options, then click Show.

• To remove a server from the list, click Remove, and then click OK to the warning message.

4 Click Done.

To set workgroup management preferences:

1 Do one of the following:

- In Windows and Mac OS 9.x, choose Edit > Preferences > File Handling.

- In Mac OS X, choose Photoshop > Preferences > File Handling.

2 Do one of the following:

- To show the Workgroup pop-up menu 🗔 at the bottom of the application window (Windows) or document window (Mac OS), select Enable Workgroup functionality.

- To hide the Workgroup pop-up menu, deselect Enable Workgroup functionality.

3 Select one of the following options for Check Out from Server:

- Never to open the local copy of the file without displaying a dialog box and without checking it out.

- Always to automatically check out the file when you open it.

- Ask to display a dialog box when you open a file that is not checked out.

4 Select one of the following options for Update from Server:

- Never to open the local copy of the file without displaying a dialog box and without downloading the latest version of the file from the server.

- Always to automatically download the latest version of the file from the server.

- Ask to display a dialog box asking if you want to download the latest version.

Logging on and off WebDAV servers

Different WebDAV servers have different authentication requirements. Some servers require you to enter a user name and password for every transaction; other servers require authentication only once per session. When the Authentication dialog box appears, enter your user name and password.

To log off all WebDAV servers:

Choose File > Workgroup > Logoff All Servers.

Opening managed files

To view a managed file, open a copy of the file from a WebDAV server. The File > Workgroup > Open command creates a local copy of the file on your hard drive.

After you have a local copy of a file, you can revert it to the version of the file on the server (for checked out files) or update it with changes from the file on the server (for non-checked out files). Reverting and updating permanently discard all changes you've made to the file.

To open a managed file:

1 Choose File > Workgroup > Open.

2 Select a server, a directory, and the file you want to open.

3 Do one of the following:

- Click Check Out if you want to open and check out at the same time. (See "Checking files out and in" on page 75.)

- Click Open if you want to open a local copy without checking it out.

To revert a checked out file to the version on the server:

1 Open your local copy of the file.

2 Do one of the following:

- Choose File > Workgroup > Revert.

- Choose Revert from the Workgroup pop-up menu ⬚ at the bottom of the application window (Windows) or document window (Mac OS).

To update a non-checked out file from the version on the server:

1 Open your local copy of the file.

2 Do one of the following:

- Choose File > Workgroup > Update.

- Choose Update from the Workgroup pop-up menu ⬚ .

Checking files out and in

Checking out a file prevents other users from making changes to it on the WebDAV server. When you're finished making edits, check in the file to update your changes to the server and release your lock on the managed file.

To check out a file:

Do one of the following:

- To check out the file that you already have open, choose File > Workgroup > Check Out. Alternately, choose Check Out from the Workgroup pop-up menu ⬚ at the bottom of the application window (Windows) or document window (Mac OS).

- To open and check out a file at the same time, choose File > Workgroup > Open. Then, locate and select the file and click Check Out. (See "Opening managed files" on page 74.)

To verify if a local file is available for check out:

1 Open your copy of the file.

2 Choose File > Workgroup > Verify State, or choose Verify State from the Workgroup pop-up menu.

To check in a file:

Do one of the following:

- To check in the file and update changes to the server, choose File > Workgroup > Check In. Alternately, choose Check In from the Workgroup pop-up menu.

- To check in the file without updating changes to the server, choose File > Workgroup > Cancel Check Out. Alternately, choose Cancel Check Out from the Workgroup pop-up menu.

Saving changes to the server

While you have a file checked out, you can save changes to the managed file on the server. This allows you to share your work with other users without giving up your lock on the file.

To save changes to the server:

1 Open your local copy of the file.

2 Do one of the following:

• Choose File > Workgroup > Save.

• Choose Save from the Workgroup pop-up menu ⬛ at the bottom of the application window (Windows) or document window (Mac OS).

Adding files to the server

Adding a file to a WebDAV server initiates workgroup management for the file; in other words, you create a managed file by adding it to a server.

To add a file to a WebDAV server:

1 Open the file you want to add to the server.

2 Do one of the following:

• Choose File > Workgroup > Save As.

• Choose Save As from the Workgroup pop-up menu ⬛ at the bottom of the application window (Windows) or document window (Mac OS).

3 Choose a server from the pop-up menu; then locate the directory to which you want to save the file.

4 Type in a filename in the Name text box, and choose a format from the Format pop-up menu.

Note: *Be sure to specify a file extension if the file will be downloaded to a computer running a Windows operating system.*

5 To check out the file, select Keep This File Checked Out for Editing.

6 Click Save.

Chapter 3: Working with Color

Familiarity with color theory and termi- nology can help you understand how color is measured and how Adobe Photoshop and Adobe ImageReady use this information to define, display, and print color values.

After you determine the appropriate color mode for your image, you can apply colors and make color and tonal adjustments.

About color modes and models (Photoshop)

A color mode determines the color model used to display and print images. Photoshop bases its color modes on established models for describing and reproducing color. Common models include HSB (hue, saturation, brightness); RGB (red, green, blue); CMYK (cyan, magenta, yellow, black); and CIE L*a*b*. Photoshop also includes modes for specialized color output such as Indexed Color and Duotone. ImageReady uses RGB mode to work with images.

In addition to determining the number of colors that can be displayed in an image, color modes affect the number of channels and the file size of an image.

You can set up the Info palette so that you can select any tool, position the pointer over any part of an image, and determine the color value under the pointer. You can customize the Info palette and color samplers to express color values using HSB, RGB, CMYK, Lab, or Grayscale modes without changing the mode of the image itself. (See the procedure to change Info palette options in "Using the Info palette (Photoshop)" on page 27.)

For more information, see "Seeing the color values of pixels (Photoshop)" in online Help.

HSB model

Based on the human perception of color, the HSB model describes three fundamental characteristics of color:

- *Hue* is the color reflected from or transmitted through an object. It is measured as a location on the standard color wheel, expressed as a degree between 0° and 360°. In common use, hue is identified by the name of the color such as red, orange, or green.

- *Saturation*, sometimes called *chroma*, is the strength or purity of the color. Saturation represents the amount of gray in proportion to the hue, measured as a percentage from 0% (gray) to 100% (fully saturated). On the standard color wheel, saturation increases from the center to the edge.

- *Brightness* is the relative lightness or darkness of the color, usually measured as a percentage from 0% (black) to 100% (white).

Although you can use the HSB model in Photoshop to define a color in the Color palette or Color Picker dialog box, there is no HSB mode available for creating and editing images.

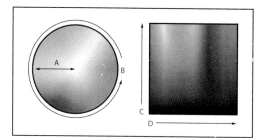

HSM model:
A. *Saturation* **B.** *Hue* **C.** *Brightness* **D.** *All hues*

RGB model

A large percentage of the visible spectrum can be represented by mixing red, green, and blue (RGB) colored light in various proportions and intensities. Where the colors overlap, they create cyan, magenta, yellow, and white.

Because the RGB colors combine to create white, they are also called *additive* colors. Adding all colors together creates white—that is, all visible wavelengths are transmitted back to the eye. Additive colors are used for lighting, video, and monitors. Your monitor, for example, creates color by emitting light through red, green, and blue phosphors.

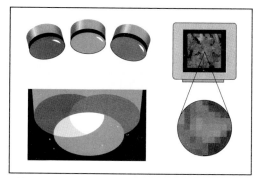

Additive colors (RGB)

RGB mode

Photoshop's RGB mode uses the RGB model, assigning an intensity value to each pixel ranging from 0 (black) to 255 (white) for each of the RGB components in a color image. For example, a bright red color might have an R value of 246, a G value of 20, and a B value of 50. When the values of all three components are equal, the result is a shade of neutral gray. When the value of all components is 255, the result is pure white; when the value is 0, pure black.

RGB images use three colors, or channels, to reproduce up to 16.7 million colors on-screen; the three channels translate to 24 (8 x 3) bits of color information per pixel. (In 16-bit-per-channel images, this translates to 48 bits per pixel, with the ability to reproduce many more colors.) In addition to being the default mode for new Photoshop images, the RGB model is used by computer monitors to display colors. This means that when working in color modes other than RGB, such as CMYK, Photoshop uses RGB mode for display on-screen.

Although RGB is a standard color model, the exact range of colors represented can vary, depending on the application or display device. Photoshop's RGB mode varies according to the working space setting that you have specified in the Color Settings dialog box. (See "About working spaces" on page 91.)

CMYK model

The CMYK model is based on the light-absorbing quality of ink printed on paper. As white light strikes translucent inks, certain visible wavelengths are absorbed while others are reflected back to your eyes.

In theory, pure cyan (C), magenta (M), and yellow (Y) pigments should combine to absorb all light and produce black. For this reason these colors are called *subtractive* colors. Because all printing inks contain some impurities, these three inks actually produce a muddy brown and must be combined with black (K) ink to produce a true black. (*K* is used instead of B to avoid confusion with blue.) Combining these inks to reproduce color is called *four-color process printing*.

The subtractive (CMY) and additive (RGB) colors are *complementary colors*. Each pair of subtractive colors creates an additive color, and vice versa.

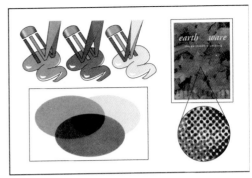

Subtractive colors (CMYK)

CMYK mode

In Photoshop's CMYK mode, each pixel is assigned a percentage value for each of the process inks. The lightest (highlight) colors are assigned small percentages of process ink colors, the darker (shadow) colors higher percentages. For example, a bright red might contain 2% cyan, 93% magenta, 90% yellow, and 0% black. In CMYK images, pure white is generated when all four components have values of 0%.

Use the CMYK mode when preparing an image to be printed using process colors. Converting an RGB image into CMYK creates a *color separation*. If you start with an RGB image, it's best to edit first and then convert to CMYK. In RGB mode, you can use the Proof Setup commands to simulate the effects of a CMYK conversion without changing the actual image data. (See "Soft-proofing colors" on page 97.) You can also use CMYK mode to work directly with CMYK images scanned or imported from high-end systems.

Although CMYK is a standard color model, the exact range of colors represented can vary, depending on the press and printing conditions. Photoshop's CMYK mode varies according to the working space setting that you have specified in the Color Settings dialog box. (See "About working spaces" on page 91.)

L*a*b model

The L*a*b color model is based on the model proposed by the Commission Internationale d'Eclairage (CIE) in 1931 as an international standard for color measurement. In 1976, this model was refined and named CIE L*a*b.

L*a*b color is designed to be *device independent*, creating consistent color regardless of the device (such as a monitor, printer, computer, or scanner) used to create or output the image.

L*a*b color consists of a *luminance* or lightness component (L) and two chromatic components: the *a* component (from green to red) and the *b* component (from blue to yellow).

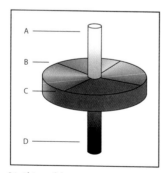

L*a*b* model:
A. Luminance=100 (white) **B.** Green to red component
C. Blue to yellow component **D.** Luminance=0 (black)

Lab mode

In Photoshop, Lab mode (the asterisks are dropped from the name) has a lightness component (L) that can range from 0 to 100. In the color picker, the *a* component (green-red axis) and the *b* component (blue-yellow axis) can range from +128 to –128. In the Color palette, the *a* component and the *b* component can range from +120 to –120.

You can use Lab mode to work with Photo CD images, edit the luminance and the color values in an image independently, move images between systems, and print to PostScript Level 2 and Level 3 printers. To print Lab images to other color PostScript devices, convert to CMYK first.

Lab color is the intermediate color model Photoshop uses when converting from one color mode to another.

Bitmap mode

This mode uses one of two color values (black or white) to represent the pixels in an image. Images in Bitmap mode are called bitmapped 1-bit images because they have a bit depth of 1.

 For more information, see "Specifying 8-bit color display (Photoshop)" in online Help.

Grayscale mode

This mode uses up to 256 shades of gray. Every pixel of a grayscale image has a brightness value ranging from 0 (black) to 255 (white). Grayscale values can also be measured as percentages of black ink coverage (0% is equal to white, 100% to black). Images produced using black-and-white or grayscale scanners typically are displayed in Grayscale mode.

Although Grayscale is a standard color model, the exact range of grays represented can vary, depending on the printing conditions. In Photoshop, Grayscale mode uses the range defined by the working space setting that you have specified in the Color Settings dialog box. (See "About working spaces" on page 91.)

These guidelines apply to converting images to and from Grayscale mode:

- You can convert both Bitmap-mode and color images to grayscale.

- To convert a color image to a high-quality grayscale image, Photoshop discards all color information in the original image. The gray levels (shades) of the converted pixels represent the luminosity of the original pixels.

You can mix information from the color channels to create a custom grayscale channel by using the Channel Mixer command.

- When converting from grayscale to RGB, the color values for a pixel are based on its previous gray value. A grayscale image can also be converted to a CMYK image (for creating process-color quadtones without converting to Duotone mode) or to a Lab color image.

Duotone mode

This mode creates duotone (two-color), tritone (three-color), and quadtone (four-color) grayscale images using two to four custom inks. (See "Printing duotones" on page 390.)

Indexed Color mode

This mode uses at most 256 colors. When converting to indexed color, Photoshop builds a color lookup table (CLUT), which stores and indexes the colors in the image. If a color in the original image does not appear in the table, the program chooses the closest one or simulates the color using available colors.

By limiting the palette of colors, indexed color can reduce file size while maintaining visual quality—for example, for a multimedia animation application or a Web page. Limited editing is available in this mode. For extensive editing you should convert temporarily to RGB mode. (See "Converting to indexed color (Photoshop)" on page 86.)

Multichannel mode

This mode uses 256 levels of gray in each channel. Multichannel images are useful for specialized printing.

These guidelines apply to converting images to Multichannel mode:

- Channels in the original image become spot color channels in the converted image.

- When you convert a color image to multi-channel, the new grayscale information is based on the color values of the pixels in each channel.

- Converting a CMYK image to multichannel creates cyan, magenta, yellow, and black spot channels.

- Converting an RGB image to multichannel creates cyan, magenta, and yellow spot channels.

- Deleting a channel from an RGB, CMYK, or Lab image automatically converts the image to Multichannel mode. (See "About color channels" on page 84 for more information on channels.)

- To export a multichannel image, save it in Photoshop DCS 2.0 format.

Color gamuts (Photoshop)

A *gamut* is the range of colors that a color system can display or print. The spectrum of colors seen by the human eye is wider than the gamut available in any color model.

Among the color models used in Photoshop, L*a*b has the largest gamut, encompassing all colors in the RGB and CMYK gamuts. Typically, RGB gamuts contain the subset of these colors that can be viewed on a computer or television monitor (which emits red, green, and blue light). Therefore, some colors, such as pure cyan or pure yellow, can't be displayed accurately on a monitor.

CMYK gamuts are smaller, consisting only of colors that can be printed using process-color inks. When colors that cannot be printed are displayed on-screen, they are referred to as out-of-gamut colors—that is, outside a CMYK gamut.

Important: The gamut for an RGB or CMYK image depends on its document profile. (See "About color management" on page 87.)

For more information, see "Identifying out-of-gamut colors (Photoshop)" in online Help.

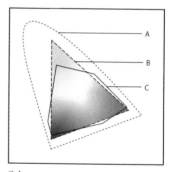

Color gamuts:
A. *A Lab color gamut* ***B.*** *An RGB color gamut*
C. *A CMYK color gamut*

Adjusting the monitor display

Although the RGB color model used by computer monitors is capable of displaying much of the visible spectrum, the video system sending data to a given monitor often limits how many colors can be displayed at once. By understanding how color data is measured in digital files and on-screen, you can better adjust color display settings to offset the limitations of your video system.

For more information, see "Specifying 8-bit color display (Photoshop)" in online Help.

Making previews display more quickly (Photoshop)

The Use Pixel Doubling preference option speeds up the preview of a tool or command's effects by temporarily doubling the size of the pixels (halving the resolution) in the preview. This option has no effect on the pixels in the file; it simply provides faster previews with the tools and commands.

To speed up previews:

1 Do one of the following:

• In Windows or Mac OS 9.x, choose Edit > Preferences > Display & Cursors.

• In Mac OS X, choose Photoshop > Preferences > Display & Cursors.

2 Select Use Pixel Doubling, and click OK.

Adjusting color display for cross-platform variations

RGB color display on a computer monitor varies with the operating system used by the computer. For example, an image appears darker on a Windows system than on a Mac OS computer (because the standard RGB color space is darker in Windows than in Mac OS). The Preview commands in ImageReady enable you to compensate for cross-platform differences in RGB color display during image preview.

In Photoshop, you can simulate cross-platform differences by using the Macintosh RGB, Windows RGB, and Monitor RGB commands in the View > Proof Setup menu. (See "Soft-proofing colors" on page 97.)

RGB color display can also vary between Photoshop and ImageReady. In Photoshop, you can select from several RGB color spaces when editing images. As a result, images created in Photoshop may use an RGB color space that differs from the monitor RGB color space used by ImageReady. You can adjust the RGB color display during image preview to compensate for differences between Photoshop and ImageReady.

To adjust RGB color display for cross-platform variations (ImageReady):

Choose View > Preview and choose an option for adjusting the color display:

• Uncompensated Color (the default option) to view the image with no color adjustment.

• Standard Macintosh Color (Windows) to view the image with color adjusted to simulate a standard Macintosh monitor.

• Standard Windows Color (Mac OS) to view the image with color adjusted to simulate a standard Windows monitor.

Note: *These options adjust color display only. No changes are made to pixels in the image.*

To adjust RGB color display to match Photoshop color display (ImageReady):

Choose View > Preview > Use Embedded Color Profile.

Note: In order to use the Use Embedded Color Profile command in ImageReady, you must save the original image, with color profile embedded, in Photoshop.

Channels and bit depth (Photoshop)

A working knowledge of color channels and bit depth is key to understanding how Photoshop stores and displays color information in images.

About color channels

Every Adobe Photoshop image has one or more *channels,* each storing information about color elements in the image. The number of default color channels in an image depends on its color mode. For example, a CMYK image has at least four channels, one each for cyan, magenta, yellow, and black information. Think of a channel as analogous to a plate in the printing process, with a separate plate applying each layer of color.

In addition to these default color channels, extra channels, called *alpha channels,* can be added to an image for storing and editing selections as masks, and spot color channels can be added to add spot color plates for printing. (See "Storing masks in alpha channels" on page 225 and "Adding spot colors (Photoshop)" on page 217.)

An image can have up to 24 channels. By default, Bitmap-mode, grayscale, duotone, and indexed-color images have one channel; RGB and Lab images have three; and CMYK images have four. You can add channels to all image types except Bitmap-mode images.

About bit depth

Bit depth—also called pixel depth or color depth—measures how much color information is available to display or print each pixel in an image. Greater bit depth (more bits of information per pixel) means more available colors and more accurate color representation in the digital image. For example, a pixel with a bit depth of 1 has two possible values: black and white. A pixel with a bit depth of 8 has 2^8, or 256, possible values. And a pixel with a bit depth of 24 has 2^{24}, or roughly 16 million, possible values. Common values for bit depth range from 1 to 64 bits per pixel.

In most cases, Lab, RGB, grayscale, and CMYK images contain 8 bits of data per color channel. This translates to a 24-bit Lab bit depth (8 bits x 3 channels); a 24-bit RGB bit depth (8 bits x 3 channels); an 8-bit grayscale bit depth (8 bits x 1 channel); and a 32-bit CMYK bit depth (8 bits x 4 channels). Photoshop can also read and import Lab, RGB, CMYK, and grayscale images that contain 16 bits of data per color channel.

Converting between bit depths

A 16-bit-per-channel image provides finer distinctions in color, but it can have twice the file size of an 8-bit-per-channel image. In addition, only the following Photoshop tools and commands are available for 16-bit-per-channel images:

- The marquee, lasso, crop, measure, zoom, hand, pen, eyedropper, history brush, slice, color sampler, clone stamp tools, healing brush tool, and patch tool, as well as the pen and shape tools (for drawing work paths only).

- The Duplicate, Feather, Modify, Levels, Auto Levels, Auto Contrast, Auto Color, Curves, Histogram, Hue/Saturation, Brightness/Contrast, Color Balance, Equalize, Invert, Channel Mixer, Gradient Map, Image Size, Canvas Size, Transform Selection, and Rotate Canvas commands, and a limited set of filters.

 For more information, see "Using filters" in online Help.

To take full advantage of Photoshop features, you can convert a 16-bit-per-channel image to an 8-bit-per-channel image.

To convert between 8 bits per channel and 16 bits per channel:

1 To convert to a 16-bit-per-channel image, first flatten the image. (See "Flattening all layers" on page 239.)

2 Choose Image > Mode > 16 Bits/Channel or 8 Bits/Channel.

Converting between color modes (Photoshop)

When you choose a different color mode for an image, you permanently change the color values in the image. For example, when you convert an RGB image to CMYK mode, RGB color values outside the CMYK gamut (defined by the CMYK working space setting in the Color Settings dialog box) are adjusted to fall within gamut. Consequently, before converting images, it's best to do the following:

- Do as much editing as possible in the image's original mode (usually RGB from most scanners, or CMYK from traditional drum scanners or if imported from a Scitex system).

- Save a backup copy before converting. Be sure to save a copy of your image that includes all layers in order to edit the original version of the image after the conversion.

- Flatten the file before converting it. The interaction of colors between layer blending modes will change when the mode changes.

To convert an image to another mode:

Choose Image > Mode and the mode you want from the submenu. Modes not available for the active image appear dimmed in the menu.

Images are flattened when converted to Multichannel, Bitmap, or Indexed Color mode, because these modes do not support layers.

For more information, see "Converting between Grayscale and Bitmap modes (Photoshop)" in online Help.

Converting to indexed color (Photoshop)

Converting to indexed color reduces the number of colors in the image to at most 256—the standard number of colors supported by the GIF and PNG-8 formats and many multimedia applications. This conversion reduces file size by deleting color information from the image.

To convert to indexed color, you must start with either a grayscale or RGB image.

To convert a grayscale or RGB image to indexed color:

1 Choose Image > Mode > Indexed Color.

Note: All visible layers will be flattened; any hidden layers will be discarded.

For grayscale images, the conversion happens automatically. For RGB images, the Indexed Color dialog box appears.

2 Select Preview the Indexed Color dialog box to display a preview of the changes.

3 Specify conversion options.

 For information on conversion options and customizing indexed color tables, see "Conversion options for indexed-color images (Photoshop)" in online Help.

Making color and tonal adjustments

When you photograph, scan, or resample images, you can often introduce problems involving color quality and tonal range. Photoshop provides a comprehensive set of tools for making color and tonal corrections and sharpening the overall focus of an image. ImageReady provides many of the basic correction tools.

 For more information, see "Making color and tonal adjustments" in online Help.

Chapter 4: Producing Consistent Color (Photoshop)

When your document must meet color standards set by clients and designers, viewing and editing color consistently becomes critical, all the way from scanning source images to creating final output. A color management system reconciles color differences among devices so that you can be reasonably certain of the colors your system ultimately produces.

Why colors sometimes don't match

No device in a publishing system is capable of reproducing the full range of colors viewable to the human eye. Each device operates within a specific color space, which can produce a certain range, or *gamut*, of colors.

The RGB (red, green, blue) and CMYK (cyan, magenta, yellow, black) color modes represent two main categories of color spaces. The gamuts of the RGB and CMYK spaces are very different; while the RGB gamut is generally larger (that is, capable of representing more colors) than CMYK, some CMYK colors still fall outside the RGB gamut. (See "Color gamuts (Photoshop)" on page 82 for an illustration.) In addition, different devices produce slightly different gamuts within the same color mode. For example, a variety of RGB spaces can exist among scanners and monitors, and a variety of CMYK spaces can exist among printing presses.

Because of these varying color spaces, colors can shift in appearance as you transfer documents between different devices. Color variations can result from different image sources (scanners and software produce art using different color spaces), differences in the way software applications define color, differences in print media (newsprint paper reproduces a smaller gamut than magazine-quality paper), and other natural variations, such as manufacturing differences in monitors or monitor age.

About color management

Because color-matching problems result from various devices and software that use different color spaces, one solution is to have a system that interprets and translates color accurately between devices. A color management system (CMS) compares the color space in which a color was created to the color space in which the same color will be output, and makes the necessary adjustments to represent the color as consistently as possible among different devices.

Note: Don't confuse color management with color adjustment or color correction. A CMS won't correct an image that was saved with tonal or color balance problems. It provides an environment where you can evaluate images reliably in the context of your final output.

Photoshop follows a color management workflow based on conventions developed by the International Color Consortium (ICC). The following elements and concepts are integral to such a color-managed workflow.

Color management engine Different companies have developed various ways to manage color. To provide you with a choice, a color management system lets you choose a *color management engine* that represents the approach you want to use. Sometimes called the *color management module (CMM)*, the color management engine is the part of the CMS that does the work of reading and translating colors between different color spaces.

Color numbers Each pixel in an image document has a set of *color numbers* that describe the pixel's location in a particular color mode—for example, red, green, and blue values for the RGB mode. However, the actual appearance of the pixel may vary when output or displayed on different devices, because each device has a particular way of translating the raw numbers into visual color. (See "Why colors sometimes don't match" on page 87.) When you apply color and tonal adjustments or convert a document to a different color space, you are changing the document's color numbers.

Color profiles An ICC workflow uses *color profiles* to determine how color numbers in a document translate to actual color appearances. A profile systematically describes how color numbers map to a particular color space, usually that of a device such as a scanner, printer, or monitor. By associating, or *tagging,* a document with a color profile, you provide a definition of actual color appearances in the document; changing the associated profile changes the color appearances. (For information on displaying the current profile name in the status bar, see "Displaying file and image information" on page 42.) Documents without associated profiles are known as *untagged* and contain only raw color numbers. When working with untagged documents, Photoshop uses the current working space profile to display and edit colors. (See "About working spaces" on page 91.)

Do you need color management?

Use the following guidelines to determine whether or not you need to use color management:

- You might not need color management if your production process is tightly controlled for one medium only, for example, if you're using a closed system where all devices are calibrated to the same specifications. You or your prepress service provider may prefer to tailor CMYK images and specify color values for a known, specific set of printing conditions.

- You also might not need color management if you are producing images for the Web or other screen-based output, since you cannot control the color management settings of monitors displaying your final output. It is helpful, however, to use the Web Graphics Defaults setting when preparing such images, because this setting reflects the average RGB space of many monitors. (See "Using predefined color management settings" on page 90.)

- You can benefit from color management if you have more variables in your production process (for example, if you're using an open system with multiple platforms and multiple devices from different manufacturers). Color management is recommended if you anticipate reusing color graphics for print and online media, if you manage multiple workstations, or if you plan to print to different domestic and international presses. If you decide to use color management, consult with your production partners—such as graphic artists and prepress service providers—to ensure that all aspects of your color management workflow integrate seamlessly with theirs.

Creating a viewing environment for color management

Your work environment influences how you see color on your monitor and on printed output. For best results, control the colors and light in your work environment by doing the following:

- View your documents in an environment that provides a consistent light level and color temperature. For example, the color characteristics of sunlight change throughout the day and alter the way colors appear on your screen, so keep shades closed or work in a windowless room. To eliminate the blue-green cast from

fluorescent lighting, consider installing D50 (5000 degree Kelvin) lighting. Ideally, view printed documents using a D50 lightbox or using the ANSI PH2.30 viewing standard for graphic arts.

- View your document in a room with neutral-colored walls and ceiling. A room's color can affect the perception of both monitor color and printed color. The best color for a viewing room is polychromatic gray. Also, the color of your clothing reflecting off the glass of your monitor may affect the appearance of colors on-screen.

- Match the light intensity in the room or variable lightbox to the light intensity of your monitor. View continuous-tone art, printed output, and images on-screen under the same intensity of light.

- Remove colorful background and user-interface patterns on your monitor desktop. Busy or bright patterns surrounding a document interfere with accurate color perception. Set your desktop to display neutral grays only.

- View document proofs in the real-world conditions under which your audience will see the final piece. For example, you might want to see how a housewares catalog looks under the incandescent lightbulbs used in homes, or view an office furniture catalog under the fluorescent lighting used in offices. However, always make final color judgments under the lighting conditions specified by the legal requirements for contract proofs in your country.

Setting up color management

Photoshop simplifies the task of setting up a color-managed workflow by gathering most color management controls in a single Color Settings dialog box. You can choose from a list of predefined color management settings, or you can adjust the controls manually to create your own custom settings. You can even save customized settings to share them with other users and other Adobe applications, such as Illustrator 9.0, that use the Color Settings dialog box.

Photoshop also uses color management policies, which determine how to handle color data that does not immediately match your current color management workflow. Policies provide guidelines on what to do when you open a document or import color data into an active document.

To specify color management settings:

1 Do one of the following:

- In Windows and Mac OS 9.x, choose Edit > Color Settings.

- In Mac OS X, choose Photoshop > Color Settings.

  To display helpful descriptions of the options that appear in the dialog box, position the pointer over a section heading or menu item. These descriptions appear in the lower area of the dialog box.

2 Do one of the following:

- To set up a predefined color management workflow, see "Using predefined color management settings" on page 90.

- To customize your own color management settings, see "Customizing color management settings" on page 92.

Using predefined color management settings

Photoshop offers a collection of predefined color management settings designed to produce consistent color for a common publishing workflow, such as preparation for Web or offset press output. In most cases, the predefined settings will provide sufficient color management for your needs. These settings can also serve as starting points for customizing your own workflow-specific settings.

To choose a predefined color management setting, choose one of the following options from the Settings menu in the Color Settings dialog box.

Color Management Off Uses passive color management techniques to emulate the behavior of applications that do not support color management. Although working space profiles are considered when converting colors between color spaces, Color Management Off does not tag documents with profiles. Use this option for content that will be output on video or as on-screen presentations; do not use this option if you work mostly with documents that are tagged with color profiles.

ColorSync Workflow (Mac OS only) Manages color using the ColorSync CMS with the profiles chosen in the ColorSync control panel. Use this option if you want to use color management with a mix of Adobe and non-Adobe applications. This color management configuration is not recognized by Windows systems, or by versions of ColorSync earlier than 3.0.

Emulate Photoshop 4 Emulates the color workflow used by the Mac OS version of Adobe Photoshop 4.0 and earlier.

Europe Prepress Defaults Manages color for content that will be output under common press conditions in Europe.

Japan Prepress Defaults Manages color for content that will be output under common press conditions in Japan.

Photoshop 5 Default Spaces Preparation of content using the default working spaces from Photoshop 5.

U.S. Prepress Defaults Manages color for content that will be output under common press conditions in the U.S.

Web Graphics Defaults Manages color for content that will be published on the World Wide Web.

When you choose a predefined configuration, the Color Settings dialog box updates to display the specific color management settings associated with the configuration.

About working spaces

Among other options, predefined color management settings specify the color profiles to be associated with the RGB, CMYK, and Grayscale color modes. The settings also specify the color profile for spot colors in a document. Central to the color management workflow, these profiles are known as *working spaces*. The working spaces specified by predefined settings represent the color profiles that will produce the best color fidelity for several common output conditions. For example, the U.S. Prepress Defaults setting uses a CMYK working space that is designed to preserve color consistency under standard Specifications for Web Offset Publications (SWOP) press conditions.

A working space acts as the color profile for untagged documents and newly created documents that use the associated color mode. For example, if Adobe RGB (1998) is the current RGB working space, each new RGB document that you create will use colors within the Adobe RGB (1998) color space. Working spaces also define the destination color space of documents converted to RGB, CMYK, or Grayscale color mode.

About color management policies

When you specify a predefined color management setting, Photoshop sets up a color management workflow that will be used as the standard for all documents and color data that you open or import. For a newly created document, the color workflow operates relatively seamlessly: the document uses the working space profile associated with its color mode for creating and editing colors.

However, it is common to encounter the following exceptions to your color-managed workflow:

- You might open a document or import color data (for example, by copying and pasting or dragging and dropping) from a document that is not tagged with a profile. This is often the case when you open a document created in an application that either does not support color management or has color management turned off.

- You might open a document or import color data from a document that is tagged with a profile different from the current working space. This may be the case when you open a document that has been created using different color management settings, or a document that has been scanned and tagged with a scanner profile.

In either case, Photoshop must decide how to handle the color data in the document. A *color management policy* looks for the color profile associated with an opened document or imported color data, and compares the profile (or lack of profile) with the current working space to make default color management decisions. If the profile is missing or does not match the working space, Photoshop displays a message that indicates the default action for the policy. In many cases you will also be provided with the opportunity to choose another action. For detailed information on the color management decisions associated with different policies, see "Specifying color management policies" on page 94.

Working with policy warnings and messages

The predefined color management workflows are set to display warning or option messages when a default color management policy is about to be used. Although you can disable the repeated display of some warnings and messages by selecting the Don't Show Again option, it is highly recommended that you continue to display all policy messages, to ensure the appropriate color management of documents on a case-by-case basis. (See "Resetting all warning dialogs" on page 51.) You should only turn off message displays if you are very confident that you understand the default policy decision and are willing to accept it for all documents that you open. You cannot undo the results of a default policy decision once a document has been saved.

Customizing color management settings

Although the predefined settings should provide sufficient color management for many publishing workflows, you may sometimes want to customize individual options in a configuration. For example, you might want to change the CMYK working space to a profile that matches the proofing system used by your printer or your service bureau.

It's important to save your custom configurations so that you can reuse and share them with other users and Adobe applications that use the same color management workflows. The color management settings that you customize in the Color Settings dialog box are contained in an associated preferences file called Color Settings.

Note: The default location of the Color Settings file varies by operating system; use your operating system's Find command to locate this file.

To customize color management settings:

1 Do one of the following:

• In Windows and Mac OS 9.x, choose Edit > Color Settings.

• In Mac OS X, choose Photoshop > Color Settings.

2 To use a preset color management configuration as the starting point for your customization, choose that configuration from the Settings menu.

3 Specify the desired color settings (working spaces and policies). As you make adjustments, the Settings menu option changes to Custom by default.

For detailed customization instructions, see "Specifying working spaces" on page 93, "Specifying color management policies" on page 94, and "Customizing advanced color management settings" on page 96.

4 Save your custom configuration so that it can be reused. (See "Saving and loading color management settings" on page 96.)

Specifying working spaces

In a color-managed workflow, each color mode must have a working space profile associated with it. (See "About working spaces" on page 91.) Photoshop ships with a standard set of color profiles that have been recommended and tested by Adobe Systems for most color management workflows. By default, only these profiles appear in the working space menus.

To display additional color profiles that you have customized or installed on your system, select Advanced Mode in the Color Settings dialog box. To appear in a working space menu, a color profile must be bidirectional, that is, contain specifications for translating both into and out of color spaces. You can also create a custom RGB, CMYK, Grayscale, or Spot working space profile to describe the color space of a particular output or display device.

For more information, see "Creating custom RGB profiles," "Creating custom CMYK profiles," and "Creating custom grayscale and spot-color profiles" in online Help.

For information about a specified RGB or CMYK working space profile, see the Description area of the Color Settings dialog box. (See "Setting up color management" on page 90.) The following information can help you specify an appropriate Gray or Spot working space:

• For images that will be printed, you can specify a Gray or Spot working space profile that is based on the characteristics of a particular dot gain. *Dot gain* occurs when a printer's halftone dots change as the ink spreads and is absorbed by paper. Photoshop calculates dot gain as the amount by which the expected dot increases or decreases. For example, a 50% halftone screen may produce an actual density of 60% on the printed page, exhibiting a dot gain of 10%. The Dot Gain 10% option represents the color space that reflects the grayscale characteristics of this particular dot gain.

Proof (no dot gain), and printed image (with dot gain)

- For images that will be used online or in video, you can also specify a Gray working space profile that is based on the characteristics of particular gamma. A monitor's *gamma setting* determines the brightness of midtones displayed by the monitor. Gray Gamma 1.8 matches the default grayscale display of Mac OS computers and is also the default grayscale space for Photoshop 4.0 and earlier. Gray Gamma 2.2 matches the default grayscale display of Windows computers.

Specifying color management policies

Each predefined color management configuration sets up a color management policy for the RGB, CMYK, and Grayscale color modes and displays warning messages to let you override the default policy behavior on a case-by-case basis. If desired, you can change the default policy behavior to reflect a color management workflow that you use more often. For more information on policies, see "About color management policies" on page 91.

To customize color management policies:

1 In the Color Settings dialog box, under Color Management Policies, choose one of the following to set the default color management policy for each color mode:

- Off if you do not want to color-manage new, imported, or opened color data.

- Preserve Embedded Profiles if you anticipate working with a mix of color-managed and non-color-managed documents, or with documents that use different profiles within the same color mode.

- Convert to Working Space if you want to force all documents to use the current working space.

For detailed descriptions of the default behaviors associated with each policy option, see the table following this procedure.

2 For Profile Mismatches, select either, both, or neither of the following:

- Ask When Opening to display a message whenever you open a document tagged with a profile other than the current working space. You will be given the option to override the policy's default behavior.

- Ask When Pasting to display a message whenever color profile mismatches occur as colors are imported into a document (via pasting, drag-and-drop, placing, and so on). You will be given the option to override the policy's default behavior.

The availability of options for Profile Mismatches depends on which policies have been specified.

3 For Missing Profiles, select Ask When Opening to display a message whenever you open an untagged document. You will be given the option to override the policy's default behavior.

The availability of options for Missing Profiles depends on which policies have been specified.

It is strongly recommended that you keep the Ask When Opening and Ask When Pasting options selected.

Policy option	Default color management behavior
Off	• New documents and existing untagged documents remain untagged. • Existing documents tagged with a profile other than the current working space become untagged. • Existing documents tagged with the current working space profile remain tagged. • For color data imported into a document using the same color mode, color numbers are preserved. • For all other import cases, colors are converted to the document's color space.
Preserve Embedded Profiles	• New documents are tagged with the current working space profile. • Existing documents tagged with a profile other than the current working space remain tagged with the original embedded profile. • Existing untagged documents use the current working space for editing but remain untagged. • For color data imported within the same color mode between either a non-color-managed source or destination, or from a CMYK document into a CMYK document, color numbers are preserved. • For all other import cases, colors are converted to the document's color space.

Policy option	Default color management behavior
Convert to Working Space	• New documents are tagged with the current working space profile. • Existing documents tagged with a profile other than the current working space are converted to and tagged with the working space profile. • Existing untagged documents use the current working space for editing but remain untagged. • For color data imported within the same color mode between either a non-color-managed source or destination, color numbers are preserved. • For all other import cases, colors are converted to the document's color space.

Customizing advanced color management settings

When you select Advanced Mode at the top of the Color Settings dialog box, you have the option of further customizing settings used for color management.

For detailed information on advanced color management settings, see "Specifying a color management engine," "Specifying a rendering intent," "Using black-point compensation," "Using dither," "Desaturating monitor colors," and "Blending RGB colors" in online Help.

Saving and loading color management settings

When you create a custom color management configuration, you should name and save the configuration to ensure that it can be shared with other users and applications that use the Color Settings dialog box, such as Adobe Illustrator and Adobe InDesign. You can also load previously saved color management configurations into the Color Settings dialog box.

To save a custom color management configuration:

1 In the Color Settings dialog box, click Save.

2 Name your color settings file, and click Save.

To ensure that the saved configuration appears in the Settings menu of the Color Settings dialog box, save the file in one of the following recommended locations:

• (Windows) Program Files/Common Files/Adobe/Color/Settings.

• (Mac OS 9.x) System Folder/Application Support/Adobe/Color/Settings.

• (Mac OS X) User/CurrentUser/Library/Application Support/Adobe/Color/Settings.

3 Enter any comments that you want to associate with the configuration, and click OK.

The comments that you enter will appear in the Description area of the Color Settings dialog box when the pointer is positioned over the configuration in the Settings menu.

To load a color management configuration:

1 In the Color Settings dialog box, click Load.

2 Locate and select the desired color settings file, and click Load.

When you load a custom color settings file, it appears as the active choice in the Settings menu of the Color Settings dialog box. If you load a settings file that has been saved outside the recommended location, it temporarily replaces the Other option in the Settings menu until another settings file is loaded.

Synchronizing color management between applications

The Color Settings dialog box represents the common color management controls shared by several Adobe applications, including Photoshop, Illustrator, and InDesign. If you modify and save over the current color settings file in any application other than Photoshop, you may be prompted to synchronize the common color settings upon starting Photoshop or upon reopening the Color Settings dialog box in Photoshop.

Synchronizing the color settings helps to ensure that color is reproduced consistently between Adobe applications that use the Color Settings dialog box. To share custom color settings between applications, be sure to save and load the settings file in the desired applications. (See "Saving and loading color management settings" on page 96.)

Soft-proofing colors

In a traditional publishing workflow, you print a hard proof of your document to preview how the document's colors will look when reproduced on a specific output device. In a color-managed workflow, you can use the precision of color profiles to *soft-proof* your document directly on the monitor—to display an on-screen preview of the document's colors as reproduced on a specified device. In addition, you can use your printer to produce a hard-proof version of this soft proof. (See "Using color management when printing" on page 388.) The following diagram shows how the source document profile, proof profile, and monitor profile are used to represent colors in a soft proof.

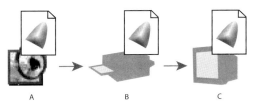

Color-managed workflow:
A. *Document space* *B.* *Proof space* *C.* *Monitor space*

Keep in mind that the reliability of the soft proof is highly dependent upon the quality of your monitor, your monitor and printer profiles, and the ambient lighting conditions of your work station. (See "Creating an ICC monitor profile" on page 102.)

To display a soft proof:

1 Choose View > Proof Setup, and choose the proof profile space that you want to simulate:

- Custom soft-proofs colors using the color profile of a specific output device. Follow the instructions after this procedure to set up the custom proof.

- Working CMYK soft-proofs colors using the current CMYK working space as defined in the Color Settings dialog box.

- Working Cyan Plate, Working Magenta Plate, Working Yellow Plate, Working Black Plate, or Working CMY Plates soft-proofs specific CMYK ink colors using the current CMYK working space.

- Macintosh RGB or Windows RGB soft-proofs colors in an image using either a standard Mac OS or Windows monitor as the proof profile space to simulate. Neither option is available for Lab or CMYK documents.

- Monitor RGB soft-proofs colors in an RGB document using your current monitor color space as the proof profile space. This option is unavailable for Lab and CMYK documents.

- Simulate Paper White previews the specific shade of white exhibited by the print medium defined by a document's profile. This option is not available for all profiles and is available only for soft-proofing, not printing.

- Simulate Ink Black previews the actual dynamic range defined by a document's profile. This option is not available for all profiles and is available only for soft-proofing, not printing.

2 Choose View > Proof Colors to turn the soft-proof display on and off. When soft proofing is on, a check mark appears next to the Proof Colors command.

When soft proofing is on, the name of the current proof profile appears next to the color mode in the document's title bar.

To create a custom proof setup:

1 Choose View > Proof Setup > Custom.

If you want the custom proof setup to be the default proof setup for documents, close all document windows before choosing the View > Proof Setup > Custom command.

2 Select Preview to display a live preview of the proof settings in the document while the Proof Setup dialog box is open.

3 To use a preset proof setup as a starting point, choose it from the Setup menu. If the desired setup does not appear in the menu, click Load to locate and load the setup.

4 For Profile, choose the color profile for the device for which you want to create the proof.

5 If the proof profile you chose uses the same color mode as the document, do one of the following:

- Select Preserve Color Numbers to simulate how the document will appear without converting colors from the document space to the proof profile space. This simulates the color shifts that may occur when the document's color values are interpreted using the proof profile instead of the document profile.

- Deselect Preserve Color Numbers to simulate how the document will appear if colors are converted from the document space to their nearest equivalents in the proof profile space in an effort to preserve the colors' visual appearances. Then specify a rendering intent for the conversion.

For more information, see "Specifying a rendering intent" in online Help.

6 If needed, select any of the following:

- Simulate Paper White to preview, in the monitor space, the specific shade of white exhibited by the print medium described by the proof profile. Selecting this option automatically selects the Simulate Ink Black option.

- Simulate Ink Black to preview, in the monitor space, the actual dynamic range defined by the proof profile.

The availability of these options depends on the proof profile chosen. Not all profiles support both options.

7 To save your custom proof setup as a preset proof setup, click Save. To ensure that the new preset appears in the View > Proof Setup menu, save the preset in the Program Files/Common Files/Adobe/Color/Proofing folder (Windows), System Folder/Application Support/Adobe/Color/Proofing folder (Mac OS 9.x), or Library/Application Support/Adobe/Color/Proofing folder (Mac OS X).

Changing the color profile of a document

In some cases you may want to convert a document's colors to a different color profile, tag a document with a different color profile without making color conversions, or remove the profile from a document altogether. For example, you may want to prepare the document for a different output destination, or you may want to correct a policy behavior that you no longer want implemented on the document. The Assign Profile and Convert to Profile commands are recommended only for advanced users.

When using the Assign Profile command, you may see a shift in color appearance as color numbers are mapped directly to the new profile space. Convert Profile, however, shifts color numbers before mapping them to the new profile space, in an effort to preserve the original color appearances.

To reassign or discard the profile of a document:

1 Choose Image > Mode > Assign Profile.

2 Select one of the following:

- Don't Color Manage This Document to remove the profile from a tagged document. Select this option only if you are sure that you want the document to become untagged.

- Working *color mode: working space* to tag the document with the current working space profile.

- Profile to reassign a different profile to a tagged document. Choose the desired profile from the menu. Photoshop tags the document with the new profile without converting colors to the profile space. This may dramatically change the appearance of the colors as displayed on your monitor.

3 To preview the effects of the new profile assignment in the document, select Preview.

To convert colors in a document to another profile:

1 Choose Image > Mode > Convert to Profile.

2 Under Destination Space, choose the color profile to which you want to convert the document's colors. The document will be converted to and tagged with this new profile.

3 Under Conversion Options, specify a color management engine, a rendering intent, and black point and dither options.

For more information, see "Customizing advanced color management settings" in online Help.

4 To flatten all layers of the document onto a single layer upon conversion, select Flatten Image.

5 To preview the effects of the conversion in the document, select Preview. This preview becomes more accurate if you select Flatten Image.

Embedding profiles in saved documents

By default, a tagged document will have its profile information embedded upon saving in a file format that supports embedded ICC profiles. Untagged documents are saved by default without embedded profiles.

You can specify whether or not to embed a profile as you save a document; you can also specify to convert colors to the proof profile space and embed the proof profile instead. However, changing the profile-embedding behavior is recommended only for advanced users who are familiar with color management.

To change the embedding behavior of a profile in a document:

1 Choose File > Save As.

2 Do one of the following:

- To toggle the embedding of the document's current color profile, select or deselect ICC Profile (Windows) or Embed Color Profile (Mac OS). This option is available only for the native Photoshop format (.psd) and PDF, JPEG, TIFF, EPS, DCS, and PICT formats.

- To toggle the embedding of the document's current proof profile, select or deselect Use Proof Setup (available for PDF, EPS, DCS 1.0, and DCS 2.0 formats only). Selecting this option converts the document's colors to the proof profile space and is useful for creating an output file for print. For information on setting up a proof profile, see "Soft-proofing colors" on page 97.

3 Name the document, choose other save options, and click Save.

Obtaining, installing, and updating color profiles

Precise, consistent color management requires accurate ICC-compliant profiles of all of your color devices. For example, without an accurate scanner profile, a perfectly scanned image may appear incorrect in another program, simply due to any difference in color space between the scanner and the program displaying the image. This misleading representation may cause you to make unnecessary, time-wasting, and potentially damaging "corrections" to an already satisfactory image. With an accurate profile, a program importing the image can correct for any gamut differences and display a scan's actual colors.

Once you obtain accurate profiles, they will work with all applications that are compatible with your color-management system. You can obtain profiles in the following ways, with the most precise methods listed first:

• Generate profiles customized for your specific devices using professional profiling equipment.

• Use the settings in the Custom CMYK dialog box to describe your device, and then save the settings as a color profile.

> For more information, see "Creating custom CMYK profiles" in online Help.

• Obtain a profile created by the manufacturer. Unfortunately, such profiles do not account for individual variations that naturally occur among machines (even identical modes from the same manufacturer) or from age.

• Substitute an available profile that may be appropriate for the device's color space. For example, many Mac OS scanners have been optimized for an Apple RGB monitor color space, so you might try using an Apple monitor profile for these devices; for a non-profiled Windows scanner, try substituting the sRGB color space. Be sure to proof images created with the profile before using the profile in production.

Adding device profiles to the color management system

You can add color profiles to your system so that they appear as choices in the Color Settings dialog box. To minimize confusion when working with profiles, delete any profiles for devices not used by you or your workgroup. Once you have added a profile to the recommended location on your system, you may need to load it or restart Photoshop so that the profile appears in the Color Settings dialog box.

Note: In Mac OS, you can organize the ColorSync Profiles folder by creating additional folders within it, or adding aliases to other folders. However, nested folders may cause conflicts with some applications, such as Adobe PressReady.

To add profiles to your system:

Copy profiles to one of the following recommended locations:

- (Windows 2000) WinNT/System/Spool/ Drivers/Color.

- (Windows NT) WinNT/System32/Color.

- (Windows 98) Windows/System/Color.

- (Mac OS 9.x) System Folder/ColorSync Profiles.

- (Mac OS X) Users/CurrentUser/Library/ ColorSync.

Note: If you use ColorSync 2.5 but have used earlier versions, some profiles may still be stored in the System Folder/Preferences/ColorSync™ Profiles folder on your hard disk. For compatibility with ColorSync 2.5 or later, store profiles in the ColorSync Profiles folder in the System Folder.

Updating profiles

The color reproduction characteristics of a color device change as it ages, so recalibrate devices periodically and generate updated profiles. Profiles should be good for approximately a month depending on the device. Some monitors automatically compensate for phosphor aging.

Also, recalibrate a device when you change any of the factors that affect calibration. For example, recalibrate your monitor when you change the room lighting or the monitor brightness setting.

Creating an ICC monitor profile

Your monitor will display color more reliably if you use color management and accurate ICC profiles. Using an ICC monitor profile helps you eliminate any color cast in your monitor, make your monitor grays as neutral as possible, and standardize image display across different monitors.

On Windows, you can use the Adobe Gamma software (installed with Photoshop) to create a monitor profile. On Mac OS, you can use the Apple calibration utility to create a monitor profile. In addition, there are hardware-based utilities that you can use to create a monitor profile. Be sure to use only one calibration utility to display your profile; using multiple utilities can result in incorrect color.

For more information, see "Calibrating versus characterizing a monitor," "About monitor calibration settings," "Guidelines for creating an ICC monitor profile," and "Calibrating with Adobe Gamma" in online Help.

Chapter 5: Selecting

To modify part of an image in Adobe Photoshop or Adobe ImageReady, you first select the area you want to edit. A selected area is indicated by a dotted selection border, also called a selection marquee. The area outside the selection border is protected while you move, copy, paint, or apply special effects to the isolated area.

You can choose from a variety of specialized tools for creating selection borders.

About selections

Since there are two different types of data in your image—bitmap and vector—you need to use separate sets of tools to make selections of each type. You can use selection borders to select pixels. When you select pixels, you are selecting resolution dependent information in the image. For more information about bitmap images and vector graphics, see "About bitmap images and vector graphics" on page 53.

You can also create selections using the pen or shape tools, which produce precise outlines called *paths*. A path is a vector shape that contains no pixels. (See "Moving, copying, and pasting selections and layers" on page 113.) You can convert paths to selections or convert selections to paths. (See "Converting between paths and selection borders (Photoshop)" on page 164.)

In Photoshop, you can use the Extract command to isolate an object from its background and erase the background to transparency. You can also make sophisticated selections using masks. (See "Saving a mask selection" on page 226.)

Making pixel selections

You can select pixels in an image by dragging with the marquee tools or lasso tools, or by targeting color areas with the magic wand tool. In Photoshop, you can also use the Color Range command. Making a new selection replaces the existing one. Additionally, you can create selections that add to a selection, subtract from a selection, select an area intersected by other selections, or select the union of a new selection and the current selection.

Using the Select menu

You can use commands in the Select menu to select all pixels, to deselect, or to reselect.

To select all pixels on a layer within the canvas boundaries:

1 Select the layer in the Layers palette.

2 Choose Select > All.

To deselect selections:

Do one of the following:

- Choose Select > Deselect.

- If you are using the rectangle marquee, rounded rectangle marquee (ImageReady), elliptical marquee, or lasso tool, click anywhere in the image outside the selected area.

To reselect the most recent selection:

Choose Select > Reselect.

Using the marquee tools

The marquee tools let you select rectangles, ellipses, rounded rectangles (ImageReady), and 1-pixel rows and columns. By default, a selection border is dragged from its corner.

To use the marquee tools:

1 Select a marquee tool:

- Rectangle marquee ⌷ to make a rectangular selection.

- (ImageReady) Rounded rectangle marquee ⌷ to select a rounded rectangle such as a Web-page button.

- Elliptical marquee ○ to make an elliptical selection.

- Single row ⇿ or single column ⸾ marquee to define the border as a 1-pixel-wide row or column.

2 In the options bar, specify whether to add a new selection ▢ , add to a selection ▨ , subtract from a selection ▣ , or select an area intersected by other selections ▣ .

3 Specify a feathering setting in the options bar. Turn anti-aliasing on or off for the rounded rectangle or elliptical marquee. (See "Softening the edges of a selection" on page 111.)

4 For the rectangle, rounded rectangle, or elliptical marquee, choose a style in the options bar:

- Normal to determine marquee proportions by dragging.

- Fixed Aspect Ratio to set a height-to-width ratio. Enter values (decimal values are valid) for the aspect ratio. For example, to draw a marquee twice as wide as it is high, enter 2 for the width and 1 for the height.

- Fixed Size to specify set values for the marquee's height and width. Enter pixel values in whole numbers. Keep in mind that the number of pixels needed to create a 1-inch selection depends on the resolution of the image. (See "About image size and resolution" on page 54.)

5 For aligning your selection to guides, a grid, slices, or document bounds, do one of the following to snap your selection:

- (Photoshop) Choose View > Snap, or choose View > Snap To and choose a command from the submenu. The marquee selection can snap to a document bound and more than one Photoshop Extra. This is controlled in the Snap To submenu. (See "Using the Snap command" on page 117.)

- (ImageReady) Choose View > Snap To > Guides.

6 Do one of the following to make a selection:

- With the rectangle, rounded rectangle, or elliptical marquee, drag over the area you want to select. Hold down Shift as you drag to constrain the marquee to a square or circle. To drag a marquee from its center, hold down Alt (Windows) or Option (Mac OS) after you begin dragging.

- With the single row or single column marquee, click near the area you want to select, and then drag the marquee to the exact location. If no marquee is visible, increase the magnification of your image view.

To reposition a rectangle, rounded rectangle, or elliptical marquee, first drag to create the border, keeping the mouse button depressed. Then hold down the spacebar and continue to drag. If you have finished drawing the border, drag from inside the selection.

Using the lasso, polygonal lasso, and magnetic lasso tools

The lasso and polygonal lasso tools let you draw both straight-edged and freehand segments of a selection border. With the magnetic lasso tool (Photoshop), the border snaps to the edges of defined areas in the image.

The magnetic lasso tool is especially useful for quickly selecting objects with complex edges set against high-contrast backgrounds.

To use the lasso tool:

1 Select the lasso tool ⌐, and select options. (See "Setting options for the lasso, polygonal lasso, and magnetic lasso tools" on page 106.)

2 Drag to draw a freehand selection border.

3 To draw a straight-edged selection border, hold down Alt (Windows) or Option (Mac OS), and click where segments should begin and end. You can switch between drawing freehand and straight-edged segments.

4 To erase recently drawn segments, hold down the Delete key until you've erased the fastening points for the desired segment.

5 To close the selection border, release the mouse without holding down Alt (Windows) or Option (Mac OS).

To use the polygonal lasso tool:

1 Select the polygonal lasso tool ⌐, and select options. (See "Setting options for the lasso, polygonal lasso, and magnetic lasso tools" on page 106.)

2 Click in the image to set the starting point.

3 Do one or more of the following:

- To draw a straight segment, position the pointer where you want the first straight segment to end, and click. Continue clicking to set endpoints for subsequent segments.

- To draw a freehand segment, hold down Alt (Windows) or Option (Mac OS), and drag. When finished, release Alt or Option and the mouse button.

- To erase recently drawn straight segments, press the Delete key.

4 Close the selection border:

- Position the polygonal lasso tool pointer over the starting point (a closed circle appears next to the pointer), and click.

- If the pointer is not over the starting point, double-click the polygonal lasso tool pointer, or Ctrl-click (Windows) or Command-click (Mac OS).

To use the magnetic lasso tool (Photoshop):

1 Select the magnetic lasso tool 🖉, and select options. (See "Setting options for the lasso, polygonal lasso, and magnetic lasso tools" on page 106.)

2 Click in the image to set the first fastening point. Fastening points anchor the selection border in place.

3 To draw a freehand segment, move the pointer along the edge you want to trace. (You can also drag with the mouse button depressed.)

The most recent segment of the selection border remains active. As you move the pointer, the active segment snaps to the strongest edge in the image, based on the detection Width set in the options bar. Periodically, the magnetic lasso tool adds fastening points to the selection border to anchor previous segments.

4 If the border doesn't snap to the desired edge, click once to add a fastening point manually. Continue to trace the edge, and add fastening points as needed.

5 To switch temporarily to the other lasso tools, do one of the following:

- To activate the lasso tool, hold down Alt (Windows) or Option (Mac OS), and drag with the mouse button depressed.

- To activate the polygonal lasso tool, hold down Alt (Windows) or Option (Mac OS), and click.

6 To erase recently drawn segments and fastening points, press the Delete key until you've erased the fastening points for the desired segment.

7 Close the selection border:

- To close the border with a freehand magnetic segment, double-click, or press Enter or Return.

- To close the border with a straight segment, hold down Alt (Windows) or Option (Mac OS), and double-click.

- To close the border, drag back over the starting point and click.

Setting options for the lasso, polygonal lasso, and magnetic lasso tools

The lasso tool options let you customize how the different lasso tools detect and select edges.

To set options for the lasso tools:

1 If needed, select the tool.

2 In the options bar, specify whether to add a new selection ▣ , add to an existing selection ▣ , subtract from a selection ▣ , or select an area intersected by other selections ▣ .

3 Specify feather and anti-aliasing options. (See "Softening the edges of a selection" on page 111.)

4 For the magnetic lasso tool (Photoshop), set any of these options:

- To specify a detection width, enter a pixel value for Width. The magnetic lasso detects edges only within the specified distance from the pointer.

- To specify the lasso's sensitivity to edges in the image, enter a value between 1% and 100% for Edge Contrast. A higher value detects only edges that contrast sharply with their surroundings; a lower value detects lower-contrast edges.

- To specify the rate at which the lasso sets fastening points, enter a value between 0 and 100 for Frequency. A higher value anchors the selection border in place more quickly.

On an image with well-defined edges, try a higher width and higher edge contrast, and trace the border roughly. On an image with softer edges, try a lower width and lower edge contrast, and trace the border more precisely.

- To change the lasso cursor to indicate the lasso width, press the Caps Lock key on the keyboard. Change the cursor while the tool is selected but not in use.

- If you are working with a stylus tablet, select or deselect the Stylus Pressure option. When the option is selected, an increase in stylus pressure will cause the edge width to decrease.

While creating a selection, you can press] to increase the magnetic lasso edge width by 1 pixel; press [to decrease the width by 1 pixel.

Using the magic wand tool

The magic wand tool lets you select a consistently colored area (for example, a red flower) without having to trace its outline. You specify the color range, or *tolerance*, for the magic wand tool's selection.

Note: You cannot use the magic wand tool on an image in Bitmap mode.

To use the magic wand tool:

1 Select the magic wand tool .

2 In the options bar, specify whether to add a new selection , add to an existing selection , subtract from a selection , or select an area intersected by other selections . The magic wand cursor changes depending on which option is selected.

3 For Tolerance, enter a value in pixels, ranging from 0 to 255. Enter a low value to select colors very similar to the pixel you click, or enter a higher value to select a broader range of colors.

4 To define a smooth edge, select Anti-aliased. (See "Softening the edges of a selection" on page 111.)

5 To select only adjacent areas using the same colors, select Contiguous. Otherwise, all pixels using the same colors will be selected.

6 To select colors using data from all the visible layers, select Use All Layers. Otherwise, the magic wand tool selects colors from the active layer only.

7 In the image, click the color you want to select. If Contiguous is selected, all adjacent pixels within the tolerance range are selected. Otherwise, all pixels in the tolerance range are selected.

Using the Color Range command (Photoshop)

The Color Range command selects a specified color or color subset within an existing selection or an entire image. If you want to replace a selection, be sure to deselect everything before applying this command.

To refine an existing selection, use the Color Range command repeatedly to select a subset of colors. For example, to select the green areas in a cyan selection, select Cyans in the Color Range dialog box, and click OK. Then reopen the Color Range dialog box, and select Greens. (The results are subtle because the technique selects parts of colors within a color mix.)

To select a color range using sampled colors:

1 Choose Select > Color Range.

2 For Select, choose the Sampled Colors tool 🖋 .

3 Select one of the display options:

• Selection to preview only the selection as you build it.

• Image to preview the entire image. For example, you might want to sample from a part of the image that isn't on-screen.

💡 *To toggle between the Image and Selection previews in the Color Range dialog box, press Ctrl (Windows) or Command (Mac OS).*

4 Position the pointer over the image or preview area, and click to sample the colors you want included.

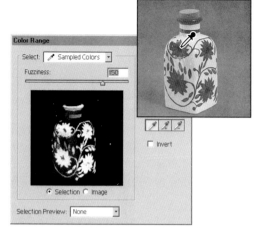

Sampling color

5 Adjust the range of colors using the Fuzziness slider or by entering a value. To decrease the range of colors selected, decrease the value. The Fuzziness option partially selects pixels by controlling the degree to which related colors are included in the selection (whereas the Tolerance option for the magic wand and paint bucket options increases the range of colors that are fully selected).

Increasing Fuzziness expands selection

6 Adjust the selection:

- To add colors, select the plus eyedropper, and click in the preview area or image.

- To remove colors, select the minus eyedropper, and click in the preview area or image.

To activate the plus eyedropper temporarily, hold down Shift. Hold down Alt (Windows) or Option (Mac OS) to activate the minus eyedropper.

7 To preview the selection in the image window, choose an option for Selection Preview:

- None to display no preview in the image window.

- Grayscale to display the selection as it would appear in a grayscale channel.

- Black Matte to display the selection in color against a black background.

- White Matte to display the selection in color against a white background.

- Quick Mask to display the selection using the current quick mask settings. (See "Creating temporary masks in Quick Mask mode (Photoshop)" on page 224.)

8 To revert to the original selection, hold down Alt (Windows) or Option (Mac OS), and click Reset.

To select a color range using preset colors:

1 Choose Select > Color Range.

2 For Select, choose a color or tonal range. The Out-of-Gamut option works only on RGB and Lab images. (An out-of-gamut color is an RGB or Lab color that cannot be printed using process color printing. See "Color gamuts (Photoshop)" on page 82.)

3 Click Selection to display the selected areas in the preview area.

4 To preview the selection in the image window, choose an option for Selection Preview:

- None to display no preview in the image window.

- Grayscale to display the selection as it would appear in a grayscale channel.

- Black Matte to display the selection in color against a black background.

- White Matte to display the selection in color against a white background.

- Quick Mask to display the selection using the current quick mask settings. (See "Creating temporary masks in Quick Mask mode (Photoshop)" on page 224.)

5 To revert to the original selection, hold down Alt (Windows) or Option (Mac OS), and click Reset.

Note: If a message appears stating "No pixels are more than 50% selected," the selection border will not be visible. You may have selected a color, such as red, when the image didn't contain the fully saturated color.

To save and load color range settings:

Use the Save and Load buttons in the Color Range dialog box to save and reuse the current settings.

Creating selections from slices (ImageReady)

If you create a slice in ImageReady, it can be converted into a selection.

To create a selection from a slice:

1 Select a slice. (See "Selecting slices" on page 293.)

2 Choose Select > Create Selection from Slice.

Adjusting pixel selections

You can adjust and refine your pixel selections using the selection tools and a variety of commands in the Select menu.

In addition, you can apply geometric transformations to change the shape of a selection border. (See "Transforming objects in two dimensions" on page 127.)

Moving, hiding, or inverting a selection

You can move a selection border around an image, hide a selection border, and invert a selection so that the previously unselected part of the image is selected.

To move a selection border:

1 Using any selection tool, select new selection ▣ from the options bar, and position the pointer inside the selection border. The pointer changes to indicate that you can move the selection ▷⬚ .

2 Drag the border to enclose a different area of the image. You can drag a selection border partly beyond the canvas boundaries. When you drag it back, the original border reappears intact. You can also drag the selection border to another image window.

To control the movement of a selection:

- To constrain the direction to multiples of 45°, begin dragging, and then hold down Shift as you continue to drag.

- To move the selection in 1-pixel increments, use an arrow key.

- To move the selection in 10-pixel increments, hold down Shift, and use an arrow key.

To hide or show selection edges:

Do one of the following:

- Choose View > Extras. This command also shows or hides: (Photoshop) selection edges, target path, slices, and notes, or (ImageReady) selection edges, slices, image maps, text bounds, text baseline, and text selection. (See "Working with Extras" on page 41.)

- Choose View > Show > Selection Edges. This toggles the view of the selection edges and affects the current selection only. The selection edges reappear when you make a different selection.

To select the unselected parts of an image:

Choose Select > Inverse.

You can use this option to select an object placed against a solid-colored background. Select the background using the magic wand tool and then inverse the selection.

Adjusting selections manually

You can use the selection tools to add to or subtract from existing pixel selections.

Before manually adding to or subtracting from a selection, set the feather and anti-aliased values in the options bar to the same settings used for the original selection. (See "Softening the edges of a selection" on page 111.)

To adjust selections numerically, see "Adjusting selections numerically" in online Help.

To add to a selection or select an additional area:

1 Make a selection.

2 Using any selection tool, do one of the following:

- Select the Add to Selection option 🔲 in the options bar, and drag.

- (ImageReady) Hold down Shift (a plus sign appears next to the pointer), and drag to add another selection.

To subtract from a selection:

1 Make a selection.

2 Using any selection tool, do one of the following:

- Select the Subtract from Selection option 🔲 in the options bar, and drag to intersect with other selections.

- Hold down Alt (Windows) or Option (Mac OS) (a minus sign appears next to the pointer), and drag to subtract another selection.

To select only an area intersected by other selections:

1 Make a selection.

2 Using any selection tool, do one of the following:

- Select the Intersect with Selection option 🔲 in the options bar, and drag.

- Hold down Alt+Shift (Windows) or Option+Shift (Mac OS) (a cross appears next to the pointer), and drag over the portion of the original selection that you want to select.

Softening the edges of a selection

You can smooth the hard edges of a selection by anti-aliasing and by feathering.

Anti-aliasing   Smooths the jagged edges of a selection by softening the color transition between edge pixels and background pixels. Since only the edge pixels change, no detail is lost. Anti-aliasing is useful when cutting, copying, and pasting selections to create composite images.

Anti-aliasing is available for the lasso, polygonal lasso, magnetic lasso, rounded rectangle marquee (ImageReady), elliptical marquee, and magic wand tools. (Select a tool to display its options bar.) You must specify this option before using these tools. Once a selection is made, you cannot add anti-aliasing.

Feathering   Blurs edges by building a transition boundary between the selection and its surrounding pixels. This blurring can cause some loss of detail at the edge of the selection.

You can define feathering for the marquee, lasso, polygonal lasso, or magnetic lasso tool as you use the tool, or you can add feathering to an existing selection. Feathering effects become apparent when you move, cut, copy, or fill the selection.

To use anti-aliasing:

1 Select the lasso, polygonal lasso, magnetic lasso, rounded rectangle marquee (ImageReady), elliptical marquee, or magic wand tool.

2 Select Anti-aliased in the options bar.

To define a feathered edge for a selection tool:

1 Select any of the lasso or marquee tools.

2 Enter a Feather value in the options bar. This value defines the width of the feathered edge and can range from 1 to 250 pixels.

To define a feathered edge for an existing selection:

1 Choose Select > Feather.

2 Enter a value for the Feather Radius, and click OK.

Note: *A small selection made with a large feather radius may be so faint that its edges are invisible and thus not selectable. If a message appears stating "No pixels are more than 50% selected," either decrease the feather radius or increase the selection's size. Or click OK to accept the mask at its current setting and create a selection where you cannot see the edges.*

A

B

C

D

Selection without feathering and with feathering:
A. *Original selection* **B.** *Feather: 0* **C.** *Feather: 10*
D. *Feather: 30*

Moving, copying, and pasting selections and layers

You can move or copy selections and layers within or between images—and also between images in other applications.

Moving selections and layers within an image

The move tool lets you drag a selection or layer to a new location in the image. With the Info palette open, you can track the exact distance of the move. You can also use the move tool to align selections and layers and distribute layers within an image.

To specify move tool options:

1 Select the move tool ▸⊕ .

2 Select any of the following in the options bar:

• Auto Select Layer to select the topmost layer that has pixels under the move tool, rather than the selected layer.

• Show Bounding Box to display the bounding box around the selected item.

To move a selection or layer:

1 Select the move tool ▸⊕ .

To activate the move tool when another tool is selected, hold down Ctrl (Windows) or Command (Mac OS). (This technique does not work with the pen tool ✎ , freeform pen ✎ , path selection tool ▸ , direct selection tool ▸ , hand tool ✋ , slice select tool ✄ , or anchor point tools ✎⁺ ✎⁻ ⌐.) Hold down Command (Mac OS) to activate the move tool when using the shape tools ▢ ▢ ◯ ◯ ╲ ✿ .

2 Do one of the following:

• Move the pointer inside the selection border, and drag the selection to a new position. If you have selected multiple areas, all move as you drag.

• Select the layer you want to move. Then drag the layer to a new position.

To align selections and layers within an image:

1 Do one of the following:

• To align the content of a layer to a selection, make a selection in the image. Then select a layer in the Layers palette.

• To align the contents of multiple layers to a selection border, make a selection in the image. Then link together the layers you want to align in the Layers palette. (See "Linking layers" on page 234.

• To align the contents of layers with the content of the active layer, link the layers you want to align to the active layer. (See "Linking layers" on page 234.)

2 Select the move tool ⊹.

3 Click one or more alignment buttons in the options bar: Align Top Edges ⬚ , Align Vertical Centers ⬚ , Align Bottom Edges ⬚ , Align Left Edges ⬚ , Align Horizontal Centers ⬚ , or Align Right Edges ⬚ .

To distribute layers within an image:

1 In the Layers palette, link three or more layers. (See "Linking layers" on page 234.)

2 Select the move tool ⊹.

3 Click one or more distribute buttons in the options bar: Distribute Top Edges ⬚ , Distribute Vertical Centers ⬚ , Distribute Bottom Edges ⬚ , Distribute Left Edges ⬚ , Distribute Horizontal Centers ⬚ , or Distribute Right Edges ⬚ .

Copying selections or layers

You can use the move tool to copy selections as you drag them within or between images, or you can copy and move selections using the Copy, Copy Merged, Cut, and Paste commands. Dragging with the move tool saves memory because the Clipboard is not used as it is with the Copy, Copy Merged, Cut, and Paste commands.

- The Copy command copies the selected area on the active layer.

- The Copy Merged command makes a merged copy of all the visible layers in the selected area.

- The Paste command pastes a cut or copied selection into another part of the image or into another image as a new layer.

(Photoshop) The Paste Into command pastes a cut or copied selection inside another selection in the same image or different image. The source selection is pasted onto a new layer, and the destination selection border is converted into a layer mask. (See "Masking layers" on page 259.)

Keep in mind that when a selection or layer is pasted between images with different resolutions, the pasted data retains its pixel dimensions. This can make the pasted portion appear out of proportion to the new image. Use the Image Size command to make the source and destination images the same resolution before copying and pasting. (See "Determining a recommended resolution for an image (Photoshop)" on page 60.)

Depending on your color management settings and the color profile associated with the file (or imported data), you may be prompted to specify how to handle color information in the file (or imported data). For more information, see "About color management policies" on page 91.

To copy a selection:

1 Select the area you want to copy.

2 Choose Edit > Copy or Edit > Copy Merged.

To copy a selection while dragging:

1 Select the move tool ⊹ , or hold down Ctrl (Windows) or Command (Mac OS) to activate the move tool.

2 Hold down Alt (Windows) or Option (Mac OS), and drag the selection you want to copy and move.

When copying between images, drag the selection from the active image window into the destination image window. If nothing is selected, the entire active layer is copied. As you drag the selection over another image window, a border highlights the window if you can drop the selection into it.

To create multiple copies of a selection within an image:

1 Select the move tool ⊹ , or hold down Ctrl (Windows) or Command (Mac OS) to activate the move tool.

2 Copy the selection:

• Hold down Alt (Windows) or Option (Mac OS), and drag the selection.

• To copy the selection and offset the duplicate by 1 pixel, hold down Alt or Option, and press an arrow key.

• To copy the selection and offset the duplicate by 10 pixels, press Alt+Shift (Windows) or Option+Shift (Mac OS), and press an arrow key.

As long as you hold down Alt or Option, each press of an arrow key creates a copy of the selection and offsets it by the specified distance from the last duplicate.

To paste one selection into another (Photoshop):

1 Cut or copy the part of the image you want to paste.

2 Select the part of the image into which you want to paste the selection. The source selection and the destination selection can be in the same image or in two different Photoshop images.

3 Choose Edit > Paste Into. The contents of the source selection appear masked by the destination selection.

In the Layers palette, the layer thumbnail for the source selection appears next to the layer mask thumbnail for the destination selection. The layer and layer mask are unlinked—that is, you can move each one independently.

Source selection pasted into destination selection

For more information on editing layer masks, see "Applying and discarding layer masks" on page 263.

4 Select the move tool ⊹ , or hold down the Ctrl (Windows) or Command (Mac OS) key to activate the move tool. Then drag the source contents until the part you want appears through the mask.

5 To reveal more or less of the image underlying the layer, click the layer mask thumbnail in the Layers palette, select a painting tool, and edit the mask:

• To hide more of the image underlying the layer, paint the mask with black.

- To reveal more of the image underlying the layer, paint the mask with white.

- To partially reveal the image underlying the layer, paint the mask with gray.

6 If you are satisfied with your results, you can choose Layer > Merge Down to merge the new layer and layer mask with the underlying layer and make the changes permanent.

Using drag and drop to copy between applications

The drag-and-drop feature lets you copy and move images between Photoshop or ImageReady and other applications.

In Windows, the application must be OLE-compliant. To duplicate an entire image by dragging and dropping, use the move tool to drag the image. To copy an OLE object that contains .psd data, use the OLE Clipboard. (See your Windows documentation.) In Mac OS, the application must support Mac OS Drag Manager.

Dragging vector artwork from Adobe Illustrator or from other applications that use the Illustrator Clipboard rasterizes the artwork—the mathematically defined lines and curves of the vector art are converted into the pixels or bits of a bitmap image. To copy the vector artwork as a path in Photoshop, hold down Ctrl (Windows) or Command (Mac OS) as you drag from Adobe Illustrator. To copy type, you must first convert it to outlines.

Using the Clipboard to copy between applications

You can often use the Cut or Copy command to copy selections between Photoshop or ImageReady and other applications. The cut or copied selection remains on the Clipboard until you cut or copy another selection.

In some cases, the contents of the Clipboard are converted to a *raster* image. Photoshop prompts you when vector artwork will be rasterized.

Note: *The image is rasterized at the resolution of the file into which you paste it.*

To change the Export Clipboard preference (Photoshop):

1 Do one of the following:

- In Windows and Mac OS 9.x, choose Edit > Preferences > General.

- In Mac OS X, choose Photoshop > Preferences > General.

2 Select Export Clipboard to save any Photoshop contents on the Clipboard when you exit from Photoshop. If you leave this deselected, the contents are deleted when you exit from the program.

To paste PostScript artwork from another application:

1 In the supporting application, select your artwork, and choose Edit > Copy.

For more information, see "About file formats" in online Help.

2 In Photoshop or ImageReady, select the image into which you'll paste the selection.

3 Choose Edit > Paste.

4 (Photoshop) In the dialog box, select from the following options:

- Paste as Pixels to have the artwork rasterized as it is pasted. Rasterizing converts mathematically defined vector artwork to pixels.

- Paste as Paths to paste the copy as a path in the Paths palette. When copying type from Illustrator, you must first convert it to outlines.

- Paste as Shape Layer to create a new shape layer that uses the path as a vector mask.

Important: When copying artwork from Adobe Illustrator, Illustrator's default Clipboard preferences may prevent the Paste dialog box from appearing in Photoshop. Select AICB in the Files and Clipboard section of Illustrator's Preferences dialog box if you want the Paste options to appear when you paste the artwork in Photoshop.

5 If you chose Paste as Pixels in the previous step, you can choose Anti-alias in the options bar to make a smooth transition between the edges of the selection and the surrounding pixels. (See "Softening the edges of a selection" on page 111.)

Note: You can use the Matting commands if you have already merged data and are trying to re-extract the rasterized data. (See "Removing fringe pixels from a selection (Photoshop)" on page 118.)

Using the Snap command

Snapping helps with precise placement of selection edges, cropping marquees, slices, shapes, and paths. You can enable or disable snapping using the Snap command. You can also specify different elements to which you want to snap when snapping is enabled.

To enable or disable snapping:

Choose View > Snap. A check mark indicates that snapping is enabled.

To specify what to snap to:

Choose View > Snap To, and choose one or more options from the submenu:

- Guides to snap to guides. (See "Using guides and the grid" on page 39.)

- (Photoshop) Grid to snap to the grid. You cannot select this option when the grid is hidden. (See "Using guides and the grid" on page 39.)

- Slices to snap to slice boundaries. You cannot select this option when slices are hidden. (See "Viewing slices" on page 291.)

- (Photoshop) Document Bounds to snap to the edges of the document.

- All to select all Snap To options.

- None to deselect all Snap To options.

A check mark indicates that the option is selected and snapping is enabled. A dot (Windows) or a dash (Mac OS) indicates that the option is selected but snapping is disabled.

To enable snapping for one Snap To option:

1 With the Snap command disabled, choose View > Snap To.

2 Choose an option. This automatically enables snapping for the selected option, and deselects all other Snap To options.

Saving and loading selections

Selections can be saved and loaded for reuse. (See "Saving a mask selection" on page 226.)

To save a selection:

Choose Select > Save Selection.

To load a saved selection (Photoshop):

1 Choose Select > Load Selection, then enter the options in the Load Selection dialog window.

2 Click OK to load selection. (See "Loading a selection into an image" on page 228.)

To load a saved selection (ImageReady):

Choose Select > Load Selection, then choose an option from the submenu.

Deleting selections

To delete a selection, choose Edit > Clear, or press Backspace (Windows) or Delete (Mac OS). To cut a selection to the Clipboard, choose Edit > Cut.

Deleting a selection on a background or on a layer with the Lock Transparency option selected in the Layers palette replaces the original location with the background color. Deleting a selection on a layer without Lock Transparency selected replaces the original area with the layer transparency.

Removing fringe pixels from a selection (Photoshop)

When you move or paste an anti-aliased selection, some of the pixels surrounding the selection border are included with the selection. This can result in a fringe or halo around the edges of the pasted selection. These Matting commands let you edit unwanted edge pixels:

- Defringe replaces the color of any fringe pixels with the colors of nearby pixels containing pure colors (those without background color). For example, if you select a yellow object on a blue background and then move the selection, some of the blue background is selected and moved with the object. Defringe replaces the blue pixels with yellow ones.

• Remove Black Matte and Remove White Matte are useful when you want to paste a selection anti-aliased against a white or black background onto a different background. For example, anti-aliased black text on a white background has gray pixels at the edges, which are visible against a colored background.

You can also remove fringe areas by using the Advanced Blending sliders in the Layer Styles dialog box to remove, or make transparent, areas from the layer. In this case, you would make the black or white areas transparent. Alt-click (Windows) or Option-click (Mac OS) on the sliders to separate them; separating the sliders allows you to remove fringe pixels and retain a smooth edge.

To decrease a fringe on a selection:

1 Choose Layer > Matting > Defringe.

2 Enter a value in the Width text box for the distance to search for replacement pixels. In most cases, a distance of 1 or 2 pixels is enough.

3 Click OK.

To remove a matte from a selection:

Choose Layer > Matting > Remove Black Matte or Layer > Matting > Remove White Matte.

Extracting objects from their background (Photoshop)

The Extract command provides a sophisticated way to isolate a foreground object and erase its background on a layer. Even objects with wispy, intricate, or undefinable edges may be clipped from their backgrounds with a minimum of manual work.

Note: For simpler cases, you can instead use the background eraser tool.

To extract an object, you use tools in the Extract dialog box. First you draw a highlight that marks the edges of the object, and define the object's interior. Then you can preview the extraction and redo it or touch up the result as needed. When you extract the object, Photoshop erases its background to transparency. Pixels on the edge of the object lose their color components derived from the background, so they can blend with a new background without producing a color halo.

You can add back opacity to the background and create other effects by using the Edit > Fade command after an extraction.

For more information, see "Blending filter effects (Photoshop)" in online Help.

To extract an object from its background:

1 In the Layers palette, select the layer containing the object you want to extract. If you select a background layer, it becomes a normal layer after the extraction.

To avoid losing the original image information, duplicate the layer or make a snapshot of the original image state.

Note: If the layer contains a selection, the extraction erases the background only in the selected area.

2 Choose Filter > Extract.

You use tools in the Extract dialog box to specify which part of the image to extract. You can resize the dialog box by dragging its lower right corner.

3 Specify options for tools in the dialog box (you can change these settings at any time):

- For Brush Size, enter a value, or drag the slider to specify the width of the edge highlighter, eraser, cleanup, and edge touchup tools.

- For Highlight, choose a preset color option, or choose Other to specify a custom color for the highlight.

- For Fill, choose a preset color option, or choose Other to specify a custom color for the area covered by the fill tool.

- If you are highlighting a well-defined edge, select Smart Highlighting. This option helps you keep the highlight on the edge, and applies a highlight that is just wide enough to cover the edge, regardless of the current brush size.

4 Adjust the view as needed:

- To magnify an area, select the zoom tool 🔍 in the dialog box, and click in the preview image. To zoom out, hold down Alt (Windows) or Option (Mac OS) as you click.

- To view a different area, select the hand tool in the dialog box, and drag in the preview image.

5 Define the edge of the object you want to extract:

- To draw a highlight that marks the edge, select the edge highlighter tool ✎ in the dialog box, and drag so that the highlight slightly overlaps both the foreground object and its background. Use Smart Highlighting to trace sharper edges. Use a large brush to cover wispy, intricate edges where the foreground blends into the background, such as hair or trees.

💡 *If you use Smart Highlighting to mark an object edge that is near another edge, decrease the brush size if conflicting edges pull the highlight off the object edge. If the object edge has a uniform color on one side and high-contrast edges on the other side, keep the object edge within the brush area but center the brush on the uniform color.*

- If the object has a well-defined interior, make sure that the highlight forms a complete enclosure. You do not need to highlight areas where the object touches the image boundaries. If the object lacks a clear interior, highlight the entire object.

- To base the highlight on a selection saved in an alpha channel, choose the alpha channel from the Channel menu. The alpha channel should be based on a selection of the edge boundary. If you modify a highlight based on a channel, the channel name in the menu changes to Custom.

- To erase the highlight, select the eraser tool 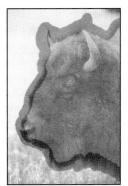 in the dialog box, and drag over the highlight. To erase the entire highlight, press Alt+Backspace (Windows) or Option+Delete (Mac OS).

6 Define the foreground area:

- If the object has a well-defined interior, select the fill tool in the dialog box. Click inside the object to fill its interior. (Clicking a filled area with the fill tool removes the fill.)

- If the object is especially intricate or lacks a clear interior, make sure that the highlight covers the entire object, and then select Force Foreground. Select the eyedropper tool in the dialog box, and click inside the object to sample the foreground color, or click in the Color text box and use a color picker to select the foreground color. This technique works best with objects that contain tones of a single color.

7 Click Preview to preview the extracted object, or skip to step 10 to extract the object without a preview.

Selected area highlighted and filled, and extracted object

Zoom in as needed, and set any preview options:

- Use Show menu options to switch between previews of the original and extracted images.

- Use Display menu options to preview the extracted object against a colored matte background or as a grayscale mask. To display a transparent background, choose None.

- Select Show Highlight or Show Fill to display the object's highlight or fill.

8 If necessary, repeat the extraction to improve the results (when you are finished, you can perform final touch-ups as described in step 9):

- To perform another extraction after adjusting the highlight and fill, repeat steps 5, 6, and 7.

- To perform another extraction with new extraction settings, change the Smooth, Force Foreground, or Color settings, and repeat step 7.

Note: *To specify the amount of smoothing of the extracted object, drag the Smooth slider or enter a value. It is usually best to begin with a zero or small value to avoid unwanted blurring of details. If there are sharp artifacts in the extraction result, you can increase the Smooth value to help remove them in the next extraction.*

9 Touch up the extraction results as needed:

• To erase background traces in the extracted area, use the cleanup tool . The tool subtracts opacity and has a cumulative effect. You can also use the cleanup tool to fill gaps in the extracted object. Hold down Alt (Windows) or Option (Mac OS) while dragging to add back opacity.

• To edit the edge of the extracted object, use the edge touchup tool . The tool sharpens edges and has a cumulative effect. If there is no clear edge, the edge touchup tool adds opacity to the object or subtracts opacity from the background.

10 Click OK to apply the final extraction. On the layer, all pixels outside the extracted object are erased to transparency.

Note: *For best results in cleaning up stray edges, use the cleanup and edge touchup tools in the Extract dialog box. You can also clean up after an extraction by using the background eraser and history brush tools in the toolbox.*

Chapter 6: Transforming and Retouching

Transformations—such as cropping, scaling, rotating, and distorting—let you change the geometry of an entire image or parts of an image. Retouching lets you correct the tone and focus of an image, remove dust and scratches, and clone pixels within or between images.

Changing the size of the work canvas

The Canvas Size command lets you add or remove work space around an existing image. You can crop an image by decreasing the canvas area. Added canvas appears in the same color or transparency as the background.

To use the Canvas Size command:

1 Choose Image > Canvas Size.

2 (Photoshop) Choose the units of measurement you want.

3 The Columns option measures width in terms of the columns specified in the Rulers & Units preferences. For more information, see "Using columns (Photoshop)" on page 38.

4 Do one of the following:

• Enter the dimensions you want the canvas to be in the Width and Height boxes.

• Select Relative, and enter the amount by which you want to increase or decrease the size of the canvas. (Enter a negative number to decrease the size of the canvas.)

5 For Anchor, click a square to indicate where to position the existing image on the new canvas.

6 Click OK.

Original canvas, and canvas added to top of image

Rotating and flipping entire images

The Rotate Canvas commands let you rotate or flip an entire image. The commands do not work on individual layers or parts of layers, paths, or selection borders.

To rotate or flip an entire image:

Choose Image > Rotate Canvas, and choose one of the following commands from the submenu:

- 180° to rotate the image by a half-turn.

- 90° CW to rotate the image clockwise by a quarter-turn.

- 90° CCW to rotate the image counterclockwise by a quarter-turn.

- Arbitrary to rotate the image by the angle you specify. If you choose this option, enter an angle between –359.99 and 359.99 in the angle text box, and then select CW or CCW to rotate clockwise or counterclockwise. Click OK.

- Flip Canvas Horizontal (Photoshop) or Flip Horizontal (ImageReady) to flip the image horizontally, along the vertical axis.

- Flip Canvas Vertical (Photoshop) or Flip Vertical (ImageReady) to flip the image vertically, along the horizontal axis.

Cropping images

Cropping is the process of removing portions of an image to create focus or strengthen the composition. You can crop an image using the crop tool and the Crop command. You can also trim pixels using the Trim command.

The crop tool provides the most options for cropping images.

To crop an image using the crop tool:

1 Select the crop tool ⊏ .

2 Set the mode of the crop tool:

- (Photoshop) To crop the image without resampling (default), make sure that all the text boxes in the options bar are empty. You can click the Clear button to quickly clear all text boxes.

- (Photoshop) To resample the image during cropping, enter a height, width, and/or resolution in the options bar.

- (ImageReady) To crop the image without resampling, make sure that Fixed Size is deselected in the options bar.

- (ImageReady) To resample the image during cropping, select Fixed Size, and enter a height and width in the options bar.

- To resample an image based on the dimensions and resolution of another image, open the other image, select the crop tool, and click Front Image in the options bar. (In ImageReady, you must select the Fixed Size option to access the Front Image button.) Then make the image you want to crop active.

Resampling during cropping combines the function of the Image > Image Size command with that of the crop tool. (See "About resampling" on page 57.)

3 Define the cropping marquee by dragging over the part of the image you want to keep. The marquee doesn't have to be precise—you can adjust it later.

4 Do the following in the options bar:

- Specify whether you want to hide or delete the cropped area. Select Hide to preserve the cropped area in the image file. You can make the hidden area visible by moving the image with the move tool. Select Delete to discard the cropped area.

Note: In Photoshop, the Hide option is not available for images that contain only a background layer. If you want to crop a background by hiding, convert the background to a regular layer first. (See "About the background layer" on page 230.) In ImageReady, cropping a background by hiding automatically converts the background to a regular layer.

- Specify whether you want to use a cropping shield to shade the area of the image that will be deleted or hidden. When Shield is selected, you can specify a color and opacity for the cropping shield. When Shield is deselected, the area outside the cropping marquee is revealed.

5 If necessary, adjust the cropping marquee:

- To move the marquee to another position, place the pointer inside the bounding box and drag.

- To scale the marquee, drag a handle. To constrain the proportions, hold down Shift as you drag a corner handle.

- To rotate the marquee, position the pointer outside the bounding box (the pointer turns into a curved arrow), and drag. To move the center point around which the marquee rotates, drag the circle at the center of the bounding box.

Note: In Photoshop, you can't rotate the marquee for an image in Bitmap mode.

6 Do one of the following:

- Press Enter (Windows) or Return (Mac OS); click the Commit button ✔ in the options bar; or double-click inside the cropping marquee.

- To cancel the cropping operation, press Esc or click the Cancel button ⊘ in the options bar.

To crop an image using the Crop command:

1 Select the part of the image you want to keep. (See "Using the marquee tools" on page 104.)

2 Choose Image > Crop.

To crop an image using the Trim command:

1 Choose Image > Trim.

2 In the Trim dialog box, select an option:

- Transparent Pixels to trim away transparency at the edges of the image, leaving the smallest image containing non-transparent pixels.

- Top Left Pixel Color to remove an area the color of the upper left pixel from the image.

- Bottom Right Pixel Color to remove an area the color of the lower right pixel from the image.

3 Select one or more areas of the image to trim away: Top, Bottom, Left, or Right.

Transforming perspective while cropping (Photoshop)

The crop tool in Photoshop has an additional option that allows you to transform the perspective in an image. This is very useful when working with images that contain *keystone distortion*. Keystone distortion occurs when an object is photographed from an angle rather than from a straight-on view. For example, if you take a picture of a a tall building from ground level, the edges of the building appear closer at the top than they do at the bottom.

Note: You cannot transform the perspective of 16-bit-per-channel images.

A   B

C   D

Steps to transform perspective:
A. Draw initial cropping marquee **B.** *Adjust cropping marquee to match the object's edges* **C.** *Extend the cropping bounds* **D.** *Final image*

To transform the perspective in an image:

1 Select the crop tool ⌗ and set the crop mode. (See "Cropping images" on page 124.)

2 Drag the cropping marquee around an object that was rectangular in the original scene (although it doesn't appear rectangular in the image). You'll use the edges of this object to define the perspective in the image. The marquee doesn't have to be precise—you'll adjust it later.

Important: You must select an object that was rectangular in the original scene or Photoshop will not be able to transform the perspective in the image.

3 Select Perspective in the options bar, and set the other options as desired. (See "Cropping images" on page 124.)

4 Move the corner handles of the cropping marquee to match the object's edges. This defines the perspective in the image, so it is important to precisely match the object's edges.

5 Drag the side handles to extend the cropping bounds while preserving the perspective.

Important: Do not move the center point of the cropping marquee. Photoshop needs to know the original center point of the image in order to perform perspective correction.

6 Do one of the following:

• Press Enter (Windows) or Return (Mac OS); click the Commit button ✔ in the options bar; or double-click inside the cropping marquee.

• To cancel the cropping operation, press Esc or click the Cancel button ⊘ in the options bar.

If Photoshop displays an error, it is probably due to improper placement of the corner handles or center point. Click Cancel to go back and adjust the cropping marquee; click Don't Crop to cancel the cropping operation. An error may also occur if you're working with a previously cropped image.

Transforming objects in two dimensions

You can scale, rotate, skew, distort, and apply perspective to entire layers, selected parts of layers, masks, paths, shapes, selection borders, and channels.

Note: Pixels are added or deleted during transformations. To calculate the color values of these pixels, Photoshop and ImageReady use the interpolation method selected in the General section of the Preferences dialog box. This option directly affects the speed and quality of the transformation. Bicubic interpolation, the default, is slowest but yields the best results. (See "Choosing an interpolation method" on page 58.)

Specifying what to transform

You can apply transformations to a selection, an entire layer, multiple layers, or a layer mask. In Photoshop, you can also apply transformations to a path, a vector shape, a vector mask, a selection border, or an alpha channel.

Note: You cannot apply transformations to16 bit-per-channel images. You can, however, apply full canvas transformations to 16-bit images using the options in the Image menu. (See "Rotating and flipping entire images" on page 123.)

To specify what to transform:

Do one of the following:

- To transform an entire layer, make the layer active, and make sure nothing is selected.

Important: You cannot transform the background layer. However, you can convert a background layer to a regular layer. (See "Adding layers and layer sets" on page 230.)

- To transform part of a layer, select the layer, and then select part of the image on that layer.

- To transform multiple layers, link the layers together in the Layers palette. (See "Linking layers" on page 234.)

- To transform a layer mask or a vector mask, unlink the mask, and select the mask thumbnail in the Layers palette. (See "Masking layers" on page 259.)

- (Photoshop) To transform a path or vector shape, use the path selection tool ▶ to select the entire path or the direct selection tool ▶ to select part of the path. If you select one or more points on a path, only those path segments connected to the points are transformed. (See "Selecting paths (Photoshop)" on page 158.)

- (Photoshop) To transform a selection border, make or load a selection. Then choose Select > Transform Selection.

• (Photoshop) To transform an alpha channel, select the channel in the Channels palette. (See "Storing masks in alpha channels" on page 225.)

Setting the reference point

All transformations are performed around a fixed point called the *reference point*. By default, this point is at the center of the item you are transforming. However, you can change the reference point or move the center point to a different location.

To set the reference point for a transformation:

1 Select a transformation command, as described in the following topics. A bounding box appears in the image.

2 In the options bar, click a square on the reference point locator ⊞ . Each square represents a point on the bounding box. For example, to set the reference point to the top left corner of the bounding box, click the top left square on the reference point locator.

To move the center point for the transformation:

1 Select a transformation command, as described in the following topics. A bounding box appears in the image.

2 Drag the center point. The center point can be outside the item you want to transform.

Applying transformations

The commands under the Transform submenu let you apply the following transformations to an item:

• Scaling enlarges or reduces an item relative to its reference point. You can scale horizontally, vertically, or both horizontally and vertically.

• Rotating turns an item around a reference point. By default, this point is at the center of the object; however, you can move it to another location.

• Skewing lets you slant an item vertically and horizontally.

• Distorting lets you stretch an item in all directions.

• Applying perspective lets you apply one-point perspective to an item.

In Photoshop, you can perform several commands in succession before applying the cumulative transformation. For example, you can choose Scale, drag a handle to scale, and then choose Distort, drag a handle to distort, and press Enter or Return to apply both transformations. In ImageReady, you can perform multiple types of transformations at the same time using the Transform > Numeric command.

To scale, rotate, skew, distort, or apply perspective:

1 Select what you want to transform. (See "Specifying what to transform" on page 127.)

2 Choose Edit > Transform > Scale, Rotate, Skew, Distort, or Perspective.

Note: (Photoshop) If you are transforming a shape or entire path, the Transform menu becomes the Transform Path menu. If you are transforming multiple path segments (but not the entire path), the Transform menu becomes the Transform Points menu.

3 In the options bar, click a square on the reference point locator ⊞ . (See "Setting the reference point" on page 128.)

4 Do one or more of the following:

• If you chose Scale, drag a handle on the bounding box. Press Shift as you drag a corner handle to scale proportionately. When positioned over a handle, the pointer becomes a double arrow.

• If you chose Rotate, move the pointer outside of the bounding border (it becomes a curved, two-sided arrow), and then drag. Press Shift to constrain the rotation to 15° increments.

• If you chose Skew, drag a side handle to slant the bounding box.

• If you chose Distort, drag a corner handle to stretch the bounding box.

• If you chose Perspective, drag a corner handle to apply perspective to the bounding box.

• For all types of transformations, enter a value in the options bar. For example, to rotate an item, specify degrees in the rotation △ text box.

5 If desired, switch to a different type of transformation by selecting a command from the Edit > Transform submenu.

When transforming a bitmap image (versus a shape or path), it becomes slightly less sharp each time you commit a transformation; therefore, performing multiple commands before applying the cumulative transformation is preferable to applying each transformation separately.

6 When you're satisfied with the results, do one of the following:

• Press Enter (Windows) or Return (Mac OS); click the Commit button ✔ in the options bar; or double-click inside the transformation marquee.

• To cancel the transformation, press Esc or click the Cancel button ⊘ in the options bar.

To flip or rotate precisely:

1 Select what you want to transform. (See "Specifying what to transform" on page 127.)

2 Choose Edit > Transform and choose one of the following commands from the submenu:

• Rotate 180° to rotate by a half-turn.

• Rotate 90° CW to rotate clockwise by a quarter-turn.

• Rotate 90° CCW to rotate counterclockwise by a quarter-turn.

• Flip Horizontal to flip horizontally, along the vertical axis.

• Flip Vertical to flip vertically, along the horizontal axis.

Note: (Photoshop) If you are transforming a shape or entire path, the Transform command becomes the Transform Path command. If you are transforming multiple path segments (but not the entire path), the Transform command becomes the Transform Points command.

To repeat a transformation:

Choose Edit > Transform > Again, Edit > Transform Path > Again, or Edit > Transform Points > Again.

To duplicate an item when transforming it:

Hold down Alt (Windows) or Option (Mac OS) when selecting the Transform command.

To apply multiple types of transformations at the same time (ImageReady):

1 Select what you want to transform. (See "Specifying what to transform" on page 127.)

2 Choose Edit > Transform > Numeric.

3 Do one or more of the following, and click OK:

• Select Position and enter values for the new location in the X (horizontal position) and Y (vertical position) text boxes. Select Relative to specify the new position in relation to the current position.

• Select Scale. Enter the dimensions in the W and H text boxes, or enter a scaling percentage in the Scale text box. Select Constrain Proportions to maintain the aspect ratio.

• Select Skew and enter degrees in the H (horizontal skew) and V (vertical skew) text boxes.

• Select Rotate. Enter degrees of rotation in the Angle text box, or drag the in the circle to the right of the text box.

Using the Free Transform command

The Free Transform command lets you apply transformations (rotate, scale, skew, distort, and perspective) in one continuous operation. Instead of choosing different commands, you simply hold down a key on your keyboard to switch between transformation types.

To freely transform:

1 Select what you want to transform. (See "Specifying what to transform" on page 127.)

2 Do one of the following:

• Choose Edit > Free Transform.

Note: (Photoshop) If you are transforming a shape or entire path, the Transform command becomes the Transform Path command. If you are transforming multiple path segments (but not the entire path), the Transform command becomes the Transform Points command.

• If you are transforming a selection, pixel-based layer, or selection border, choose the move tool ⊕. Then select Show Bounding Box in the options bar.

• If you are transforming a vector shape or path, select the path selection tool ▸. Then select Show Bounding Box in the options bar.

3 Do one or more of the following:

- To scale by dragging, drag a handle. Press Shift as you drag a corner handle to scale proportionately.

- To scale numerically, enter percentages in the W and H text boxes in the options bar. In Photoshop, click the link button 🔗 to maintain the aspect ratio.

- To rotate by dragging, move the pointer outside of the bounding border (it becomes a curved, two-sided arrow ↻), and then drag. Press Shift to constrain the rotation to 15° increments.

- To rotate numerically, enter degrees in the rotation text box △ in the options bar.

- To distort relative to the center point of the bounding border, press Alt (Windows) or Option (Mac OS), and drag a handle ⬉ .

- To distort freely, press Ctrl (Windows) or Command (Mac OS), and drag a handle.

- To skew, press Ctrl+Shift (Windows) or Command+Shift (Mac OS), and drag a side handle. When positioned over a side handle, the pointer becomes a white arrowhead with a small double arrow ⬂ .

- To skew numerically, enter degrees in the H (horizontal skew) and V (vertical skew) text boxes in the options bar.

- To apply perspective, press Ctrl+Alt+Shift (Windows) or Command+Option+Shift (Mac OS), and drag a corner handle. When positioned over a corner handle, the pointer becomes a gray arrowhead ▶ .

- To change the reference point, click a square on the reference point locator ⊞ in the options bar. (See "Setting the reference point" on page 128.)

- To move an item, enter values for the new location of the reference in the X (horizontal position) and Y (vertical position) text boxes in the options bar. In Photoshop, click the Relative Positioning button △ to specify the new position in relation to the current position.

💡 *To undo the last handle adjustment, choose Edit > Undo.*

4 Do one of the following:

- Press Enter (Windows) or Return (Mac OS); click the Commit button ✔ in the options bar; or double-click inside the transformation marquee.

- To cancel the transformation, press Esc or click the Cancel button ⊘ in the options bar.

💡 *When transforming a bitmap image (versus a shape or path), it becomes slightly less sharp each time you commit a transformation; therefore, performing multiple commands before applying the cumulative transformation is preferable to applying each transformation separately.*

Transforming objects in three dimensions

The 3D Transform filter lets you manipulate a flat, two-dimensional image as if it were a solid, three-dimensional object. Take, for example, a perspective photograph of a cereal box. You specify the corners of the box using a wire frame, and you can then manipulate the box as if it were a three-dimensional object. You can reposition the box, turn or rotate it, shrink or enlarge it, and change its field of view.

Transforming and manipulating objects

You can transform a two-dimensional object into a cube, sphere, or cylinder and manipulate it using wire frames based on that shape. Cylinders can include anything from simple objects, such as a can of soup, to shapes whose sides are lathed, such as a bottle or a lamp.

You can create and manipulate any grouping of cubes, spheres, and cylinders in the same image. For example, you can create and rotate a box, two balls, and a bottle together in the same image.

To add a wire frame:

1 Choose Filter > Render > 3D Transform.

2 Select one of these tools in the dialog box:

- Cube ⬤ to map the image (such as a file cabinet) to a cubic surface.

- Sphere ⊕ to map the image (such as a globe or ball) to a spherical surface.

- Cylinder ⬚ to map the image (such as a can or bottle) to a cylindrical surface.

3 Drag to create a cubic, cylindrical, or spherical wire frame over the image preview.

Note: The anchor points should line up with the corners of the box, or the top and bottom of the sphere or cylinder you want to manipulate.

To move or reshape the wire frame:

1 Select the selection tool ▸ or direct selection tool ▸ in the 3D Transform dialog box.

2 Do either of the following:

- Drag an edge of the wire frame to move the entire frame.

- With the direct selection tool, drag an anchor point on the wire frame to move that anchor point.

Note: The wire frame turns red if you try to make a wire frame that would be impossible to re-create in three dimensions.

3 If you are creating a complex cylinder, do any of the following:

- To add an anchor point to a cylinder, select the add anchor point tool ⬦⁺ in the dialog box, and click the right side of the wire frame. For example, you can add an anchor point to more closely fit the cylindrical wire frame to a picture of a bottle.

- To change an added anchor point from a smooth anchor point to a corner anchor point and vice versa, select the convert anchor point tool ⌐, and click the point. A smooth anchor point creates a gentle curve when you adjust it; a corner anchor point creates a sharp corner.

- To delete an added anchor point, select the delete anchor point tool ✑⁻, and click the point.

4 For Field of View, enter a value between 1 and 130. Alternatively, drag the slider to the left to increase the apparent field of view, right to decrease it. This can make the wire frame fit the image better. If you know the field of view angle used to photograph the image, you can enter it here.

To delete a wire frame:

1 Select the selection tool ➤ in the 3D Transform dialog box.

2 Select the wire frame, and press Backspace (Windows) or Delete (Mac OS).

To manipulate the object in three dimensions:

Do any of the following in the 3D Transform dialog box:

- To move the object, click the pan camera tool ⊹ in the dialog box, and drag the object.

- To rotate the object in any direction, click the trackball tool ◐, and drag the object.

- For Dolly Camera, enter a value between 0 and 99. Alternatively, drag the slider to the left to magnify the transformed object, right to shrink it. This has the same effect as if you were dollying, or moving, the camera further from or closer to the image.

- For Field of View, enter a value between 1 and 130, or drag the slider to the left to increase the apparent field of view, right to decrease it.

The 3D Transform dialog box previews only the active layer. As you manipulate an object in three dimensions, you can align it with the contents of underlying layers.

To align an object with an underlying layer:

1 Duplicate the layer with which you want to align. (See "Working with layered images" on page 231.)

2 Within the existing stacking order, place this duplicate layer directly under the layer you are transforming.

3 Merge the layer to be transformed with the duplicated layer.

4 With the Display Background option enabled in the 3D Transform options, manipulate the object on the layer.

5 When the layer is aligned, disable the Display Background option, and click OK.

Modifying the preview image

Use the zoom and hand tools in the 3D Transform dialog box to change your preview of an image. These actions do not modify the transformation itself, only your view of it.

To magnify or shrink the preview image:

1 Select the zoom tool 🔍 in the 3D Transform dialog box.

2 Click the image to zoom in, or Alt-click (Windows) or Option-click (Mac OS) to zoom out.

To move the view of the preview image:

Select the hand tool ✋ in the 3D Transform dialog box, and drag the preview image. This works only if you are zoomed in on the image.

Setting 3D rendering options

You can set the resolution and anti-aliasing of rendered images and specify whether to show the background from the original image in the 3D preview.

To set 3D rendering options:

1 Click Options in the 3D Transform dialog box.

2 Do any of the following:

- For Resolution, choose the quality of the rendered image. The setting has little effect on the image quality of cubes, but will produce smoother curved surfaces in cylinders and spheres.

- For Anti-aliasing, choose the level of anti-aliasing to apply to the rendered image.

- Select Display Background to include the portions of the original image outside of the wire frame in the preview and with the rendered image. Turn this option off to separate the transformed object from the original background.

Cloning and repairing images

You can use the clone stamp tool, pattern stamp tool, healing brush tool, and patch tool to clone pixels and repair images.

Using the clone stamp tool

The clone stamp tool takes a sample of an image, which you can then apply over another image or part of the same image. Each stroke of the tool paints on more of the sample.

Example of altering an image with the cloning tool

To use the clone stamp tool:

1 Select the clone stamp tool 🔳, and do the following in the options bar:

- Choose a brush and set brush options. (See "Working with brushes" on page 172.)

- Specify a blending mode, opacity, and flow. (See "Setting options for painting and editing tools" on page 185.)

- Determine how you want to align the sampled pixels. If you select Aligned, you can release the mouse button without losing the current sampling point. As a result, the sampled pixels are applied continuously, no matter how many times you stop and resume painting. If you deselect Aligned, the sampled pixels are applied from the initial sampling point each time you stop and resume painting.

- Select Use All Layers to sample data from all visible layers; deselect Use All Layers to sample only from the active layer.

2 Set the sampling point by positioning the pointer in any open image and Alt-clicking (Windows) or Option-clicking (Mac OS).

Note: If you are sampling from one image and applying to another, both images must be in the same color mode.

3 Drag in the image.

Using the pattern stamp tool

The pattern stamp tool lets you paint with a pattern. You can select a pattern from the pattern libraries or create your own patterns.

To use the pattern stamp tool:

1 Select the pattern stamp tool 🗿 , and do the following in the options bar:

- Choose a brush and set brush options. (See "Working with brushes" on page 172.)

- Specify a blending mode, opacity, and flow. (See "Setting options for painting and editing tools" on page 185.)

- Select a pattern from the Pattern pop-up palette. (See "Creating and managing patterns" on page 196.)

- Determine how you want to align the sampled pixels. If you select Aligned, you can release the mouse button without losing the current sampling point. As a result, the sampled pixels are applied continuously, no matter how many times you stop and resume painting. If you deselect Aligned, the sampled pixels are applied from the initial sampling point each time you stop and resume painting.

- Select Impressionist to apply the pattern with an impressionistic effect.

2 Drag in the image.

Using the healing brush tool (Photoshop)

The healing brush tool lets you correct imperfections, causing them to disappear into the surrounding image. Like the cloning tools, you use the healing brush tool to paint with sampled pixels from an image or pattern. However, the healing brush tool also matches the texture, lighting, and shading of the sampled pixels to the source pixels. As a result, the repaired pixels blend seamlessly into the rest of the image.

Sampled pixels and healed image

To use the healing brush tool:

1 Select the healing brush tool ✐ .

2 Click the brush sample in the options bar and set brush options in the pop-up palette:

- For more information on the Diameter, Hardness, Spacing, Angle, and Roundness options, see "Customizing brush tips (Photoshop)" on page 174.

- If you're using a pressure-sensitive digitizing tablet, choose an option from the Size menu to vary the size of the healing brush over the course of a stroke. Choose Pen Pressure to base the variation on the pen pressure. Choose Stylus Wheel to base the variation on the position of the pen thumbwheel. Choose Off to not vary the size.

3 Choose a blending mode from the Mode pop-up menu in the options bar:

- Choose Replace to preserve noise, film grain, and texture at the edges of the brush stroke.

- For more information on the Normal, Multiply, Screen, Darken, Lighten, Color, and Luminosity modes, see "Selecting a blending mode" on page 185.

4 Choose a source to use for repairing pixels in the options bar: Sampled to use pixels from the current image, or Pattern to use pixels from a pattern. If you chose Pattern, select a pattern from the Pattern pop-up palette. (See "Creating and managing patterns" on page 196.)

Note: The Pattern option is not available for 16-bit images.

5 Determine how you want to align the sampled pixels:

- If you select Aligned in the options bar, you can release the mouse button without losing the current sampling point. As a result, the sampled pixels are applied continuously, no matter how many times you stop and resume painting.

- If you deselect Aligned in the options bar, the sampled pixels are applied from the initial sampling point each time you stop and resume painting.

6 For the healing brush tool in sampling mode, set the sampling point by positioning the pointer in any open image and Alt-clicking (Windows) or Option-clicking (Mac OS).

Note: If you are sampling from one image and applying to another, both images must be in the same color mode unless one of the images is in Grayscale mode.

7 Drag in the image.

The sampled pixels are melded with the existing pixels each time you release the mouse button. Look in the status bar to view the status of the melding process.

💡 *If there is a strong contrast at the edges of the area you want to heal, make a selection before you use the healing brush tool. The selection should be bigger than the area you want to heal but precisely follow the boundary of contrasting pixels. When you paint with the healing brush tool, the selection will prevent colors from bleeding in from the outside.*

Using the patch tool (Photoshop)

The patch tool lets you repair a selected area with pixels from another area or a pattern. Like the healing brush tool, the patch tool matches the texture, lighting, and shading of the sampled pixels to the source pixels. You can also use the patch tool to clone isolated areas of an image.

When repairing with pixels from the image, select a small area to produce the best result.

Sampled pixels and source pixels

Patched image

To repair an area using sampled pixels:

1 Select the patch tool ⬭.

2 Do one of the following:

• Drag in the image to select the area you want to repair, and select Source in the options bar.

• Drag in the image to select the area from which you want to sample, and select Destination in the options bar.

Note: *You can also make a selection prior to selecting the patch tool.*

3 To adjust the selection, do one of the following:

• Shift-drag in the image to add to the existing selection.

• Alt-drag (Windows) or Option-drag (Mac OS) in the image to subtract from the existing selection.

• Alt-Shift-drag (Windows) or Option-Shift-drag (Mac OS) in the image to select an area intersected by the existing selection.

4 Position the pointer inside the selection, and do one of the following:

• If Source is selected in the options bar, drag the selection border to the area from which you want to sample. When you release the mouse button, the originally selected area is patched with the sampled pixels.

• If Destination is selected in the options bar, drag the selection border to the area you want to patch. When you release the mouse button, the newly selected area is patched with the sampled pixels.

To repair an area using a pattern:

1 Select the patch tool ⬭ .

2 Drag in the image to select the area you want to repair.

Note: You can also make a selection prior to selecting the patch tool.

3 To adjust the selection, do one of the following:

- Shift-drag in the image to add to the existing selection.

- Alt-drag (Windows) or Option-drag (Mac OS) in the image to subtract from the existing selection.

- Alt-Shift-drag (Windows) or Option-Shift-drag (Mac OS) in the image to select an area intersected by the existing selection.

4 Select a pattern from the Pattern pop-up palette in the options bar, and click Use Pattern.

Retouching images

You can retouch images using the smudge, focus, toning, and sponge tools.

Note: These tools cannot be used with Bitmap, Indexed Color mode, or 16-bit-per-channel images.

Using the smudge tool

The smudge tool simulates the actions of dragging a finger through wet paint. The tool picks up color where the stroke begins and pushes it in the direction you drag.

To use the smudge tool:

1 Select the smudge tool ⬭ .

2 Do the following in the options bar:

- Choose a brush and set brush options. (See "Working with brushes" on page 172.)

- Specify a blending mode and strength. (See "Setting options for painting and editing tools" on page 185.)

- Select Use All Layers to smudge using color data from all visible layers. If this is deselected, the smudge tool uses colors from only the active layer.

- Select Finger Painting to smudge using the foreground color at the beginning of each stroke. If this is deselected, the smudge tool uses the color under the pointer at the beginning of each stroke.

3 Drag in the image to smudge color.

💡 *In Photoshop, press Alt (Windows) or Option (Mac OS) as you drag with the smudge tool to use the Finger Painting option.*

Using the focus tools

The focus tools consist of the blur tool and the sharpen tool. The blur tool softens hard edges or areas in an image to reduce detail. The sharpen tool focuses soft edges to increase clarity or focus. For information on other ways to adjust sharpness, see "Sharpening images" on page 168 and "Improving performance with filters" on page 342.

To use the blur or sharpen tool:

1 Select the blur tool ⬤ or sharpen tool △ .

2 Do the following in the options bar:

- Choose a brush and set brush options. (See "Working with brushes" on page 172.)

- Specify a blending mode and strength. (See "Setting options for painting and editing tools" on page 185.)

- Select Use All Layers to blur or sharpen using data from all visible layers. If this is deselected, the tool uses data from only the active layer.

3 Drag over the part of the image you want to blur or sharpen.

Using the toning tools

The toning tools consist of the dodge tool and the burn tool. Used to lighten or darken areas of the image, the dodge and burn tools are based on a traditional photographer's technique for regulating exposure on specific areas of a print. Photographers hold back light to lighten an area on the print (dodging) or increase the exposure to darken areas on a print (burning).

To use the dodge or burn tool:

1 Select the dodge tool 🔍 or burn tool 🖐 .

2 Do the following in the options bar:

- Choose a brush and set brush options. (See "Working with brushes" on page 172.)

- Select what to change in the image: Midtones to change the middle range of grays; Shadows to change the dark areas; Highlights to change the light areas.

- Specify the exposure for the tool. (See "Specifying opacity, flow, strength, or exposure" on page 188.)

- (Photoshop) Click the airbrush button ✐ to use the brush as an airbrush. Alternately, select the Airbrush option in the Brushes palette. (See "Creating airbrush effects (Photoshop)" on page 183.)

3 Drag over the part of the image you want to modify.

Using the sponge tool

The sponge tool subtly changes the color saturation of an area. In Grayscale mode, the tool increases or decreases contrast by moving gray levels away from or toward the middle gray.

To use the sponge tool:

1 Select the sponge tool ⬤ .

2 Do the following in the options bar:

- Choose a brush and set brush options. (See "Working with brushes" on page 172.)

- Select how to change the color: Saturate to intensify the color's saturation; Desaturate to dilute the color's saturation.

- Specify the flow for the tool. (See "Specifying opacity, flow, strength, or exposure" on page 188.)

3 Drag over the part of the image you want to modify.

Using the Liquify command

The Liquify command lets you interactively scramble, push, pull, rotate, reflect, pucker, and bloat any area of an image. The distortions you create can be subtle or drastic, which makes the Liquify command a powerful tool for retouching images as well as creating artistic effects.

Note: The Liquify command is available only for 8-bit images in RGB Color, CMYK Color, Lab Color, and Grayscale image modes.

Using the Liquify dialog box

The Liquify dialog box provides tools and options for distorting an image.

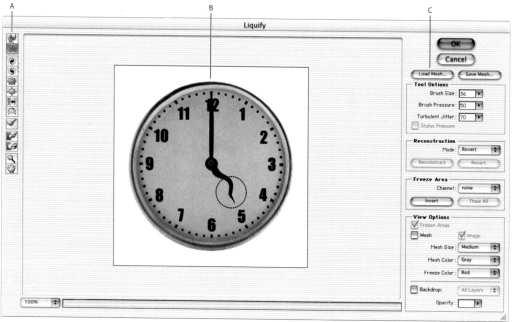

Liquify dialog box:
A. Toolbox B. Preview image C. Options

Displaying the Liquify dialog box Choose Filter > Liquify.

Magnifying and reducing the preview image
Select the zoom tool 🔍 in the Liquify dialog box, and click or drag in the preview image to zoom in; hold down Alt (Windows) or Option (Mac OS), and click or drag in the preview image to zoom out. Alternatively, you can specify a magnification level in the Zoom text box at the bottom of the dialog box.

Navigating in the preview image Select the hand tool 🖑 in the Liquify dialog box, and drag in the preview image. Alternately, hold down the spacebar, and drag in the preview image.

Using a mesh Adding a mesh helps you see and keep track of distortions. To add a mesh, select Mesh in the View Options section of the dialog box, and choose a mesh size, mesh color, and freeze color. To hide the mesh, deselect Mesh.

When Mesh is selected, you can show or hide the preview image. Select Image in the View Options section of the dialog box to show the preview image; deselect Image to view only the mesh.

Displaying layers in the preview image To show only the active layer in the preview image, deselect Add Backdrop (Windows) or Backdrop (Mac OS) in the View Options section of the dialog box. To show additional layers in the preview image, select Add Backdrop (Windows), or Backdrop (Mac OS), specify an overlay opacity, and choose an option from the pop-up menu.

Note: Only the active layer is distorted, even if other layers are displayed.

Distorting images

Several tools in the Liquify dialog box distort the brush area when you hold down the mouse button or drag. The distortion is concentrated at the center of the brush area, and the effect intensifies as you hold down the mouse button or repeatedly drag over an area.

To distort an image:

1 Select the layer you want to distort. To change only part of the current layer, select that area.

2 Choose Filter > Liquify.

Note: If a type layer, or a shape layer is selected, you must rasterize the layer before proceeding, making the type or shape uneditable. To distort type without rasterizing the type layer, use the Warp options for the type tool.

3 Freeze areas of the image that you don't want to alter. (See "Freezing and thawing areas" on page 143.)

4 In the Tool Options section of the dialog box, do the following:

• Specify a brush size and brush pressure. Using a low brush pressure makes changes occur more slowly, so it's easier to stop them at exactly the right moment.

• Specify a Turbulent Jitter to control how tightly the turbulence tool scrambles pixels.

- (Photoshop) Select Stylus Pressure to use pressure readings from a stylus tablet. (This option is available only when you are working with a stylus tablet.) When Stylus Pressure is selected, the brush pressure for the tools is the stylus pressure multiplied by the Brush Pressure value.

5 Use any of the following tools to distort the preview image:

- The warp tool 🖐 pushes pixels forward as you drag.

- The turbulence tool ≋ smoothly scrambles pixels. It is useful for creating fire, clouds, waves, and similar effects.

- The twirl clockwise tool ↻ rotates pixels clockwise as you hold down the mouse button or drag.

- The twirl counterclockwise tool ↺ rotates pixels counterclockwise as you hold down the mouse button or drag.

- The pucker tool 🞑 moves pixels toward the center of the brush area as you hold down the mouse button or drag.

- The bloat tool ✛ moves pixels away from the center of the brush area as you hold down the mouse button or drag.

- The shift pixels tool ⛗ moves pixels perpendicular to the stroke direction. Drag to move pixels to the left, and Alt-drag (Windows) or Option-drag (Mac OS) to move pixels to the right.

- The reflection tool 🔲 copies pixels to the brush area. Drag to reflect the area perpendicular to the direction of the stroke (to the left of the stroke). Alt-drag (Windows) or Option-drag (Mac OS) to reflect the area in the direction opposite to that of the stroke (for example, the area above a downward stroke). Usually, Alt-dragging or Option-dragging gives better results when you have frozen the area you want to reflect. Use overlapping strokes to create an effect similar to a reflection in water.

💡 *Shift-click with the warp, shift pixels, and reflection tools to create the effect of dragging in a straight line from the previous point you clicked.*

6 After distorting the preview image, you can use the reconstruct tool 🖌 or other controls to fully or partially reverse the changes or to change the image in new ways. (See "Reconstructing distortions" on page 143.)

7 Do one of the following:

- Click OK to close the Liquify dialog box and apply the changes to the active layer.

- Click Cancel to close the Liquify dialog box without applying changes to the layer.

- Hold down Alt (Windows) or Option (Mac OS) and click Reset to revert all distortions to the preview image.

💡 *You can use the Edit > Fade command to create additional effects. (See "Blending filter effects (Photoshop)" on page 340.)*

Freezing and thawing areas

You can use tools or alpha channels to freeze areas of the preview image to protect them from further changes, or to thaw the frozen areas.

Certain reconstruction modes change unfrozen areas in relation to the distortions in frozen areas. (See "Reconstructing distortions" on page 143.) You can hide or show the mask for frozen areas, change the mask color, and use a Brush Pressure option to create partial freezes and thaws.

To define which areas can be edited:

Do any of the following in the Liquify dialog box:

- To use the freeze tool ![freeze tool icon] to protect an area in the preview image from further editing, select the tool and drag over the area. Shift-click to freeze in a straight line between the current point and the previous point that you clicked or Shift-clicked.

The degree of freezing depends on the current brush pressure. If the frozen areas mask is displayed, the tint of the mask indicates the degree of freezing. If the brush pressure is less than 100%, you can fully freeze an area by dragging more than once. If you use other tools to distort and reconstruct partially frozen areas, the effects are proportionate to the degree of freezing. For example, if you drag the warp tool over an area that is 50% frozen and continue dragging over an unfrozen area, the frozen area shows half the distortion that occurs in the unfrozen area.

- To use an alpha channel to define a frozen area, choose the channel from the Channel menu in the Freeze Area section of the dialog box.

- To thaw a frozen area, making it editable, select the thaw tool ![thaw tool icon], and drag over the area. Shift-click to thaw in a straight line between the current point and the previous point that you clicked or Shift-clicked. Brush pressure has the same effect on the thaw tool as it has on the freeze tool.

- To thaw all frozen areas, click Thaw All in the Freeze Area section of the dialog box.

- To thaw all frozen areas and freeze the remaining areas, click Invert in the Freeze Area section of the dialog box. If you used an alpha channel to define the frozen area, the alpha channel name in the Channel menu changes to Custom.

To show or hide frozen areas:

Select or deselect Frozen Areas in the View Options section of the dialog box.

To change the color of frozen areas:

Choose a color from the Freeze Color pop-up menu in the View Options section of the dialog box.

Reconstructing distortions

After you distort the preview image, you can use a variety of controls and reconstruction modes to reverse changes or redo the changes in new ways. Reconstruction modes include reverting to the original state, extending distortions in frozen areas into unfrozen areas, and repeating distortions sampled from a starting point.

To restore a preview image to a previous state:

After distorting the preview image, do one of the following:

- To change one or more unfrozen areas back to their state when you opened the Liquify dialog box, choose Revert from the Mode menu in the Reconstruction section of the dialog box. Then select the reconstruct tool ![reconstruct tool icon], and hold down the mouse button or drag over the areas. The restoration occurs more quickly at the brush center.

- To change all unfrozen areas back to their state when you opened the Liquify dialog box, choose Revert from the Mode menu in the Reconstruction section of the dialog box, and click Reconstruct.

- To restore the entire preview image to its state when you opened the dialog box, click Revert in the Reconstruction section of the dialog box.

To extend distortions in frozen areas into unfrozen areas:

1 Freeze part of the areas you have changed. (For reconstruction, the image borders are also treated as if they are frozen.)

2 Choose one of these reconstruction modes from the Mode menu in the Reconstruction section of the dialog box:

- Rigid to maintain right angles in the pixel grid (as shown by the mesh) at the edges between frozen and unfrozen areas, sometimes producing near-discontinuities at the edges. This restores the unfrozen areas to something close to their original appearance. (To restore their original appearance, use Revert reconstruction mode.)

- Stiff acts like a weak magnetic field. At the edges between frozen and unfrozen areas, the unfrozen areas continue the distortions in the frozen areas. As the distance from frozen areas increases, the distortions lessen.

- Smooth to propagate the distortions in frozen areas throughout unfrozen areas, with smoothly continuous distortions.

- Loose to produce effects similar to Smooth, with even greater continuity between distortions in frozen and unfrozen areas.

A   B

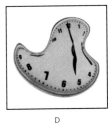

C   D

Reconstruction based on distortions in frozen areas:
A. Original image B. Distorted with frozen areas
C. Reconstructed in Rigid mode (using button)
D. Thawed, edges reconstructed in Smooth mode (using tool)

3 Do one of the following:

- To reconstruct one or more unfrozen areas, select the reconstruct tool , and hold down the mouse button or drag over the area. Pixels move more quickly at the brush center. Shift-click to reconstruct in a straight line between the current point and the previous point that you clicked or Shift-clicked.

- To reconstruct all unfrozen areas, click Reconstruct. The image changes until reconstruction in the current mode is complete. To partially reconstruct the unfrozen areas, press Esc or press Command+period (Mac OS) during reconstruction.

To reconstruct areas to match distortions from the image location where the mouse button is initially pressed:

1 After distorting the preview image, choose one of these reconstruction modes from the Mode menu in the Reconstruction section of the dialog box:

- Displace to reconstruct unfrozen areas to match the displacement at the starting point for the reconstruction. You can use Displace to move all or part of the preview image to a different location.

- Amplitwist to reconstruct unfrozen areas to match the displacement, rotation, and overall scaling that exist at the starting point.

- Affine to reconstruct unfrozen areas to match all local distortions that exist at the starting point, including displacement, rotation, horizontal and vertical scaling, and skew.

2 Select the reconstruct tool , and in the preview image, hold down the mouse button or drag from a starting point.

This spreads the distortion sampled at the starting point. (If there is no distortion, the effect is the same as using Revert mode.) Pixels move more quickly at the brush center. You can set new starting points and use the reconstruct tool repeatedly to create a variety of effects.

Note: The Reconstruct button is not available in Displace, Amplitwist, and Affine reconstruction modes.

Saving and loading distortions

You can save the distortion mesh from one image and apply it to other images.

To save a distortion mesh:

1 After distorting the preview image, click Save Mesh.

2 Specify a name and location for the mesh file, and click Save.

To apply a distortion mesh to a preview image:

Click Load Mesh, select the mesh file you want to apply, and click Open. If the image and distortion mesh aren't the same size, the mesh is scaled to fit the image.

Chapter 7: Drawing

The drawing tools let you create and edit vector shapes. You can work with shapes in shape layers and as paths; you can also create rasterized shapes, which can be edited with the painting tools. The drawing tools provide an easy way to create buttons, navigation bars, and other items used on Web pages.

About drawing and painting

When creating graphics on a computer, there is a distinction between painting and drawing. *Painting* involves changing the colors of pixels using a painting tool. You can apply colors gradually, with soft edges and transitions, and manipulate individual pixels using powerful filter effects. However, once you apply a brush stroke, there is no simple way to select the entire brush stroke and move it to a new location in the image.

Drawing, on the other hand, involves creating shapes that are defined as geometric objects (also called *vector objects*). For example, if you draw a circle using the ellipse tool, the circle is defined by a specific radius, location, and color. You can quickly select the entire circle and move it to a new location, or you can edit the outline of the circle to distort its shape. (See "About bitmap images and vector graphics" on page 53.)

Working with shapes provides several advantages:

- Shapes are object-oriented—you can quickly select, resize, and move a shape, and you can edit a shape's outline (called a *path*) and attributes (such as stroke, fill color, and style). You can use shapes to make selections and create libraries of custom shapes with the Preset Manager.

- Shapes are resolution-independent—they maintain crisp edges when resized, printed to a PostScript printer, saved in a PDF file, or imported into a vector-based graphics application.

Drawing shapes and paths

You use the drawing tools to create shape layers, work paths, and rasterized shapes.

About the drawing tools

Keep in mind the following similarities and differences when using the drawing tools in Photoshop and ImageReady:

- The rectangle tool ▢, rounded rectangle tool ▢, ellipse tool ◯, and line tool ╲ are available in both Photoshop and ImageReady.

- The pen tool ✎, freeform pen tool ✎, polygon tool ◯, custom shape tool ✑, add anchor point tool ✎⁺, delete anchor point tool ✎⁻, and convert point tool ⋏ are available only in Photoshop.

- In Photoshop, you can use the drawing tools to create a work path; in ImageReady, you can't create a work path.

- In Photoshop, you can draw multiple shapes in a layer and specify how overlapping shapes interact. In ImageReady, you can only draw one shape in a layer.

- In Photoshop, you can edit shapes after you draw them. In ImageReady, you can move and transform shapes, but you can't edit them.

Creating shape layers

You create a *shape layer* using a shape tool or a pen tool. The shape is automatically filled with the current foreground color; however, you can easily change the fill to a different color, a gradient, or a pattern. The shape's outline is stored in a vector mask that is linked to the layer.

In Photoshop, you can draw multiple shapes in a layer and specify how overlapping shapes interact.

To create a new shape layer:

1 Select a shape tool or a pen tool, and click the Shape Layers button 🔲 in the options bar.

2 To apply a style to the shape layer, select a preset style from the Style pop-up menu. (See "Applying preset styles" on page 246.)

3 To change the color of the shape layer, click the color swatch in the options bar and choose a color.

4 Set additional tool-specific options, and draw a shape. For more information, see "Using the shape tools" on page 150 and "Using the pen tools (Photoshop)" on page 152.

To draw multiple shapes in a layer (Photoshop):

1 Select the layer to which you want to add shapes.

2 Select a drawing tool, and set tool-specific options.

3 Choose one of the following in the options bar:

- Add to Shape Area 🔲 to add the new area to the existing shapes or path.

- Subtract from Shape Area 🔲 to remove the overlapping area from the existing shapes or path.

- Intersect Shape Areas 🔲 to restrict the area to the intersection of the new area and the existing shapes or path.

- Exclude Overlapping Shape Areas 🔲 to exclude the overlap area in the consolidated new and existing areas.

💡 *Use the following keyboard shortcuts while drawing with a shape tool: Hold down Shift to temporarily select the Add to Shape Area option; hold down Alt (Windows) or Option (Mac OS) to temporarily select the Subtract from Shape Area option.*

4 Draw in the image. You can easily switch between drawing tools by clicking a tool button in the options bar.

Creating a work path (Photoshop)

A *work path* is a temporary path that appears in the Paths palette and defines the outline of a shape. You can use paths in several ways:

- You can use a path as a vector mask to hide areas of a layer. (See "Masking layers" on page 259.)

- You can convert a path to a selection. For more information, see "Converting between paths and selection borders (Photoshop)" on page 164.

- You can edit a path to change its shape. For more information, see "Editing paths (Photoshop)" on page 157.

- You can designate a saved path as a clipping path to make part of an image transparent when exporting the image to a page-layout or vector-editing application.

Create a new path in the Paths palette before you begin drawing to automatically save the work path as a named path.

To create a new work path:

1 Select a shape tool or a pen tool, and click the Paths button in the options bar.

2 Set tool-specific options, and draw the path. For more information, see "Using the shape tools" on page 150 and "Using the pen tools (Photoshop)" on page 152.

3 Draw additional path components if desired. You can easily switch between drawing tools by clicking a tool button in the options bar. Choose a path area option to determine how overlapping path components intersect:

- Add to Path Area to add the new area to overlapping path areas.

- Subtract from Path Area to remove the new area from the overlapping path area.

- Intersect Path Areas to restrict the path to the intersection of the new area and the existing area.

- Exclude Overlapping Path Areas to exclude the overlap area in the consolidated path.

Use the following keyboard shortcuts while drawing with a shape tool: Hold down Shift to temporarily select the Add to Path Area option; hold down Alt (Windows) or Option (Mac OS) to temporarily select the Subtract from Path Area option.

For more information on working with paths, see "Using the Paths palette (Photoshop)" on page 156.

Creating rasterized shapes

As the name implies, rasterized shapes are not vector objects. Creating a rasterized shape is the same as making a selection and filling it with the foreground color. You cannot edit a rasterized shape as a vector object.

To create a rasterized shape:

1 Select a layer. You cannot create a rasterized shape on a vector-based layer (a shape layer or a type layer).

2 Select a shape tool, and click the Fill Pixels button in the options bar.

3 Set the following options in the options bar:

- Mode to control how the shape will affect the existing pixels in the image. (See "Selecting a blending mode" on page 185.)

- Opacity to determine to what degree the shape will obscure or reveal the pixels beneath it. A shape with 1% opacity appears nearly transparent, while one with 100% opacity appears completely opaque.

- Anti-Aliased to blend the shape's edge pixels with the surrounding pixels.

4 Set additional tool-specific options, and draw a shape. For more information, see "Using the shape tools" on page 150 and "Using the pen tools (Photoshop)" on page 152.

Note: In Photoshop, you can easily switch between drawing tools by clicking a tool button in the options bar.

Using the shape tools

You use the shape tools to draw lines, rectangles, rounded rectangles, and ellipses in an image. In Photoshop, you can also draw polygons and create custom shape libraries to reuse and share custom shapes.

Setting shape tool options

Each shape tool provides specific options; for example, you can set options that allow you to draw a rectangle with fixed dimensions or a line with arrowheads.

(Photoshop) Click the inverted arrow to display options for the selected shape.

To set tool-specific options:

1 Select the rectangle tool ▢ , rounded rectangle tool ▢ , ellipse tool ◯ , polygon tool ◯ (Photoshop), line tool ╲ , or custom shape tool 🐾 (Photoshop).

2 Set tool options in the options bar. The available options vary by tool. In Photoshop, click the inverted arrow ▾ next to the shape buttons to view the options:

Arrowheads Start and End Renders a line with arrowheads. Select Start, End, or both to specify on which end of the line arrows are rendered. In ImageReady, click Shape to define the shape of the arrowhead; in Photoshop, the shape options appear in the pop-up dialog box. Enter values for Width and Length to specify the proportions of the arrowhead as a percentage of the line width (10% to 1000% for Width, and 10% to 5000% for Length). Enter a value for the concavity of the arrowhead (from –50% to +50%). The concavity value defines the amount of curvature on the widest part of the arrowhead, where the arrowhead meets the line.

Note: In Photoshop, you can also edit an arrowhead directly using the vector selection and drawing tools.

Circle (Photoshop) Constrains an ellipse to a circle.

Corner Radius (ImageReady) Specifies the corner radius for rendering a rounded rectangle.

Defined Proportions (Photoshop) Renders a custom shape based on the proportions with which it was created.

Defined Size (Photoshop) Renders a custom shape based on the size at which it was created.

Fixed Size Renders a rectangle, rounded rectangle, ellipse, or custom shape as a fixed shape based on the values you enter in the Width and Height text boxes.

From Center (Photoshop) Renders a rectangle, rounded rectangle, ellipse, or custom shape from the center.

Indent Sides By (Photoshop) Renders a polygon as a star. Enter a percentage in the text box to specify the portion of the star's radius taken up by the points. A 50% setting creates points that are half the total radius of the star; a larger value creates sharper, thinner points; a smaller value creates fuller points.

Proportional (Photoshop) Renders a rectangle, rounded rectangle, or ellipse as a proportional shape based on the values you enter in the Width and Height text boxes.

Radius (Photoshop) For rounded rectangles, specifies the corner radius. For polygons, specifies the distance from the center of a polygon to the outer points.

Sides (Photoshop) Specifies the number of sides in a polygon.

Smooth Corners or Smooth Indents (Photoshop) Renders a polygon with smooth corners or indents.

Snap to Pixels (Photoshop) Snaps edges of a rectangle or rounded rectangle to the pixel boundaries.

Square (Photoshop) Constrains a rectangle or rounded rectangle to a square.

Unconstrained (Photoshop) Lets you set the width and height of a rectangle, rounded rectangle, ellipse, or custom shape by dragging.

Weight Determines the width of a line in pixels.

Using preset shapes (Photoshop)

When you're using the custom shape tool, you can choose from a variety of preset shapes. You can also save shapes that you create as preset shapes.

To select a preset shape:

1 Select the custom shape tool.

2 Select a shape from the Shape pop-up palette. (See "Using pop-up palettes" on page 25.)

To save a shape or path as a custom shape:

1 In the Paths palette, select a path—either a vector mask for a shape layer, a work path, or a saved path.

2 Choose Edit > Define Custom Shape, and enter a name for the new custom shape in the Shape Name dialog box. The new shape appears in the Shape pop-up palette.

3 To save the new custom shape as part of a new library, select Save Shapes from the pop-up palette menu.

You can also use the Preset Manager to manage libraries of custom shapes. For more information, see "Managing libraries with the Preset Manager (Photoshop)" on page 49.

Controlling a shape as you draw it

You can use the following modifier keys to manipulate a shape while dragging:

- Hold down the spacebar to move the shape without changing its size or proportions.

- (ImageReady) Hold down Shift to constrain a rectangle or rounded rectangle to a square, to constrain an ellipse to a circle, or to constrain the line angle to a multiple of 45°.

Using the pen tools (Photoshop)

You can create or edit straight lines, curves, or freeform lines and shapes using the pen tools. The pen tools can be used in conjunction with the shape tools to create complex shapes.

Drawing with the pen tool

The pen tool lets you create straight lines and smooth flowing curves with greater precision than is possible with the freeform pen tool. For most users, the pen tool provides the best control and greatest accuracy for drawing.

To draw with the pen tool:

1 Select the pen tool ✎ .

2 Set the following tool-specific options:

- To add an anchor point when you click a line segment and delete an anchor point when you click it, select Auto Add/Delete in the options bar. (See "Adding, deleting, and converting anchor points" on page 162.)

- To preview path segments as you draw, click the inverted arrow ▾ next to the shape buttons in the options bar, and select Rubber Band.

3 Position the pen pointer where you want to begin to draw, and click to define the first anchor point.

4 Click or drag to set anchor points for additional segments. (See "Drawing straight segments with the pen tool" on page 152 and "Drawing curves with the pen tool" on page 153.)

5 Complete the path:

- To end an open path, Ctrl-click (Windows) or Command-click (Mac OS) away from the path.

- To close a path, position the pen pointer over the first anchor point. A small loop appears next to the pen tip when it is positioned correctly. Click to close the path.

For more information on closed and open paths, see "About anchor points, direction lines, direction points, and components" on page 157.

Drawing straight segments with the pen tool

The simplest segment you can draw with the pen tool is a straight segment, made by clicking to create anchor points.

To draw straight segments:

1 Position the pen pointer where you want the straight segment to begin, and click to define the first anchor point.

2 Click again where you want the first segment of the straight line to end, or Shift-click to constrain the angle of the segment to a multiple of 45°.

3 Continue clicking to set anchor points for additional segments. The last anchor point is always a solid square, indicating it is selected. Previously defined anchor points become hollow squares as you add further anchor points. If the Auto Add/Delete option is selected, you can click an existing point to delete it.

Drawing curves with the pen tool

You create curves by dragging the pen tool in the direction you want the curve to go. Keep these guidelines in mind when drawing curves:

- Always drag the first direction point in the direction of the bump of the curve, and drag the second direction point in the opposite direction to create a single curve. Dragging both direction points in the same direction creates an "S" curve.

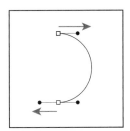 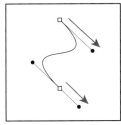

Drag in the opposite direction to create a smooth curve. Drag in the same direction to create an "S" curve.

- When drawing a series of smooth curves, draw one curve at a time, placing anchor points at the beginning and end of each curve, not at the tip of the curve. Use as few anchor points as possible, placing them as far apart as possible. This decreases the file size and reduces the potential for printing errors.

For more information on how paths are constructed, see "About anchor points, direction lines, direction points, and components" on page 157.

To draw a curve:

1 Position the pointer where you want the curve to begin, and hold down the mouse button. The first anchor point appears, and the pointer changes to an arrowhead.

2 Drag in the direction you want the curve segment to be drawn. As you drag, the pointer leads one of two direction points. Hold down the Shift key to constrain the tool to multiples of 45°, and release the mouse button once you have positioned the first direction point.

The length and slope of the direction line determine the shape of the curve segment. You can adjust one or both sides of the direction line later.

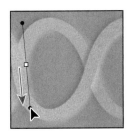 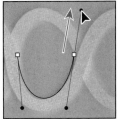

Drag in the direction of the curve to set the first anchor point. Drag in the opposite direction to complete the curve segment.

3 Position the pointer where you want the curve segment to end, and drag in the opposite direction to complete the segment.

4 Do one of the following:

• To draw the next segment of a smooth curve, position the pointer where you want the next segment to end, and drag away from the curve.

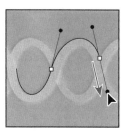

*Drag away from the curve
to create the next segment.*

• To change the direction of the curve sharply, release the mouse button, then Alt-drag (Windows) or Option-drag (Mac OS) the direction point in the direction of the curve. Release Alt (Windows) or Option (Mac OS) and the mouse button, reposition the pointer where you want the segment to end, and drag in the opposite direction to complete the curve segment.

• To break out the direction lines of an anchor point, Alt-drag (Windows) or Option-drag (Mac OS) the lines.

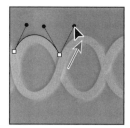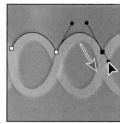

Alt-drag or Option-drag the direction point toward the curve. Release the key, and drag in the opposite direction.

Drawing with the freeform pen tool

The freeform pen tool lets you draw as if you were drawing with a pencil on paper. Anchor points are added automatically as you draw. You do not determine where the points are positioned, but you can adjust them once the path is complete.

The magnetic pen is an option of the freeform tool that lets you draw a path that snaps to the edges of defined areas in your image. You can define the range and sensitivity of the snapping behavior, as well as the complexity of the resulting path. The magnetic pen and magnetic lasso tools share many of the same options.

To draw with the freeform pen tool:

1 Select the freeform pen tool 🖊.

2 To control how sensitive the final path is to the movement of your mouse or stylus, click the inverted arrow ▾ next to the shape buttons in the options bar, and enter a value between 0.5 and 10.0 pixels for Curve Fit. A higher value creates a simpler path with fewer anchor points.

3 Drag the pointer in the image. As you drag, a path trails behind the pointer. When you release the mouse, a work path is created.

4 To continue the existing freehand path, position the freeform pen pointer on an endpoint of the path, and drag.

5 To complete the path, release the mouse. To create a closed path, click the initial point of the path (a circle appears next to the pointer when it is aligned). For more information on closed and open paths, see "About anchor points, direction lines, direction points, and components" on page 157.

To draw using the magnetic pen options:

1 To convert the freeform pen tool to the magnetic pen tool ✑ , select Magnetic in the options bar, or click the inverted arrow next to the shape buttons in the options bar, select Magnetic, and set the following:

- For Width, enter a pixel value between 1 and 256. The magnetic pen detects edges only within the specified distance from the pointer.

- For Contrast, enter a percentage value between 1 and 100 to specify the contrast between pixels required to be considered an edge. Use a higher value for low contrast images.

- For Frequency, enter a value between 5 and 40 to specify the rate at which the pen sets anchor points. A higher value anchors the path in place more quickly.

- If you are working with a stylus tablet, select or deselect Pen Pressure. When this option is selected, an increase in pen pressure causes the width to decrease.

2 Click in the image to set the first fastening point.

3 To draw a freehand segment, move the pointer or drag along the edge you want to trace.

The most recent segment of the border remains active. As you move the pointer, the active segment snaps to the strongest edge in the image, connecting the pointer to the last fastening point. Periodically, the magnetic pen adds fastening points to the border to anchor previous sections.

4 If the border doesn't snap to the desired edge, click once to add a fastening point manually and to keep the border from moving. Continue to trace the edge and add fastening points as needed. If needed, press Delete to remove the last fastening point.

5 To dynamically modify the properties of the magnetic pen, do one of the following:

- Alt-drag (Windows) or Option-drag (Mac OS) to draw a freehand path.

- Alt-click (Windows) or Option-click (Mac OS) to draw straight segments.

- Press the [key to decrease the magnetic pen width by 1 pixel; press the] key to increase the pen width by 1 pixel.

6 Complete the path:

- Press Enter or Return to end an open path.

- Double-click to close the path with a magnetic segment.

- Hold down Alt (Windows) or Option (Mac OS), and double-click to close the path with a straight segment.

Editing shape layers

A shape layer is a fill layer linked to a vector mask. You can easily change the fill to a different color, a gradient, or a pattern by editing the shape's fill layer. You can also edit the shape's vector mask to modify the shape outline, and apply a style to the layer.

To change the color of a shape:

Double-click the shape layer's thumbnail in the Layers palette, and choose a different color using the color picker.

To fill a shape with a pattern or gradient:

1 Select a shape layer in the Layers palette.

2 Do one of the following:

• Choose Layer > Change Layer Content > Gradient, and set gradient options.

• Choose Layer > Change Layer Content > Pattern, and set pattern options.

For more information, see "Using adjustment layers and fill layers (Photoshop)" on page 256.

To modify the outline of a shape:

Click the shape layer's vector mask thumbnail in the Layers palette or Paths palette. Then change the shape using the shape and pen tools.

For more information, see "Moving, reshaping, copying, and deleting path components" on page 160.

Using the Paths palette (Photoshop)

The Paths palette lists the name and a thumbnail image of each saved path, the current work path, and the current vector mask. Decreasing the size of thumbnails or turning them off lets you list more paths in the palette, and turning thumbnails off can improve performance. To view a path, you must first select it in the Paths palette.

To display the Paths palette:

Choose Window > Paths.

To select or deselect a path in the palette:

Do one of the following:

• To select a path, click the path name in the Paths palette. Only one path can be selected at a time.

• To deselect a path, click in the blank area of the Paths palette or press Esc.

To change the size of path thumbnails:

1 Choose Palette Options from the Paths palette menu.

2 Select a size, or select None to turn off the display of thumbnails.

To change a path's stacking order:

1 Select the path in the Paths palette.

2 Drag the path up or down in the Paths palette. When the heavy black line appears in the desired location, release the mouse button.

Note: You cannot change the order of vector masks in the Paths palette.

Editing paths (Photoshop)

A path is composed of one or more *path components*—collections of one or more anchor points joined by segments.

Because they take up less disk space than pixel-based data, paths can be used for long-term storage of simple masks. Paths can also be used to clip sections of your image for export to an illustration or page-layout application. (See "Using image clipping paths to create transparency" on page 377.)

About anchor points, direction lines, direction points, and components

A path consists of one or more straight or curved segments. *Anchor points* mark the endpoints of the path segments. On curved segments, each selected anchor point displays one or two *direction lines*, ending in *direction points*. The positions of direction lines and points determine the size and shape of a curved segment. Moving these elements reshapes the curves in a path.

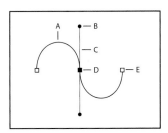

A path:
A. *Curved line segment* **B.** *Direction point*
C. *Direction line* **D.** *Selected anchor point*
E. *Unselected anchor point*

A path can be *closed*, with no beginning or end (for example, a circle), or *open*, with distinct *endpoints* (for example, a wavy line).

Smooth curves are connected by anchor points called *smooth points*. Sharply curved paths are connected by *corner points*.

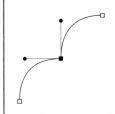

Smooth point, and corner point

When you move a direction line on a smooth point, the curved segments on both sides of the point adjust simultaneously. By comparison, when you move a direction line on a corner point, only the curve on the same side of the point as the direction line is adjusted.

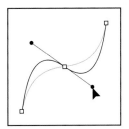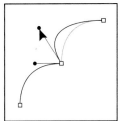

Adjusting a smooth point, and a corner point

A path does not have to be all one connected series of segments. It can contain more than one distinct and separate *path component*. Each shape in a shape layer is a path component, as described by the layer's clipping path.

Separate path components selected

Selecting paths (Photoshop)

Selecting a path component or path segment displays all of the anchor points on the selected portion, including any direction lines and direction points if the selected segment is curved. Direction points appear as filled circles, selected anchor points as filled squares, and unselected anchor points as hollow squares.

To select a path:

1 Do one of the following:

- To select a path component (including a shape in a shape layer), select the path selection tool ![path selection tool] , and click anywhere inside the path component. If a path consists of several path components, only the path component under the pointer is selected.

To display the bounding box along with the selected path, select Show Bounding Box in the options bar.

- To select a path segment, select the direct selection tool ![direct selection tool] , and click one of the segment's anchor points or drag a marquee over part of the segment.

Drag a marquee to select segments.

2 To select additional path components or segments, select the path selection tool or the direct selection tool, then hold down Shift while selecting additional paths or segments.

When the direct selection tool is selected, you can select the entire path or path component by Alt-clicking (Windows) or Option-clicking (Mac OS) inside the path. To activate the direct selection tool when any other tool is selected, position the pointer over an anchor point, and press Ctrl (Windows) or Command (Mac OS).

To change the overlap mode for the selected path component:

Using the path selection tool, drag a marquee to select existing path areas, then choose a shape area option in the options bar:

- Add to Shape Area 🔲 to add the path area to overlapping path areas.

- Subtract from Shape Area 🔲 to remove the path area from overlapping path areas.

- Intersect Shape Areas 🔲 to restrict the area to the intersection of the selected path area and overlapping path areas.

- Exclude Overlapping Shape Areas 🔲 to exclude the overlap area.

To show or hide the selected path component:

Do one of the following:

- Choose View > Show > Target Path.

- Choose View > Extras. This command also shows or hides a grid, guides, selection edges, annotations, and slices.

Moving, reshaping, and deleting path segments

You can move, reshape, or delete individual segments in a path, and you can add or delete anchor points to change the configuration of segments.

Note: *You can also apply a transformation, such as scaling, rotating, flipping, or distorting, to a segment or anchor point. See "Applying transformations" on page 128.*

To move a straight segment:

1 Select the direct selection tool ▶, and select the segment you want to adjust. To adjust the angle or length of the segment, select an anchor point.

2 Drag the selected segment to its new position.

To move a curved segment:

1 Select the direct selection tool ▶, and select the points or segments you want to move. Be sure to select both points anchoring the segment.

2 Drag the selected anchor points or segments to new positions. Hold down Shift as you drag to constrain the movement to multiples of 45°.

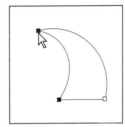

Select points anchoring a curve. Then drag to move the curve.

To reshape a curved segment:

1 Select the direct selection tool ▶, and select the curved segment you want to adjust. Direction lines appear for that segment.

2 Adjust the curve:

- To adjust the position of the segment, drag the segment.

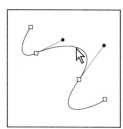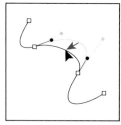

Click to select the curve segment. Then drag to adjust.

- To adjust the shape of the segment on either side of a selected anchor point, drag the anchor point or the direction point. Hold down Shift as you drag to constrain movement to multiples of 45°.

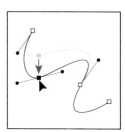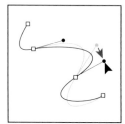

Drag the anchor point, or drag the direction point.

To delete a segment:

1 Select the direct selection tool ⬦, and select the segment you want to delete.

2 Press Backspace (Windows) or Delete (Mac OS) to delete the selected segment. Pressing Backspace or Delete again erases the rest of the path component.

Moving, reshaping, copying, and deleting path components

You can reposition a path component (including a shape in a shape layer) anywhere within an image. You can copy components within an image or between two Photoshop images. Using the path selection tool, you can merge overlapping components into a single component. All vector objects, whether they are described by a saved path, a work path, or a vector mask, can be moved, reshaped, copied, or deleted.

You can also use the Copy and Paste commands to duplicate vector objects between a Photoshop image and an image in another application, such as Adobe Illustrator.

To move a path or path component:

1 Select the path name in the Paths palette, and use the path selection tool ⬧ to select the path in the image. To select multiple path components, Shift-click each additional path component to add it to the selection.

2 Drag the path to its new location. If you move any part of a path beyond the canvas boundaries, the hidden part of the path is still available.

Note: If you drag a path so that the move pointer is over another open image, the path will be copied to that image.

To reshape a path component:

1 Select the path name in the Paths palette, and use the direct selection tool ⬦ to select an anchor point in the path.

2 Drag the point or its handles to a new location. (See "Adding, deleting, and converting anchor points" on page 162.)

To merge overlapping path components:

1 Select the path name in the Paths palette, and select the path selection tool ▶.

2 Click Combine in the options bar to create a single component from all overlapping components.

To copy a path component or path:

Do any of the following:

- To copy a path component as you move it, select the path name in the Paths palette, and click a path component with the path selection tool ▶. Then Alt-drag (Windows) or Option-drag (Mac OS) the selected path.

- To copy a path without renaming it, drag the path name in the Paths palette to the New Path button ▣ at the bottom of the palette.

- To copy and rename a path, Alt-drag (Windows) or Option-drag (Mac OS) the path in the Paths palette to the New Path button at the bottom of the palette. Or select the path to copy, and choose Duplicate Path from the Paths palette menu. Enter a new name for the path in the Duplicate Path dialog box, and click OK.

- To copy a path or path component into another path, select the path or path component you want to copy, and choose Edit > Copy. Then select the destination path, and choose Edit > Paste.

To copy path components between two Adobe Photoshop files:

1 Open both images.

2 Use the path selection tool ▶ to select the entire path or the path components in the source image you want to copy.

3 To copy the path component, do any of the following:

- Drag the path component from the source image to the destination image. The path component is copied to the active path in the Paths palette.

- In the source image, select the path's name in the Paths palette and choose Edit > Copy to copy the path. In the destination image, choose Edit > Paste. You can also use this method to combine paths in the same image.

- To paste the path component into the center of the destination image, select the path component in the source image, and choose Edit > Copy. In the destination image, choose Edit > Paste.

To delete a path component:

1 Select the path name in the Paths palette, and click a path component with the path selection tool ▶.

2 Press backspace (Windows) or Delete (Mac OS) to delete the selected path component.

Aligning and distributing path components

You can both align and distribute path components that are described in a single path. For example, you can align the left edges of several shapes contained in a single layer or distribute several components in a work path along their horizontal centers.

***Note:** To align shapes that are on separate layers, use the move tool. (See "Moving selections and layers within an image" on page 113.)*

To align components:

Use the path selection tool to select the components you want to align, and select one of the alignment options from the options bar: Top, Vertical Center, Bottom, Left, Horizontal Center, or Right.

To align or distribute components:

Select at least three components you want to distribute, then select one of the distribute options from the options bar: Top, Vertical Center, Bottom, Left, Horizontal Center, or Right.

Adding, deleting, and converting anchor points

The add anchor point and delete anchor point tools let you add and delete anchor points on a shape. The convert direction point tool lets you convert a smooth curve to a sharp curve or to a straight segment, and vice versa. If you have selected Auto Add/Delete in the options bar for the pen tool or freeform pen tool, when you click a line segment, a point is added, and when you click an existing point, it is deleted.

To add an anchor point:

1 Select the add anchor point tool (), and position the pointer on the path where you want the anchor point added (a plus sign appears next to the pointer).

2 Do one of the following:

- To add an anchor point without changing the shape of the segment, click the path.
- To add an anchor point and change the shape of the segment, drag to define direction lines for the anchor point.

To delete an anchor point:

1 Select the delete anchor point tool, and position the pointer on the anchor point you want deleted (a minus sign appears next to the pointer).

2 Delete the anchor point:

- Click the anchor point to delete it and to reshape the path to fit the remaining anchor points.
- Drag the anchor point to delete it and to change the shape of the segment.

To convert between a smooth point and a corner point:

1 Select the convert point tool ⌐, and position the pointer over the anchor point you want changed.

💡 *To activate the convert point tool while the direct selection tool is selected, position the pointer over an anchor point, and press Ctrl+Alt (Windows) or Command+Option (Mac OS).*

2 Convert the point:

- To convert a smooth point to a corner point without direction lines, click the smooth anchor point.

- To convert a smooth point to a corner point with direction lines, make sure the direction lines are visible. Then drag a direction point to break the pair of direction lines.

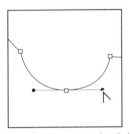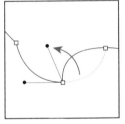

Drag direction point to break direction lines.

- To convert a corner point to a smooth point, drag away from the corner point to make direction lines appear.

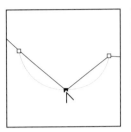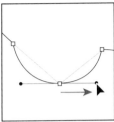

Click to create a corner point. Drag to create a smooth point.

Managing paths (Photoshop)

When you use a pen or shape tool to create a work path, the new path appears as the Work Path in the Paths palette. The Work Path is temporary; you must save it to avoid losing its contents. If you deselect the Work Path without saving it and start drawing again, a new path will replace the existing one.

When you use a pen or shape tool to create a new shape layer, the new path appears as a vector mask in the Paths palette. Vector masks are linked to their parent layer; you must select the parent layer in the Layers palette in order to list the clipping path in the Paths palette. You can remove a clipping path from a layer and convert a clipping path to a rasterized mask. For more information, see "Creating and editing vector masks" on page 262.

Paths saved with an image appear when you open it again. In Windows, the Photoshop, JPEG, DCS, EPS, PDF, and TIFF formats support paths. In Mac OS, all available file formats support paths.

Note: *Paths in formats other than those listed here generally don't survive a transition from Mac OS to Windows and back to Mac OS.*

To create a new path in the Paths palette:

Do one of the following:

- To create a path without naming it, click the New Path button ▣ at the bottom of the Paths palette.

- To create and name a path, make sure no work path is selected. Choose New Path from the Paths palette menu, or Alt-click (Windows) or Option-click (Mac OS) the New Path button at the bottom of the palette. Enter a name for the path in the New Path dialog box, and click OK.

To save a work path:

Do one of the following:

- To save without renaming, drag the *Work Path* name to the New Path button ▣ at the bottom of the Paths palette.

- To save and rename, choose Save Path from the Paths palette menu, enter a new path name in the Save Path dialog box, and click OK.

To rename a saved path:

Double-click the path's name in the Paths palette, type a new name, and press Enter (Windows) or Return (Mac OS).

Note: *You cannot rename a vector mask; double-clicking a vector mask creates a copy of it. However, you can rename the copy.*

To delete a path:

1 Select the path name in the Paths palette.

2 Do one of the following:

- Drag the path to the Trash button ▦ at the bottom of the Paths palette.

- Choose Delete Path from the Paths palette menu.

- Click the Trash button at the bottom of the Paths palette, and click Yes.

To delete a path without being asked to confirm, Alt-click (Windows) or Option-click (Mac OS) the Trash button at the bottom of the Paths palette.

Converting between paths and selection borders (Photoshop)

Because of their smooth outlines, you can convert paths into precise selection borders. You also can convert selection borders into paths, using the direct selection tool for fine-tuning.

Converting paths to selection borders

You can define any closed path as a selection border. A closed path that overlaps a selected area can be added to, subtracted from, or combined with the current selection.

To convert a path to a selection border using the current Make Selection settings:

1 Select the path in the Paths palette.

2 To convert the path, do one of the following:

• Click the Load Path as a Selection button ○ at the bottom of the Paths palette.

• Ctrl-click (Windows) or Command-click (Mac OS) the path thumbnail in the Paths palette.

To convert a path to a selection border and specify settings:

1 Select the path in the Paths palette.

2 Do one of the following:

• Alt-click (Windows) or Option-click (Mac OS) the Load Path as a Selection button ○ at the bottom of the Paths palette.

• Alt-drag (Windows) or Option-drag (Mac OS) the path to the Load Path as a Selection button.

• Choose Make Selection from the Paths palette menu.

3 In the Make Selection dialog box, select a Rendering option:

• Feather Radius to define how far inside and outside the selection border the feather edge extends. Enter a value in pixels.

• Anti-aliased to create a finer transition between the pixels in the selection and the surrounding pixels. Make sure the Feather Radius is set to 0.

For more information on these options, see "Softening the edges of a selection" on page 111.

4 Select an Operation option:

• New Selection to select only the area defined by the path.

• Add to Selection to add the area defined by the path to the original selection.

• Subtract from Selection to remove the area defined by the path from the original selection.

• Intersect with Selection to select the area common to both the path and the original selection. If the path and selection do not overlap, nothing is selected.

5 Click OK.

Converting selection borders to paths

Any selection made with a selection tool can be defined as a path.

The Make Work Path command eliminates any feathering applied to the selection. It can also alter the shape of the selection, depending on the complexity of the path and the tolerance value you choose in the Make Work Path dialog box.

To convert a selection to a path using the current Make Work Path settings:

Make the selection, and click the Make Work Path button ⟡ at the bottom of the Paths palette.

To convert a selection to a path and specify settings:

1 Make the selection, and do one of the following:

• Alt-click (Windows) or Option-click (Mac OS) the Make Work Path button ⌁ at the bottom of the Paths palette.

• Choose Make Work Path from the Paths palette menu.

2 Enter a Tolerance value or use the default value in the Make Work Path dialog box.

Tolerance values can range from 0.5 to 10 pixels and determine how sensitive the Make Work Path command is to slight changes in the selection shape. The higher the tolerance value, the fewer the anchor points used to draw the path and the smoother the path. If the path is used as a clipping path and you have problems printing the image, use a higher tolerance value. (See "Printing image clipping paths" on page 378.)

3 Click OK. The path appears at the bottom of the Paths palette.

Adding color to paths (Photoshop)

You can add color values to a path by filling or stroking it. Filling a path is the same as creating a rasterized shape using the shape tools. (See "Creating rasterized shapes" on page 149.)

🄰 For more information, see "Filling paths with color" and "Stroking to paint path borders" in online Help.

Chapter 8: Painting

The painting tools, gradient tools, paint bucket tool, and Fill command let you change the color of pixels and create colored areas in an image. You can select colors using the Color palette, Swatches palette, or color picker.

Using the painting tools (Photoshop)

Photoshop provides the brush tool and the pencil tool to let you paint with the current foreground color. By default, the brush tool creates soft strokes of color and the pencil tool creates hard-edged, freehand lines. However, you can change these default characteristics by resetting the tool's brush options. You can also use the brush tool as an airbrush to apply sprays of color to an image.

To use the brush tool or pencil tool:

1 Specify a foreground color. (See "Choosing foreground and background colors" on page 201.)

2 Select the brush tool ✐ or pencil tool ✐.

3 Do the following in the options bar:

- Choose a brush and set brush options. (See "Working with brushes" on page 172.)

- Specify a blending mode. (See "Selecting a blending mode" on page 185.)

- Specify an opacity. (See "Specifying opacity, flow, strength, or exposure" on page 188.)

- For the brush tool, specify a flow rate. (See "Specifying opacity, flow, strength, or exposure" on page 188.)

- Click the airbrush button ✎ to use the brush as an airbrush. Alternately, select the Airbrush option in the Brushes palette. (See "Creating airbrush effects (Photoshop)" on page 183.)

- For the pencil tool, select Auto Erase to paint the background color over areas containing the foreground color. (See "Using the Auto Erase option" on page 171.)

4 Do one or more of the following:

- Drag in the image to paint.

- To draw a straight line, click a starting point in the image. Then hold down Shift, and click an ending point.

- When using the brush tool as an airbrush, hold down the mouse button without dragging to build up color.

Using the painting tools (ImageReady)

ImageReady provides the paintbrush tool, pencil tool, and airbrush tool to let you paint the current foreground color on an image. The three tools create different effects:

- The paintbrush tool creates soft strokes of color.

- The pencil tool creates hard-edged freehand lines.

- The airbrush tool applies gradual tones (including sprays of color) to an image, simulating traditional airbrush techniques. The edges of the stroke are more diffused than those created with the paintbrush tool.

To use the paintbrush tool, pencil tool, or airbrush tool:

1 Specify a foreground color. (See "Choosing foreground and background colors" on page 201.)

2 Select the paintbrush tool ✐ , pencil tool ✐ , or airbrush tool ✐ .

3 Do the following in the options bar:

- Choose a preset brush. (See "Working with brushes" on page 172.)

- Specify a blending mode. (See "Selecting a blending mode" on page 185.)

- For the paintbrush tool and pencil tool, specify an opacity. (See "Specifying opacity, flow, strength, or exposure" on page 188.)

- For the airbrush tool, specify a paint flow. (See "Specifying opacity, flow, strength, or exposure" on page 188.)

- For the pencil tool, select Auto Erase to paint the background color over areas containing the foreground color. (See "Using the Auto Erase option" on page 171.)

4 Do one or more of the following:

- Drag in the image to paint.

- To draw a straight line, click a starting point in the image. Then hold down Shift, and click an ending point.

- When using the brush tool as an airbrush, hold down the mouse button without dragging to build up color.

Erasing

The eraser and magic eraser tools let you erase areas of an image to transparency or to the background color. The background eraser tool (Photoshop) lets you erase to transparency on a layer. You can also use the Auto Erase option with the pencil tool to erase the foreground color to the background color as you paint.

💡 *If you want to erase the background of an object with intricate or wispy edges, use the Extract command. (See "Extracting objects from their background (Photoshop)" on page 119.)*

Using the eraser tool

The eraser tool changes pixels in the image as you drag through them. If you're working in the background or in a layer with transparency locked, the pixels change to the background color; otherwise, the pixels are erased to transparency. You can also use the eraser to return the affected area to a state selected in the History palette.

To use the eraser tool:

1 Select the eraser tool ✐ .

2 Do the following in the options bar:

• Choose a brush and set brush options (Photoshop), or choose a preset brush (ImageReady). (See "Working with brushes" on page 172.) This option is not available for Block mode.

• Choose a mode for the eraser—Brush (Photoshop), Paintbrush (ImageReady), Airbrush (ImageReady), Pencil, or Block.

• Specify an opacity to define the strength of the erasure. An opacity of 100% erases pixels completely. A lower opacity erases pixels partially. (This option is not available for Block mode in Photoshop.)

• (Photoshop) In Brush mode, specify a flow rate. (See "Specifying opacity, flow, strength, or exposure" on page 188.)

• (Photoshop) In Brush mode, click the airbrush button ✍ to use the brush as an airbrush. Alternately, select the Airbrush option in the Brushes palette. (See "Creating airbrush effects (Photoshop)" on page 183.)

• (Photoshop) To erase to a saved state or snapshot of the image, click the left column of the state or snapshot in the History palette, then select Erase to History in the options bar.

🖳   For more information, see "Painting with a state or snapshot of an image (Photoshop)" in online Help.

💡   *(Photoshop) To temporarily use the eraser tool in Erase to History mode, hold down Alt (Windows) or Option (Mac OS) as you drag in the image.*

3 Drag through the area you want to erase.

Using the magic eraser tool

When you click in a layer with the magic eraser tool, the tool automatically changes all similar pixels. If you're working in the background, or in a layer with locked transparency, the pixels change to the background color; otherwise, the pixels are erased to transparency. You can choose to erase contiguous pixels only or all similar pixels on the current layer.

Example of erasing similar pixels

To use the magic eraser tool:

1 Select the magic eraser tool 🩹 .

2 Do the following in the options bar:

• Enter a tolerance value to define the range of colors that can be erased. A low tolerance erases pixels within a range of color values very similar to the pixel you click. A high tolerance erases pixels within a broader range.

• Select Anti-aliased to smooth the edges of the area you erase.

- Select Contiguous to erase only pixels contiguous to the one you click, or deselect to erase all similar pixels in the image.

- Select Use All Layers to sample the erased color using combined data from all visible layers.

- Specify an opacity to define the strength of the erasure. An opacity of 100% erases pixels completely. A lower opacity erases pixels partially.

3 Click in the part of the layer you want to erase.

Using the background eraser tool (Photoshop)

The background eraser tool lets you erase pixels on a layer to transparency as you drag; this allows you to erase the background while maintaining the edges of an object in the foreground. By specifying different sampling and tolerance options, you can control the range of the transparency and the sharpness of the boundaries. The background eraser samples the color in the center of the brush, also called the hot spot, and deletes that color wherever it appears inside the brush. It also performs color extraction at the edges of any foreground objects, so that color halos are not visible if the foreground object is later pasted into another image.

Note: The background eraser overrides the lock transparency setting of a layer.

To use the background eraser tool:

1 In the Layers palette, select the layer containing the areas you want to erase.

2 Select the background eraser tool 🗑 .

3 Click the brush sample in the options bar and set brush options in the pop-up palette:

- For more information on the Diameter, Hardness, Spacing, Angle, and Roundness options, see "Customizing brush tips (Photoshop)" on page 174.

- If you're using a pressure-sensitive digitizing tablet, choose options from the Size and Tolerance menus to vary the size and tolerance of the background eraser over the course of a stroke. Choose Pen Pressure to base the variation on the pen pressure. Choose Stylus Wheel to base the variation on the position of the pen thumbwheel. Choose Off to not vary the size or tolerance.

4 Do the following in the options bar:

- Choose a Limits mode for erasing: Discontiguous to erase the sampled color wherever it occurs under the brush; Contiguous to erase areas that contain the sampled color and are connected to one another; Find Edges to erase connected areas containing the sampled color while better preserving the sharpness of shape edges.

- For Tolerance, enter a value or drag the slider. A low tolerance limits erasure to areas that are very similar to the sampled color. A high tolerance erases a broader range of colors.

- Select Protect Foreground Color to prevent the erasure of areas that match the foreground color in the toolbox.

- Choose a Sampling option: Continuous to sample colors continuously as you drag; Once to erase only areas containing the color that you first click; Background Swatch to erase only areas containing the current background color.

5 Drag through the area you want to erase. The background eraser tool pointer appears as a brush shape with a cross hair indicating the tool's hot spot ⊕.

Using the Auto Erase option

The Auto Erase option for the pencil tool lets you paint the background color over areas containing the foreground color.

To use the Auto Erase option:

1 Specify foreground and background colors. (See "Choosing foreground and background colors" on page 201.)

2 Select the pencil tool ✎.

3 Select Auto Erase in the options bar.

4 Drag over the image.

If the center of the cursor is over the foreground color when you begin dragging, the area is erased to the background color. If the center of the cursor is over an area that doesn't contain the foreground color when you begin dragging, the area is painted with the foreground color.

Using the art history brush tool (Photoshop)

The art history brush tool lets you paint with stylized strokes, using the source data from a specified history state or snapshot. By experimenting with different paint style, size, and tolerance options, you can simulate the texture of painting with different colors and artistic styles.

Like the history brush, the art history brush uses a specified history state or snapshot as the source data. The history brush, however, paints by recreating the specified source data, while the art history brush uses that data along with the options you set to create different colors and artistic styles.

💡 *For a variety of visual effects, experiment with applying filters or filling an image with a solid color before painting with the art history brush tool. Also try increasing the size of the image by a factor of 4 to soften the details.*

Example of using the art history brush tool:
A. Original B. White fill C. Large brush D. Small brush

To use the art history brush tool:

1 In the History palette, click the left column of the state or snapshot to use as the source for the art history brush tool. A brush icon appears next to the source history state.

2 Select the art history brush tool ✍.

3 Do the following in the options bar:

- Choose a brush and set brush options. (See "Working with brushes" on page 172.)

- Specify a blending mode and opacity for the paint. (See "Setting options for painting and editing tools" on page 185.)

- Choose an option from the Style menu to control the shape of the paint stroke.

- For Area, enter a value to specify the area covered by the paint strokes. The greater the size, the larger the covered area and more numerous the strokes.

- For Tolerance, enter a value or drag the slider to limit the regions where paint strokes can be applied. A low tolerance lets you paint unlimited strokes anywhere in the image. A high tolerance limits paint strokes to areas that differ considerably from the color in the source state or snapshot.

4 Drag in the image to paint.

Working with brushes

Working with brushes is an important part of using the painting and editing tools. The brush you select determines many characteristics of the resulting stroke. Photoshop and ImageReady provide a variety of preset brushes to fill a wide range of uses. In Photoshop, you can also create custom brushes using the Brushes palette.

Using the Brushes palette (Photoshop)

The Brushes palette lets you select preset brushes and design custom brushes.

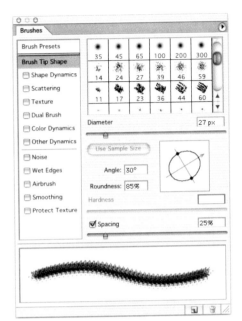

Brushes palette with Brush Tip Shape options displayed

Displaying the Brushes palette Choose
Window > Brushes, or click the palette button
on the right side of the options bar for the painting
tools, erasing tools, toning tools, and focus tools.

Displaying options in the Brushes palette Select
an item name on the left side of the palette. The
available options for the selected item appear on
the right side of the palette.

> Click the checkbox to the left of the item name
> to enable or disable the item without viewing its
> options.

Selecting preset brushes

The Brush pop-up palette in the options bar for
the painting and editing tools lets you view, select,
and load preset brushes. In Photoshop, you can
also use the Brushes palette to view, select, and
load preset brushes.

To display the Brush pop-up palette:

1 Select a painting tool or editing tool.

2 Click the brush sample in the options bar.

To select a preset brush:

1 Click a brush in the Brush pop-up palette or
Brushes palette.

*Note: If you are using the Brushes palette, be sure
that Brush Presets on the left side palette is selected
to view the loaded presets.*

2 (Photoshop) Specify a Master Diameter for the
brush by dragging the slider or entering a value.
If the brush has a dual tip, both the primary and
dual brush tips are scaled. (See "Creating dual
brushes (Photoshop)" on page 180.)

3 (Photoshop) Click Use Sample Size to use the
original diameter of the brush tip. This option is
available only if the brush tip shape is based on a
sample.

**To change how preset brushes are displayed
(Photoshop):**

Choose a display option from the Brush pop-up
palette menu or Brushes palette menu:

• Text Only to view the brushes as a list.

- Small or Large Thumbnail to view the brushes as thumbnails.

- Small or Large List to view the brushes as a list with thumbnails.

- Stroke Thumbnail to view a sample brush stroke with each brush thumbnail.

💡 *To dynamically preview brush strokes in the Brushes palette, position the pointer over a brush until the tool tip appears, then move the pointer over different brushes. The preview area at the bottom of the palette will display sample brush strokes.*

To load a library of preset brushes:

Choose one of the following from the Brush pop-up palette menu or Brushes palette menu:

- Load Brushes to add a library to the current list. Select the library file you want to use, and click Load.

- Replace Brushes to replace the current list with a different library. Select the library file you want to use, and click Load.

- A library file (displayed at the bottom of the palette menu). Click OK to replace the current list, or click Append to append the current list.

Note: *You can also use the Preset Manager to load and reset brush libraries. For more information, see "Managing libraries with the Preset Manager (Photoshop)" on page 49.*

To return to the default library of preset brushes:

Choose Reset Brushes from the Brush pop-up palette menu or Brushes palette menu. You can either replace the current list or append the default library to the current list.

Customizing brush tips (Photoshop)

A brush stroke is made up of many individual brush marks. The brush tip you select determines the shape, diameter, and other characteristics of a brush mark. You can customize brush tips by editing their options and create new brush tip shapes by sampling pixels in an image.

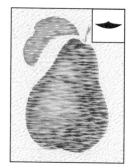

Pear painted with custom brush shown in inset

To create a new brush tip shape:

1 Use the rectangle marquee ⬚ with Feather set to 0 px to select part of an image to use as a custom brush.

The brush shape can be up to 2500 pixels by 2500 pixels in size. To be most effective, the shape should appear on a solid white background. If you want to define a brush with soft edges, select pixels with gray values. (Colored brush shapes appear as gray values.)

2 Choose Edit > Define Brush.

3 Name the brush, and click OK.

To set brush tip shape options:

1 In the Brushes palette, select Brush Tip Shape on the left side of the palette.

2 Select the brush tip you want to customize, and set one or more of the following options:

Diameter Controls the size of the brush. Enter a value in pixels or drag the slider.

Brush strokes with different diameter values

Use Sample Size Resets the brush to its original diameter. This option is only available if the brush tip shape was created by sampling pixels in an image.

Angle Specifies the angle by which an elliptical or sampled brush's long axis is rotated from horizontal. Type a value in degrees, or drag the horizontal axis in the preview box.

Angled brushes create a chiseled stroke

Roundness Specifies the ratio between the brush's short and long axes. Enter a percentage value, or drag the points in the preview box. A value of 100% indicates a circular brush, a value of 0% indicates a linear brush, and intermediate values indicate elliptical brushes.

Hardness Controls the size of the brush's hard center. Type a number, or use the slider to enter a value that is a percentage of the brush diameter.

Brush strokes with different hardness values

Spacing Controls the distance between the brush marks in a stroke. To change the spacing, type a number, or use the slider to enter a value that is a percentage of the brush diameter. When this option is deselected, the speed of the cursor determines the spacing.

 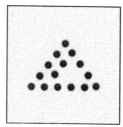

Increasing the spacing makes the brush skip

💡 *While using a preset brush, press the [key to decrease the brush width; press the] key to increase the width. For hard round, soft round, and calligraphic brushes, press Shift+ the [key to decrease the brush hardness; press Shift+ the] key to increase the brush hardness.*

About brush dynamics (Photoshop)

The Brushes palette provides many options for adding dynamic (or changing) elements to preset brush tips. For example, you can set options that vary the size, color, and opacity of brush marks over the course of a stroke.

You work with two components when adding dynamics elements to a brush:

• Jitter percentages specify the randomness of dynamic elements. At 0%, an element does not change over the course of a stroke; at 100%, an element has the maximum amount of randomness.

• Options in the Control pop-up menus specify how you want to control the variance of dynamic elements. You can choose to not control the variance of an element, to fade an element over the specified number of steps, or to vary an element based of pen pressure, pen tilt, or position of the pen thumbwheel.

Note: Pen controls are only are available only when you're using a pressure-sensitive digitizing tablet such as the Wacom® tablet. A warning icon appears if you select a pen control but have not installed a tablet.

Specifying brush shape dynamics (Photoshop)

Shape dynamics determine the variance of brush marks in a stroke.

Brush stokes without shape dynamics and with shape dynamics

To edit shape dynamics for a brush:

1 In the Brushes palette, select Shape Dynamics on the left side of the palette. Be sure to click the name, rather than the check box, to select the item.

2 Set one or more of the following options:

Size Jitter and Control Specifies how the size of brush marks vary in a stroke. For more information, see "About brush dynamics (Photoshop)" on page 176.

To specify the maximum percentage of jittering, type a number or use the slider to enter a value. To specify how you want to control the size variance of brush marks, choose an option from the Control pop-up menu:

- Off to not control the size variance of brush marks.

- Fade to fade the size of brush marks between the initial diameter and the minimum diameter in the specified number of steps. Each step is equal to one mark of the brush tip. The value can range from 1 to 9999. For example, entering 10 steps produces a fade in 10 increments.

- Pen Pressure, Pen Tilt, or Stylus Wheel to vary the size of brush marks between the initial diameter and the minimum diameter based on the pen pressure, pen tilt, or position of the pen thumbwheel.

Minimum Diameter Specifies the minimum percentage by which brush marks can scale when Size Jitter or Size Control is enabled. Type a number, or use the slider to enter a value that is a percentage of the brush tip diameter.

Tilt Scale Specifies the scale factor applied to the height of the brush prior to rotation when Size Control is set to Pen Tilt. Type a number, or use the slider to enter a value that is a percentage of the brush diameter.

Angle Jitter and Control Specifies how the angle of brush marks varies in a stroke. For more information, see "About brush dynamics (Photoshop)" on page 176.

To specify the maximum percentage of jittering, type a number or use the slider to enter a value that is a percentage of 360 degrees. To specify how you want to control the angle variance of brush marks, choose an option from the Control pop-up menu:

- Off to not control the angle variance of brush marks.

- Fade to fade the angle of brush marks between 0 and 360 degrees in the specified number of steps.

- Pen Pressure, Pen Tilt, or Stylus Wheel to vary the angle of brush marks between 0 and 360 degrees based on the pen pressure, pen tilt, or position of the pen thumbwheel.

- Initial Direction to base the angle of brush marks on the initial direction of the brush stroke.

- Direction to base the angle of brush marks on the direction of the brush stroke.

Roundness Jitter and Control Specifies how the roundness of brush marks varies in a stroke. For more information, see "About brush dynamics (Photoshop)" on page 176.

To specify the maximum percentage of jittering, type a number or use the slider to enter a value that is a percentage indicating the ratio between the brush's short and long axes. To specify how you want to control the roundness variance of brush marks, choose an option from the Control pop-up menu:

- Off to not control the roundness variance of brush marks.

- Fade to fade the roundness of brush marks between 100% and the Minimum Roundness value in the specified number of steps.

- Pen Pressure, Pen Tilt, or Stylus Wheel to vary the roundness of brush marks between 100% and the Minimum Roundness value based on the pen pressure, pen tilt, or position of the pen thumbwheel.

Minimum Roundness Specifies the minimum roundness for brush marks when Roundness Jitter or Roundness Control is enabled. Type a number, or use the slider to enter a value that is a percentage indicating the ratio between the brush's short and long axes.

Specifying brush scattering (Photoshop)

Brush scattering determines the number and placement of marks in a stroke.

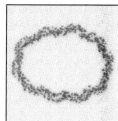

Brush strokes without scattering and with scattering

To edit scattering options for a brush:

1 In the Brushes palette, select Scattering on the left side of the palette. Be sure to click the name, rather than the check box, to select the item.

2 Set one or more of the following options:

Scatter and Control Specifies how brush marks are distributed in a stroke. When Both Axis is selected, brush marks are distributed in a radial direction. When Both Axis is deselected, brush marks are distributed perpendicular to the stroke path.

To specify the maximum percentage of scattering, type a number or use the slider to enter a value. To specify how you want to control the scattering variance of brush marks, choose an option from the Control pop-up menu:

- Off to not control the scattering variance of brush marks.

- Fade to fade the scattering of brush marks from the maximum scattering to no scattering in the specified number of steps.

- Pen Pressure, Pen Tilt, or Stylus Wheel to vary the scattering of brush marks based on the pen pressure, pen tilt, or position of the pen thumbwheel.

Count Specifies the number of brush marks applied at each spacing interval. Type a number, or use the slider to enter a value.

Note: If you increase the count without increasing the spacing or scattering values, painting performance may decrease.

Count Jitter and Control Specifies how the number of brush marks varies for each spacing interval. For more information, see "About brush dynamics (Photoshop)" on page 176.

To specify the maximum percentage of brush marks applied at each spacing interval, type a number or use the slider to enter a value.
To specify how you want to control the count variance of brush marks, choose an option from the Control pop-up menu:

- Off to not control the count variance of brush marks.

- Fade to fade the number of brush marks from the Count value to 1 in the specified number of steps.

- Pen Pressure, Pen Tilt, or Stylus Wheel to vary the number of brush marks based on the pen pressure, pen tilt, or position of the pen thumbwheel.

Creating textured brushes (Photoshop)

A textured brush uses a pattern to make strokes look like they are painted on textured canvas.

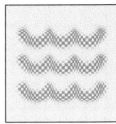

Brush strokes without texture and with texture

To edit texture options for a brush:

1 In the Brushes palette, select Texture on the left side of the palette. Be sure to click the name, rather than the check box, to select the item.

2 Click the pattern sample, and select a pattern from the pop-up palette.

3 Set one or more of the following options:

Invert Inverts the high and low points in the texture based on the tones in the pattern. When Invert is selected, the lightest areas in the pattern are the low points in the texture and therefore receive the least paint; the darkest areas in the pattern are the high points in the texture and therefore receive the most paint. When Invert is deselected, the lightest areas in the pattern receive the most paint; the darkest areas in the pattern receive the least paint.

Scale Specifies the scale of the pattern. Type a number, or use the slider to enter a value that is a percentage of the pattern size.

Texture Each Tip Specifies whether or not to render each tip individually as it is painted. When this option is not selected, the Depth variance options are not available.

Mode Specifies the blending mode used to combine the brush and the pattern. (See "Selecting a blending mode" on page 185.)

Depth Specifies how deep the paint penetrates into the texture. Type a number, or use the slider to enter a value. At 100%, the low points in the texture do not receive any paint. At 0%, all points in the texture receive the same amount of paint, therefore hiding the pattern.

Minimum Depth Specifies the minimum depth paint can penetrate when Depth Control is set to Fade, Pen Pressure, Pen Tilt, or Stylus Wheel and Texture Each Tip is selected.

Depth Jitter and Control Specifies how the depth varies when Texture Each Tip is selected. For more information, see "About brush dynamics (Photoshop)" on page 176.

To specify the maximum percentage of jitter, type a number or use the slider to enter a value. To specify how you want to control the depth variance of brush marks, choose an option from the Control pop-up menu:

• Off to not control the depth variance of brush marks.

• Fade to fade from the Depth Jitter percentage to the Minimum Depth percentage in the specified number of steps.

• Pen Pressure, Pen Tilt, or Stylus Wheel to vary the depth based on the pen pressure, pen tilt, or position of the pen thumbwheel.

Creating dual brushes (Photoshop)

A dual brush uses two tips to create brush marks. You set options for the primary tip in the Brush Tip Shape section of the Brushes palette. You set options for the secondary tip in the Dual Brush section of the Brushes palette.

Brush strokes created with a single tip and with dual tips

To edit dual tip options for a brush:

1 In the Brushes palette, select Dual Brush on the left side of the palette. Be sure to click the name, rather than the check box, to select the item.

2 Select a blending mode to use when combining brush marks from the primary tip and the dual tip. (See "Selecting a blending mode" on page 185.)

3 Select a tip for the dual brush from the list below the Mode pop-up menu.

4 Set one or more of the following options:

Diameter Controls the size of the dual tip. Enter a value in pixels, drag the slider, or click Use Sample Size to use the original diameter of the brush tip. (The Use Sample Size option is only available if the brush tip shape was created by sampling pixels in an image.)

Spacing Controls the distance between the dual tip brush marks in a stroke. To change the spacing, type a number, or use the slider to enter a value that is a percentage of the tip diameter.

Scatter Specifies how dual tip brush marks are distributed in a stroke. When Both Axis is selected, dual tip brush marks are distributed in a radial direction. When Both Axis is deselected, dual tip brush marks are distributed perpendicular to the stroke path. To specify the maximum percentage of scattering, type a number or use the slider to enter a value.

Count Specifies the number of dual tip brush marks applied at each spacing interval. Type a number, or use the slider to enter a value.

Specifying color dynamics (Photoshop)

Color dynamics determine how the color of paint changes over the course of a stroke.

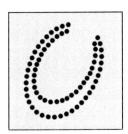 

Brush strokes without color dynamics and with color dynamics

To edit color dynamics for a brush:

1 In the Brushes palette, select Color Dynamics on the left side of the palette. Be sure to click the name, rather than the check box, to select the item.

2 Set one or more of the following options:

Foreground/Background Jitter and Control
Specifies how paint varies between the foreground color and background color. For more information, see "About brush dynamics (Photoshop)" on page 176.

To specify a percentage by which the color of the paint can vary, type a number or use the slider to enter a value. To specify how you want to control the color variance of brush marks, choose an option from the Control pop-up menu:

- Off to not control the color variance of brush marks.

- Fade to vary the color of paint between the foreground color and the background color in the specified number of steps.

- Pen Pressure, Pen Tilt, or Stylus Wheel to vary the color of paint between the foreground color and the background color based on the pen pressure, pen tilt, or position of the pen thumbwheel.

Hue Jitter Specifies a percentage by which the hue of the paint can vary in a stroke. Type a number, or use the slider to enter a value. A lower value changes the hue while maintaining a close proximity to the hue of the foreground color. A higher value increases the difference between hues.

Saturation Jitter Specifies a percentage by which the saturation of the paint can vary in a stroke. Type a number, or use the slider to enter a value. A lower value changes the saturation while maintaining a close proximity to the saturation of the foreground color. A higher value increases the difference between saturation levels.

Brightness Jitter Specifies a percentage by which the brightness of the paint can vary in a stroke. Type a number, or use the slider to enter a value. A lower value changes the brightness while maintaining a close proximity to the brightness of the foreground color. A higher value increases the difference between brightness levels.

Purity Increases or decreases the saturation of the color. Type a number, or use the slider to enter a percentage between −100 and 100. At −100, the color is fully desaturated; at 100, the color is fully saturated.

Specifying paint dynamics (Photoshop)

Paint dynamics determine how paint changes over the course of a stroke.

Brush strokes without paint dynamics and with paint dynamics

To edit paint dynamics for a brush:

1 In the Brushes palette, select Other Dynamics on the left side of the palette. Be sure to click the name, rather than the check box, to select the item.

2 Set one or more of the following options:

Opacity Jitter and Control Specifies how the opacity of paint varies in a brush stroke, up to (but not exceeding) the opacity value specified in the options bar. For more information, see "About brush dynamics (Photoshop)" on page 176.

To specify a percentage by which the opacity of the paint can vary, type a number or use the slider to enter a value. To specify how you want to control the opacity variance of brush marks, choose an option from the Control pop-up menu:

- Off to not control the opacity variance of brush marks.

- Fade to fade the opacity of paint from the opacity value in the options bar to 0 in the specified number of steps.

- Pen Pressure, Pen Tilt, or Stylus Wheel to vary the opacity of paint based on the pen pressure, pen tilt, or the position of the pen thumbwheel.

Flow Jitter and Control Specifies how the flow of paint varies in a brush stroke, up to (but not exceeding) the flow value specified in the options bar. For more information, see "About brush dynamics (Photoshop)" on page 176.

To specify a percentage by which the flow of the paint can vary, type a number or use the slider to enter a value. To specify how you want to control the flow variance of brush marks, choose an option from the Control pop-up menu:

- Off to not control the flow variance of brush marks.
- Fade to fade the flow of paint from the flow value in the options bar to 0 in the specified number of steps.
- Pen Pressure, Pen Tilt, or Stylus Wheel to vary the flow of paint based on the pen pressure, pen tilt, or the position of the pen thumbwheel.

Adding noise to brush strokes (Photoshop)

The Noise option adds additional randomness to individual brush tips. This option is most effective when applied to soft brush tips (brush tips that contain gray values).

To enable or disable noise in brush strokes:

In the Brushes palette, select Noise on the left side of the palette. A check mark indicates that the option is enabled.

Using wet brush edges (Photoshop)

The Wet Edges option causes paint to build up along the edges of the brush stroke, creating a watercolor effect.

To enable or disable wet brush edges:

In the Brushes palette, select Wet Edges on the left side of the palette. A check mark indicates that the option is enabled.

Creating airbrush effects (Photoshop)

The Airbrush option in the Brushes palette lets you apply gradual tones to an image, simulating traditional airbrush techniques.

Note: The Airbrush option in the Brushes palette corresponds to the Airbrush option in the options bar.

To enable or disable the Airbrush option:

In the Brushes palette, select Airbrush on the left side of the palette. A check mark indicates that the option is enabled.

Note: The Airbrush option in the Brushes palette corresponds to the Airbrush option in the options bar.

Smoothing brush strokes (Photoshop)

The Smoothing option produces smoother curves in brush strokes. This option is most effective when you are painting quickly with a stylus; however, it may produce a slight lag time in stroke rendering.

To enable or disable smoothing in brush strokes:

In the Brushes palette, select Smoothing on the left side of the palette. A check mark indicates that the option is enabled.

Protecting texture in brush strokes (Photoshop)

The Protect Texture option applies the same pattern and scale to all brush presets that have a texture. Select this option to simulate a consistent canvas texture when painting with multiple, textured brush tips.

To enable or disable the Protect Texture option:

In the Brushes palette, select Protect Texture on the left side of the palette. A check mark indicates that the option is enabled.

Copying textures between tools (Photoshop)

When you specify a texture for the current tool, you can copy the texture's pattern and scale to all tools that support textures. For example, you can copy the current texture pattern and scale for the brush tool to the pencil, clone stamp, pattern stamp, history brush, art history brush, eraser, dodge, burn, and sponge tools.

To copy a texture pattern and scale to other painting and editing tools:

Choose Copy Texture to Other Tools from the Brushes palette menu.

Clearing brush options (Photoshop)

You can easily clear all brush options for a tool using the Clear Brush Controls command.

To clear brush options:

Choose Clear Brush Controls from the Brushes palette menu.

Creating and managing preset brushes (Photoshop)

After you customize a brush, you can save it as a preset brush. Preset brushes appear in the Brushes palette, Brush pop-up palette in the options bar, and Preset Manager. You can create libraries of preset brushes, rename preset brushes, and delete preset brushes.

Note: New preset brushes are saved in a Preferences file so that they persist between editing sessions. If this file is deleted or damaged, or if you reset brushes to the default library, the new presets will be lost. To permanently save new preset brushes, save them in a library.

To create a new preset brush:

1 Customize a brush.

2 Do one of the following in the Brushes palette or Brush pop-up palette:

- Choose New Brush from the palette menu, enter a name for the preset brush, and click OK.
- Click the Create New Brush button ⊡ .

To rename a preset brush:

Do one of the following:

- Select a brush in the Brush pop-up palette or Brushes palette, and choose Rename Brush from the palette menu. Enter a new name for the brush, and click OK.

• If the Brushes palette is set to display brushes as thumbnails, double-click a brush, enter a new name, and click OK.

• If the Brushes palette is set to display brushes as a list or text only, double-click a brush, enter a new name inline, and press Enter (Windows) or Return (Mac OS).

To delete a preset brush:

Do one of the following:

• In the Brush pop-up palette or Brushes palette, select a brush, and choose Delete Brush from the palette menu.

• In the Brush pop-up palette or Brushes palette, Alt-click (Windows) or Option-click (Mac OS) the brush you want to delete.

• In the Brushes palette, select a brush and click the Trash button 🗑 , or drag a brush to the Trash button.

To save a set of preset brushes as a library:

1 Choose Save Brushes from the Brush pop-up palette menu or Brushes palette menu.

2 Choose a location for the brush library, enter a filename, and click Save.

You can save the library anywhere. However, if you place the library file in the Presets/Brushes folder inside the Photoshop program folder, the library name will appear at the bottom of the Brush pop-up palette menu and Brushes palette menu after you restart Photoshop.

Note: *You can also use the Preset Manager to rename, delete, and save libraries of preset brushes. For more information, see "Managing libraries with the Preset Manager (Photoshop)" on page 49.*

Setting options for painting and editing tools

You set options for a painting or editing tool in the options bar.

Selecting a blending mode

The blending mode specified in the options bar controls how pixels in the image are affected by a painting or editing tool. It's helpful to think in terms of the following colors when visualizing a blending mode's effect:

• The *base color* is the original color in the image.

• The *blend color* is the color being applied with the painting or editing tool.

• The *result color* is the color resulting from the blend.

To select a blending mode for a tool:

Choose from the Mode pop-up menu in the options bar.

Normal Edits or paints each pixel to make it the result color. This is the default mode. (Normal mode is called *Threshold* when you're working with a bitmapped or indexed-color image.)

Dissolve Edits or paints each pixel to make it the result color. However, the result color is a random replacement of the pixels with the base color or the blend color, depending on the opacity at any pixel location.

Behind Edits or paints only on the transparent part of a layer. This mode works only in layers with Lock Transparency deselected and is analogous to painting on the back of transparent areas in a sheet of acetate.

Clear Edits or paints each pixel and makes it transparent. This mode is available for the line tool \ (when fill region □ is selected), the paint bucket tool ◇ , the brush tool ✎ , the pencil tool ✐ , the Fill command, and the Stroke command. You must be in a layer with Lock Transparency deselected to use this mode.

Darken Looks at the color information in each channel and selects the base or blend color—whichever is darker—as the result color. Pixels lighter than the blend color are replaced, and pixels darker than the blend color do not change.

Multiply Looks at the color information in each channel and multiplies the base color by the blend color. The result color is always a darker color. Multiplying any color with black produces black. Multiplying any color with white leaves the color unchanged. When you're painting with a color other than black or white, successive strokes with a painting tool produce progressively darker colors. The effect is similar to drawing on the image with multiple magic markers.

Color Burn Looks at the color information in each channel and darkens the base color to reflect the blend color by increasing the contrast. Blending with white produces no change.

Linear Burn Looks at the color information in each channel and darkens the base color to reflect the blend color by decreasing the brightness. Blending with white produces no change.

Lighten Looks at the color information in each channel and selects the base or blend color—whichever is lighter—as the result color. Pixels darker than the blend color are replaced, and pixels lighter than the blend color do not change.

Screen Looks at each channel's color information and multiplies the inverse of the blend and base colors. The result color is always a lighter color. Screening with black leaves the color unchanged. Screening with white produces white. The effect is similar to projecting multiple photographic slides on top of each other.

Color Dodge Looks at the color information in each channel and brightens the base color to reflect the blend color by decreasing the contrast. Blending with black produces no change.

Linear Dodge Looks at the color information in each channel and brightens the base color to reflect the blend color by increasing the brightness. Blending with black produces no change.

Overlay Multiplies or screens the colors, depending on the base color. Patterns or colors overlay the existing pixels while preserving the highlights and shadows of the base color. The base color is not replaced but is mixed with the blend color to reflect the lightness or darkness of the original color.

Soft Light Darkens or lightens the colors, depending on the blend color. The effect is similar to shining a diffused spotlight on the image.

If the blend color (light source) is lighter than 50% gray, the image is lightened as if it were dodged. If the blend color is darker than 50% gray, the image is darkened as if it were burned in. Painting with pure black or white produces a distinctly darker or lighter area but does not result in pure black or white.

Hard Light Multiplies or screens the colors, depending on the blend color. The effect is similar to shining a harsh spotlight on the image.

If the blend color (light source) is lighter than 50% gray, the image is lightened, as if it were screened. This is useful for adding highlights to an image. If the blend color is darker than 50% gray, the image is darkened, as if it were multiplied. This is useful for adding shadows to an image. Painting with pure black or white results in pure black or white.

Vivid Light Burns or dodges the colors by increasing or decreasing the contrast, depending on the blend color. If the blend color (light source) is lighter than 50% gray, the image is lightened by decreasing the contrast. If the blend color is darker than 50% gray, the image is darkened by increasing the contrast.

Linear Light Burns or dodges the colors by decreasing or increasing the brightness, depending on the blend color. If the blend color (light source) is lighter than 50% gray, the image is lightened by increasing the brightness. If the blend color is darker than 50% gray, the image is darkened by decreasing the brightness.

Pin Light Replaces the colors, depending on the blend color. If the blend color (light source) is lighter than 50% gray, pixels darker than the blend color are replaced, and pixels lighter than the blend color do not change. If the blend color is darker than 50% gray, pixels lighter than the blend color are replaced, and pixels darker than the blend color do not change. This is useful for adding special effects to an image.

Difference Looks at the color information in each channel and subtracts either the blend color from the base color or the base color from the blend color, depending on which has the greater brightness value. Blending with white inverts the base color values; blending with black produces no change.

Exclusion Creates an effect similar to but lower in contrast than the Difference mode. Blending with white inverts the base color values. Blending with black produces no change.

Hue Creates a result color with the luminance and saturation of the base color and the hue of the blend color.

Saturation Creates a result color with the luminance and hue of the base color and the saturation of the blend color. Painting with this mode in an area with no (0) saturation (gray) causes no change.

Color Creates a result color with the luminance of the base color and the hue and saturation of the blend color. This preserves the gray levels in the image and is useful for coloring monochrome images and for tinting color images.

Luminosity Creates a result color with the hue and saturation of the base color and the luminance of the blend color. This mode creates an inverse effect from that of the Color mode.

Specifying opacity, flow, strength, or exposure

You can specify opacity, flow, strength, or exposure for the following tools:

- Opacity specifies the maximum amount of paint coverage applied by the brush, paintbrush, pencil, clone stamp, pattern stamp, history brush, art history brush, gradient, and paint bucket tools.

- Flow specifies how quickly paint is applied by the brush tool.

- Strength specifies the strength of strokes applied by the smudge, blur, sharpen, and sponge tools.

- Exposure specifies the amount of exposure used by the dodge and burn tools.

To specify opacity, flow, strength, or exposure:

Enter a value, or drag the slider for Opacity, Flow, Strength, or Exposure in the options bar.

Opacity, flow, strength, or exposure can range from 1% to 100%. For transparent paint or a weak effect, specify a low percentage value; for more opaque paint or a strong effect, specify a high value.

Press a number key to set a tool's opacity, flow, strength, or exposure in multiples of 10% (pressing 1 sets to 10%, pressing 0 sets to 100%).

Using the gradient tool (Photoshop)

The gradient tool creates a gradual blend between multiple colors. You can choose from preset gradient fills or create your own.

Note: The gradient tool cannot be used with images in Bitmap, indexed-color, or 16-bits per channel mode.

Applying a gradient fill

You fill an area with a gradient by dragging in the image. The starting point (where the mouse is pressed) and ending point (where the mouse is released) affect the gradient appearance, depending on the gradient tool used.

To apply a gradient fill:

1 To fill part of the image, select the desired area. Otherwise, the gradient fill is applied to the entire active layer.

2 Select the gradient tool .

3 Choose a gradient fill in the options bar:

- Click the triangle next to the gradient sample to pick a preset gradient fill.

- Click inside the gradient sample to view the Gradient Editor. Select a preset gradient fill, or create a new gradient fill. Then click OK. (See "Creating smooth gradient fills" on page 189.)

4 Select an option for applying the gradient fill in the options bar:

- Linear gradient ▭ to shade from the starting point to the ending point in a straight line.

- Radial gradient ▣ to shade from the starting point to the ending point in a circular pattern.

- Angle gradient ◩ to shade in a counter-clockwise sweep around the starting point.

- Reflected gradient ▤ to shade using symmetric linear gradients on either side of the starting point.

- Diamond gradient ◈ to shade from the starting point outward in a diamond pattern. The ending point defines one corner of the diamond.

5 Do the following in the options bar:

- Specify a blending mode and opacity for the paint. (See "Setting options for painting and editing tools" on page 185.)

- To reverse the order of colors in the gradient fill, select Reverse.

- To create a smoother blend with less banding, select Dither.

- To use a transparency mask for the gradient fill, select Transparency. (See "Specifying the gradient transparency" on page 191.)

6 Position the pointer in the image where you want to set the starting point of the gradient, and drag to define the ending point. To constrain the line angle to a multiple of 45°, hold down Shift as you drag.

Creating smooth gradient fills

The Gradient Editor dialog box lets you define a new gradient by modifying a copy of an existing gradient. You can also add intermediate colors to a gradient, creating a blend between more than two colors.

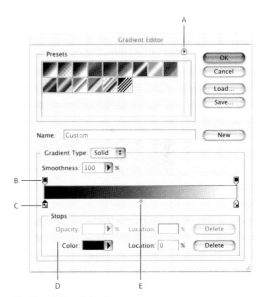

Gradient Editor dialog box:
A. Palette menu B. Opacity stop C. Color stop
D. Adjust values or delete the selected opacity or color stop
E. Midpoint

To create a smooth gradient:

1 Select the gradient tool ▭ .

2 Click inside the gradient sample in the options bar to display the Gradient Editor dialog box.

3 To base the new gradient on an existing gradient, select a gradient in the Presets section of the dialog box.

4 Choose Solid from the Gradient Type pop-up menu.

5 To define the starting color of the gradient, click the left color stop under the gradient bar. The triangle above the stop turns black, indicating that the starting color is being edited.

6 To choose a color, do one of the following:

• Double-click the color stop, or click the color swatch in the Stops section of the dialog box. Choose a color, and click OK. For information on choosing a color, see "Using the Adobe Color Picker" on page 205.

• Choose an option from the Color pop-up menu in the Stops section of the dialog box.

• Position the pointer over the gradient bar (the pointer turns into the eyedropper), and click to sample a color, or click anywhere in the image to sample a color from the image.

7 To define the ending color, click the right color stop under the gradient bar. Then choose a color as described in step 5.

8 To adjust the location of the starting point or ending point, do one of the following:

• Drag the corresponding color stop left or right to the location you want.

• Click the corresponding color stop, and enter a value for Location in the Stops section of the dialog box. A value of 0% places the point at the far left end of the gradient bar, a value of 100% at the far right end.

9 To adjust the location of the midpoint (where the gradient displays an even mix of the starting and ending colors), drag the diamond below the gradient bar to the left or right, or click the diamond and enter a value for Location.

10 To delete the color stop you are editing, click Delete.

11 To set the smoothness for the entire gradient, enter a value in the Smoothness text box, or drag the Smoothness pop-up slider.

12 If desired, set transparency values for the gradient. (See "Specifying the gradient transparency" on page 191.)

13 Enter a name for the new gradient.

14 To save the gradient as a preset, click New after you have finished creating the gradient.

Note: New presets are saved in a Preferences file so that they persist between editing sessions. If this file is deleted or damaged, or if you reset presets to the default library, the new presets will be lost. To permanently save new presets, save them in a library. (See "Managing gradients" on page 192.)

To add intermediate colors to a gradient:

In the Gradient Editor dialog box, click below the gradient bar to define another color stop. Specify the color and adjust the location and midpoint for the intermediate point as you would for a starting or ending point. To remove an intermediate color, drag the color stop down and off the gradient bar, or select the color stop and click the Delete button.

Specifying the gradient transparency

Each gradient fill contains settings that control the opacity of the fill at different locations on the gradient. For example, you can set the starting color to 100% opacity and have the fill gradually blend into an ending color with 50% opacity. The checkerboard pattern indicates the amount of transparency in the gradient preview.

To specify the gradient transparency:

1 Create a gradient as described in steps 1 through 10 of "Creating smooth gradient fills" on page 189.

2 To adjust the starting opacity, click the left opacity stop above the gradient bar. The triangle below the stop turns black, indicating that the starting transparency is being edited.

3 In the Stops section of the dialog box, enter a value in the Opacity text box, or drag the Opacity pop-up slider.

4 To adjust the opacity of the endpoint, click the right transparency stop above the gradient bar. Then set the opacity as described in step 3.

5 To adjust the location of the starting or ending opacity, do one of the following:

- Drag the corresponding opacity stop to the left or right.

- Select the corresponding opacity stop, and enter a value for Location.

6 To adjust the location of the midpoint opacity (the point midway between the starting and ending opacities), do one of the following:

- Drag the diamond above the gradient bar to the left or right.

- Select the diamond and enter a value for Location.

7 To delete the opacity stop you are editing, click Delete.

8 To add an intermediate opacity to the mask, click above the gradient bar to define a new opacity stop. You can then adjust and move this opacity as you would for a starting or ending opacity. To remove an intermediate opacity, drag its transparency stop up and off the gradient bar.

9 To create a preset gradient, enter a name in the Name text box and click New. This creates a new gradient preset with the transparency setting you specified.

Creating noise gradient fills

In addition to creating smooth gradients, the Gradient Editor dialog box lets you define a new noise gradient. A noise gradient is a gradient that contains randomly distributed colors within the range of colors that you specify.

Gradient with different Noise values:
A. 10% noise B. 50% noise C. 90% noise

To create a noise gradient:

1 Select the gradient tool ▉ .

2 Click in the gradient sample in the options bar to display the Gradient Editor dialog box.

3 To base the new gradient on an existing gradient, select a gradient in the Presets section of the dialog box.

4 Choose Noise from the Gradient Type pop-up menu.

5 To set the roughness for the entire gradient, enter a value in the Roughness text box, or drag the Roughness pop-up slider.

6 To define the color model, choose a color model from the Color Model list.

7 To adjust the range of colors, drag the sliders. For each color component of the color model you've selected, you can drag the sliders to define the range of acceptable values. For example, if you choose the HSB model, you can restrict the gradient to blue-green hues, high saturation, and medium brightness.

8 Set the options to restrict colors or to add transparency.

9 To randomize a gradient that conforms to the settings, click the Randomize button until you find a setting you like.

10 To create a preset gradient, enter a name in the Name text box and click New. This creates a new preset gradient with the settings you specified.

Managing gradients

By saving and loading libraries of gradients, you can customize the gradient list that appears in the options bar and the Gradient Editor dialog box. You can also rename presets, delete presets, and change the display of the gradient list.

Note: You can use the Preset Manager to manage gradient libraries. For more information, see "Managing libraries with the Preset Manager (Photoshop)" on page 49.

To save a set of preset gradients as a library:

1 Click Save in the Gradient Editor dialog box.

2 Choose a location for the gradient library, enter a filename, and click Save.

You can save the library anywhere. However, if you place the library file in the Presets/Gradients folder inside the Photoshop program folder, the library name will appear at the bottom of the palette menu after you restart Photoshop.

To load a library of preset gradients:

Do one of the following:

• Click Load to add a library to the current list. Select the library file you want to use, and click Load.

- Choose Replace Gradients from the palette menu to replace the current list with a different library. Select the library file you want to use, and click Load.

- Choose a library file from the bottom of the palette menu. Click OK to replace the current list, or click Append to append the current list.

To return to the default library of preset gradients:

Choose Reset Gradients from the palette menu. You can either replace the current list or append the default library to the current list.

To change how preset gradients are displayed:

Choose a display option from the palette menu:

- Text Only to view the gradients as a list.

- Small or Large Thumbnail to view the gradients as thumbnails.

- Small or Large List to view the gradients as a list with thumbnails.

To rename a preset gradient:

Do one of the following:

- If the palette is set to display gradients as thumbnails, double-click a gradient, enter a new name, and click OK.

- If the palette is set to display gradients as a list or text only, double-click a gradient, enter a new name inline, and press Enter (Windows) or Return (Mac OS).

Using the paint bucket tool

The paint bucket tool fills adjacent pixels that are similar in color value to the pixels you click.

Note: The paint bucket tool cannot be used with images in Bitmap mode.

To use the paint bucket tool:

1 Specify a foreground color. (See "Choosing foreground and background colors" on page 201.)

2 Select the paint bucket tool ♢.

3 (Photoshop) Specify whether to fill the selection with the foreground color or with a pattern. (See "Filling and stroking selections and layers" on page 194.)

4 Specify a blending mode and opacity for the paint. (See "Setting options for painting and editing tools" on page 185.)

5 Enter the tolerance for the fill.

The tolerance defines how similar in color a pixel must be to be filled. Values can range from 0 to 255. A low tolerance fills pixels within a range of color values very similar to the pixel you click. A high tolerance fills pixels within a broader range.

6 To smooth the edges of the filled selection, select Anti-aliased. (See "Softening the edges of a selection" on page 111.)

7 To fill only pixels contiguous to the one you click, select Contiguous; leave unselected to fill all similar pixels in the image.

8 To fill pixels based on the merged color data from all visible layers, select All Layers. (See "Sampling from layers" on page 236.)

9 Click the part of the image you want to fill. All specified pixels within the specified tolerance are filled with the foreground color or pattern.

If you're working on a layer and don't want to fill transparent areas, make sure that the layer's transparency is locked in the Layers palette. (See "Locking layers" on page 235.)

Filling and stroking selections and layers

Photoshop and ImageReady provide a variety of ways to fill a selection or a layer with colors and patterns. You can also paint a border around a selection or a layer. Layer styles allow you to fill or stroke a selection or layer to create a live editable effect, while you can also paint a fill or border to create a softer effect. (See "Managing layers" on page 236.)

To increase the contrast between your image and the surrounding work canvas, you can fill the canvas with a color.

Filling a selection or layer with colors or patterns

You can fill a selection or layer with the foreground color, the background color, or a pattern. In Photoshop, you can use patterns from the pattern libraries provided or create your own patterns. You can also fill a shape using the Color, Gradient, or Pattern Overlay effects or the Solid Color,

Gradient, or Pattern fill layers on the Layers palette. When you use fill layers to fill a selection, you can easily change the type of layer being used. For more information, see "Using adjustment layers and fill layers (Photoshop)" on page 256.

To fill a selection or a layer with a foreground or background color:

1 Specify a foreground or background color. (See "Choosing foreground and background colors" on page 201.)

2 Select the area you want to fill. To fill an entire layer, select the layer in the Layers palette.

3 Choose Edit > Fill to fill the selection or layer. Or to fill a path, select the path and choose Fill Path from the Paths palette menu.

4 In the Fill dialog box, for Use, choose one of the following options or select a Custom Pattern:

- Foreground Color, Background Color, Black, 50% Gray, or White to fill the selection with the specified color.

To apply a foreground color fill only to the areas that contain pixels, press Alt+Shift+Backspace (Windows) or Option+Shift+Delete (Mac OS). This preserves the transparency of the layer. To apply a background color fill only to the areas that contain pixels, press Ctrl+Shift+Backspace (Windows) or Command+Shift+Delete (Mac OS).

- Pattern to fill the selection with a pattern. Click the inverted arrow ▾ next to the pattern sample and select a pattern from the pop-up palette. You can load additional patterns using the pop-up palette menu. Select the name of a library of patterns or choose Load Patterns and navigate to the folder containing the patterns you want to use.

- History to restore the selected area to a state or snapshot of the image. (See "Making a snapshot of an image (Photoshop)" on page 35.)

Note: If you fill a CMYK image using the Black option, Photoshop fills all the channels with 100% black. This may result in more ink than is allowable by the printer. For best results when filling a CMYK image, use the Foreground option with the foreground color set to an appropriate black.

5 Specify the blending mode and opacity for the paint. (See "Setting options for painting and editing tools" on page 185.)

6 If you're working in a layer and want to fill only areas containing pixels, choose Preserve Transparency.

7 If you are filling a path, enter a Feather Radius value to blend the edges of the filled path and select Anti-aliased if you want to anti-alias the path.

To fill the work canvas:

1 Set the foreground color you want to use for the canvas.

2 Select the paint bucket tool ⬦ .

3 In the options bar, set Fill to Foreground.

4 Hold down Shift, and click in the work canvas.

Note: You need to be in full screen mode and viewing the menus to fill the work canvas.

To fill a selection with a pattern:

1 Select the part of the image you want to fill.

2 Do one of the following:

- Choose Edit > Fill. In the Fill dialog box, for Use, choose Pattern, select a pattern from the pop-up palette, and click OK.

If Pattern is dimmed, you need to load a pattern library before you can select this option. (See "Managing libraries with the Preset Manager (Photoshop)" on page 49.)

- Select the paint bucket tool ⬦ . In the options bar, choose Pattern from the Fill pop-up menu and select a pattern from the Pattern pop-up palette. Then click to fill the selected area with the pattern.

Note: You can load additional pattern libraries into the pop-up palette prior to making a selection. (See "Creating and managing patterns" on page 196.)

Stroking a selection or layer with color

You can use the Stroke command to paint a colored border around a selection, layer, or path. This allows you to create a softer border than one created using the Stroke layer style. The Stroke layer style provides a resolution-independent method to stroke a shape. (See "Managing layers" on page 236.) You can use the Stroke layer effect when you want to stroke the entire layer. If you want a quick way to create a stroke on the current layer—without necessarily following the edge of the layer—use the Stroke command.

To stroke a selection or layer:

1 Specify a foreground color. (See "Choosing foreground and background colors" on page 201.)

2 Select the area or layer you want to stroke.

3 Choose Edit > Stroke.

4 In the Stroke dialog box, specify the width of the hard-edged border.

5 For Location, specify whether to place the border inside, outside, or centered over the selection or layer boundaries.

6 Specify an opacity and a blending mode. (See "Setting options for painting and editing tools" on page 185.)

7 If you're working in a layer and want to stroke only areas containing pixels, select the Preserve Transparency option. (See "Locking layers" on page 235.)

To stroke a path:

1 Select the path in the Paths palette.

2 Choose Stroke Path from the palette menu.

3 In the Stroke Path dialog box, choose a tool to stroke the path.

Creating and managing patterns

A pattern is an image that is repeated, or *tiled*, during application. Photoshop and ImageReady come with a variety of preset patterns. In Photoshop, you can create new patterns and save them in libraries for use with different tools and commands. In ImageReady, you can define a single pattern, called the User Defined Pattern, which you can use to fill selections and layers.

Defining patterns

You use the Edit > Define Pattern command to create new patterns based on a selection.

To define a preset pattern:

1 Use the rectangle marquee tool ⬚ on any open image to select an area to use as a pattern. Feather must be set to 0 px. Note that large images may become unwieldy.

2 Choose Edit > Define Pattern.

3 (Photoshop) Enter a name for the pattern in the Pattern Name dialog box.

Note: If you are using a pattern from one image and applying it to another, Photoshop converts the color mode.

To use a preset pattern from the PostScript Patterns folder:

1 Choose File > Open. Each preset file in the PostScript Patterns folder (which comes with Photoshop) contains a single pattern in the Adobe Illustrator format. You can scale and render these patterns at any resolution.

2 Select the pattern file you want to use, and click Open.

3 Select any rasterizing options. (See "Opening and importing images" on page 64.)

4 Make a rectangular selection around the pattern, or make no selection to use the whole image.

5 Choose Edit > Define Pattern.

6 (Photoshop) Enter a name for the pattern in the Pattern Name dialog box.

Managing patterns (Photoshop)

Preset patterns are displayed in pop-up palettes in the options bar for the paint bucket, pattern stamp, healing brush, and patch tools, as well as in the Layer Style dialog box. You can load, reset, and save libraries of preset patterns, and rename and delete individual preset patterns.

Note: You can also use the Preset Manager to load, reset, and save libraries of preset patterns, and rename and delete individual preset patterns. For more information, see "Managing libraries with the Preset Manager (Photoshop)" on page 49.

To change how patterns are displayed:

Choose a display option from a Pattern pop-up palette menu.

To load a library of patterns:

Choose one of the following from a Pattern pop-up palette menu:

- Load Patterns to add a library to the current list. Select the library file you want to use, and click Load.

- Replace Patterns to replace the current list with a different library. Select the library file you want to use, and click Load.

- A library file (displayed at the bottom of the palette menu). Click OK to replace the current list, or click Append to append the current list.

To rename a preset pattern:

1 Select the pattern you want to rename, and choose Rename Pattern from the palette menu.

2 Enter a new name for the pattern, and click OK.

To delete a preset pattern:

Do one of the following:

- Select the pattern you want to delete, and choose Delete Pattern from the palette menu.

- Hold down Alt (Windows) or Option (Mac OS), position the pointer over a pattern (the pointer turns into scissors), and click.

To save a set of preset patterns as a library:

1 Choose Save Patterns from a Pattern pop-up palette menu.

2 Choose a location for the pattern library, enter a filename, and click Save.

You can save the library anywhere. However, if you place the library file in the Presets/Patterns folder inside the Photoshop program folder, the library name will appear at the bottom of the Pattern pop-up palette menus after you restart Photoshop.

To return to the default library of patterns:

Choose Reset Patterns from a Pattern pop-up palette menu. You can either replace the current list or append the default library to the current list.

💡 *If you receive a pattern stamp tool preset that uses an undefined pattern, or if you erase the preset you're using by resetting or replacing the pattern library, choose New Pattern from the Pattern pop-up palette menu to redefine the pattern.*

Using the Pattern Maker

The Pattern Maker lets you create an infinite variety of patterns based on a selection or the contents of the Clipboard. Because the pattern is based on the pixels in a sample, it shares visual characteristics with the sample. For example, if you sample an image of grass, the Pattern Maker generates a tileable pattern that is different from the sample but still appears to be grass. You can generate multiple patterns from the same sample, and save pattern tiles as preset patterns for future use in Photoshop and ImageReady.

Note: The Pattern Maker command is available only for 8-bit images in RGB Color, CMYK Color, Lab Color, and Grayscale image modes.

Generating patterns

The Pattern Maker generates patterns by rearranging the pixels in a sampled area to create a tile. The size of a tile can vary, from 1 pixel by 1 pixel to the dimensions of the active layer. If the tile is smaller than the active layer, the pattern is made up of multiple tiles that are laid out in a grid to fill the layer. If the tile is the same size as the active layer, it comprises the entire pattern.

Original image. Pixels in selected area are sampled to create a tile.

A   B

Generated pattern:
A. *Single tile* **B.** *Tiled pattern*

Note: If the transparency of the active layer is locked, the Pattern Maker does not change the transparency of the layer when it tiles with a generated pattern.

To generate a pattern:

1 Do one of the following:

• Select the layer that contains the area from which you want to generate the pattern. The layer you select will be replaced by the generated pattern, so it's a good idea to make a copy of the layer first.

• To generate a pattern in a new layer or file, select the pixels from which you want to generate the pattern, and choose Edit > Copy. Then add a layer to the image, or create a new file with the dimensions you want the final image to have.

Note: You cannot generate a pattern from a non-rectangular sample. If you make a non-rectangular selection, Photoshop uses the bounding box of the selected area to create a rectangular sample.

2 Choose Filter > Pattern Maker.

3 Do one of the following:

• If you are generating a pattern in the same layer that contains the sample, select the rectangular marquee tool ⌊⌉ in the Pattern Maker dialog box, and select the area from which you want to generate the pattern. To move the selection marquee, drag it to a different location.

• If you are generating a pattern in a new layer or file, select Use Clipboard as Sample in the Pattern Maker dialog box.

4 Specify the dimensions of tiles in the generated pattern by doing one of the following:

• Enter pixel values in the Width and Height text boxes, or drag the pop-up sliders.

• Click Use Image Size to use the image size as the tile size. Selecting this option produces a pattern with a single tile.

5 To offset the tiles in the generated pattern, choose a direction from the Offset pop-up menu and specify an offset amount by entering a value in the Amount text box or dragging the Amount pop-up slider. The offset amount is a percentage of the tile dimension in the specified direction.

6 Click Generate. The preview area is tiled with the generated pattern. (See "Previewing patterns" on page 200.)

You can view the status of the current generation in the Photoshop status bar. Press Esc to cancel the generation.

7 Click Generate Again to generate additional patterns using the same options, or adjust the options and then click Generate Again.

You can navigate through the generated tiles using the Tile History panel. (See "Reviewing tiles and pattern previews" on page 200.)

8 When you are satisfied with a pattern preview and you have saved the tiles that you might want to use in the future, click OK. (See "Reviewing tiles and pattern previews" on page 200.)

Previewing patterns

The Pattern Maker dialog box provides tools and options for previewing generated patterns. You can magnify and navigate in the preview image just as you do in the Photoshop document window. You can also show or hide tile boundaries and switch between previewing the original image and the generated pattern.

To magnify and reduce the preview image:

1 Select the zoom tool ⚲ in the Pattern Maker dialog box.

2 Click in the preview image to zoom in, or hold down Alt (Windows) or Option (Mac OS), and click in the preview image to zoom out.

The magnification level appears at the bottom of the dialog box.

To navigate in the preview image:

Select the hand tool ✋ in the Pattern Maker dialog box, and drag in the preview image. Alternately, hold down the spacebar, and drag in the preview image.

To display tile boundaries in the preview image:

Select Tile Boundaries in the Preview section of the Pattern Maker dialog box. To choose a different color for tile boundaries, click the color swatch.

To switch between the generated pattern and the original image:

Choose an option from the Show pop-up menu in the Preview section of the Pattern Maker dialog box.

When previewing the original image, you change the sample area using the rectangular marquee tool. The new sample will be used for the next generation.

Reviewing tiles and pattern previews

The Tile History section of the Pattern Maker dialog box lets you review all the pattern previews you have generated. You can navigate through pattern previews, delete pattern previews, and save tiles as preset patterns.

Important: *When you save a tile as a preset pattern, only a single tile is saved, not the full, generated pattern.*

To navigate through tiles and pattern previews:

Do one of the following:

• Click the First Tile button ⏮ , Previous Tile button ◀ , Next Tile button ▶ , or Last Tile button ⏭ .

• Type the number of the pattern preview you want to view, and press Enter (Windows) or Return (Mac OS).

If the Update Pattern Preview option is selected, the full pattern is regenerated in the preview area. If the Update Pattern Preview option is deselected, only the tile thumbnail changes.

Deselect Update Pattern Preview to quickly review tiles. When you find the desired tile, select Update Pattern Preview to regenerate the preview.

To delete a tile and pattern preview:

Navigate to the tile you want to delete, and click the Trash button 🗑 .

To save a tile as a preset pattern:

1 Navigate to the tile you want to save, and click the Preset button 🖫 .

2 Enter a preset name, and click OK.

You can create and manage libraries of presets using the Preset Manager. (See "Managing libraries with the Preset Manager (Photoshop)" on page 49.)

Specifying pattern smoothness and detail

The Smoothness and Sample Detail options in the Pattern Maker dialog box let you control the parameters that Photoshop uses to generate a pattern. The default settings work well for most samples, so don't change these settings unless you get a poor result.

Smoothness If the pixels in the sample lack contrast, the Pattern Maker may introduce unwanted edges into the generated pattern. Increasing the Smoothness value decreases the prominence of edges within a generated tile.

Generated pattern with Smoothness of 1 and Smoothness of 3

Sample Detail If the sample contains details that are cut up in the generated pattern, increase the Sample Detail value.

Example of sampled image

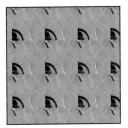

Generated pattern with Sample Detail of 5 and Sample Detail of 15

Note: *Increasing the Smoothness and Sample Detail values results in slower pattern generation.*

Choosing foreground and background colors

Photoshop uses the *foreground* color to paint, fill, and stroke selections and the *background* color to make gradient fills and fill in the erased areas of an image. The foreground and background colors are also used by some special effects filters.

You can designate a new foreground or background color using the eyedropper tool, the Color palette, the Swatches palette, or the Adobe Color Picker.

The default foreground color is black, and the default background color is white. (In an alpha channel, the default foreground is white, and the background is black.)

Using color settings in the toolbox

The current foreground color appears in the upper color selection box in the toolbox; the current background color appears in the lower box.

The Info palette, the Color palette, and the Adobe Color Picker let you display color values using a number of color models. (See "About color modes and models (Photoshop)" on page 77.)

To change the foreground or background color:

1 Do one of the following:

• To change the foreground color, click the upper color selection box in the toolbox.

• To change the background color, click the lower color selection box in the toolbox.

2 Choose a color in the Adobe Color Picker. (See "Using the Adobe Color Picker" on page 205.)

To reverse the foreground and background colors:

Click the Switch Colors icon ↳ in the toolbox.

To restore the default foreground and background colors:

Click the Default Colors icon ▪ in the toolbox.

Using the eyedropper tool

The eyedropper tool samples color to designate a new foreground or background color. You can sample from the active image or from anywhere else on the screen.

You can also specify the area sampled by the eyedropper tool. For example, you can set the eyedropper to sample the color values of a 3-by-3-pixel area under the pointer. Modifying the sample size of the eyedropper affects the color readouts displayed in the Info palette.

To select the foreground or background color:

1 Select the eyedropper tool ✐ .

2 To change the sample size of the eyedropper, choose an option from the Sample Size menu:

• Point Sample to read the precise value of the pixel you click.

• 3 by 3 Average or 5 by 5 Average to read the average value of the specified number of pixels within the area you click.

3 Do one of the following:

• To select a new foreground color, click in the image. Alternately, position the pointer over the image, press the mouse button, and drag anywhere on the screen. The foreground color selection box changes dynamically as you drag. Release the mouse button to pick the new color.

- To select a new background color, Alt-click (Windows) or Option-click (Mac OS) in the image. Alternately, position the pointer over the image, press Alt (Windows) or Options (Mac OS), press the mouse button, and drag anywhere on the screen. The background color selection box changes dynamically as you drag. Release the mouse button to pick the new color.

To use the eyedropper tool temporarily while using any painting tool, hold down Alt (Windows) or Option (Mac OS).

Using the Color palette

The Color palette displays the color values for the current foreground and background colors. Using the sliders in the Color palette, you can edit the foreground and background colors according to several different color models. You can also choose a foreground or background color from the spectrum of colors displayed in the color ramp at the bottom of the palette.

The Color palette may display the following alerts when you select a color:

- In Photoshop, an exclamation point inside a triangle ⚠ appears above the left side of the color ramp when you choose a color that cannot be printed using CMYK inks. For more information, see "Identifying out-of-gamut colors (Photoshop)" on page 148.

- A cube 🔲 appears above the left side of the color ramp when you choose a color that is not Web-safe. For more information, see "Using Web-safe colors" on page 207.

To display the Color palette:

Choose Window > Color, or click the Color palette tab.

To change the color model of the color sliders:

Choose a Sliders option from the Color palette menu. For more information on the different color models, see "About color modes and models (Photoshop)" on page 77.

To change the spectrum displayed in the color ramp:

1 Choose an option from the Color palette menu:

- RGB Spectrum, CMYK Spectrum (Photoshop), or Grayscale Ramp to display the spectrum of the specified color model.

- Current Colors to display the spectrum of colors between the current foreground color and the current background color.

2 To display only Web-safe colors, choose Make Ramp Web Safe. (See "Using Web-safe colors" on page 207.)

To change the spectrum of the color ramp quickly, Shift-click in the color ramp until you see the spectrum you want.

To select the foreground or background color:

1 To edit the foreground or background color, make sure that its color selection box is active (outlined in black). To make the foreground or background color selection box active, click the box.

2 Do one of the following:

- Drag the color sliders. By default, the slider colors change as you drag. In Photoshop, you can turn off this feature to improve performance by deselecting Dynamic Color Sliders in the General section of the Preferences dialog box.

- Enter values next to the color sliders.

- Click the color selection box, choose a color using the color picker, and click OK.

- Position the pointer over the color ramp (the pointer becomes the eyedropper), and click to sample a color. Alt-click to apply the sample to the non-active color selection box.

Using the Swatches palette

You can choose a foreground or background color from the Swatches palette, or you can add or delete colors to create a custom swatch library. Creating libraries of swatches can help you group related or special swatches and manage palette size.

Note: You can also use the Preset Manager to manage libraries. For more information, see "Managing libraries with the Preset Manager (Photoshop)" on page 49.

To display the Swatches palette:

Choose Window > Swatches, or click the Swatches palette tab.

To change how swatches are displayed (Photoshop):

Choose a display option from the Swatches palette menu:

- Small Thumbnail to display a thumbnail of each swatch. This is the default view.

- Small List to display the name and thumbnail of each swatch.

To select a foreground or background color:

Do one of the following:

- To choose a foreground color, click a color in the Swatches palette.

- To choose a background color, Ctrl-click (Windows) or Command-click (Mac OS) a color in the Swatches palette.

To load a library of swatches:

Choose one of the following from the Swatches palette menu:

- Load Swatches to add a library to the current list. Select the library file you want to use, and click Load.

- Replace Swatches to replace the current list with a different library. Select the library file you want to use, and click Load.

- A library file (displayed at the bottom of the palette menu). Click OK to replace the current list, or click Append to append the current list.

To add a color to the Swatches palette:

Do one of the following:

- Make the color you want to add the foreground color, and click the New Swatch button ⬛ in the Swatches palette. Alternately, choose New Swatch from the Swatches palette menu.

- (Photoshop) Make the color you want to add the foreground color. Position the pointer over an empty space in the bottom row of the Swatches palette (the pointer turns into the paint bucket tool), and click to add the color. Enter a name for the new color and click OK.

- (ImageReady) Drag the foreground color selection box or the background color selection box from the toolbox to the Swatches palette.

- (ImageReady) Drag a swatch from the Color Table palette to the Swatches palette.

Note: New colors are saved in the Preferences file so that they persist between editing sessions. To permanently save a color, save it in a library.

To duplicate a color in the Swatches palette (ImageReady):

Select the color you want to duplicate, and choose New Swatch from the Swatches palette menu.

To delete a color from the Swatches palette:

Do one of the following:

- Drag a swatch to the Trash button 🗑 .

- (Photoshop) Hold down Alt (Windows) or Option (Mac OS), position the pointer over a swatch (the pointer turns into scissors), and click.

- (ImageReady) Select a swatch, and choose Delete Swatch from the Swatches palette menu.

To save a set of swatches as a library:

1 Choose Save Swatches from the Swatches palette menu.

2 Choose a location for the swatch library, enter a filename, and click Save.

You can save the library anywhere. However, if you place the library file in the Presets/Swatches folder inside the Photoshop program folder, the library name will appear at the bottom of the Swatches palette menu after you restart the application.

To return to the default library of swatches:

Choose Reset Swatches from the Swatches palette menu. You can either replace the current list or append the default library to the current list.

Using the Adobe Color Picker

You can use the Adobe Color Picker to select the foreground or background color by choosing from a color spectrum or by defining colors numerically. In addition, you can select colors based on the HSB, RGB, Lab, and CMYK color models, choose to use only Web-safe colors, and choose from several custom color systems. For more information, see "About color modes and models (Photoshop)" on page 77. By default, the program uses the Adobe Color Picker.

To display the Adobe Color Picker:

Do one of the following:

- Click the foreground or background color selection box in the toolbox.

- Click the active color selection box in the Color palette.

Specifying a color using the color field and color slider

With the HSB, RGB, and Lab color modes, you can use the color field and the color slider in the Color Picker dialog box to select a color. The color slider displays the range of color levels available for the selected color component (for example, R, G, or B). The color field displays the range for the remaining two components—one on the horizontal axis, one on the vertical.

For example, if the current color is black and you click the red component (R) using the RGB color model, the color slider displays the range of color for red (0 is at the bottom of the slider and 255 is at the top). The color field displays the values for blue along its horizontal axis, for green along its vertical axis.

To specify a color using the color field and color slider:

1 Click a component next to the HSB, RGB, or Lab values.

2 Select a color:

- Drag the white triangles along the slider.

- Click inside the color slider.

- Click inside the color field.

When you click in the color field, a circular marker indicates the color's position in the field.

As you adjust the color using the color field and color slider, the numerical values change to reflect the new color. The color rectangle to the right of the color slider displays the new color in the top section of the rectangle. The original color appears at the bottom of the rectangle.

Specifying a color using numeric values

In the Adobe Color Picker, you can select a color in any of the four color models by specifying numeric values for each color component.

To specify a color using numeric values:

Do one of the following:

- (Photoshop) In CMYK color mode (the mode PostScript printers use), specify each component value as a percentage of cyan, magenta, yellow, and black.

- In RGB color mode (the mode your monitor uses), specify component values from 0 to 255 (0 is black, and 255 is the pure color).

- In HSB color mode, specify saturation and brightness as percentages; specify hue as an angle from 0° to 360° that corresponds to a location on the color wheel. For more information on the color wheel, see "About color modes and models (Photoshop)" on page 77.

- (Photoshop) In Lab mode, enter a lightness value (L) from 0 to 100 and a axis (green to magenta) and b axis (blue to yellow) values from -120 to $+120$.

Using Web-safe colors

The *Web-safe colors* are the 216 colors used by browsers regardless of the platform. The browser will change all colors in the image to these colors when displaying the color on an 8-bit screen. The 216 colors are a subset of the Mac OS 8-bit color palettes. By working only with these colors, you can be sure that art you prepare for the Web will not dither on a system set to display in 256 colors.

To identify Web-safe colors in the Adobe Color Picker:

• Click the Only Web Colors option in the lower left corner of the color picker, and then choose any color in the color picker. Any color you pick with this option selected is Web-safe.

• Choose a color in the color picker. If you choose a non-Web color, an alert cube ⬡ appears next to the color rectangle in the color picker. Click the alert cube to select the closest Web color. (If no alert cube appears, the color you chose is Web-safe.)

To select a Web-safe color using the Color palette:

1 Click the Color palette tab, or choose Window > Color to view the Color palette.

2 Choose an option for selecting a Web-safe color:

• Choose Make Ramp Web Safe from the Color palette menu. With this option selected, any color you choose in the Color palette is Web-safe.

• Choose Web Color Sliders from the Color palette menu (Photoshop), or choose any Slider option from the Color palette menu (ImageReady). By default, Web Color Sliders snap to Web-safe colors (indicated by tick marks) when you drag them. (To override Web-safe color selection, Alt-drag (Windows) or Option-drag (Mac OS) the sliders.) If you choose a non-Web color, an alert cube ⬡ appears above the color ramp on the left side of the Color palette. Click the alert cube to select the closest Web color. In ImageReady, drag around the alert icon to select other close Web colors. (If no alert cube appears, the color you chose is Web-safe.)

Note: In Photoshop, you must choose Web Color Sliders from the Color palette menu to view the Web-safe alert cube. In ImageReady, you can view the alert cube with any color slider option.

Recognizing nonprintable colors (Photoshop)

Some colors in the RGB, HSB, and Lab color models, such as neon colors, cannot be printed because they have no equivalents in the CMYK model. When you select a nonprintable color, an alert triangle appears in the Color Picker dialog box and in the Color palette. The closest CMYK equivalent is displayed below the triangle. (See "Identifying out-of-gamut colors (Photoshop)" on page 148.)

Note: The alert triangle is not available if you've chosen to use Web-safe sliders.

Printable colors are determined by your current CMYK working space as defined in the Color Settings dialog box.

To select the closest CMYK equivalent for a nonprintable color:

Click the alert triangle ⚠ that appears in the Color Picker dialog box or the Color palette.

Choosing custom colors (Photoshop)

The Adobe Color Picker lets you choose custom colors from the PANTONE® MATCHING SYSTEM®, the TRUMATCH® SWATCHING SYSTEM™, the FOCOLTONE® COLOUR SYSTEM, the TOYO Color Finder™ 1050 system, the ANPA-COLOR™ system, HKS® color system, and the DIC Color Guide.

To ensure that the final printed output is the color you want, consult your printer or service bureau and choose your custom color based on a printed color swatch. Manufacturers recommend that you get a new swatch book each year to compensate for fading inks and other damage.

Important: Photoshop prints custom colors to CMYK (process color) plates in every image mode except Duotone. To print true spot color plates, create spot color channels. (See "Adding spot colors (Photoshop)" on page 217.)

To choose a custom color:

1 Open the Adobe Color Picker, and click Custom.

The Custom Colors dialog box displays the color closest to the color currently selected in the Color Picker.

2 For Book, choose a color system. (See "Choosing a custom color system (Photoshop)" on page 208.)

3 Locate the color you want by entering the ink number or by dragging the triangles along the scroll bar.

4 Click the desired color patch in the list.

Choosing a custom color system (Photoshop)

The Adobe Color Picker supports various color systems:

PANTONE Used for printing solid-color and CMYK inks. The PANTONE MATCHING SYSTEM includes 1,114 solid colors. To select a color, use a PANTONE Color guide, printed on coated, uncoated, and matte stocks.

To simulate a PANTONE solid color in CMYK, use the PANTONE Solid to Process Guide, which displays a visual comparison of 1,089 solid PANTONE colors beside the closest process color match.

PANTONE process guides let you choose from over 3,000 CMYK combinations, printed coated and uncoated stocks.

TRUMATCH Provides predictable CMYK color matching with more than 2000 achievable, computer-generated colors. TRUMATCH colors cover the visible spectrum of the CMYK gamut in even steps. The TRUMATCHCOLORFINDER displays up to 40 tints and shades of each hue, each originally created in four-color process and each reproducible in four colors on electronic image-setters. In addition, four-color grays using different hues are included.

FOCOLTONE Consists of 763 CMYK colors. FOCOLTONE colors help avoid prepress trapping and registration problems by showing the overprints that make up the colors.

A swatch book with specifications for process and spot colors, overprint charts, and a chip book for marking up layouts are available from FOCOLTONE.

TOYO Color Finder 1050 Consists of more than 1000 colors based on the most common printing inks used in Japan. The *TOYO Color Finder 1050 Book* contains printed samples of Toyo colors and is available from printers and graphic arts supply stores.

ANPA-COLOR Commonly used for newspaper applications. The *ANPA-COLOR ROP Newspaper Color Ink Book* contains samples of the ANPA colors.

DIC Color Guide Commonly used for printing projects in Japan.

HKS Used for printing projects in Europe. Each color has a specified CMYK equivalent. You can select from HKS E (for continuous stationary), HKS K (for gloss art paper), HKS N (for natural paper), and HKS Z (for newsprint). Color samplers for each scale are available.

Using other color pickers

In addition to the default Adobe Color Picker, you can use the built-in color pickers on your system or a plug-in color picker to select colors. Any plug-in color pickers you install appear under Color Picker in the General section of the Preferences dialog box. For information on installing and using a plug-in color picker, see the documentation that came with the plug-in.

To use the Windows Color Picker (Windows):

1 Choose Edit > Preferences > General.

2 Choose Windows from the Color Picker menu, and click OK.

For more information, see your Windows documentation.

To use the Apple Color Picker (Mac OS):

1 Do one of the following:

• In Mac OS 9.x, choose Edit > Preferences > General.

• (Photoshop) In Mac OS X, choose Photoshop > Preferences > General.

• (ImageReady) In Mac OS X, choose ImageReady > Preferences > General.

2 For Color Picker, choose Apple, and click OK.

The exact appearance of the Apple Color Picker varies between different system software versions. For more information, see your Mac OS documentation.

To return to the Adobe Color Picker after using another color picker:

1 Do one of the following:

• In Windows and Mac OS 9.x, choose Edit > Preferences > General.

• (Photoshop) In Mac OS X, choose Photoshop > Preferences > General.

• (ImageReady) In Mac OS X, choose ImageReady > Preferences > General.

2 Choose Adobe from the Color Picker menu, and click OK.

Chapter 9: Using Channels and Masks

Each image in Adobe Photoshop has channels that store information about the image's color. You can create additional channels to store spot colors for printing with special inks and to store masks for sophisticated selections.

About channels

Channels are grayscale images that store different types of information:

- *Color information channels* are created automatically when you open a new image. The image's color mode determines the number of color channels created. For example, an RGB image has four default channels: one for each of the red, green, and blue colors plus a composite channel used for editing the image.

- You can create *alpha channels* to store selections as 8-bit grayscale images. You use alpha channels to create and store masks, which let you manipulate, isolate, and protect specific parts of an image. In addition to supporting alpha channels from Photoshop, you can save, load, and delete selections as alpha channels in ImageReady 7.0.

- You can create *spot color channels* to specify additional plates for printing with spot color inks.

An image can have up to 24 channels. The file size required for a channel depends on the pixel information in the channel. Certain file formats, including TIFF and Photoshop formats, compress channel information and can save space. The uncompressed size of a file, including alpha channels and layers, appears as the rightmost value in the status bar at the bottom of the window when Document Sizes is chosen from the pop-up menu.

Note: As long as you save a file in a format supporting the image's color mode, the color channels are preserved. Alpha channels are preserved only when you save a file in Adobe Photoshop, PDF, PICT, Pixar, TIFF, or Raw formats. DCS 2.0 format only preserves spot channels. Saving in other formats may cause channel information to be discarded. (See "About file formats" on page 373.)

Using the Channels palette (Photoshop)

The Channels palette lets you create and manage channels and monitor the effects of editing. The palette lists all channels in the image—composite channel first (for RGB, CMYK, and Lab images), then individual color channels, spot color channels, and finally alpha channels. A thumbnail of the channel's contents appears to the left of the channel name; the thumbnail automatically updates as you edit the channel.

Viewing channels

You can use the palette to view any combination of individual channels. For example, you can view an alpha channel and the composite channel together to see how changes made in the alpha channel relate to the entire image. By default, individual channels are displayed in grayscale.

To display the Channels palette:

1 Choose Windows > Channels, or click the Channels palette tab.

2 Use the scroll bars or resize the palette to see additional channels.

When a channel is visible in the image, an eye icon 👁 appears to its left in the palette.

To show or hide a channel:

Click in the eye column next to the channel to show or hide that channel. (Click the composite channel to view all default color channels. The composite channel is displayed whenever all the color channels are visible.)

To show or hide multiple channels, drag through the eye column in the Channels palette.

These guidelines apply to channels you display:

- In RGB, CMYK, or Lab images, you can view the individual channels in color. (In Lab images, only the *a* and *b* channels appear in color.)

- If more than one channel is active, the channels always appear in color.

- In alpha channels, selected pixels appear as white; unselected pixels appear as black (partially transparent or selected pixels appear as gray). These are the channel default options.

- If you display an alpha channel at the same time as color channels, the alpha channel appears as a transparent color overlay, analogous to a printer's rubylith or a sheet of acetate. To change the color of this overlay or set other alpha channel options, see "Creating alpha channels (Photoshop)" on page 226.

Changing the display of the palette

You can show the individual color channels in color (rather than grayscale) in the Channels palette and specify the size of the thumbnails. Using thumbnails is the most convenient way of tracking channel contents; however, turning off the display of thumbnails can improve performance.

To show color channels in color:

1 Do one of the following:

- In Windows and Mac OS 9.x, choose Edit > Preferences > Display & Cursors.

- In Mac OS X, choose Photoshop > Preferences > Display & Cursors.

2 Select Color Channels in Color, and click OK.

To resize or hide channel thumbnails:

1 Choose Palette Options from the Channels palette menu.

2 Select a display option:

- Click a thumbnail size. Smaller thumbnails reduce the space required by the palette—helpful when you're working on smaller monitors.

- Click None to turn off the display of thumbnails.

Selecting and editing channels

You can select one or more channels in the Channels palette. The names of all selected, or *active*, channels are highlighted. Any editing changes you make apply to the active channels.

To select a channel:

Click the channel name. Shift-click to select (or deselect) multiple channels.

To edit a channel:

Use a painting or editing tool to paint in the image. Paint with white to add the selected channel's color at 100% intensity. Paint with a value of gray to add the channel's color at a lower intensity. Paint with black to fully remove the channel's color.

Managing channels (Photoshop)

You can rearrange channels, duplicate a channel within or between images, split a channel into separate images, merge channels from separate images into one new image, and delete alpha and spot channels when you're finished with them.

Rearranging and renaming channels

The default color channels normally appear at the top of the Channels palette, followed by the spot color channels, and then the alpha channels. You cannot move or rename the default channels, but you can rearrange and rename spot and alpha channels to suit the way you work.

Spot colors are overprinted in the order they appear in the Channels palette.

To change the order of alpha or spot channels:

Drag the channel up or down. When a line appears in the position you want, release the mouse button.

Note: You can move alpha or spot channels above the default color channels only if the image is in Multi-channel mode.

To rename an alpha or spot channel:

Double-click the channel's name in the Channels palette, and enter a new name.

Duplicating channels

You might duplicate an image's channel to make a backup before editing the channel. Or you might duplicate alpha channels to a new image to create a library of selections to load into the current image one by one—thus keeping the file smaller.

If you are duplicating alpha channels between images, the channels must have identical pixel dimensions. (See "Creating new images" on page 63.)

Note: You cannot duplicate a channel to a Bitmap-mode image.

To duplicate a channel using the Duplicate command:

1 In the Channels palette, select the channel to duplicate.

2 Choose Duplicate Channel from the Channels palette menu.

3 Type a name for the duplicate channel.

4 For Document, do one of the following:

• Choose a destination. Only open images with pixel dimensions identical to the current image are available. To duplicate the channel in the same file, select the channel's current file.

• Choose New to copy the channel to a new image, creating a multichannel image containing a single channel. Type a name for the new image.

5 To reverse the selected and masked areas in the duplicate channel, select Invert.

To duplicate a channel within an image by dragging:

1 In the Channels palette, select the channel you want to duplicate.

2 Drag the channel onto the New Channel button ⊟ at the bottom of the palette.

To duplicate a channel to another image by dragging or pasting:

1 In the Channels palette, select the channel you want to duplicate.

2 Make sure that the destination image is open.

Note: The destination image does not have to be the same pixel dimensions as the duplicated channel.

3 Do one of the following:

• Drag the channel from the Channels palette into the destination image window. The duplicated channel appears at the bottom of the Channels palette.

• Choose Select > All, then choose Edit > Copy. Select the channel in the destination image and choose Edit > Paste. The pasted channel overwrites the existing channel.

Splitting channels into separate images

You can split the channels of a flattened image into separate images. The original file is closed, and the individual channels appear in separate grayscale image windows. The title bars in the new windows show the original filename plus the channel abbreviation (Windows) or full name (Mac OS). Any changes since the last save are retained in the new images and lost in the original.

💡 *Splitting channels is useful when you want to retain individual channel information in a file format that doesn't preserve channels.*

Note: Only flattened images can be split. (See "Flattening all layers" on page 239.)

To split channels into separate images:

Choose Split Channels from the Channels palette menu.

Merging channels

Multiple grayscale images can be combined into a single image. Some grayscale scanners let you scan a color image through a red filter, a green filter, and a blue filter to generate red, green, and blue images. Merging lets you combine the separate scans into a single, color image.

Note: You can also blend the data in one or more channels into an existing or new channel. (See "Mixing color channels (Photoshop)" on page 216.)

The images you want to merge must be in Grayscale mode, have the same pixel dimensions, and be open. (See "Changing the pixel dimensions of an image" on page 59.) The number of grayscale images you have open determines the color modes available when merging channels. For example, you can't merge the split channels from an RGB image into a CMYK image, because CMYK requires four channels and RGB requires only three.

Note: If you are working with DCS files that have accidentally lost their links (and so cannot be opened, placed, or printed), open the channel files, and merge them into a CMYK image. Then resave the file as a DCS EPS file.

To merge channels:

1 Open the grayscale images containing the channels you want to merge, and make one of the images active.

You must have more than one image opened for the Merge Channels option to be available.

2 Choose Merge Channels from the Channels palette menu.

3 For Mode, choose the color mode you want to create. If an image mode is unavailable, it is dimmed. The number of channels appropriate for the mode appears in the Channels text box.

4 If necessary, enter a number in the Channels text box.

If you enter a number that is incompatible with the selected mode, Multichannel mode is automatically selected. This creates a a multichannel image with two or more channels.

5 Click OK.

6 For each channel, make sure the image you want is open. If you change your mind about image type, click Mode to return to the Merge Channels dialog box.

7 If merging into a multichannel image, click Next, and repeat step 6 to select the remaining channels.

Note: All channels of a multichannel image are alpha channels.

8 When you are finished selecting channels, click OK.

The selected channels are merged into a new image of the specified type, and the original images are closed without any changes. The new image appears in an untitled window.

Note: You cannot split and recombine (merge) an image with spot color channels. The spot color channel will be added as an alpha channel.

Deleting channels

You may want to delete spot or alpha channels you no longer need before saving an image. Complex alpha channels can substantially increase the disk space required for an image.

To delete a channel (Photoshop):

1 Select the channel in the Channels palette.

2 Do one of the following:

• Alt-click (Windows) or Option-click (Mac OS) the Trash button 🗑 .

• Drag the channel name in the palette to the Trash button.

• Choose Delete Channel from the Channels palette menu.

• Click the Trash button at the bottom of the palette. Then click Yes.

To delete a channel (ImageReady):

Choose Select > Delete Channel, and choose the channel from the submenu.

Note: When deleting a channel from a file with layers, visible layers are flattened and hidden layers are discarded. This is done because removing a color channel converts the image to Multichannel mode, which does not support layers.

Mixing color channels (Photoshop)

The Channel Mixer command lets you modify a color channel using a mix of the current color channels. With this command, you can do the following:

• Make creative color adjustments not easily done with the other color adjustment tools.

• Create high-quality grayscale images by choosing the percentage contribution from each color channel.

• Create high-quality sepia-tone or other tinted images.

• Convert images to and from alternative color spaces, such as YCbCr, which is used in digital video.

• Swap or duplicate channels.

To mix color channels:

1 In the Channels palette, select the composite color channel.

2 Choose Image > Adjustments > Channel Mixer.

3 For Output Channel, choose the channel in which to blend one or more existing (or *source*) channels. (See "Restricting blending to channels (Photoshop)" on page 243.)

4 Drag any source channel's slider to the left to decrease the channel's contribution to the output channel or to the right to increase it, or enter a value between −200% and +200% in the text box. Using a negative value inverts the source channel before adding it to the output channel.

5 Drag the slider or enter a value for the Constant option. This option adds a black or white channel of varying opacity—negative values act as a black channel, positive values act as a white channel.

6 Select Monochrome to apply the same settings to all the output channels, creating a color image that contains only gray values.

Use the Channel Mixer with the Monochrome option applied to control the amount of detail and contrast in the images you plan to convert to grayscale.

If you select and then deselect the Monochrome option, you can modify the blend of each channel separately, creating a handtinted appearance.

Adding spot colors (Photoshop)

Spot colors are special premixed inks used instead of, or in addition to, the process color (CMYK) inks. Each spot color requires its own plate on the press. (Because a varnish requires a separate plate, it is considered a spot color, too.) For information on printing spot color plates, see "Printing color separations" on page 394.

If you are planning to print an image with spot colors, you need to create spot channels to store the colors. To export spot channels, save the file in DCS 2.0 format or PDF. (See "Saving files in Photoshop EPS format (Photoshop)" on page 367.)

Note: *ImageReady supports Photoshop spot color channels as alpha channels.*

About spot colors

Note the following when working with spot colors:

- For spot color graphics that have crisp edges and knock out the underlying image, consider creating the additional artwork in a page-layout or illustration application.

- To apply spot color as a tint throughout an image, convert the image to Duotone mode and apply the spot color to one of the duotone plates. You can use up to four spot colors, one per plate. (See "Printing color separations" on page 394.)

- The names of the spot colors print on the separations.

- Spot colors are overprinted on top of the fully composited image. Each spot color is overprinted in the order it appears in the Channels palette.

- You cannot move spot colors above a default channel in the Channels palette except in Multi-channel mode.

- Spot colors cannot be applied to individual layers.

- Printing an image with a spot color channel to a composite color printer will print the spot color at an opacity indicated by the solidity setting.

- You can merge spot channels with color channels, splitting the spot color into its color channel components.

Creating spot channels

You can create a new spot channel or convert an existing alpha channel to a spot channel.

To create a new spot channel:

1 Choose Window > Channels to display the Channels palette.

2 To fill a selected area with a spot color, make or load a selection.

3 Do one of the following to create a channel:

• Ctrl-click (Windows) or Command-click (Mac OS) the New Channel button ▣ in the Channels palette.

• Choose New Spot Channel from the Channels palette menu.

If you made a selection, that area is filled with the currently specified spot color.

4 Click the color box, and choose a color. (See "Using the Adobe Color Picker" on page 205.)

If you select a custom color, your print service provider can more easily provide the proper ink to reproduce the image. For more information, see "Choosing custom colors (Photoshop)" on page 208.

5 For Solidity, enter a value between 0% and 100%.

This option lets you simulate on-screen the solidity of the printed spot color. A value of 100% simulates an ink that completely covers the inks beneath (such as a metallic ink); 0% simulates a transparent ink that completely reveals the inks beneath (such as a clear varnish). You can also use this option to see where an otherwise transparent spot color (such as a varnish) will appear.

Note: *The Solidity and color choice options affect only the on-screen preview and the composite print. They have no effect on the printed separations.*

6 To enter a name for the spot channel, choose a custom color in step 4, and the channel automatically takes the name of that color.

Be sure to name spot colors so they'll be recognized by other applications reading your file. Otherwise the file might not print.

To convert an alpha channel to a spot channel:

1 Do one of the following:

• Double-click the alpha channel thumbnail in the Channels palette.

• Select the alpha channel in the Channels palette, and choose Channel Options from the palette menu.

2 If needed, rename the channel.

3 Select Spot Color.

4 Click the color box, choose a color in the Color Picker dialog box, and click OK. (See "Using the Adobe Color Picker" on page 205.)

5 Click OK. The areas of the channel containing grayscale values are converted to spot color.

6 Choose Image > Adjustments > Invert to apply the color to the selected area of the channel.

Modifying spot channels

You can edit a spot channel to add or remove color in it, change a spot channel's color or on-screen color solidity, and merge a spot channel with the image's color channels.

For information on rearranging, duplicating, or deleting spot channels, see "Managing channels (Photoshop)" on page 213.

To edit a spot channel:

1 Select the spot channel in the Channels palette.

2 Use a painting or editing tool to paint in the image. Paint with black to add more spot color at 100% opacity; paint with gray to add spot color with lower opacity.

Note: Unlike the Solidity option in the Spot Channel Options dialog box, the Opacity option in the painting or editing tool's options determines the actual density of ink used in the printed output.

To change a spot channel's options:

1 Do one of the following:

• Double-click the spot channel thumbnail in the Channels palette.

• Select the spot channel in the Channels palette, and choose Channel Options from the palette menu.

2 Click the color box, and choose a color. (See "Using the Adobe Color Picker" on page 205.)

By selecting a custom color, your print service can more easily provide the proper ink to reproduce the image. For more information, see "Choosing custom colors (Photoshop)" on page 208.

3 For Solidity, enter a value between 0% and 100%.

This option lets you simulate on-screen the solidity of the printed spot color. A value of 100% simulates an ink that completely covers the inks beneath (such as a metallic ink); 0% simulates a transparent ink that completely reveals the inks beneath (such as a clear varnish). You can also use this option to see where an otherwise transparent spot color (such as a varnish) will appear.

Note: The Solidity and color choice options affect only the on-screen preview and the composite print. They have no effect on the printed separations.

To merge spot channels:

1 Select the spot channel in the Channels palette.

2 Choose Merge Spot Channel from the palette menu.

The spot color is converted to and merged with the color channels. The spot channel is deleted from the palette.

Merging spot channels flattens layered images. The merged composite reflects the preview spot color information, including the Solidity settings. For example, a spot channel with a solidity of 50% will produce different merged results than the same channel with a solidity of 100%.

In addition, the resulting merged spot channels usually don't reproduce the same colors as the original spot channels, because CMYK inks can't represent the range of colors available from spot color inks.

Adjusting overlapping spot colors

To prevent overlapping spot colors from either printing over or knocking out the underlying spot color, remove one of the spot colors where they overlap.

Use a printed sample of the overprinted inks to adjust your screen display to help you predict how colors will look when printed.

Note: In some cases, such as varnish and bump plates, you may want colors to overprint.

To adjust overlapping spot colors:

1 In the Channels palette, select the spot channel with the color you want to print.

2 Choose Select > Load Selection.

💡 *To quickly select an image in a channel, hold down Ctrl (Windows) or Command (Mac OS), and click the channel in the Channels palette.*

3 For Channel, choose the spot channel from step 1, and click OK.

4 To create a trap when knocking out the underlying color, choose Select > Modify > Expand or Contract, depending on whether the overlapping spot color is darker or lighter than the spot color beneath it. For more information on trapping, see "Creating color traps" on page 390.

5 In the Channels palette, select the underlying spot channel that contains areas you want to knock out. Press Backspace (Windows) or Delete (Mac OS).

💡 *This method can be used to knock out areas from any channels under a spot color, such as the CMYK channels.*

6 If a spot color in one channel overlaps more than one other spot color, repeat this process for each channel that contains areas you want removed.

Using channel calculations to blend layers and channels (Photoshop)

You can use the blending effects associated with layers to combine channels within and between images into new images using the Apply Image command (on single and composite channels) and the Calculations command (on single channels). These commands offer two additional blending modes not available in the Layers palette—Add and Subtract. Although it's possible to create new combinations of channels by copying channels into layers in the Layers palette, you may find it quicker to use the calculation commands to blend channel information.

The calculation commands perform mathematical operations on the corresponding pixels of two channels (the pixels with identical locations on the image) and then combine the results in a single channel. Two concepts are fundamental to understanding how the calculation commands work.

- Each pixel in a channel has a brightness value from 0 (off or black) to 255 (on or white). The Calculations and Apply Image commands manipulate these values to produce the resulting composite pixels.

- These commands overlay the pixels in two or more channels. Thus, the images used for calculations must have the same pixel dimensions. (See "Changing image size and resolution" on page 57 for information on adjusting an image's pixel dimensions.)

Using the Apply Image command

The Apply Image command lets you blend one image's layer and channel (the *source*) with a layer and channel of the active image (the *destination*).

To use the Apply Image command:

1 Open the source and destination images, and select the desired layer and channel in the destination image. The pixel dimensions of the images must match for image names to appear in the Apply Image dialog box.

Note: If the color modes of the two images differ (for example, one image is RGB and the other is CMYK), you can copy a single channel to another channel between images, but you cannot copy a composite channel to a composite channel in another image.

2 Choose Image > Apply Image.

3 Choose the source image, layer, and channel you want to combine with the destination. To use all layers in the source image, select Merged for Layer.

4 Select Preview to preview the results in the image window.

5 Select Invert to use the negative of the channel contents in the calculation.

6 For Blending, choose a blending option.

For information on the Add and Subtract options, see "About the Add and Subtract blending modes" on page 222. For information on other blending options, see "Selecting a blending mode" on page 185.

7 Enter an opacity to specify the effect's strength.

8 Select Preserve Transparency to apply the results only to opaque areas in the result layer.

9 Select Mask if you want to apply the blending through a mask. Then choose the image and layer containing the mask. For Channel, you can choose any color or alpha channel to use as the mask. You can also use a mask based on the active selection or the boundaries of the chosen layer (Transparency). Select Invert to reverse the masked and unmasked areas of the channel. (See "Using channel calculations to blend layers and channels (Photoshop)" on page 220.)

Using the Calculations command

The Calculations command lets you blend two individual channels from one or more source images. You can then apply the results to a new image or to a new channel or selection in the active image. You cannot apply the Calculations command to composite channels.

To use the Calculations command:

1 Open the source image or images.

Note: If you are using more than one source image, the images must have the same pixel dimensions.

2 Choose Image > Calculations.

3 Select Preview to preview the results in the image window.

4 Choose the first source image, layer, and channel. To use all the layers in the source image, choose Merged for Layer.

5 Select Invert to use the negative of the channel contents in the calculation. For Channel, choose Gray to get the same effect as would be obtained by converting the image to a grayscale image.

6 Choose the second source image, layer, and channel, specifying further options as described in step 5.

7 For Blending, choose a blending mode.

For information on the Add and Subtract modes, see "About the Add and Subtract blending modes" on page 222. For information on other blending modes, see "Selecting a blending mode" on page 185.

8 Enter an opacity to specify the effect's strength.

9 Select Mask if you want to apply the blending through a mask. Then choose the image and layer containing the mask. For Channel, you can choose any color or alpha channel to use as the mask. You can also use a mask based on the active selection or the boundaries of the chosen layer (Transparency). Select Invert to reverse the masked and unmasked areas of the channel.

10 For Result, specify whether to place the blending results in a new document, or in a new channel or selection in the active image.

About the Add and Subtract blending modes

The Add and Subtract blending modes are available only for the Apply Image and Calculations commands.

Add Adds the pixel values in two channels. This is a good way to combine nonoverlapping images in two channels.

Because higher pixel values represent lighter colors, adding channels with overlapping pixels lightens the image. Black areas in both channels remain black $(0 + 0 = 0)$. White in either channel results in white $(255 + \text{any value} = 255 \text{ or greater})$.

Add mode divides the sum of the pixel values by the Scale amount and then adds the Offset value to the sum. For example, if you wanted to find the average of the pixels in two channels, you would add them, divide by 2, and enter no Offset value.

The Scale factor may be any number between 1.000 and 2.000. Entering a higher Scale value darkens the image.

The Offset value lets you lighten or darken the pixels in the destination channel by any brightness value between +255 and −255. Negative values darken the image; positive values lighten the image.

Subtract Subtracts the pixel values in the source channel from the corresponding pixels in the target channel. As with Add mode, the result is then divided by the Scale factor and added to the Offset value.

The Scale factor may be any number between 1.000 and 2.000. The Offset value lets you lighten or darken the pixels in the destination channel by any brightness value between +255 and –255.

About masks (Photoshop)

Masks let you isolate and protect areas of an image as you apply color changes, filters, or other effects to the rest of the image. When you select part of an image, the area that is not selected is "masked" or protected from editing. You can also use masks for complex image editing such as gradually applying color or filter effects to an image.

In addition, masks let you save and reuse time-consuming selections as alpha channels. (Alpha channels can be converted to selections and then used for image editing.) Because masks are stored as 8-bit grayscale channels, you can refine and edit them using the full array of painting and editing tools.

When a mask channel is selected in the Channels palette, foreground and background colors appear as grayscale values. (See "Creating temporary masks in Quick Mask mode (Photoshop)" on page 224.)

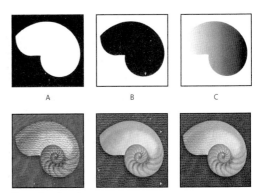

Examples of masks:
A. Opaque mask used to protect the background and color the shell B. Opaque mask used to protect the shell and color the background C. Semitransparent mask used to color the background and part of the shell

In Photoshop, you can create masks, all stored at least temporarily as grayscale channels, in the following ways:

• Quick Mask mode lets you create and view a temporary mask for an image. Temporary masks are useful when you don't want to save the mask for later use. (See "Creating temporary masks in Quick Mask mode (Photoshop)" on page 224.)

• Alpha channels let you save and load a selection to be used as a mask. (See "Storing masks in alpha channels" on page 225.)

• Layer masks and vector masks let you produce a mix of soft and hard masking edges on the same layer. By making changes to the layer mask or the vector masks, you can apply a variety of special effects. (See "Masking layers" on page 259.)

Creating temporary masks in Quick Mask mode (Photoshop)

Quick Mask mode lets you edit any selection as a mask without using the Channels palette and while viewing your image. The advantage of editing your selection as a mask is that you can use almost any Photoshop tool or filter to modify the mask. For example, if you create a rectangular selection with the marquee tool, you can enter Quick Mask mode and use the paintbrush to extend or contract the selection, or you can use a filter to distort the edges of the selection. You can also use selection tools, because the quick mask is not a selection.

Start with a selected area and use Quick Mask mode to add to or subtract from it to make the mask. Alternatively, create the mask entirely in Quick Mask mode. Color differentiates the protected and unprotected areas. When you leave Quick Mask mode, the unprotected areas become a selection.

A temporary Quick Mask channel appears in the Channels palette while you work in Quick Mask mode. However, you do all mask editing in the image window.

To create a temporary mask:

1 Using any selection tool, select the part of the image you want to change.

2 Click the Quick Mask mode button  in the toolbox.

Selected area, and Quick Mask mode applied

A color overlay (similar to a rubylith) covers and protects the area outside the selection. The original selection is left unprotected by this mask. By default, Quick Mask mode colors the protected area using a red, 50% opaque overlay.

3 To edit the mask, select a painting or editing tool from the toolbox, or select a filter or adjustment command from the menu bar. By default, painting with black adds to the mask, shrinking the selection. Painting with white removes areas from the mask, expanding the selection. Painting with gray or another color creates a semitransparent area, useful for feathering or anti-aliased effects.

4 Click the Standard mode button ▣ in the toolbox to turn off the quick mask and return to your original image. A selection border now surrounds the unprotected area of the quick mask.

If a feathered mask is converted to a selection, the boundary line runs halfway between the black pixels and the white pixels of the mask gradient. The selection boundary indicates the pixels transition from being less than 50% selected to more than 50% selected.

5 Apply the desired changes to the image. Changes affect only the selected area.

6 Choose Select > Deselect to deselect the selection, or save the selection.

To change the Quick Mask options:

1 Double-click the Quick Mask mode button ![icon] in the toolbox.

2 Choose from the following display options:

• Masked Areas to have masked areas appear black (opaque) and to have selected areas appear white (transparent). Painting with black increases the masked area; painting with white increases the selected area.

With this option, the Quick Mask button in the toolbox appears as a white circle on a gray background ![icon].

• Selected Areas to have masked areas appear white (transparent) and to have selected areas appear black (opaque). Painting with white increases the masked area; painting with black increases the selected area.

With this option, the Quick Mask button in the toolbox appears as a gray circle on a white background ![icon].

To toggle between the Masked Areas and Selected Areas options for quick masks, Alt-click (Windows) or Option-click (Mac OS) the Quick Mask mode button.

3 To choose a new mask color, click the color box, and choose a new color. (See "Using the Adobe Color Picker" on page 205.)

4 To change the opacity, enter a value between 0% and 100%.

Both the color and opacity settings affect only the appearance of the mask and have no effect on how underlying areas are protected. Changing these settings may make the mask more easily visible against the colors in the image.

You can convert this temporary mask to a permanent alpha channel by switching to standard mode and choosing Select > Save Selection.

Storing masks in alpha channels

In addition to the temporary masks of Quick Mask mode, you can create more permanent masks by storing them in *alpha channels*. This allows you to use the masks again in the same image or in a different image.

You can create an alpha channel in Photoshop and then add a mask to it. You can also save an existing selection in a Photoshop or ImageReady image as an alpha channel that will appear in the Channels palette in Photoshop.

About alpha channels (Photoshop)

An alpha channel has these properties:

• Each image (except 16-bit images) can contain up to 24 channels, including all color and alpha channels.

• All channels are 8-bit grayscale images, capable of displaying 256 levels of gray.

• You can specify a name, color, mask option, and opacity for each channel. (The opacity affects the preview of the channel, not the image.)

- All new channels have the same dimensions and number of pixels as the original image.

- You can edit the mask in an alpha channel using painting tools, editing tools, and filters.

- You can convert alpha channels to spot color channels.

Creating alpha channels (Photoshop)

You can create a new alpha channel and then use painting tools, editing tools, and filters to add the mask to it.

To create an alpha channel using current options:

1 Click the New Channel button ⊡ at the bottom of the Channels palette. The new channel is named according to the sequence in which it was created.

2 Use a painting or editing tool to paint in the image. Paint with black to add to the channel; paint with white to remove from the channel; paint with a lower opacity or a color to add to the channel with lower opacities.

To create an alpha channel and specify options:

1 Do one of the following:

- Alt-click (Windows) or Option-click (Mac OS) the New Channel button ⊡ at the bottom of the palette.

- Choose New Channel from the Channels palette menu.

2 Type a name for the channel.

3 Select display options for the channel, as described in steps 2 through 4 of the procedure for changing Quick Mask options in "Creating temporary masks in Quick Mask mode (Photoshop)" on page 224. Alpha channel options are identical to Quick Mask options.

4 Click OK. A new channel appears at the bottom of the Channels palette and is the only channel visible in the image window.

5 Click the eye icon 👁 next to a color channel or the composite color channel to display the image with a color overlay.

6 Use a painting or editing tool to paint in the image. Paint with black to add to the new channel, paint with white to remove from the new channel, or paint with a lower opacity or a color to add to the new channel with lower opacities.

Saving a mask selection

You can save any selection as a mask in a new or existing alpha channel.

To save a selection to a new channel with default options (Photoshop):

1 Select the area or areas of the image that you want to isolate.

2 Click the Save Selection button ◻ at the bottom of the Channels palette. A new channel appears, named according to the sequence in which it was created.

To save a selection to a new or existing channel:

1 Select the area or areas of the image that you want to isolate.

2 Choose Select > Save Selection.

3 Do the following in the Save Selection dialog box, and click OK:

- (Photoshop) Choose a destination image for the selection in the Document menu. By default, the selection is placed in a channel in your active image. You can choose to save the selection to a channel in another open image with the same pixel dimensions or to a new image.

- Choose a destination channel for the selection from the Channel pop-up menu. By default, the selection is saved in a new channel. You can choose to save the selection to any existing channel in the selected image or to a layer mask if the image contains layers.

- If you're saving the selection as a new channel, enter a name for the channel in the Name text box. In ImageReady, you can change the default channel name if desired.

- If you're saving the selection to an existing channel, select how to combine the selections: Replace Channel to replace the current selection in the channel; Add to Channel to add the selection to the current channel contents; Subtract from Channel to delete the selection from the channel contents; Intersect with Channel to keep the areas of the new selection that intersect with the channel contents.

In Photoshop, you can select the channel in the Channels palette to see the saved selection displayed in grayscale. A selection saved in ImageReady will appear in a new or existing channel in the Photoshop Channels palette.

Modifying alpha channels (Photoshop)

You can edit an alpha channel to add or remove color in it, and you can specify settings for the masking colors and opacity.

See "Managing channels (Photoshop)" on page 213 for information on rearranging, duplicating, or deleting alpha channels.

To edit an alpha channel:

Use a painting or editing tool to paint in the image. Paint with black to add to the channel, paint with white to remove from the channel, or paint with a lower opacity or a color to add to the channel with lower opacities.

To change an alpha channel's options:

1 Do one of the following:

- Select the channel in the Channels palette, and choose Channel Options from the palette menu.

- Double-click the channel thumbnail in the Channels palette.

2 Enter a new name for the channel.

3 Choose display options, as described in steps 2 through 4 of the procedure on Quick Mask options in "Creating temporary masks in Quick Mask mode (Photoshop)" on page 224.

See "Modifying spot channels" on page 219 for information on changing Spot Color channel options.

Note: You cannot modify options for the default color channels.

Loading a selection into an image

You can reuse a previously saved selection by loading it into an image. In Photoshop, you can also load the selection into an image when you have finished modifying an alpha channel.

To load a saved selection using shortcuts (Photoshop):

Do one of the following in the Channels palette:

• Select the alpha channel, click the Load Selection button ○ at the bottom of the palette, and then click the composite color channel near the top of the palette.

• Drag the channel containing the selection you want to load onto the Load Selection button.

• Ctrl-click (Windows) or Command-click (Mac OS) the channel containing the selection you want to load.

• To add the mask to an existing selection, press Ctrl+Shift (Windows) or Command+Shift (Mac OS), and click the channel.

• To subtract the mask from an existing selection, press Ctrl+Alt (Windows) or Command+Option (Mac OS), and click the channel.

• To load the intersection of the saved selection and an existing selection, press Ctrl+Alt+Shift (Windows) or Command+Option+Shift (Mac OS), and select the channel.

To load a saved selection into an image (Photoshop):

1 Choose Select > Load Selection. For Document, the active filename is selected.

2 For Channel, choose the channel containing the selection you want to load.

3 Click Invert to make the nonselected areas selected and vice versa.

4 If the destination image already has a selection, indicate how to combine the selections. (For information on these options, see "Saving a mask selection" on page 226.)

To load a saved selection into an image (ImageReady):

Choose Select > Load Selection, then choose an option from the submenu.

To load a selection from another image (Photoshop):

1 Open the two images you want to use.

Note: The images must have identical pixel dimensions. (See "Changing the pixel dimensions of an image" on page 59.)

2 Make the destination image active, and choose Select > Load Selection.

3 For Document, choose the source image.

4 For Channel, choose the channel containing the selection you want to use as a mask.

5 Click Invert if you want to make the nonselected areas selected and vice versa.

6 If the destination image already has a selection, indicate how to combine the selections. (For information on these options, see "Saving a mask selection" on page 226.)

Chapter 10: Using Layers

Layers allow you to organize your work into distinct levels. You can use layers to composite images and create artistic effects.

About layers

Layers allow you to work on one element of an image without disturbing the others. Think of layers as sheets of acetate stacked one on top of the other. Where there is no image on a layer, you can see through to the layers below. You can change the composition of an image by changing the order and attributes of layers. In addition, special features such as adjustment layers, fill layers, and layer styles let you create sophisticated effects.

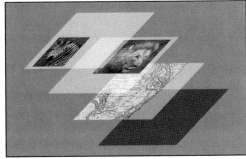

Illustration of how transparent areas on a layer let you see through to the layers below

Using the Layers palette

The Layers palette lists all layers, layer sets, and layer effects in an image. You can accomplish many tasks—such as creating, hiding, displaying, copying, and deleting layers—using the buttons in the Layers palette. You can access additional commands and options in the Layers palette menu and the Layers menu.

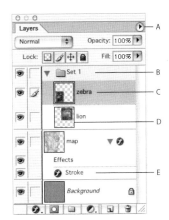

Photoshop Layers palette:
A. Layers palette menu B. Layer set C. Layer
D. Layer thumbnail E. Layer effect

Displaying the Layers palette Choose Window > Layers.

Using the Layers palette menu Click the triangle ⊙ in the upper right corner of the palette to access commands for working with layers.

Changing the size of layer thumbnails Choose Palette Options from the Layers palette menu, and select a thumbnail size.

Turn off thumbnails to improve performance and save monitor space.

Expanding and collapsing layer sets Click the triangle to the left of a layer set folder. In Photoshop, press Alt (Windows) or Option (Mac OS) when clicking the triangle to expand or collapse all effects applied to layers contained within the set. In ImageReady, press Alt (Windows) or Option (Mac OS) when clicking the triangle to expand or collapse all sets.

Creating layers and layer sets

A new image in Photoshop or ImageReady has a single layer. The number of additional layers, layer sets, and layer effects you can add to an image is limited only by your computer's memory.

About the background layer

When you create a new image with a white background or a colored background, the bottommost image in the Layers palette is *Background*. An image can have only one background. You cannot change the stacking order of a background, its blending mode, or its opacity. However, you can convert a background to a regular layer.

When you create a new image with transparent content, the image does not have a background layer. The bottommost layer is not constrained like the background layer; you can move it anywhere in the Layers palette, and change its opacity and blending mode.

To convert a background into a layer:

1 Double-click Background in the Layers palette, or choose Layer > New > Layer from Background.

2 Set layer options as desired. (See "Adding layers and layer sets" on page 230.)

3 Click OK.

To convert a layer into a background:

1 Select a layer in the Layers palette.

2 Choose Layer > New > Background from Layer.

Note: You cannot create a background by renaming a regular layer Background—you must use the Background from Layer command.

Adding layers and layer sets

You can create empty layers and add content to them, or you can create new layers from existing content. When you create a new layer, it appears either above the selected layer or within the selected layer set in the Layers palette.

Layer sets help you organize and manage layers. You can use layer sets to easily move layers as a group, to apply attributes and masks to groups of layers, and to reduce clutter in the Layers palette. You cannot create a new layer set within an existing layer set.

To add a new layer or layer set using default options:

Click the New Layer button ⬛ or New Layer Set button ⬛ in the Layers palette.

To add a new layer or layer set and specify options:

1 Do one of the following:

- Choose Layer > New > Layer or Layer > New > Layer Set.

- Choose New Layer or New Layer Set from the Layers palette menu.

- Alt-click (Windows) or Option-click (Mac OS) the New Layer button or New Layer Set button in the Layers palette.

- Ctrl-click (Windows) or Command-click (Mac OS) the New Layer button or New Layer Set button in the Layers palette to add a layer below the currently selected layer.

2 Set layer options, click OK:

- Name to specify a name for the layer or layer set. (See "Renaming layers" on page 236.)

- Group with Previous Layer to create a clipping group. This option is not available for layer sets. (See "Creating clipping groups" on page 264.)

- Color to assign a color to the layer or layer set. (See "Color coding layers" on page 237.)

- Mode to specify a blending mode for the layer or layer set. (See "Choosing a blending mode" on page 240.)

- Opacity to specify an opacity for the layer or layer set. (See "Setting layer opacity" on page 240.)

- (Photoshop) Fill with *Mode*-neutral color to fill the layer with a preset, neutral color. (See "Filling new layers with a neutral color" on page 241.)

To convert a selection into a new layer:

1 Make a selection. (See "Making pixel selections" on page 103.)

2 Do one of the following:

- Choose Layer > New > Layer Via Copy to copy the selection into a new layer.

- Choose Layer > New > Layer Via Cut to cut the selection and paste it into a new layer.

To create a new layer set from linked layers:

Choose Layer > New > Layer Set from Linked. (See "Linking layers" on page 234.)

Working with layered images

There are many advantages to working with layered images. You can quickly select, hide, duplicate, lock, and change the appearance of images using layers.

Selecting layers

If an image has multiple layers, you must choose which layer you want to work on. Any changes you make to the image affect only the *active* layer. You select a layer to make it active, and only one layer can be active at a time. The name of the active layer appears in the title bar of the document window, and a paintbrush icon appears next to the layer in the Layers palette.

If you don't see the desired results when using a tool or applying a command, you may not have the correct layer selected. Check the Layers palette to make sure that you're working on the desired layer.

To select a layer:

Do one of the following:

- Click a layer in the Layers palette.

- Select the move tool, right-click (Windows) or Control-click (Mac OS) in the image, and choose a layer from the context menu. The context menu lists all the layers that contain pixels under the current pointer location.

You can also select layers interactively as you use the move tool. If Auto Select Layer is selected in the Move tool options, the topmost layer containing pixels under the cursor will be selected. (See "Moving selections and layers within an image" on page 113.)

Displaying the contents of layers

You can use the Layers palette to selectively hide and display the contents of layers, layer sets, and layer effects. You can also specify how transparent areas are displayed in the image.

To change the visibility of a layer, layer set, or layer effect:

Do one of the following:

- In the Layers palette, click the eye icon 👁 next to a layer, layer set, or layer effect to hide its content in the document window. Click in the column again to redisplay the content.

- Alt-click (Windows) or Option-click (Mac OS) an eye icon to display only the content for that layer or layer set. Alt/Option-click in the eye column again to redisplay all content.

- Drag through the eye column to change the visibility of multiple items in the Layers palette.

Note: Only visible layers are printed.

To change the display of transparency:

1 Do one of the following:

- (Photoshop) In Windows and Mac OS 9.x, choose Edit > Preferences > Transparency & Gamut; in Mac OS X, choose Photoshop > Preferences > Transparency & Gamut.

- (ImageReady) In Windows and Mac OS 9.x, choose Edit > Preference > Transparency; in Mac OS X, choose ImageReady > Preferences > Transparency.

2 Choose a size and color for the transparency checkerboard, or choose None for Grid Size to hide the transparency checkerboard.

3 (Photoshop) Select Use Video Alpha to enable Photoshop to send transparency information to your computer's video board. This option requires hardware support—make sure that your computer's video board allows images to be overlaid on top of a live video signal.

4 Click OK.

Duplicating layers

Duplicating layers is an easy way to copy content within an image or between images. When duplicating layers between images, keep in mind that the layer's content will appear smaller or larger if it is copied to a file with different resolution. (See "About image size and resolution" on page 54.)

To duplicate a layer or layer set within an image:

1 Select a layer or layer set in the Layers palette.

2 Do one of the following:

• Drag the layer to the New Layer button ⬛ , or drag the layer set to the New Layer Set button ⬛ .

• Choose Duplicate Layer or Duplicate Layer Set from the Layers menu or the Layers palette menu. In Photoshop, enter a name for the layer or layer set, and click OK.

• (Photoshop) Press Alt (Windows) or Option (Mac OS), and drag the layer or layer set to the New Layer button or the New Layer Set button. Enter a name for the layer or layer set, and click OK.

To duplicate a layer or layer set between images:

1 Open the source and destination images.

2 In the Layers palette of the source image, select a layer or layer set.

3 Do one of the following:

• Drag the layer or layer set from the Layers palette into the destination image.

• Select the move tool ▸⊕ , and drag from the source image to the destination image. The duplicate layer or layer set appears above the active layer in the Layers palette of the destination image. Shift-drag to position the image content in the same location it occupied in the source image (if the source and destination images have the same pixel dimensions) or at the center of the document window (if the source and destination images have different pixel dimensions).

• (Photoshop) Choose Duplicate Layer or Duplicate Layer Set from the Layers menu or the Layers palette menu. Choose the destination document from the Document pop-up menu, and click OK.

• Choose Select > All to select all of the pixels on the layer, and choose Edit > Copy. Then choose Edit > Paste in the destination image.

To create a new document from a layer or layer set (Photoshop):

1 Select a layer or layer set in the Layers palette.

2 Choose Duplicate Layer or Duplicate Layer Set from the Layers menu or the Layers palette menu.

3 Choose New from the document pop-up menu, and click OK.

Changing the stacking order of layers

The stacking order in the Layers palette determines whether the content of a layer or layer set appears in front of or behind other elements in the image.

To change the order of layers and layer sets:

Do one of the following:

• Drag the layer or layer set up or down in the Layers palette. Release the mouse button when the highlighted line appears where you want to place the layer or layer set.

- To move a layer into a layer set, drag a layer to the layer set folder ▣ . The layer is placed at the bottom of the layer set.

- Select a layer or layer set, choose Layer > Arrange, and choose a command from the submenu. If the selected item is in a layer set, the command applies to the stacking order within the layer set. If the selected item is not in a layer set, the command applies to the stacking order within the Layers palette.

Note: *By definition, the background layer is always at the bottom of the stacking order. Therefore, the Send to Back command places the selected item directly above the background layer. (See "About the background layer" on page 230.)*

Linking layers

By linking two or more layers or layer sets, you can move their contents together. You can also copy, paste, align, merge, apply transformations to, and create clipping groups from linked layers.

To link layers:

1 Select a layer or layer set in the Layers palette.

2 Click in the column immediately to the left of any layers you want to link to the selected layer. A link icon ▣ appears in the column.

To unlink layers:

In the Layers palette, click the link icons to remove them.

Repositioning the contents of layers

You can reposition the contents of layers and layer sets using the move tool. (See "Moving selections and layers within an image" on page 113.) You can also align and distribute the contents of layers using commands in the Layers menu.

Note: *The align and distribute commands affect only those layers that contain pixels of greater than 50% opacity.*

To align the contents of layers:

1 Do one of the following:

- To align the content of a layer to a selection border, make a selection in the image. Then select a layer in the Layers palette.

- To align the contents of multiple layers to a selection border, make a selection in the image. Then link together the layers you want to align in the Layers palette. (See "Linking layers" on page 234.)

- To align the contents of layers to the content of the active layer, link the layers you want to align to the active layer. (See "Linking layers" on page 234.)

2 Choose Layer > Align Linked or Layer > Align To Selection, and choose a command from the submenu:

- Top Edges to align the top pixel on the linked layers to the top pixel on the active layer or the top edge of the selection border.

- Vertical Centers to align the vertical center pixel on the linked layers to the vertical center pixel on the active layer or the vertical center of the selection border.

- Bottom Edges to align the bottom pixel on the linked layers to the bottom pixel on the active layer or the bottom edge of the selection border.

- Left Edges to align the left pixel on the linked layers to the left pixel on the active layer or the left edge of the selection border.

- Horizontal Centers to align the horizontal center pixel on the linked layers to the horizontal center pixel on the active layer or the horizontal center of the selection border.

- Right Edges to align the right pixel on the linked layers to the right pixel on the active layer or the right edge of the selection border.

To distribute layers:

1 In the Layers palette, link three or more layers. (See "Linking layers" on page 234.)

2 Choose Layer > Distribute Linked, and choose an option from the submenu:

- Top Edges to space the linked layers evenly starting from the top pixel on each layer.

- Vertical Centers to space the linked layers evenly starting from the vertical center pixel on each layer.

- Bottom Edges to space the linked layers evenly starting from the bottom pixel on each layer.

- Left Edges to space the linked layers evenly starting from the left pixel on each layer.

- Horizontal Centers to space the linked layers evenly starting from the horizontal center pixel on each layer.

- Right Edges to space the linked layers evenly starting from the right pixel on each layer.

Locking layers

You can fully or partially lock layers to protect their contents. When a layer is locked, a lock icon displays to the right of the layer name. The lock icon is solid when the layer is fully locked; it is hollow when the layer is partially locked.

To lock all properties of a layer or layer set:

1 Select a layer or layer set.

2 Do one of the following:

- Click the Lock All 🔒 option in the Layers palette.

- (ImageReady) Choose Layer Options from the Layers palette menu, and select the Lock All option.

Note: When a layer in a locked layer set has individual lock options applied to it, the lock icon is dimmed 🔒 .

To partially lock a layer:

1 Select a layer.

2 Click one or more lock options in the Layers palette. In ImageReady, you can also choose Layer Options from the Layers palette menu, and select one or more lock options:

- Lock Transparency ▨ to confine editing to the opaque portions of the layer. This option is equivalent to the Preserve Transparency option in earlier versions of Photoshop.

- Lock Image 🖌 to prevent modification of the layer's pixels using the painting tools.

- Lock Position ✛ to prevent the layer's pixels from being moved.

Note: For type layers, Lock Transparency and Lock Image are selected by default and cannot be deselected.

To apply lock options to all linked layers or all layers in a layer set:

1 Select a linked layer or a layer set.

2 Choose Lock All Linked Layers or Lock All Layers in Set from the Layers menu or the Layers palette menu.

3 Select lock options, and click OK.

Unifying layers (ImageReady)

The unify buttons in the Layers palette determine how the changes you make to a layer in the active rollover state or animation frame apply to the other states in a rollover or frames in an animation. When a unify button is selected, changes apply to all states and frames; when a button is deselected, changes apply to only the active state or frame. (See "Unifying and matching layers rollovers and animations" on page 314.)

Sampling from layers

The default behavior of the magic wand, smudge, blur, sharpen, paint bucket, clone stamp tool, and healing brush tool is to sample color only from pixels on the active layer. This means you can smudge or sample in a single layer even when other layers are visible, and you can sample from one layer and paint in another one.

Alternatively, you can choose to paint using sampled data from all visible layers. For example, you can use the clone stamp tool to clone an area containing pixels from all the visible layers.

To sample from all visible layers:

1 Select the magic wand tool ✎ , smudge tool 💧 , blur tool ◌ , sharpen tool △, paint bucket tool ◌ , clone stamp tool 🎯 , or healing brush tool ✐ .

2 In the options bar, select Use All Layers.

Note: When you are using tools that sample image data, painting or editing in a new layer where there are no pixels produces the best results when Use All Layers is selected.

Managing layers

After you add layers to an image, you can use the Layers palette to manage them.

Renaming layers

As you add layers to an image, it's helpful to rename layers based on their content. Using descriptive layer names allows you to easily identify layers in the Layers palette.

To rename a layer or layer set:

1 Do one of the following:

• Double-click the layer or layer set's name in the Layers palette, and enter a new name.

- Press Alt (Windows) or Option (Mac OS), and double-click the layer or layer set's name in the Layers palette. Enter a new name in the Name text box, and click OK.

- (Photoshop) Select a layer or layer set, and choose Layer Properties or Layer Set Properties from the Layers menu or the Layers palette menu. Enter a new name in the Name text box, and click OK.

- (ImageReady) Select a layer or layer set, and choose Layer Options or Layer Set Options from the Layers menu or the Layers palette menu. Enter a new name in the Name text box, and click OK.

- (ImageReady) Select a layer or layer set, and choose Window > Layer Options/Style. Enter a new name in the Name text box.

Color coding layers

Color coding layers and layer sets makes it easier to locate related layers in the Layers palette.

To assign a color to a layer or layer set:

1 Do one of the following:

- Press Alt (Windows) or Option (Mac OS), and double-click the layer or layer set's name in the Layers palette.

- (Photoshop) Select a layer or layer set, and choose Layer Properties or Layer Set Properties from the Layers menu or the Layers palette menu.

- (ImageReady) Select a layer or layer set, and choose Layer Options or Layer Set Options from the Layers menu or the Layers palette menu.

2 Choose a color from the Color pop-up menu, and click OK.

Rasterizing layers

You cannot use the painting tools or filters on layers that contain vector data (such as type layers, shape layers, and vector masks) and generated data (such as fill layers). However, you can rasterize these layers to convert their contents into a flat, raster image.

To rasterize a single layer:

1 Select the layer you want to rasterize.

2 Choose Layer > Rasterize, and choose an option from the submenu.

To rasterize multiple layers:

Do one of the following:

- Link the layers you want to rasterize, and choose Layer > Rasterize > Linked Layers. (See "Linking layers" on page 234.)

- To rasterize all layers that contain vector and generated data, choose Layer > Rasterize > All Layers.

Deleting layers

Deleting layers that you no longer need reduces the size of your image file.

To delete a layer or layer set:

1 Select a layer or layer set in the Layers palette.

2 Do one of the following:

• To delete the layer or layer set without confirmation, drag it to the Trash button or Alt-click (Windows) or Option-click (Mac OS) the Trash button.

• To delete the layer or layer set with confirmation, click the Trash button. Alternately, choose Delete Layer or Delete Layer Set from the Layers menu or the Layers palette menu.

To delete linked layers (Photoshop):

Do one of the following:

• To delete the linked layers with confirmation, choose Delete Linked Layers from the Layers menu or the Layers palette menu. Alternately, Ctrl-click (Windows) or Command-click (Mac OS) the Trash button.

• To delete the linked layers without confirmation, Ctrl-Alt-click (Windows) or Command-Option-click (Mac OS) the Trash button.

To delete hidden layers (Photoshop):

Choose Delete Hidden Layers from the Layers menu or the Layers palette menu.

Merging layers

When you have finalized the content of layers, you can merge them to create partial versions of your composite image. The intersection of all transparent areas in the merged layers remains transparent. Merging layers helps manage the size of image files.

Note: You cannot use an adjustment layer or fill layer as the target layer for a merge. (See "Merging adjustment layers or fill layers" on page 259.)

In addition to merging layers, you can stamp layers. Stamping allows you to merge the contents of more than one layer into a target layer while leaving the other layers intact. Typically, the selected layer will stamp down to the layer below it.

To merge two layers or layer sets:

1 Position the layers or layer sets you want to merge next to each other in the Layers palette, and make sure that the visibility for both items is enabled.

2 Select the top item in the pair.

3 Do one of the following:

• If the top item is a layer, choose Merge Down from the Layers menu or the Layers palette menu.

• If the top item is a layer set, choose Merge Layer Set from the Layers menu or the Layers palette menu.

To merge a clipping group:

1 Hide any layers you do not want to merge.

2 Select the base layer in the group.

3 Choose Merge Group from the Layers menu or the Layers palette menu.

To merge all visible linked layers:

Choose Merge Linked from the Layers palette or the Layers palette menu.

To merge all the visible layers and layer sets in an image:

Choose Merge Visible from the Layers palette or the Layers palette menu.

To create a new layer from all visible layers, while keeping the original layers intact:

Hold down Alt (Windows) or Option (Mac OS), and choose Layer > Merge Visible.

To stamp layers:

1 Position the layer you want to stamp to above the layer you want to stamp from, and make sure that the visibility for both items is enabled.

2 Select the top item in the pair.

3 Press Ctrl+Alt+E (Windows) or Command+Option+E (Mac OS).

The selected layer is stamped with the contents of the other layer.

To stamp linked layers:

Select one of the linked layers, and press Ctrl+Alt+E (Windows) or Command+Option+E (Mac OS). The selected layer is stamped with the contents from the other linked layers.

To stamp all visible layers:

Select the layer or layer set that you want to contain the new contents, and press Shift+Ctrl+Alt+E (Windows) or Shift+Command+Option+E (Mac OS).

Flattening all layers

In a flattened image, all visible layers are merged into the background, which greatly reduces the file size. Flattening an image discards all hidden layers and fills the remaining transparent areas with white. In most cases, you won't want to flatten a file until you have finished editing the individual layers.

Note: Converting an image between some color modes flattens the file. Be sure to save a copy of your file that includes all layers if you want to edit the original image after the conversion.

To flatten an image:

1 Make sure that all the layers you want to keep are visible.

2 Choose Layer > Flatten Image, or choose Flatten Image from the Layers palette menu.

Tracking file size

File size depends on the pixel dimensions of an image and the number of layers contained in the image. Images with more pixels may produce more detail when printed, but they require more disk space to store and may be slower to edit and print. You should keep track of your file sizes to make sure the files are not becoming too large for your purposes. If the file is becoming too large, reduce the number of layers in the image or change the image size.

You can view file size information for an image at the bottom of the application window (Windows) or document window (Mac OS). For more information, see "Displaying file and image information" on page 42.

Setting opacity and blending options

A layer's opacity and blending options determine how its pixels interact with pixels on other layers.

Setting layer opacity

A layer's opacity determines to what degree it obscures or reveals the layer beneath it. A layer with 1% opacity appears nearly transparent, while one with 100% opacity appears completely opaque.

To specify opacity for a layer or layer set:

1 Select a layer or layer set in the Layers palette.

Note: You cannot change the opacity of a background layer or a locked layer.

2 Do one of the following:

• In the Layers palette, enter a value in the Opacity text box or drag the Opacity pop-up slider.

• (Photoshop) Double-click a layer thumbnail, choose Layer > Layer Style > Blending Options, or choose Blending Options from the Layers palette menu. Enter a value in the Opacity text box or drag the Opacity pop-up slider.

Note: To view blending options for a text layer in Photoshop, choose Layer > Layer Style > Blending Options, or choose Blending Options from the Layers palette menu.

• (ImageReady) Double-click a layer thumbnail, and enter a value in the Opacity text box or drag the Opacity pop-up slider.

Choosing a blending mode

A layer's blending mode determines how its pixels blend with underlying pixels in the image. You can create a variety of special effects using blending modes.

By default, the blending mode of a layer set is Pass Through, which means that the layer set has no blending properties of its own. When you choose a different blending mode for a layer set, you effectively change the order in which the entire image is composited. All of the layers in the layer set are composited first. The composited layer set is then treated as a single image, and blended with the rest of the image using the selected blending mode. Thus, if you choose a blending mode other than Pass Through for the layer set, none of the adjustment layers or layer blending modes inside the layer set will apply to layers outside the set.

For a description of each blending mode, see "Selecting a blending mode" on page 185.

Note: *There is no Clear blending mode for layers. In addition, the Color Dodge, Color Burn, Darken, Lighten, Difference, and Exclusion modes are unavailable for Lab images.*

To specify a blending mode for a layer or layer set:

1 Select a layer or layer set in the Layers palette.

2 Choose a blending mode:

- In the Layers palette, choose an option from the Blend Mode pop-up menu.

- (Photoshop) Double-click a layer thumbnail, choose Layer > Layer Style > Blending Options, or choose Blending Options from the Layers palette menu. Choose an option from the Blend Mode pop-up menu.

Note: *To view blending options for a text layer in Photoshop, choose Layer > Layer Style > Blending Options, or choose Blending Options from the Layers palette menu.*

- (ImageReady) Double-click a layer thumbnail, and choose an option from the Blend Mode pop-up menu.

Filling new layers with a neutral color

Some filters (such as the Lighting Effects filter) cannot be applied to layers with no pixels. Selecting Fill with *Mode*-neutral color in the New Layer dialog box resolves this problem by first filling the layer with a preset, neutral color. The neutral color is assigned based on the layer's blending mode and is invisible. If no effect is applied, filling with a neutral color has no effect on the remaining layers. The Fill with Neutral Color option is not available for layers that use the Normal, Dissolve, Hue, Saturation, Color, or Luminosity modes.

Specifying fill opacity

In addition to setting opacity for a layer, which affects any layer styles and blending modes applied to the layer, you can specify a fill opacity for layers. Fill opacity affects pixels painted in a layer or shapes drawn on a layer without affecting the opacity of any layer effects that have been applied to the layer.

To specify fill opacity for a layer:

Do one of the following:

- (Photoshop) In the Layers palette, enter a value in the Fill Opacity text box or drag the Fill Opacity pop-up slider.

- (Photoshop) Double-click a layer thumbnail, choose Layer > Layer Style > Blending Options, or choose Blending Options from the Layers palette menu. Enter a value in the Fill Opacity text box.

Note: *To view blending options for a text layer in Photoshop, choose Layer > Layer Style > Blending Options, or choose Blending Options from the Layers palette menu.*

- (ImageReady) Choose Window > Layer Options/Style, and enter a value in the Fill Opacity text box. If the Fill Opacity text box is not showing, choose Show Options from the Layer Options palette menu or click the Show Options button ⬍ on the palette's tab.

Specifying knockout options

Knockout options let you specify which layers "punch through" to reveal content from other layers. For example, you can use a text layer to knock out a color adjustment layer and reveal a portion of the image using the original colors.

To create a knockout effect, you need to decide which layer will create the shape of the knockout, which layers will be punched through, and which layer will be revealed. If you want to reveal a layer other than the *Background*, you can place the layers you want to use in a layer set or clipping group.

Africa text with shallow knockout to lion layer

To create a knockout:

1 Do one of the following in the Layers palette:

- Place layer that will create the knockout above the layers that will be punched through, and make the layer you want to reveal the *Background*. (Choose Layer > New > Background from Layer to convert a regular layer to the *Background*.)

- Place the layers you want to use in a layer set. The top layer in the set will punch through to the bottom layer in the set or the *Background*. If you want to reveal the *Background*, make sure the blending mode of the layer set is set to Pass Through (the default).

- Place the layers you want to use in a clipping group. The top layer in the group will punch through to the bottom layer in the group or the *Background*. (See "Creating clipping groups" on page 264.) If you want to reveal the bottom layer in the group, make sure the Blend Clipped Layers as Group option for the bottom layer is selected. (See "Grouping blend effects" on page 243.)

2 Select the top layer (the layer that will create the the knockout).

3 Do one of the following:

- (Photoshop) Double-click a layer thumbnail, choose Layer > Layer Style > Blending Options, or choose Blending Options from the Layers palette menu.

Note: To view blending options for a text layer, choose Layer > Layer Style > Blending Options, or choose Blending Options from the Layers palette menu.

• (ImageReady) Choose Window > Layer Options/Style. In the Layer Options palette, if the advanced options are not showing, choose Show Options from the palette menu or click the Show Options button ◆ to view all of the options.

4 Choose an option from the Knockout pop-up menu:

• Shallow to knock out to the first possible stopping point such as the bottom of the layer set or clipping group containing the knockout option.

• Deep to knock out to the *Background*. If there is no *Background*, Deep knocks out to transparency.

5 Lower the fill opacity or change the blending mode to create the knockout effect. (See "Specifying fill opacity" on page 241 and "Choosing a blending mode" on page 240.)

6 Click OK.

Restricting blending to channels (Photoshop)

You can restrict blending effects to a specified channel when blending a layer or layer set. By default, all channels are included when blending a layer or layer set. The channel selections vary based on the type of image you are editing. For example, if you are editing a RGB image, the channel choices are R, G, and B. If you are editing a CMYK image, the channel choices are C, M, Y, and K. (See "About color channels" on page 84.)

When using an RGB image, for example, you can choose to exclude the Red channel from blending; in the composite image, only information contained in the Green and Blue channels are affected.

To exclude channels from blending:

1 Double-click a layer thumbnail, choose Layer > Layer Style > Blending Options, or choose Blending Options from the Layers palette menu.

Note: To view blending options for a text layer, choose Layer > Layer Style > Blending Options, or choose Blending Options from the Layers palette menu.

2 In the Advanced Blending section of the Layer Style dialog box, deselect any channels you do not want to include when the layer is blended.

Grouping blend effects

By default, layers in a clipping group are blended with the underlying layers using the blending mode of the bottommost layer in the group. However, you can choose to have the blending mode of the bottommost layer apply only to that layer, allowing you to maintain the original blending appearance of the clipped layers. (See "Creating clipping groups" on page 264.)

You can also apply the blending mode of a layer to layer effects that modify opaque pixels, such as Inner Glow or Color Overlay, without changing layer effects that modify only transparent pixels, such as Outer Glow or Drop Shadow.

To specify the scope of blending options:

1 Select the layer that you want to affect.

2 Do one of the following:

• (Photoshop) Double-click a layer thumbnail, choose Layer > Layer Style > Blending Options, or choose Blending Options from the Layers palette menu.

Note: To view blending options for a text layer, choose Layer > Layer Style > Blending Options, or choose Blending Options from the Layers palette menu.

• (ImageReady) Choose Window > Layer Options/Style to display the Layer Options palette. If advanced options are not showing in the Layer Options palette, choose Show Options from the palette menu, or click the Show Options button ⬍ .

3 Specify the scope of blending options:

• Select Blend Interior Effects as Group to apply the blending mode of the layer to layer effects that modify opaque pixels, such as Inner Glow, Satin, Color Overlay, and Gradient Overlay.

Blend Interior Effects as Group option deselected, and selected

• Select Blend Clipped Layers as Group to apply the blending mode of the base layer to all layers in the clipping group. Deselecting this option, which is always selected by default, maintains the original blending mode and appearance of each layer in the group.

Blend Clipped Layers as Group option deselected, and selected

• Select Transparency Shapes Layers to restrict layer effects and knockouts to opaque areas of the layer. Deselecting this option, which is always selected by default, applies these effects throughout the layer.

• Select Layer Mask Hides Effects to restrict layer effects to the area defined by the layer mask.

• Select Vector Mask Hides Effects to restrict layer effects to the area defined by the vector mask.

4 (Photoshop) Click OK.

Specifying a range for blending layers (Photoshop)

The sliders in the Blending Options dialog box let you control which pixels from the active layer and which pixels from the underlying visible layers appear in the final image. For example, you can drop dark pixels out of the active layer or force bright pixels from the underlying layers to show through. You can also define a range of partially blended pixels to produce a smooth transition between blended and unblended areas.

To define a range for the blending operation:

1 Double-click a layer thumbnail, choose Layer > Layer Style > Blending Options, or choose Blending Options from the Layers palette menu.

Note: *To view blending options for a text layer, choose Layer > Layer Style > Blending Options, or choose Blending Options from the Layers palette menu.*

2 In the Advanced Blending section of the Layer Style dialog box, choose an option from the Blend If pop-up menu.

- Gray to specify a blending range for all channels.

- An individual color channel (for example, red, green, or blue in an RGB image) to specify blending in that channel. (See "About color channels" on page 84.)

3 Use the This Layer and Underlying Layer sliders to set the brightness range of the blended pixels— measured on a scale from 0 (black) to 255 (white). Drag the white slider to set the high value of the range. Drag the black slider to set the low value of the range.

To define a range of partially blended pixels, hold down Alt (Windows) or Option (Mac OS), and drag one half of a slider triangle. The two values that appear above the divided slider indicate the partial blending range.

Keep the following guidelines in mind when specifying blending ranges:

- Use the This Layer sliders to specify the range of pixels on the active layer that will blend, and therefore, appear in the final image. For example, if you drag the white slider to 235, pixels with brightness values higher than 235 will remain unblended and will be excluded from the final image.

- Use the Underlying Layer sliders to specify the range of pixels in the underlying visible layers that will blend in the final image. Blended pixels are combined with pixels in the active layer to produce composite pixels, while unblended pixels show through overlying areas of the active layer. For example, if you drag the black slider to 19, pixels with brightness values lower than 19 will remain unblended and will show through the active layer in the final image.

Using layer effects and styles

Layer styles let you quickly apply effects to a layer's content. You can scan through a variety of predefined layer styles and apply a style with just a click of the mouse, or you can create a custom style by applying multiple effects to a layer.

About layer effects and styles

Photoshop and ImageReady provide a variety of effects—such as shadows, glows, bevels, overlays, and strokes—that let you quickly change the appearance of a layer's contents. Layer effects are linked to the layer contents. When you move or edit the contents of the layer, the effects are modified correspondingly. For example, if you apply a drop shadow effect to a text layer, the shadow will change automatically when you edit the text.

The effects that you apply to a layer become part of the layer's custom *style*. When a layer has a style, an "f" icon ⓕ appears to the right of the layer's name in the Layers palette. You can expand the style in the Layers palette to view all the effects that comprise the style and edit the effects to change the style.

When you save a custom style, it becomes a preset style. Preset styles appear in the Styles palette and can be applied with just a click of the mouse. Photoshop and ImageReady provide a variety of preset styles to fill a wide range of uses.

Illustration of a layer without a style

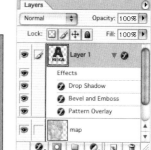

Illustration of a layer with a style

Note: *You cannot apply layer effects and styles to a background, a locked layer, or to a layer set.*

Applying preset styles

The Styles palette, Layer Styles dialog box (Photoshop), and Layer Styles pop-up palette in the options bar for the pen and shape tool let you view and select preset layer styles. By default, applying a preset style replaces the current layer style. However, you can add the attributes of a second style to those of the current style using a keyboard modifier.

The layer styles that come with Photoshop and ImageReady are grouped into libraries by function. For example, one library contains styles for creating Web buttons; another library contains styles adding effects to text.

To display the Styles palette:

Choose Window > Styles.

To apply a preset style to a layer:

Do one of the following:

- Click a style in the Styles palette to apply it to the currently selected layer.

- Drag a style from the Styles palette onto a layer in the Layers palette.

- Drag a style from the Styles palette to the document window, and release the mouse button when the pointer is over the layer content to which you want to apply the style.

Note: Hold down Shift while clicking or dragging to add the style to (instead of replace) any existing effects on the destination layer.

- (Photoshop) Double-click a layer thumbnail in the Layers palette, and click on the word *Styles* in the Layer Styles dialog box (top item in the list on the left side of the dialog box). Click the style you want to apply, and click OK.

- When using a shape or pen tool, select a style from the pop-up palette in the options bar before drawing the shape.

To load a library of preset styles:

1 Click the triangle ⊙ in the Styles palette, Layer Style dialog box (Photoshop), or Layer Style pop-up palette in the options bar (Photoshop).

2 Do one of the following:

- Choose Load Styles (Photoshop) or Append Styles (ImageReady) to add a library to the current list. Then select the library file you want to use, and click Load.

- Choose Replace Styles to replace the current list with a different library. Then select the library file you want to use, and click Load.

- Choose a library file (displayed at the bottom of the palette menu). Then click OK to replace the current list, or click Append to append the current list.

Note: You can also use the Preset Manager to load and reset style libraries. For more information, see "Managing libraries with the Preset Manager (Photoshop)" on page 49.

To return to the default library of preset styles:

1 Click the triangle ⊙ in the Styles palette, Layer Styles dialog box (Photoshop), or Layer Styles pop-up palette in the options bar (Photoshop).

2 Choose Reset Styles. You can either replace the current list or append the default library to the current list.

To change how preset styles are displayed:

1 Click the triangle ⊙ in the Styles palette, Layer Styles dialog box (Photoshop), or Layer Styles pop-up palette in the options bar (Photoshop).

2 Choose a display option from the palette menu:

- (Photoshop) Select Text Only to view the layer styles as a list.

- Select Small or Large Thumbnail to view the layer styles as thumbnails.

- Select Small or (Photoshop) Large List to view the layer styles as a list, with a thumbnail of the selected layer style displayed.

Creating custom styles

You can create custom style using one or more of the following effects:

Drop Shadow Adds a shadow that falls behind the contents on the layer.

Inner Shadow Adds a shadow that falls just inside the edges of the layer's content, giving the layer a recessed appearance.

Outer Glow and Inner Glow Add glows that emanate from the outside or inside edges of the layer's content.

Bevel and Emboss Adds various combinations of highlights and shadows to a layer.

Satin Applies shading to the interior of a layer that reacts to the shape of the layer, typically creating a satiny finish.

Color, Gradient, and Pattern Overlay Fills the layer's content with a color, gradient, or pattern.

Stroke Outlines the object on the current layer using color, a gradient, or a pattern. It is particularly useful on hard-edged shapes such as type.

To apply a custom style to a layer:

1 Do one of the following:

- Click the Layer Styles button ⊘ in the Layers palette and choose an effect from the list.

- Choose an effect from the Layer > Layer Style submenu.

- (Photoshop) Double-click a layer thumbnail in the Layers palette, and select an effect on the left side of the dialog box.

2 Set effect options in the Layer Style dialog box (Photoshop) or the context-sensitive Layer Options/Style palette (ImageReady). (See "Editing styles" on page 249.)

3 To add additional effects to the style, do one of the following:

- Repeat steps 1 and 2.

- (Photoshop) Select additional effects in the Layer Style dialog box. Click the check box to the left of the effect name to add the effect without selecting it.

Displaying layer styles

When a layer has a style, an "f" icon ⊘ appears to the right of the layer's name in the Layers palette. You can show or hide the style's effects in the image and in the Layers palette.

To hide or show all layer styles in an image:

Choose Layer > Layer Style > Hide All Layer Effects or Show All Layer Effects.

To expand or collapse layer styles in the Layers palette:

Do one of the following:

- Click the triangle ▷ next to the layer styles icon ⬤ to expand the list of layer effects applied to that layer.

- Click the inverted triangle ▽ to collapse the layer effects.

- To expand or collapse all of the layer styles applied within a layer set, hold Alt (Windows) or Option (Mac OS) and click the triangle or inverted triangle for the set. The layer styles applied to all layers within the layer set expand or collapse correspondingly.

Editing styles

You edit a layer's style by adjusting its effect settings. In Photoshop, effect settings appear in the Layer Style dialog box. In ImageReady, effect settings appear in the context-sensitive Layer Options/Style palette—the name of the palette changes depending on the effect you select.

Note: ImageReady provides a subset of the effect settings provided by Photoshop.

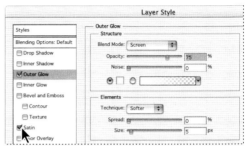

Photoshop Layer Style dialog box. Click a check box to apply the default settings without displaying the effect's options.

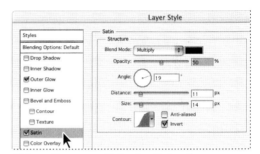

Click an effect name to display the effect's options.

To edit a layer style:

1 Do one of the following:

- In the Layers palette, double-click an effect displayed below the layer name. (Click the inverted triangle ▽ next to the "f" icon ⬤ to display the effects contained in the style.)

- (Photoshop) Double-click a layer thumbnail, and select the effect you want to edit on the left side of the dialog box.

2 Set one or more of the following options in the Layer Style dialog box (Photoshop) or the context-sensitive Layer Options/Style palette (ImageReady). The available options depend on the selected effect:

In Photoshop, you can edit multiple effects without closing the Layer Style dialog box. Select an effect on the left side of the dialog box to display an effect's options.

Angle Determines the lighting angle at which the effect is applied to the layer. In Photoshop, you can drag in the document window to adjust the angle of a Drop Shadow, Inner Shadow, or Satin effect.

Anti-alias Blends the edge pixels of a contour or gloss contour. Most useful on shadows with a small size and complicated contour.

Blend Mode Determines how the layer style blends with the underlying layers, which may or may not include the active layer. For example, an inner shadow blends with the active layer because the effect is drawn on top of that layer, but a drop shadow blends only with the layers beneath the active layer. In most cases, the default mode for each effect produces the best results. (See "Choosing a blending mode" on page 240.)

Choke Shrinks the boundaries of the matte of an Inner Shadow or Inner Glow prior to blurring.

Color Specifies the color of a shadow, glow, or highlight. You can click the color box and choose a color. (See "Using the Adobe Color Picker" on page 205.)

Contour With solid color glows, contour allows you to create rings of transparency. With gradient filled glows, contour allows you to create variations in the repetition of the gradient color and opacity. With bevel and emboss, contour allows you to sculpt the ridges, valleys, and bumps that are shaded in the embossing process. With shadows, allows you to specify the fade. For more information, see "Modifying layer effects with contours (Photoshop)" on page 252.

Distance Specifies the offset distance for a shadow or satin effect. In Photoshop, you can drag in the document window to adjust the offset distance.

Depth Specifies the depth of a bevel and is a ratio of size. It also specifies the depth of a pattern.

Global Angle Turns on global lighting for the effect. Global lighting applies the same angle to all effects with the Global Angle option selected, giving the appearance of a consistent light source shining on the image. (See "Applying global lighting" on page 253.) Deselect Global Angle to assign a local angle to Drop Shadow, Inner Shadow, and Bevel effects.

Gloss Contour Creates a glossy, metal-like appearance and is applied after shading a bevel or emboss.

Gradient Specifies the gradient of a layer effect. In Photoshop, click the gradient to display the Gradient Editor or click the inverted arrow ▾ and choose a gradient from the pop-up palette. In Photoshop, you can edit a gradient or create a new gradient using the Gradient Editor. (See "Creating smooth gradient fills" on page 189.) In ImageReady, click the inverted arrow ▾ next to the gradient sample and select a gradient from the list, or choose a gradient type from the pop-up list. You can edit the color or opacity in the Gradient Overlay panel the same way you do in the Gradient Editor. For some effects, you can specify additional gradient options. Reverse flips the orientation of the gradient, Align With Layer uses the bounding box of the layer to calculate the gradient fill. Scale scales the application of the gradient. You can also use the mouse to move the center of the gradient by clicking and dragging in the image window. Style specifies the shape of the gradient.

Highlight or Shadow Mode Specifies the blending mode of a bevel or emboss highlight or shadow.

Jitter Varies the application of a gradient's color and opacity.

Layer Knocks Out Drop Shadow Controls the drop shadow's visibility in a semitransparent layer.

Noise Specifies the amount of random elements in the opacity of a glow or shadow as you enter a value or drag the slider.

Opacity Sets the opacity of the layer effect as you enter a value or drag the slider.

Pattern Specifies the pattern of a layer effect. In ImageReady, click the inverted arrow ▼ next to the pattern sample and choose a pattern from the list. In Photoshop, click the pop-up palette and choose a pattern. Click the New preset button ▣ to create a new preset pattern based on the current settings. Click Snap to Origin to position the origin of the pattern with that of the document if Link With Layer is selected, or to position the origin with the top left corner of the layer if it is deselected. Select Link With Layer to specify that

the pattern moves with the layer as it is relocated, and drag the Scale slider or enter a value to specify the size of the pattern. You can drag a pattern in the layer to position it while in this panel. The position can be reset with the Snap to Origin button. There must be at least one pattern loaded for the pattern option to be available. You can also load patterns using the Preset Manager.

Position Specifies the position of a stroke effect as Outside, Inside, or Center.

Range Controls which portion or range of the glow is targeted for the contour.

Size Specifies the amount of blur or the size of the shadow.

Soften Blurs the results of shading before compositing to reduce unwanted artifacts.

Source Specifies the glow source for an inner glow. Choose Center to apply a glow that emanates from the center of the layer's content, or Edge to apply a glow that emanates from the inside edges of the layer's content.

Spread Expands the boundaries of the matte prior to blurring.

Style Specifies the style of a bevel: Inner Bevel to create a bevel on the inside edges of the layer contents, Outer Bevel to create a bevel on the outside edges of the layer contents, Emboss to create the effect of embossing the layer contents against the underlying layers, Pillow Emboss to create the effect of stamping the edges of the layer contents into the underlying layers, or Stroke Emboss to confine the emboss to the boundaries of a stroke effect applied to the layer. (Note that the Stroke Emboss effect will not be visible if no stroke is applied to the layer.)

Technique For bevel and emboss, Smooth blurs the edges of a matte slightly and is useful for all types of mattes, whether their edges are soft or hard. It does not preserve detailed features at larger sizes. Chisel Hard uses a distance measurement technique and is primarily useful on hard-edged mattes from anti-aliased shapes such as type. It preserves detailed features better than the Smooth technique. Chisel Soft uses a modified distance measurement technique and, while not as accurate as Chisel Hard, it is more useful on a larger range of mattes. It preserves features better than the Smooth technique. For glows, Softer applies a blur and is useful on all types of mattes, whether their edges are soft or hard. At larger sizes, it does not preserve detailed features. Precise uses a distance measurement technique to create a glow and is primarily useful on hard-edged mattes from anti-aliased shapes such as type. It preserves features better than the Softer technique.

Texture Allows you to specify a pattern used to texture the bevel effect. Scale allows you to scale the size of the texture. Link With Layer specifies that the texture moves with the layer as it is relocated. Invert inverts the texture. Depth varies the degree and direction (up/down) to which the texturing is applied. Snap to Origin controls the

snap of the pattern's origin with that of the document if Link With Layer is disabled and with the top left corner of the layer if it is selected. You can also drag the texture with the mouse to position it while in this panel.

Modifying layer effects with contours (Photoshop)

You can use contours to shape the appearance of an effect over a given range in the Drop Shadow, Inner Shadow, Inner Glow, Outer Glow, Bevel and Emboss, and Satin effects when creating custom layer styles. For example, a Linear contour on a Drop Shadow causes the opacity to drop off in a linear transition while a Custom contour can be used to create a unique shadow transition. Custom contours created in Photoshop can be used in ImageReady.

You can select, reset, delete, or change the preview of contours in the contour pop-up palette and Preset Manager. For more information, see "Using pop-up palettes" on page 25 and "Managing libraries with the Preset Manager (Photoshop)" on page 49.

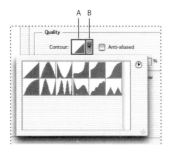

Detail of Layer Style dialog box for Drop Shadow effect:
A. *Click to display the Contour Editor dialog box*
B. *Click to display the pop-up palette*

To create a custom contour:

1 Select the Drop Shadow, Inner Shadow, Inner Glow, Outer Glow, Bevel and Emboss, Contour, or Satin effect in the Layer Style dialog box. (See "Editing styles" on page 249.)

2 Click the contour thumbnail in the Layer Style dialog box.

3 Click the contour to add points and drag to adjust the contour. Or enter values for Input and Output.

4 To create a sharp corner instead of a smooth curve, select a point and click Corner.

5 To save the contour to a file, click Save and name the contour.

6 To store a contour as a preset, choose New.

7 Click OK. New contours are added at the bottom of the pop-up palette.

To load contours from the Contour Editor dialog box:

Click the contour in the Layer Style dialog box, and in the Contour Editor dialog box, choose Load. Go to the folder where the contour library you want to load is located and click Open.

To delete a contour in the Contour Editor dialog box:

Click the inverted arrow ▾ next to the currently selected contour to view the pop-up palette. Press Alt (Windows) or Option (Mac OS), and click the contour you want to delete.

Applying global lighting

Using global light gives the appearance of a consistent light source shining on the image.

To set a global lighting angle:

To set a global lighting angle for all layers, do one of the following:

- Choose Layer > Layer Style > Global Light. In the Global Light dialog box, enter a value or drag the angle radius to set the Angle and Altitude, and click OK.

- (Photoshop) In the Layer Style dialog box for Drop Shadow, Inner Shadow, or Bevel, select Use Global Light. For Angle, enter a value or drag the slider, and click OK.

- (ImageReady) In the Bevel and Emboss or Drop Shadow palette, select Use Global Angle. For Angle and Altitude, enter a value or drag the angle radius.

The new lighting angle appears as the default for each layer effect that uses the global lighting angle.

Creating and managing preset styles

After you customize a layer style, you can save it as a preset style. Preset styles appear in the Styles palette, Layer Styles dialog box (Photoshop), Layer Styles pop-up palette in the options bar for the pen and shape tool, and Preset Manager. (See "Applying preset styles" on page 246.) You can also create libraries of preset styles, rename preset styles, and delete preset styles.

To create a new preset style:

1 In the Layers palette, select the layer that contains the style you want to save as a preset.

2 Do one of the following:

- Drag the selected layer into the Styles palette or onto the New Item button ⬛ in the Styles palette.

- Click an empty area of the Styles palette.

- Press Alt (Windows) or Option (Mac OS) and click the New Item button at the bottom of the Styles palette.

- Choose New Style from the Styles palette menu.

- (Photoshop) Double-click the layer thumbnail, and click New Style in the Layer Style dialog box.

3 Enter a name for the preset style, set style options, and click OK.

> *To create a preset style from a single effect, drag the effect from the Layers palette to the Styles palette.*

To rename a preset style:

Do one of the following:

- Double-click a style in the Styles palette. If the Styles palette is set to display styles as thumbnails, enter a new name in the dialog box, and click OK. Otherwise, type a new name directly in the Style palette, and press Enter (Windows) or Return (Mac OS).

- (Photoshop) Select a style is the Styles section of the Layer Styles dialog box. (See "Applying preset styles" on page 246.) Then choose Rename Style from the pop-up menu, enter a new name, and click OK.

- (Photoshop) When using a shape or pen tool, select a style from the Layer Style pop-up palette in the options bar. Then choose Rename Style from the pop-up palette menu.

To delete a preset style:

Do one of the following:

- Drag a style to the trash button 🗑 at the bottom of the Styles palette.

- Press Alt (Windows) or Option (Mac OS) and click the layer style in the Styles palette.

- (Photoshop) Select a style is the Styles section of the Layer Styles dialog box. (See "Applying preset styles" on page 246.) Then choose Delete Style from the pop-up menu.

- (Photoshop) When using a shape or pen tool, select a style from the Layer Style pop-up palette in the options bar. Then choose Delete Style from the pop-up palette menu.

To save a set of preset styles as a library:

1 Do one of the following:

- Choose Save Styles from the Styles palette menu.

- (Photoshop) Select Styles on the left side of the Layer Styles dialog box. (See "Applying preset styles" on page 246.) Then choose Save Styles from the pop-up menu.

- (Photoshop) When using a shape or pen tool, click the layer style thumbnail in the options bar. Then choose Save Styles from the pop-up palette menu.

2 Choose a location for the style library, enter a filename, and click Save.

You can save the library anywhere. However, if you place the library file in the Presets/Styles folder inside the Photoshop program folder, the library name will appear at the bottom of the Styles palette menu when you restart the application.

Note: You can also use the Preset Manager to rename, delete, and save libraries of preset styles. For more information, see "Managing libraries with the Preset Manager (Photoshop)" on page 49.

Copying and pasting styles

Copying and pasting styles is an easy way to apply the same effects to multiple layers.

To copy layer styles between layers:

1 In the Layers palette, select the layer containing the style you want to copy.

2 Choose Layer > Layer Style > Copy Layer Style.

3 Do one of the following:

- To paste into a single layer, select the destination layer in the palette, and choose Layer > Layer Style > Paste Layer Style.

- To paste into multiple layers, link the destination layers. (See "Linking layers" on page 234.) Then choose Layer > Layer Style > Paste Layer Style to Linked.

The pasted layer style will replace the existing layer style on the destination layer or layers.

To copy layer styles between layers by dragging:

Do one of the following:

- In the Layers palette, rag a single layer effect from one layer to another to duplicate the layer effect, or drag the Effects bar from one layer to another to duplicate the layer style.

- Drag one or more layer effects from the Layers palette to the image to apply the resulting layer style to the highest layer in the Layers palette that contains pixels at the drop point.

Scaling layer effects (Photoshop)

A layer style may have been tuned to look best on a target resolution with features of a given size. Using Scale Effects allows you to scale the effects contained in the layer style without scaling the object to which the layer style is applied.

To scale a layer effect:

1 Select the layer in the Layers palette.

2 Choose Layer > Layer Style > Scale Effects.

3 Enter a percentage or drag the slider.

4 Select Preview to preview the changes in the image.

5 Click OK.

Removing layer effects

You can remove individual effects from a layer style and remove a style from the layer.

To remove an effect from a style:

1 In the Layers palette, expand the layer style so you can see its effects.

2 Do one of the following:

- Drag the effect to the Trash button.

- (ImageReady) Select the effect, and choose Delete Effect from the Layers palette menu.

To remove a style from a layer:

1 In the Layers palette, select the layer containing the style you want to remove.

2 Do one of the following:

- In the Layers palette, drag the Effects bar to the Trash button.

- Choose Layer > Layer Style > Clear Layer Style.

- Select the layer, then click the Clear style button ⊘ at the bottom of the Styles palette.

- (ImageReady) Select an effect in the Layers palette, and choose Delete All Effects from the Layers palette menu.

Converting layer styles to layers

To customize or fine-tune the appearance of layer styles, you can convert the layer styles to regular image layers. Once you have converted a layer style to image layers, you can enhance the result by painting or applying commands and filters. However, you can no longer edit the layer style on the original layer, and the layer style will no longer update as you change the original image layer.

Note: The layers produced by this process may not result in artwork that exactly matches the version using layer styles. In Photoshop, you may see an alert when you create the new layers.

To convert a layer style to image layers:

1 In the Layers palette, select the layer containing the layer style you want to convert.

2 Choose Layer > Layer Style > Create Layers.

You can now modify and restack the new layers in the same way as regular layers. Some effects— for example, Inner Glow—convert to layers within a clipping group.

Using adjustment layers and fill layers (Photoshop)

Adjustment layers and fill layers add another level of flexibility to working with layers. Adjustment layers allow you to experiment with color and apply tonal adjustments to an image; fill layers allow you to quickly add color, patterns, and gradient elements to an image. If you change your mind about the results, you can go back and edit or remove the adjustment or fill at any time.

Original, adjustment layer applied to zebra only, and adjustment layer applied to entire image

About adjustment layers and fill layers

Adjustment layers let you experiment with color and tonal adjustments to an image without permanently modifying the pixels in the image. The color and tonal changes reside within the adjustment layer, which acts as a veil through which the underlying image layers appear. Keep in mind that an adjustment layer affects all the layers below it. This means that you can correct multiple layers by making a single adjustment, rather than making the adjustment to each layer separately.

Note: Adjustment layers can be applied and edited only in Photoshop; however, they can be viewed in ImageReady.

Fill layers let you fill a layer with a solid color, a gradient, or a pattern. Unlike adjustment layers, fill layers do not affect the layers underneath them.

Creating adjustment layers or fill layers

Adjustment layers and fill layers have the same opacity and blending mode options as image layers and can be rearranged, deleted, hidden, and duplicated in the same manner as image layers. By default, adjustment layers and fill layers have layer masks, as indicated by the mask icon to the left of the layer thumbnail. If a path is active when you create the adjustment or fill layer, a vector mask is created instead of a layer mask.

To confine the effects of an adjustment layer to a group of layers, create a clipping group consisting of these layers. You can place the adjustment layers in or at the base of the clipping group. The adjustment will be confined to the layers inside the group. (See "Creating clipping groups" on page 264.) Alternatively, you can create a layer set, and have the set use any blending mode other than Pass Through.

To create an adjustment layer or fill layer:

1 Do one of the following:

- Click the New Adjustment Layer button ⊘ at the bottom of the Layers palette, and choose the layer type you want to create.

- Choose Layer > New Fill Layer, and choose an option from the submenu. Then name the layer, set other layer options, and click OK. (See "Setting opacity and blending options" on page 240 and "Creating clipping groups" on page 264.)

- Choose Layer > New Adjustment Layer, and choose an option from the submenu. Then name the layer, set other layer options, and click OK. (See "Setting opacity and blending options" on page 240 and "Creating clipping groups" on page 264.)

Note: To confine the effects of the adjustment layer or fill layer to a selected area, make a selection, create a closed path and select it, or select an existing closed path. When you use a selection, you create an adjustment layer or fill layer confined by a layer mask. When you use a path, you create an adjustment layer or fill layer confined by a vector mask.

2 Choose from the following layer properties, and then click OK.

Solid Color Specify a color. (See "Using the Adobe Color Picker" on page 205.)

Gradient Click the gradient to display the Gradient Editor, or click the inverted arrow ▼ and choose a gradient from the pop-up palette. (See "Creating smooth gradient fills" on page 189.) Set additional options if desired. Style specifies the shape of the gradient. Angle specifies the angle at which the gradient is applied. Scale changes the size of the gradient. Reverse flips the orientation of the gradient. Dither reduces banding by applying dithering to the gradient. Align With Layer uses the bounding box of the layer to calculate the gradient fill. You can use the mouse to move the center of the gradient by clicking and dragging in the image window.

Pattern Click the pattern, and choose a pattern from the pop-up palette. Click Scale and enter a value or drag the slider to scale the pattern. Click Snap to Origin to position the origin of the pattern with that of the document window. (See "Using rulers, columns, the measure tool, guides, and the grid" on page 37.) Select Link With Layer to specify that the pattern moves with the fill layer as it is relocated. When Link With Layer is selected, you can drag in the image to position the pattern while the Pattern Fill dialog box is open.

Levels Specify values for the highlights, shadows, and midtones.

Curves Adjust the intensity values of pixels along a 0–255 scale while keeping up to 15 other values constant.

Color Balance Drag a slider toward a color you want to increase in the image; drag a slider away from a color you want to decrease in the image.

Brightness/Contrast Specify values for Brightness and Contrast.

Hue/Saturation Choose which colors to edit, and specify values for Hue, Saturation, and Lightness.

Selective Color Choose the color you want to adjust, and drag the sliders to increase or decrease the components in the selected color.

Channel Mixer Modify a color channel. For more information, see "Mixing color channels (Photoshop)" on page 216.

Gradient Map Choose a gradient and set gradient options.

Invert Invert adjustment layers don't have options.

Threshold Specify a threshold level.

Posterize Specify the number of tonal levels for each color channel.

For more information on Levels, Curves, Color Balance, Brightness/Contrast, Hue/Saturation, Selective Color, Gradient Map, Invert, Threshold, and Posterize, see "Making Color and Tonal Adjustments" in online Help.

Editing adjustment layers or fill layers

Once you create an adjustment or fill layer, you can easily edit the settings, or dynamically replace it with a different adjustment or fill type. You can also edit the mask of an adjustment layer or fill layer to control the effect that the layer has on the image. By default, all areas of an adjustment or fill layer are "unmasked" and, therefore, are showing. (See "Creating and editing layer masks" on page 260.)

To edit an adjustment or fill layer:

1 Do one of the following:

• Double-click the adjustment or fill layer's thumbnail in the Layers palette.

• Choose Layer > Layer Content Options.

2 Make the desired adjustments, and click OK.

Note: Inverted adjustment layers do not have editable settings.

To change the content of an adjustment or fill layer:

1 Select the adjustment layer or fill layer that you want to change.

2 Choose Layer > Change Layer Content and select a different fill or adjustment layer from the list.

Merging adjustment layers or fill layers

You can merge an adjustment or fill layer several ways: with the layer below it, with the layers in its own grouped layer, with the layers it is linked to, and with all other visible layers. You cannot, however, use an adjustment layer or fill layer as the target layer for a merge. When you merge an adjustment layer or fill layer with the layer below it, the adjustments are rasterized and become permanently applied within the merged layer. (See "Merging layers" on page 238.) You can also rasterize a fill layer without merging it. (See "Rasterizing layers" on page 237.)

Adjustment layers and fill layers whose masks contain only white values do not add significantly to the file size, so it is not necessary to merge these adjustment layers to conserve file space.

Masking layers

You can use masks to protect sections of layers from being edited and to show or hide sections of an image.

About masking layers

Masks control how different areas within a layer or layer set are hidden and revealed. By making changes to the mask, you can apply a variety of special effects to the layer without actually affecting the pixels on that layer. You can then apply the mask and make the changes permanent or remove the mask without applying the changes.

There are two types of masks:

- Layer masks are bitmap images and are resolution-dependent and are created with the painting or selection tools.

- (Photoshop) Vector masks are resolution-independent and are created with the pen or shape tools.

In the Layers palette, both the layer and vector masks appear as an additional thumbnail to the right of the layer thumbnail. For the layer mask, this thumbnail represents the grayscale channel that is created when you add the layer mask. (See "Storing masks in alpha channels" on page 225.) The vector mask thumbnail represents a path that clips out the contents of the layer.

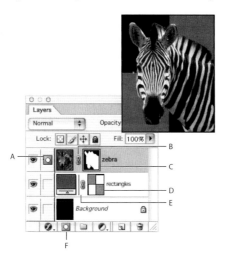

Layer palette:
A. Layer mask selected B. Layer mask link icon
C. Layer mask D. Vector mask
E. Vector mask link icon F. New Layer Mask

Creating and editing layer masks

You can obscure an entire layer or layer set, or just a selected part of it, using a layer mask. You can also edit a layer mask to add or subtract from the masked region. A layer mask is a grayscale image, so what you paint in black will be hidden, what you paint in white will show, and what you paint in gray shades will show in various levels of transparency.

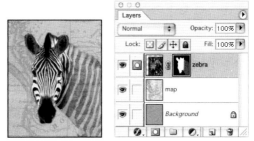

Background painted with black, head painted with white, neck painted with gray

To add a mask that shows or hides the entire layer:

1 Choose Select > Deselect to clear any selection borders in the image.

2 In the Layers palette, select the layer or layer set to which to add a mask.

3 Do one of the following:

- To create a mask that reveals the entire layer, click the New Layer Mask button in the Layers palette, or choose Layer > Add Layer Mask > Reveal All.

- To create a mask that hides the entire layer, Alt click (Windows) or Option-click (Mac OS) the New Layer Mask button, or choose Layer > Add Layer Mask > Hide All.

To add a mask that shows or hides a selection:

1 In the Layers palette, select the layer or layer set to which to add a mask.

2 Select the area in the image, and do one of the following:

• Click the New Layer Mask button ▣ in the Layers palette to create a mask that reveals the selection.

• Choose Layer > Add Layer Mask > Reveal Selection or Hide Selection.

To edit a layer mask:

1 Click the layer mask thumbnail in the Layers palette to make it active.

2 Select any of the editing or painting tools.

Note: The foreground and background colors default to grayscale values when the mask is active.

3 Do one of the following:

• To subtract from the mask and reveal the layer, paint the mask with white.

• To make the layer partially visible, paint the mask with gray.

• To add to the mask and hide the layer or layer set, paint the mask with black.

To edit the layer instead of the layer mask, select it by clicking its thumbnail in the Layers palette. The paintbrush icon ✍ appears to the left of the thumbnail to indicate that you are editing the layer.

To paste a copied selection into a layer mask, Alt-click (Windows) or Option-click (Mac OS) the layer mask thumbnail in the Layers palette to select and display the mask channel. Choose Edit > Paste, drag the selection in the image to produce the desired masking effect, and choose Select > Deselect. Click the layer thumbnail in the Layers palette to deselect the mask channel.

To select and display the layer mask channel (Photoshop):

Do one of the following:

• Alt-click (Windows) or Option-click (Mac OS) the layer mask thumbnail to view only the grayscale mask. The eye icons in the Layers palette are dimmed because all layers or layer sets are hidden. To redisplay the layers, Alt-click or Option-click the layer mask thumbnail, or click an eye icon.

• Hold down Alt+Shift (Windows) or Option+Shift (Mac OS), and click the layer mask thumbnail to view the mask on top of the layer in a rubylith masking color. Hold down Alt+Shift or Option+Shift, and click the thumbnail again to turn off the color display.

To disable or enable a layer mask:

Do one of the following:

• Shift-click the layer mask thumbnail in the Layers palette.

• Select the layer with the layer mask you want to disable or enable, and choose Layer > Disable Layer Mask or Layer > Enable Layer Mask.

A red *X* appears over the mask thumbnail in the Layers palette when the mask is disabled, and the layer's content appears without masking effects.

To change the rubylith display for a layer mask (Photoshop):

1 Do one of the following:

- Alt-click (Windows) or Option-click (Mac OS) the layer mask thumbnail to select the layer mask channel; then double-click the layer mask thumbnail.

- Double-click the layer mask channel in the Channels palette.

2 To choose a new mask color, in the Layer Mask Display Options dialog box, click the color swatch, and choose a new color. (See "Using the Adobe Color Picker" on page 205.)

3 To change the opacity, enter a value between 0% and 100%.

Both the color and opacity settings affect only the appearance of the mask and have no effect on how underlying areas are protected. For example, you might want to change these settings to make the mask more easily visible against the colors in the image.

4 Click OK.

Creating and editing vector masks

A vector mask creates a sharp-edged shape on a layer and is useful any time you want to add a design element with clean, defined edges. Once you create a layer with a vector mask, you can apply one or more layer styles to it, edit them if needed, and instantly have a usable button, panel, or other Web design element.

To add a vector mask that shows or hides the entire layer (Photoshop):

1 In the Layers palette, select the layer to which you want to add a vector mask.

2 Do one of the following:

- To create a vector mask that reveals the entire layer, choose Layer > Add Vector Mask > Reveal All.

- To create a vector mask that hides the entire layer, choose Layer > Add Vector Mask > Hide All.

To add a vector mask that shows the contents of a shape (Photoshop):

1 In the Layers palette, select the layer to which to add a vector mask.

2 Select a path or use one of the shape or pen tools to draw a work path. For more information, see "Creating a work path (Photoshop)" on page 148.

3 Choose Layer > Add Vector Mask > Current Path.

To edit a vector mask (Photoshop):

Click the vector mask thumbnail in the Layers palette or the thumbnail in the Paths palette. Then change the shape using the shape and pen tools.

To remove a vector mask:

Do one of the following in the Layers palette:

• Drag the vector mask thumbnail to the Trash button 🗑 .

• (Photoshop) Select the layer with the vector mask you want to delete, and choose Layer > Delete Vector Mask.

To disable or enable a vector mask:

Do one of the following:

• Shift-click the vector mask thumbnail in the Layers palette.

• (Photoshop) Select the layer with the vector mask you want to disable or enable, and choose Layer > Disable Vector Mask or Layer > Enable Vector Mask.

A red *X* appears over the mask thumbnail in the Layers palette when the mask is disabled, and the layer's content appears without masking effects.

To convert a vector mask to a layer mask (Photoshop):

Select the layer with the vector mask you want to convert, and choose Layer > Rasterize > Vector Mask.

Important: Once you rasterize a vector mask, it cannot be changed back into a vector object.

Unlinking layers and masks

By default, a layer or layer set is linked to its layer mask or vector mask, as indicated by the link icon between the thumbnails in the Layers palette. The layer and its mask move together in the image when you move either one with the move too!. Unlinking them lets you move them independently and shift the mask's boundaries separately from the layer.

To unlink a layer from its mask:

Click the link icon in the Layers palette.

To reestablish the link between a layer and its mask:

Click between the layer and mask path thumbnails in the Layers palette.

Applying and discarding layer masks

When you have finished creating a layer mask, you can either apply the mask and make the changes permanent or discard the mask without applying changes. Because layer masks are stored as alpha channels, applying and discarding layer masks can help reduce file size. (See "Storing masks in alpha channels" on page 225.)

To apply or discard a layer mask:

1 Click the layer mask thumbnail in the Layers palette.

2 To remove the layer mask and make changes permanent, click the Trash button 🗑 at the bottom of the Layers palette, then click Apply (Photoshop) or Yes (ImageReady).

3 To remove the layer mask without applying the changes, click the trash button at the bottom of the Layers palette, then click Discard (Photoshop) or No (ImageReady).

You can also apply or discard layer masks using the Layer menu.

Selecting opaque areas on a layer

By loading a layer mask, you can quickly select all the opaque areas on a layer—that is, the areas within the layer boundaries. This is useful when you want to exclude transparent areas from a selection. You can also load the boundaries of a layer mask as a selection.

To load a layer or layer mask's boundaries as a selection:

Do one of the following:

• In the Layers palette, Ctrl-click (Windows) or Command-click (Mac OS) the layer or layer mask thumbnail.

• To add the pixels to an existing selection, press Ctrl+Shift (Windows) or Command+Shift (Mac OS), and click the layer or layer mask thumbnail in the Layers palette.

• To subtract the pixels from an existing selection, press Ctrl+Alt (Windows) or Command+Option (Mac OS), and click the layer or layer mask thumbnail in the Layers palette.

• To load the intersection of the pixels and an existing selection, press Ctrl+Alt+Shift (Windows) or Command+Option+Shift (Mac OS), and click the layer or layer mask thumbnail in the Layers palette.

To move all the contents of a layer, you can use the move tool without loading a transparency mask.

Creating clipping groups

In a clipping group, the bottommost layer, or *base layer*, acts as a mask for the entire group. For example, you might have a shape on one layer, a texture on the overlying layer, and some text on the topmost layer. If you define all three layers as a clipping group, the texture and the text appear only through the shape on the base layer, and take on the opacity of the base layer.

Note that only successive layers can be included in a clipping group. The name of the base layer in the group is underlined, and the thumbnails for the overlying layers are indented. Additionally, the overlying layers display a clipping group icon ↓. The Blend Clipped Layers As Group option in the Layer Style dialog box (Photoshop) or the Layer Options palette (ImageReady) determines whether the blending mode of the base affects the whole group or just the base. (See "Grouping blend effects" on page 243.)

Clipping group with Layer 1 and lion layers

To create a clipping group:

1 Do one of the following:

• Hold down Alt (Windows) or Option (Mac OS), position the pointer over the line dividing two layers in the Layers palette (the pointer changes to two overlapping circles), and click.

• Select a layer in the Layers palette, and choose Layer > Group with Previous.

• Link together the desired layers in the Layers palette. (See "Linking layers" on page 234.) Then choose Layer > Group Linked.

The clipping group is assigned the opacity and mode attributes of the bottommost layer in the group.

To remove a layer from a clipping group:

Do one of the following:

• Hold down Alt (Windows) or Option (Mac OS), position the pointer over the line separating two grouped layers in the Layers palette (the pointer changes to two overlapping circles), and click.

• In the Layers palette, select a layer in the clipping group, and choose Layer > Ungroup. This command removes the selected layer and any layers above it from the clipping group.

To ungroup all layers in a clipping group:

1 In the Layers palette, select the base layer in the clipping group.

2 Choose Layer > Ungroup.

Chapter 11: Using Type

Typography gives visual form to language. Adobe Photoshop and Adobe ImageReady let you add type to images with flexibility and precision. You can create and edit type directly on-screen (instead of in a dialog box) and quickly change the font, style, size, and color of the type. You can apply changes to individual characters and set formatting options for entire paragraphs, including alignment, justification, and word-wrapping. You can create designs that include Chinese, Japanese, and Korean type (if you have the correct system software installed on your computer).

About type

Type consists of mathematically defined shapes that describe the letters, numbers, and symbols of a *typeface*. Many typefaces are available in more than one format, the most common formats being Type 1 (also called PostScript fonts), TrueType, OpenType, and CID (Japanese only).

When you add type to an image, the characters are composed of pixels and have the same resolution as the image file—zooming in on characters shows jagged edges. However, Photoshop and ImageReady preserve the vector-based type outlines and use them when you scale or resize type, save a PDF or EPS file, or print the image to a PostScript printer. As a result, it's possible to produce type with crisp, resolution-independent edges.

Creating type

You can create horizontal or vertical type anywhere in an image. Depending on how you use the type tools, you can enter *point type* or *paragraph type*. Point type is useful for entering a single word or a line of characters; paragraph type is useful for entering and formatting the type as one or more paragraphs.

Type entered as point type (top) and in a bounding box

When you create type, a new type layer is added to the Layers palette. In Photoshop, you can also create a selection border in the shape of the type.

Note: *In Photoshop, a type layer is not created for images in Multichannel, Bitmap, or Indexed Color mode, because these modes do not support layers. In these image modes, type appears on the background.*

About using the type tools (Photoshop)

Clicking in an image with a type tool puts the type tool in edit mode. You can enter and edit characters when the tool is in edit mode; however, you must commit changes to the type layer before you can perform some operations. To determine if a type tool is in edit mode, look in the options bar—if you see the Commit button ✔ and Cancel button ⊘, the type tool is in edit mode.

To commit changes to a type layer:

Do one of the following:

- Click the Commit button ✔ in the options bar.
- Press the Enter key on the numeric keypad.
- Press Ctrl+Enter on the main keyboard (Windows) or Command+Return (Mac OS).
- Select any tool in the toolbox, click in the Layers, Channels, Paths, Actions, History, or Styles palette, or select any available menu command.

Entering point type

When you enter point type, each line of type is independent—the length of a line grows or shrinks as you edit it, but it doesn't wrap to the next line. The type you entered appears in a new type layer.

To enter point type:

1 Do one of the following:

- (Photoshop) Select the horizontal type tool T or the vertical type tool ↓T.
- (ImageReady) Select the type tool T.

2 Click in the image to set an insertion point for the type. The small line through the I-beam marks the position of the type *baseline*. For horizontal type, the baseline marks the line on which the type rests; for vertical type, the baseline marks the center axis of the type characters.

> *To show the baseline in ImageReady, choose View > Show > Text Baseline.*

3 Select additional type options in the options bar, Character palette, and Paragraph palette. (See "Formatting characters" on page 274 and "Formatting paragraphs" on page 283.)

4 Enter the characters you want. Press Enter on the main keyboard (Windows) or Return (Mac OS) to begin a new line.

5 Commit the type layer. (See "About using the type tools (Photoshop)" on page 268.)

Entering paragraph type

When you enter paragraph type, the lines of type wrap to fit the dimensions of the bounding box. You can enter multiple paragraphs and select a paragraph justification option.

You can resize the bounding box, which causes the type to reflow within the adjusted rectangle. You can adjust the bounding box while you're entering type or after you create the type layer. You can also rotate, scale, and skew type using the bounding box.

To enter paragraph type:

1 Do one of the following:

- (Photoshop) Select the horizontal type tool T or the vertical type tool ↓T.

- (ImageReady) Select the type tool T.

2 Do one of the following:

- Drag diagonally to define a bounding box for the type.

- Hold down Alt (Windows) or Option (Mac OS) as you click or drag to display the Text Box Size dialog box. Enter values for Width and Height, and click OK.

3 Select additional type options in the options bar, Character palette, Paragraph palette, and Layer > Type submenu. (See "Formatting characters" on page 274 and "Formatting paragraphs" on page 283.)

4 Enter the characters you want. Press Enter on the main keyboard (Windows) or Return (Mac OS) to begin a new paragraph. If you enter more type than can fit in the bounding box, the overflow icon ⊞ appears on the bounding box.

5 (Photoshop) If desired, resize, rotate, or skew the bounding box.

6 (Photoshop) Commit the type layer. (See "About using the type tools (Photoshop)" on page 268.)

The type you entered appears in a new type layer.

To resize or transform a type bounding box:

1 Display the bounding box handles:

- (Photoshop) With the type tool active, select the type layer in the Layers palette, and click in the text flow in the image.

- (ImageReady) With the type tool active, select the type layer. If the bounding box handles don't appear, make sure that the Text Bounds option is selected in the View > Show submenu.

2 Drag to achieve the desired effect:

- To resize the bounding box, position the pointer over a handle—the pointer turns into a double arrow ⤡—and drag. Shift-drag to maintain the proportion of the bounding box.

- (Photoshop) To rotate the bounding box, position the pointer outside of the bounding border—the pointer turns into a curved, two-sided arrow ↻—and drag. Shift-drag to constrain the rotation to 15° increments. To change the center of rotation, Ctrl-drag (Windows) or Command-drag (Mac OS) the center point to a new location. The center point can be outside the bounding box.

- (Photoshop) To skew the bounding box, hold down Ctrl+Shift (Windows) or Command+Shift (Mac OS) and drag a side handle. The pointer turns into an arrowhead with a small double arrow ▸⤢.

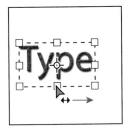

Illustration of skewing type using the bounding box

- (Photoshop) To scale the type as you resize the bounding box, Ctrl-drag (Windows) or Command-drag (Mac OS) a corner handle.

Note: *You can also transform type layers using the transformation commands in the Edit menu, except for Perspective and Distort.*

To show or hide the type bounding box (ImageReady):

Do one of the following:

- Choose View > Show > Text Bounds.

- Choose View > Extras. This command shows or hides all selected items in the View > Show submenu. (See "Working with Extras" on page 41.)

Creating a type selection border (Photoshop)

When you use the horizontal type mask tool T or vertical type mask tool $\lceil T \rceil$, you create a selection in the shape of the type. Type selections appear on the active layer, and can be moved, copied, filled, or stroked just like any other selection.

To create a type selection border:

1 Select the layer on which you want the selection to appear. For best results, create the type selection border on a normal image layer, not a type layer.

2 Select the horizontal type mask tool T or the vertical type mask tool $\lceil T \rceil$.

3 Select additional type options, and enter type at a point or in a bounding box. (See "Entering point type" on page 268 and "Entering paragraph type" on page 268.)

The type selection border appears in the image on the active layer.

Working with type layers

Once you create a type layer, you can edit the type and apply layer commands to it. You can change the orientation of the type, apply anti-aliasing, convert between point type and paragraph type, create a work path from type, or convert type to shapes. You can move, restack, copy, and change the layer options of a type layer as you do for a normal layer. You can also make the following changes to a type layer and still edit the type:

- Apply transformation commands from the Edit menu, except for Perspective and Distort. (To apply the Perspective or Distort commands, or to transform part of the type layer, you must rasterize the type layer, making the type uneditable.)

- Use layer styles.

- Use fill shortcuts. To fill with the foreground color, press Alt+Backspace (Windows) or Option+Delete (Mac OS); to fill with the background color, press Ctrl+Backspace (Windows) or Command+Delete (Mac OS).

- Warp type to conform to a variety of shapes.

Editing text in type layers

You can insert new text, change existing text, and delete text in type layers.

To edit text in a type layer:

1 Select the horizontal type tool T or the vertical type tool $\lceil T \rceil$.

2 Select the type layer in the Layers palette, or click in the text flow to automatically select a type layer.

3 Position the insertion point in the text, and do one of the following:

- Click to set the insertion point.

- Select one or more characters you want to edit.

4 Enter text as desired.

5 Commit the changes to the type layer. (See "About using the type tools (Photoshop)" on page 268.)

Rasterizing type layers

Some commands and tools—such as filter effects and painting tools—are not available for type layers. You must rasterize the type prior to applying the command or using the tool. *Rasterizing* converts the type layer to a normal layer and makes its contents uneditable as text. A warning message appears if you choose a command or tool that requires a rasterized layer. Some warning messages provide an OK button that you can click to rasterize the layer.

To convert a type layer to a normal layer:

1 Select the type layer in the Layers palette.

2 Choose Layer > Rasterize > Type.

Changing type layer orientation

The orientation of a type layer determines the direction of type lines in relation to the document window (for point type) or the bounding box (for paragraph type). When a type layer is vertical, the type lines flow up and down; when a type layer is horizontal, the type lines flow from left to right. Don't confuse the orientation of a type layer with the direction of characters in a type line. (See "Rotating vertical type" on page 281.)

To change the orientation of a type layer:

1 Select the type layer in the Layers palette.

2 Do one of the following:

- Select a type tool and click the Text Orientation button ↓**T** in the options bar.

- Choose Layer > Type > Horizontal, or choose Layer > Type > Vertical.

- Choose Change Text Orientation from the Character palette menu.

Specifying anti-aliasing

Anti-aliasing lets you produce smooth-edged type by partially filling the edge pixels. As a result, the edges of the type blend into the background.

Anti-aliasing None, and Strong

When creating type for online use, consider that anti-aliasing greatly increases the number of colors in the original image. This limits your ability to reduce the number of colors in the image and thus reduce the optimized file size, and may cause stray colors to appear along the edges of the type. When file size and limiting the number of colors is most important, leaving type without anti-aliased edges may be preferable, despite the jagged edges. Also, consider using larger type than you would use for printed works. Larger type can be easier to view online and gives you more freedom in deciding whether to apply anti-aliasing to type.

Note: When you use anti-aliasing, type may be rendered inconsistently at small sizes and low resolutions (such as the resolution used for Web graphics). To reduce this inconsistency, deselect the Fractional Width option in the Character palette menu.

Anti-aliasing options include:

- None to apply no anti-aliasing.
- Sharp to make type appear the most sharp.
- Crisp to make type appear somewhat sharp.

- Strong to make type appear heavier.
- Smooth to make type appear smoother.

To apply anti-aliasing to a type layer:

1 Select the type layer in the Layers palette.

2 Do one of the following:

- Choose an option from the anti-aliasing menu ªa in the options bar or the Character palette.
- Choose Layer > Type, and choose an option from the submenu.

Converting between point type and paragraph type

You can convert point type to paragraph type to adjust the flow of characters within a bounding box. Or you can convert paragraph type to point type to make each text line flow independently from the others.

When you convert from paragraph type to point type, a carriage return is added at the end of each line of type (with the exception of the last line).

Important: When you convert paragraph type to point type, all characters that overflow the bounding box are deleted. To avoid losing text, adjust the bounding box so that all type is visible prior to conversion.

To convert between point type and paragraph type:

1 Select the type layer in the Layers palette.

2 Choose Layer > Type > Convert to Point Text, or Layer > Type > Convert to Paragraph Text.

Warping type layers

Warping allows you to distort type to conform to a variety of shapes; for example, you can warp type in the shape of an arc or a wave. The warp style you select is an attribute of the type layer—you can change a layer's warp style at any time to change the overall shape of the warp. Warping options give you precise control over the orientation and perspective of the warp effect.

Note: You cannot warp type layers that include Faux Bold formatting or use fonts that do not include outline data (such as bitmap fonts).

Example of type warped with Fish style

To warp type:

1 Select a type layer.

2 Do one of the following:

- Select a type tool, and click the Warp button in the options bar.

- Choose Layer > Type > Warp Text.

3 Choose a warp style from the Style pop-up menu.

4 Select the orientation of the warp effect—Horizontal or Vertical.

5 If desired, specify values for additional warping options:

- Bend to specify how much warp is applied to the layer.

- Horizontal Distortion and Vertical Distortion to apply perspective to the warp.

To unwarp type:

1 Select a type layer that has warping applied to it.

2 Select a type tool, and click the Warp button in the options bar; or choose Layer > Type > Warp Text.

3 Choose None from the Style pop-up menu, and click OK.

Creating a work path from type (Photoshop)

Creating a work path from type lets you work with characters as vector shapes. A *work path* is a temporary path that appears in the Paths palette. Once you create a work path from a type layer, you can save and manipulate it like any other path. (See "Selecting paths (Photoshop)" on page 158.) You cannot edit characters in the path as text; however, the original type layer remains intact and editable.

To create a work path from type:

Select a type layer, and choose Layer > Type > Create Work Path.

Note: You cannot create work paths from fonts that don't include outline data (such as bitmap fonts).

Converting type to shapes (Photoshop)

When you convert type to shapes, the type layer is replaced by a layer with a vector mask. You can edit the vector mask and apply styles to the layer; however, you cannot edit characters in the layer as text. (See "Creating and editing vector masks" on page 262.)

To convert type to shapes:

Select a type layer, and choose Layer > Type > Convert to Shapes.

Note: You cannot create shapes from fonts that don't include outline data (such as bitmap fonts).

Formatting characters

Photoshop and ImageReady give you precise control over individual characters in type layers, including font, size, color, leading, kerning, tracking, baseline shift, and alignment. You can set type attributes before you enter characters or reset them to change the appearance of selected characters in a type layer.

Selecting characters

Before you can format individual characters, you must select them. You can select one character, a range of characters, or all characters in a type layer.

To select characters:

1 Do one of the following:

- (Photoshop) Select the horizontal type tool T or the vertical type tool ↓T .

- (ImageReady) Select the type tool T .

2 Select the type layer in the Layers palette, or click in the text flow to automatically select a type layer.

3 Position the insertion point in the text, and do one of the following:

- Drag to select one or more characters.

- Click in the text and then shift-click to select a range of characters.

- Choose Select > All to select all the characters in the layer.

- Double-click a word to select it. Triple-click a line to select it. Quadruple-click a paragraph to select it. Quintuple-click anywhere in the text flow to select all characters in a bounding box.

- To use the arrow keys to select characters, hold down Shift and press the Right arrow or Left arrow key. To use the arrow keys to select words, hold down Shift+Ctrl (Windows) or Shift+Command (Mac OS) and press the Right arrow or Left arrow key.

4 To select all the characters in a layer without positioning the insertion point in the text flow, select the type layer in the Layers palette, and then double-click the layer's type icon T .

Note: In Photoshop, selecting and formatting characters in a type layer puts the type tool into edit mode. (See "About using the type tools (Photoshop)" on page 268.)

To show or hide selection highlighting (ImageReady):

Do one of the following:

- Choose View > Show > Text Selection.

• Choose View > Extras. This command shows or hides all selected items in the View > Show submenu. (See "Working with Extras" on page 41.)

Using the Character palette

The Character palette provides options for formatting characters. Some formatting options are also provided in the options bar.

To display the Character palette:

Do one of the following:

• Choose Window > Character, or click the Character palette tab if the palette is visible but not active.

• With a type tool selected, click the palette button [image] in the options bar.

Choosing a font

A font is a complete set of characters—letters, numbers, and symbols—that share a common weight, width, and style. When you select a font, you can select the *font family* and its *type style* independently. The font family is a collection of fonts sharing an overall typeface design; for example, Times. A type style is a variant version of an individual font in the font family, for example, Regular, Bold, or Italic. The range of available type styles varies with each font. If a font doesn't include the style you want, you can apply *faux* styles—simulated versions of bold, italic, super-script, subscript, all caps, and small caps styles.

In addition to the fonts installed on your system, Photoshop uses font files in these local folders:

Windows Program Files/Common Files/ Adobe/Fonts

Mac OS 9.x System Folder/Application Support/ Adobe/Fonts

Mac OS X Library/Application Support/ Adobe/Fonts

If you install a Type 1, TrueType, OpenType, or CID font into the local Fonts folder, the font appears in Adobe applications only.

To choose a font family and style:

1 Choose a font family from the Font Family pop-up menu in the Character palette or options bar. If more than one copy of a font is installed on your computer, an abbreviation follows the font name: (T1) for Type 1 fonts, (TT) for TrueType fonts, or (OT) for OpenType fonts.

In Photoshop, you can choose a font family and style by typing the desired name in the text box. As you type, the name of the first font or style beginning with that letter appears. Continue typing until the correct font or style name appears. Be sure to deselect the font name before entering new type in the image.

2 Do one of the following:

• Choose a font style from the Font Style pop-up menu in the Character palette or options bar.

- If the font family you chose does not include a bold or italic style, click the Faux Bold button **T** or the Faux Italic button *T* in the Character palette to apply a simulated style. Alternately, choose Faux Bold or Faux Italic from the Character palette menu.

Note: You cannot apply Faux Bold formatting to warped type. (See "Warping type layers" on page 273.)

Choosing a type size

The *type size* determines how large the type appears in the image:

- In Photoshop, the default unit of measurement for type is *points*. One PostScript point is equal to 1/72 of an inch in a 72-ppi image; however, you can switch between using the PostScript and traditional definitions of point size. You can change the default unit of measurement for type in the Units & Rulers section of the Preferences dialog box.

- In ImageReady, *pixels* are the only unit of measurement for type. This is because the ImageReady application is tailored to creating images for online media, in which pixels are the standard unit of measurement.

To choose a type size:

In the Character palette or options bar, enter or select a new value for Size **T**. To use an alternate unit of measurement, enter the unit (in, cm, mm, pt, px, or pica) after the value in the Size text box. The value you enter is converted to the default unit of measurement.

To specify the default unit of measurement for type (Photoshop):

1 Do one of the following:

- In Windows and Mac OS 9.x, choose Edit > Preferences > Units & Rulers.

- In Mac OS X, choose Photoshop > Preferences > Units & Rulers.

2 Select a unit of measurement for Type.

To specify the point size definition (Photoshop):

1 Do one of the following:

- In Windows and Mac OS 9.x, choose Edit > Preferences > Units & Rulers.

- In Mac OS X, choose Photoshop > Preferences > Units & Rulers.

2 Select an option for Point/Pica Size. Traditional points are slightly smaller than PostScript points.

Changing the type color

The type you enter gets its color from the current foreground color; however, you can change the type color before or after you enter type. When editing existing type layers, you can change the color of individual, selected characters or all type in a layer.

To change the type color:

Do one of the following:

- Click the Color selection box in the options bar or Character palette, and select a color using the color picker. In ImageReady, you can also select an option from the Color selection box pop-up menu: Foreground Color, Background Color, Other (to use the color picker), or a color from the pop-up palette.

- Use fill shortcuts. To fill with the foreground color, press Alt+Backspace (Windows) or Option+Delete (Mac OS); to fill with the background color, press Ctrl+Backspace (Windows) or Command+Delete (Mac OS).

- Apply an overlay layer style to the type layer to apply a color, pattern, or gradient on top of the existing color. (See "Using layer effects and styles" on page 246.) In ImageReady, you can drag a color from the toolbox color selection box, the Color palette, the Color Table palette, or the Swatches palette, and drop it onto a type layer to automatically apply a color overlay style. Applying an overlay layer style affects all characters in the type layer; you cannot use this method to change the color of individual characters.

- Click the foreground color selection box in the toolbox, and select a color using the color picker. Or click a color in the Color palette, the Swatches palette, or the Color Table palette (ImageReady). To use this method to change the color of an existing type layer, you must first select characters on that layer.

Specifying leading

The amount of space between lines of type is called *leading*. For Roman type, leading is measured from the baseline of one line of type to the baseline of the next line. The *baseline* is the invisible line on which most type lies. You can apply more than one leading amount within the same paragraph; however, the largest leading value in a line of type determines the leading value for that line.

You can use other options to set leading for Chinese, Japanese, or Korean type.

 For more information, see "Specifying how leading is measured" in online Help.

5-point type with 6-point leading, and with 12-point leading

To change the leading:

In the Character palette, do one of the following:

- Choose the desired leading from the Leading menu 🅐.

- Select the existing leading value, and enter a new value.

To change the default auto leading percentage:

1 Display the Paragraph palette.

2 Choose Justification from the palette menu.

3 For Auto Leading, specify a new default percentage.

Specifying kerning and tracking

Kerning is the process of adding or subtracting space between specific letter pairs. You can control kerning manually, or you can use automatic kerning to turn on the kerning built into the font by the font designer. *Tracking* is the process of creating an equal amount of spacing across a range of letters.

Positive kerning or tracking values move characters apart (adding to the default spacing); negative values move characters closer together (reducing the default spacing). Kerning and tracking values are measured in units that are 1/1000 of an *em space*. The width of an em space is relative to the current type size. In a 1-point font, 1 em corresponds to 1 point; in a 10-point font, 1 em corresponds to 10 points. Because kerning and tracking units are 1/1000 em, 100 units in a 10-point font are equivalent to 1 point.

Default, and tracking set to 350

To use a font's built-in kerning information:

In the Character palette, choose Metrics (Photoshop) or Auto (ImageReady) from the Kerning menu .

Note: The Metrics option replaces the Auto Kern option in previous versions of Photoshop.

To adjust kerning manually:

1 Click with a type tool to set an insertion point between two characters.

Note: If a range of type is selected, you can't manually kern the characters. Instead, use tracking.

2 In the Character palette, enter or select a numeric value for Kerning .

3 Commit the changes to the type layer. (See "About using the type tools (Photoshop)" on page 268.)

To specify tracking:

In the Character palette, enter or select a numeric value for Tracking .

Adjusting horizontal or vertical scale

Horizontal scale and *vertical scale* specify the proportion between the height and width of the type. Unscaled characters have a value of 100%. You can adjust scale to compress or expand selected characters in both width and height.

To adjust the horizontal or vertical scale of type:

In the Character palette, enter a new percentage for Horizontal Scale **T** or Vertical Scale **T** .

Specifying baseline shift

Baseline shift controls the distance that type appears from its baseline, either raising or lowering the selected type to create superscripts or subscripts.

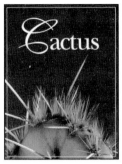 

Default, and baseline shift of 10 points

To specify baseline shift:

In the Character palette, enter a value for Baseline Shift $A_\uparrow^a$. A positive value moves horizontal type above and vertical type to the right of the baseline; a negative value moves type below or to the left of the baseline.

To show or hide the baseline (ImageReady):

Do one of the following:

• Choose View > Show > Text Baseline.

• Choose View > Extras. This command shows or hides all selected items in the View > Show submenu. (See "Working with Extras" on page 41.)

Changing case

You can enter or format type as uppercase characters, either all caps or small caps. When you format type as small caps, Photoshop and ImageReady use the small caps designed as part of the font, if available. If the font does not include small caps, Photoshop and ImageReady generate faux small caps.

To change the case of type:

Do one of the following:

• Click the All Caps button TT or the Small Caps button Tr in the Character palette.

• Choose All Caps or Small Caps from the Character palette menu. A check mark indicates that the option is selected.

Note: Selecting Small Caps will not change characters that were originally typed in uppercase.

Making characters superscript or subscript

You can enter or format type as superscript or subscript characters. Superscript characters are reduced in size and shifted above the type baseline; subscript characters are reduced in size and shifted below the type baseline. If the font does not include superscript or subscript characters, Photoshop generates faux superscript or subscript characters.

To specify superscript or subscript characters:

Do one of the following:

• Click the Superscript button T^1 or the Subscript button T_1 in the Character palette.

- Choose Superscript or Subscript from the Character palette menu. A check mark indicates that the option is selected.

Applying underline and strikethrough

You can apply a line under horizontal type, or to the left or right of vertical type. You can also apply a line through horizontal or vertical type. The line is always the same color as the type color.

To apply an underline or strikethrough:

Choose an option:

- Click the Underline button T in the Character palette to apply an underline beneath horizontal type.

- Choose Underline Left or Underline Right from the Character palette menu to apply an underline to the left or right of vertical type. You can apply an underline to the left or right, but not to both sides. A check mark indicates that an option is selected.

Note: *The Underline Left and Underline Right options only appear in the Character palette menu when a type layer that contains vertical type is selected.*

- Click the Strikethrough button T in the Character palette to apply a horizontal line through horizontal type or a vertical line through vertical type. Alternately, choose Strikethrough from the Character palette menu.

Using ligatures and old style numerals

When working with OpenType fonts, you can use ligatures and old style typographic numerals in your type, if the font provides them. *Ligatures* are typographic replacements for certain pairs of characters, such as "fi" and "fl." Old style numerals are shorter than regular numerals, and some old style numerals descend below the type baseline.

In Photoshop, you can also use alternate ligatures when working with OpenType fonts that provide them. Alternate ligatures are extra ligatures that aren't in regular use, such as "st."

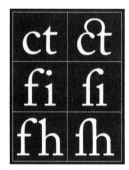

Type with Ligatures option unselected and selected

To use ligatures or old style numerals:

Choose Ligatures or Old Style from the Character palette menu. A check mark indicates that the option is selected.

To use alternate ligatures (Photoshop):

Choose Alternate Ligatures from the Character palette menu. A check mark indicates that the option is selected.

Using fractional character widths

By default, type is displayed using fractional character widths. This means that the spacing between characters varies, with fractions of whole pixels between some characters. In most situations, fractional character widths provide the best spacing for type appearance and readability. However, for type in small sizes (less than 20 points) displayed online, fractional character widths can cause type to run together or have too much extra space, making it difficult to read.

You can turn off fractional character widths to fix type spacing in whole-pixel increments and prevent small type from running together. The fractional character width setting applies to all characters on a type layer—you cannot set the option for selected characters.

To turn fractional character widths on or off:

Choose Fractional Widths from the Character palette menu. A check mark indicates that the option is selected.

Viewing text using the operating system layout

The System Layout command lets you preview text using the operating system's default text handling. This is useful when designing user interface elements, such as dialog boxes and menus.

To turn system layout on or off:

Choose System Layout from the Character palette menu. A check mark indicates that the option is selected.

Rotating vertical type

When working with vertical type, you can rotate the direction of characters by 90°. Rotated characters appear upright; unrotated characters appear sideways (perpendicular to the type line).

Original, and type without vertical rotation

To rotate characters in vertical type:

Choose Rotate Character from the Character palette menu. A check mark indicates that the option is selected.

Note: You cannot rotate double-byte characters (full width characters only available in Chinese, Japanese, and Korean fonts). Any double-byte characters in the selected range will not be rotated.

Checking for spelling errors (Photoshop)

When you spell-check a document, Photoshop questions any words that aren't in its dictionary. If a questioned word is spelled correctly, you can confirm its spelling by adding the word to the dictionary. If a questioned word is misspelled, you can correct it.

To check and correct spelling:

1 In the Character palette, choose a language from the pop-up menu at the bottom of the palette. This sets the dictionary for spell-checking.

2 Do one of the following:

• Select a type layer.

• To check specific text, select the text.

• To check a word, place an insertion point in the word.

3 Choose Edit > Check Spelling.

4 As Photoshop finds unfamiliar words and other possible errors, do one of the following:

• Click Ignore to continue checking spelling without changing text. Click Ignore All to ignore the word for the rest of the spell-check.

• To correct a misspelling, make sure the correctly spelled word is in the Change To text box and click Change. If the suggested word is not the word you want, you can select a different word in the Suggestions text box or enter the word in the Change To text box.

• To correct a repeated misspelling in a document, make sure the correctly spelled word is in the Change To text box and click Change All.

• Click Add to have Photoshop store the unrecognized word in the dictionary, so that subsequent occurrences are not flagged as misspellings.

• If you selected a type layer and want to spell-check only that layer, deselect Check All Layers.

Finding and replacing text (Photoshop)

You can search for a single character, a word, or group of words. Once you find what you're looking for, you can change it to something else.

To find and replace a word:

1 Select the layer that contains the text you want to find and replace.

2 Choose Edit > Find and Replace.

3 In the Find What box, type or paste the text you want to find. To change the text, type the new text in the Change To text box.

4 Select Case Sensitive if you want to search for a word or words that exactly match the case of the text in the Find What text box. For example, a search for "PrePress" will not find "Prepress" or "PREPRESS."

5 Select Whole Word Only if you want to disregard the search text if it is embedded within a larger word. For example, if you are searching for "any" as a whole word, "many" will be disregarded.

6 Click Find Next to begin the search.

7 Click the button that reflects what you want to do next.

• Change replaces the found text with the revised text. To repeat the search, select Find Next.

• Change/Find replaces the found text with the revised text and then searches for the next occurrence.

• Change All searches for and replaces all occurrences of the found text.

Formatting paragraphs

A paragraph is any range of type with a carriage return at the end. You use the Paragraph palette to set options that apply to entire paragraphs, such as the alignment, indentation, and space between lines of type. For point type, each line is a separate paragraph. For paragraph type, each paragraph can have multiple lines, depending on the dimensions of the bounding box.

Selecting paragraphs and showing the Paragraph palette

You can use the Paragraph palette to set formatting options for a single paragraph, multiple paragraphs, or all paragraphs in a type layer.

To select paragraphs for formatting:

Select the horizontal type tool T or the vertical type tool ↓T and do one of the following:

- Click in a paragraph to apply formatting to a single paragraph.

- Make a selection within a range of paragraphs to apply formatting to multiple paragraphs.

- Select the type layer in the Layers palette to apply formatting to all paragraphs in the layer.

To show the Paragraph palette:

Do one of the following:

- Choose Window > Paragraph, or click the Paragraph palette tab if the palette is visible but not active.

- With a type tool selected, click the palette button ▤ in the options bar.

Aligning and justifying type

You can *align* type to one edge of a paragraph (left, center, or right for horizontal type; top, center, or bottom for vertical type) and *justify* type to both edges of a paragraph. Alignment options are available for both point type and paragraph type; justification options are only available for paragraph type.

To specify alignment:

In the Paragraph palette or options bar, click an alignment option. The options for horizontal type are:

≡ Aligns type to the left, leaving the right edge of the paragraph ragged.

≡ Aligns type to the center, leaving both edges of the paragraph ragged.

≡ Aligns type to right, leaving the left edge of the paragraph ragged.

The options for vertical type are:

▥ Aligns type to the top, leaving the bottom edge of the paragraph ragged.

▥ Aligns type to the center, leaving both the top and bottom edges of the paragraph ragged.

▥ Aligns type to bottom, leaving the top edge of the paragraph ragged.

To specify justification for paragraph type:

In the Paragraph palette, click a justification option. The options for horizontal type are:

≡ Justifies all lines except the last, which is left-aligned.

≡ Justifies all lines except the last, which is center-aligned.

≡ Justifies all lines except the last, which is right-aligned.

≡ Justifies all lines including the last, which is force-justified.

The options for vertical type are:

⦙⦙ Justifies all lines except the last, which is top-aligned.

⦙⦙ Justifies all lines except the last, which is center-aligned.

⦙⦙ Justifies all lines except the last, which is bottom-aligned.

⦙⦙ Justifies all lines including the last, which is force-justified.

Indenting paragraphs

Indentation specifies the amount of space between type and the bounding box or line that contains the type. Indentation affects only the selected paragraph or paragraphs, so you can easily set different indentations for paragraphs.

To specify paragraph indentation:

In the Paragraph palette, enter a value for an indentation option:

- Left Indent ⇥ to indent from the left edge of the paragraph. For vertical type, this option controls the indentation from the top of the paragraph.

- Right Indent ⇤ to indent from the right edge of the paragraph. For vertical type, this option controls the indentation from the bottom of the paragraph.

- First Line Indent ⇥ to indent the first line of type in the paragraph. For horizontal type, the first line indent is relative to the left indent; for vertical type, the first line indent is relative to the top indent. To create a first line hanging indentation, enter a negative value.

Changing space above or below paragraphs

You can control the space above and below paragraphs using the paragraph spacing options.

To specify paragraph spacing:

In the Paragraph palette, enter a value for Space Before ⇤ and Space After ⇥.

Specifying hanging punctuation

Hanging punctuation controls whether punctuation marks fall inside or outside the margins. If hanging punctuation is turned on for Roman fonts, periods, commas, single-quotation marks, double-quotation marks, apostrophes, hyphens, em dashes, en dashes, colons, and semicolons appear outside the margins.

To use hanging punctuation for Roman fonts:

Choose Roman Hanging Punctuation from the Paragraph palette menu. A check mark indicates that the option is selected.

Note: When you use Roman Hanging Punctuation, any double-byte punctuation marks available in Chinese, Japanese, and Korean fonts in the selected range will not hang.

 For more information, see "Using burasagari" in online Help.

Controlling hyphenation and justification

The settings you choose for hyphenation and justification affect the horizontal spacing of lines and the aesthetic appeal of type on a page. Hyphenation options determine whether words can be hyphenated and, if they can, what breaks are allowable. Justification options determine word, letter, and glyph spacing.

 For more information, see "Controlling hyphenation and justification" in online Help.

Working with composition

The appearance of type on the page depends on a complex interaction of processes called *composition*. Using the word spacing, letter spacing, glyph spacing, and hyphenation options you've selected, Photoshop and ImageReady evaluate possible line breaks and choose the one that best supports the specified parameters.

 For more information, see "Working with composition" in online Help.

Setting options for Chinese, Japanese, and Korean type (Photoshop)

Photoshop provides several options for working with Chinese, Japanese, and Korean (CJK) type. Characters in CJK fonts are often referred to as *double-byte characters.*

 For more information, see "Setting options for Chinese, Japanese, and Korean type" in online Help.

Chapter 12: Designing Web Pages

Adobe Photoshop and Adobe ImageReady provide you with a comprehensive environment for designing complex, image-rich Web pages. You can use the tools and techniques you're already familiar with to design Web pages that include images, text, and sophisticated effects—such as rollovers, image maps, and animations—quickly and easily. Best of all, you never have to view or edit the underlying HTML and JavaScript.

About designing Web pages with Photoshop and ImageReady

When designing Web pages using Adobe Photoshop and Adobe ImageReady, keep in mind the tools and features that are available in each application.

- Photoshop provides tools for creating and manipulating static images for use on the Web. You can divide an image into slices, add links and HTML text, optimize the slices, and save the image as a Web page.

- ImageReady provides many of the same image-editing tools as Photoshop. In addition, it includes tools and palettes for advanced Web processing and creating dynamic Web images like animations and rollovers.

When you save an image for use as a Web page, you can choose to generate an HTML file. This file contains information that tells a Web browser what to display when it loads the page. It can contain pointers to images (in the form of GIF, PNG, JPEG, and WBMP files), HTML text, linking information, and JavaScript code for creating rollover effects.

You can integrate your Web production process by opening Photoshop files directly in Adobe GoLive. Slices, URLs, and other Web features in Photoshop files are accessible in GoLive for management and editing. You can also open Photoshop files in GoLive as page templates. Page templates display as a shaded preview and provide a visual guide for building a Web page in GoLive. For more information on using GoLive, see the *Adobe GoLive User Guide*.

Note: You can preview most Web effects directly in Photoshop or ImageReady. However, the appearance of an image on the Web depends on the operating system, color display system, and browser used to display the image. Be sure to preview images in different browsers, on different operating systems, and with different color bit depths. (See "Previewing an image in a browser" on page 48.)

Creating and viewing slices

A slice is a rectangular area of an image that you can use to create links, rollovers, and animations in the resulting Web page. Dividing an image into slices lets you selectively optimize it for Web viewing.

About slices

You use slices to divide a source image into functional areas. When you save the image as a Web page, each slice is saved as an independent file that contains its own settings, color palette, links, rollover effects, and animation effects. You can use slices to achieve faster download speeds. Slices are also advantageous when working with images that contain different types of data. For example, if one area of an image needs to be optimized in GIF format to support an animation, but the rest of the image is better optimized in JPEG format, you can isolate the animation using a slice.

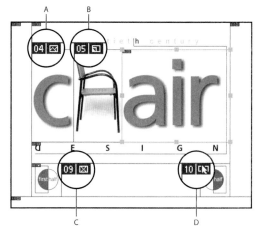

Web page divided into slices:
*A. Image slice **B.** Layer-based slice **C.** No Image slice*
D. Slice that contains a rollover

You set how the Photoshop or ImageReady application generates HTML code for aligning slices—either using tables or cascading style sheets—in the Output Settings dialog box. You can also set how slice files are named. (See "Setting output options" on page 360.)

Types of slices

Slices you create using the slice tool are called *user slices*; slices you create from a layer are called *layer-based slices*. When you create a new user slice or layer-based slice, additional *auto slices* are generated to account for the remaining areas of the image. In other words, auto slices fill the space in the image that is not defined by user slices or layer-based slices. Auto slices are regenerated every time you add or edit user slices or layer-based slices.

User slices, layer-based slices, and auto slices look different—user slices and layer-based slices are defined by a solid line, while auto slices are defined by a dotted line. In addition, each type of slice displays a distinct icon. You can choose to show or hide auto slices, which makes your work with user- and layer-based slices easier to view.

A *subslice* is a type of auto slice that is generated when you create overlapping slices. Subslices indicate how the image will be divided when you save the optimized file. Although subslices are numbered and display a slice symbol, you cannot select or edit them separately from the underlying slice. Subslices are regenerated every time you arrange the stacking order of slices.

Creating user slices

You can create user slices with the slice tool or from guides, and in ImageReady, from a selection.

To create a slice with the slice tool:

1 Select the slice tool ✐ . Any existing slices automatically display in the document window.

2 Choose a style setting in the options bar:

- Normal to determine slice proportions by dragging.

- Fixed Aspect Ratio to set a height-to-width ratio. Enter whole numbers or decimals for the aspect ratio. For example, to create a slice twice as wide as it is high, enter 2 for the width and 1 for the height.

- Fixed Size to specify the slice's height and width. Enter pixel values in whole numbers.

3 Drag over the area where you want to create a slice. Shift-drag to constrain the slice to a square. Alt-drag (Windows) or Option-drag (Mac OS) to draw from the center. Use snap to align a new slice to a guide or another slice in the image. (See "Moving and resizing user slices" on page 293.)

To create slices from guides:

1 Add guides to an image. (See "Using guides and the grid" on page 39.)

2 Do one of the following:

- (Photoshop) Select the slice tool, and click Slices From Guides in the options bar.

- (ImageReady) Choose Slices > Create Slices from Guides.

When you create slices from guides, any existing slices are deleted.

To create a slice from a selection (ImageReady):

1 Select a portion of the image.

2 Choose Select > Create Slice from Selection.

ImageReady creates a user slice based on the selection marquee. If the selection is feathered, the slice covers the full selection (including the feathered edges). If the selection is nonrectangular, the slice covers a rectangular area large enough to enclose the full selection.

Creating layer-based slices

When you create a slice from a layer, the slice area encompasses all the pixel data in the layer. If you move the layer or edit the layer's content, the slice area automatically adjusts to encompass the new pixels.

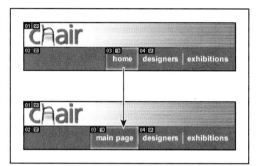

Example of how a layer-based slice is updated when the source layer is modified

Layer-based slices are especially useful when working with rollovers. If you apply an effect to the layer—such as a drop shadow or glow— to create a rollover state, the slice automatically adjusts to encompass the new pixels. However, do not use a layer-based slice when you plan to move the layer over a large area of the image during an animation, because the slice dimension may exceed a useful size.

To create a slice from a layer:

1 Select a layer in the Layers palette.

2 Choose Layer > New Layer Based Slice.

Converting auto slices to user slices

You can move, duplicate, combine, divide, resize, delete, arrange, align, and distribute user slices. You can also apply different optimization settings to user slices. In contrast, all auto slices in an image are linked and share the same optimization settings. This is because auto slices are regenerated every time you create or edit a user slice or layer-based slice.

Converting an auto slice to a user slice prevents it from being changed when regeneration occurs. Dividing, combining, linking, and setting options for auto slices automatically converts them to user slices.

To convert an auto slice to a user slice:

1 Select an auto slice. In ImageReady, you can select multiple slices. (See "Selecting slices" on page 293.)

2 Do one of the following:

• (Photoshop) With the slice select tool selected, click Promote to User Slice in the options bar.

• (ImageReady) Choose Slices > Promote to User-slice(s).

Converting layer-based slices to user slices

Because a layer-based slice is tied to the pixel content of a layer, the only way to move, combine, divide, resize, and align it is to edit the layer. You can convert a layer-based slice to a user slice to unlink it from the layer.

To convert a layer-based slice to a user slice:

1 Select a layer-based slice. In ImageReady, you can select multiple slices. (See "Selecting slices" on page 293.)

2 Do one of the following:

• (Photoshop) Click Promote to User Slice in the options bar.

• (ImageReady) Choose Slices > Promote to User-slice(s).

Viewing slices

You can view slices in Photoshop, the Photoshop Save for Web dialog box, and ImageReady. The following characteristics can help you identify and differentiate between slices:

Slice lines Define the boundary of the slice. Solid lines indicate that the slice is a user slice or layer-based slice; dotted lines indicate that the slice is an auto slice.

Slice colors Differentiate user slices and layer-based slices from auto slices. By default, user slices and layer-based slices have blue symbols, while auto slices have gray symbols.

In addition, ImageReady and the Photoshop Save for Web dialog box use color adjustments to dim unselected slices. These adjustments are for display purposes only and do not affect the final image's color. By default, the color adjustment for auto slices is twice the amount of that for user-slices.

Slice numbers Slices are numbered from left to right and top to bottom, beginning in the upper left corner of the image. If you change the arrangement or total number of slices, slice numbers are updated to reflect the new order.

Slice symbols Indicate whether a user slice has Image ⊠ or No Image ⊠ content; if the slice is a layer-based slice ⊡; if the slice is linked ▯; or if the slice includes a rollover effect ⊡.

To show or hide slices:

Do one of the following:

• Choose View > Show > Slices. To hide and show slices along with other items, use the Extras command. For more information, see "Working with Extras" on page 41.

• (ImageReady) Click the Toggle Slices Visibility button ⊡.

To show or hide auto slices:

Do one of the following:

• Select the slice select tool, and click Show Auto Slices or Hide Auto Slices in the options bar.

• (ImageReady) Choose View > Show > Auto Slices.

To show or hide slice numbers (Photoshop):

1 Do one of the following:

• In Windows and Mac OS 9.x, choose Edit > Preferences > Guides, Grid, & Slices.

• In Mac OS X, choose Photoshop > Preferences > Guides, Grid, & Slices.

2 Under Slices, click Show Slice Numbers.

To show or hide slice numbers and slice symbols (ImageReady):

1 Choose Edit > Preferences > Slices.

2 Under Numbers and Symbols, select a size for display symbols:

- None to display no numbers or symbols.

- The small icon to display small numbers and symbols.

- The large icon to display large numbers and symbols.

3 For Opacity, enter a value, or choose a value from the pop-up slider to change the opacity of the numbers and symbols display.

To show slice lines only (ImageReady):

1 Choose Edit > Preferences > Slices.

2 Under Slice Lines, select Show Lines Only.

To change the color of slice lines:

1 Do one of the following:

- (Photoshop) In Windows and Mac OS 9.x, choose Edit > Preferences > Guides, Grid, & Slices; in Mac OS X, choose Photoshop > Preferences > Guides, Grid, & Slices.

- (ImageReady) In Windows and Mac OS 9.x, choose Edit > Preferences > Slices; in Mac OS X, choose ImageReady > Preferences > Slices.

2 Under Slice Lines, choose a color from the Line Color pop-up menu.

Changing the color of slice lines automatically changes the color of selected slice lines to a contrasting color.

To change slice color adjustments (ImageReady):

1 Do one of the following:

- In Windows and Mac OS 9.x, choose Edit > Preferences > Slices.

- In Mac OS X, choose ImageReady > Preferences > Slices.

2 Enter a value, or choose a value from the Color Adjustments pop-up slider for User slices, Auto slices, or both. (The User slices option controls color adjustments for both user slices and layer-based slices.)

The value determines by how much the brightness and contrast of unselected slices are dimmed.

Selecting and modifying slices

You can move, duplicate, combine, divide, resize, delete, arrange, align, and distribute user slices. There are fewer options for modifying layer-based slices and auto slices; however, you can promote a layer-based slice or an auto slice to a user slice at any time.

In Photoshop, you cannot combine, align, or distribute slices. Jump to ImageReady to access these slice-editing capabilities.

Using the Slice palette (ImageReady)

To display the Slice palette:

Choose Window > Slice, or click the palette button on the right side of the options bar for the slice select tool.

Selecting slices

You select a slice with the slice select tool in order to apply modifications to it. In the Photoshop Save for Web dialog box and in ImageReady, you can select multiple slices.

To select a slice:

Do one of the following:

- Select the slice select tool ![icon], and click on a slice in the image. When working with overlapping slices, click the visible section of an underlying slice to select it.

  💡 *To toggle between the slice tool and the slice select tool, hold down Ctrl (Windows) or Command (Mac OS).*

- (ImageReady) Select a slice in the Rollovers palette. (See "Using the Rollovers palette" on page 315.)

To select multiple slices (ImageReady):

With the slice select tool ![icon], do one of the following:

- Shift-click to add slices to the selection.
- Click in an auto slice or outside the image area, and drag across the slices you want to select. (Clicking in a user slice and dragging moves the slice.)

In ImageReady, you can save, load, and delete slice selections. Using slice selections lets you reselect specific slices quickly and accurately.

To save a slice selection (ImageReady):

1 Select one or more slices.

2 Choose Slices > Save Slice Selection.

3 Enter a name in the Selection Name text box, and click OK.

To load a slice selection (ImageReady):

Choose Slices > Load Slice Selection, and select the name of the slice selection you want to load from the submenu.

Note: You must save a slice selection before you can load it.

To delete a slice selection (ImageReady):

Choose Slices > Delete Slice Selection, and select the name of the slice selection you want to delete from the submenu. Deleting a slice selection does not delete the slices themselves.

Moving and resizing user slices

You can move and resize user slices in Photoshop and ImageReady, but not in the Photoshop Save for Web dialog box. You can also move and resize slices using numeric coordinates. (See "Resizing and moving slices using numeric coordinates" on page 299.)

To move or resize a user slice:

1 Select a user slice. In ImageReady, you can select and move multiple slices.

2 Do one of the following:

- To move a slice, move the pointer inside the slice selection border, and drag the slice to a new position. Press Shift to restrict movement to a vertical, horizontal, or 45° diagonal line.

- To resize a slice, grab a side or a corner handle of the slice, and drag to resize the slice. In ImageReady, if you select and resize adjacent slices, common edges shared by the slices are resized together.

To snap slices to a guide or another user slice:

1 Select the options you want from the View > Snap To submenu, and choose View > Snap. (See "Using the Snap command" on page 117.) A check mark indicates that the option is turned on.

2 Move the selected slices as desired. The slices snap to any guide or slice within 4 pixels.

Dividing user slices and auto slices

The Divide Slice dialog box lets you divide slices horizontally, vertically, or both. In Photoshop, you can divide only one slice; in ImageReady, you can divide multiple slices at the same time. Duplicate slices are always user slices, regardless of whether the original is a user slice or an auto slice.

Note: You cannot divide layer-based slices.

To divide slices:

1 Select a slice. In ImageReady, you can select multiple slices.

2 Do one of the following:

- (Photoshop) With the slice select tool selected, click Divide Slice in the options bar.
- (ImageReady) Choose Slices > Divide Slice(s).
- (ImageReady) Choose Divide Slice(s) from the Slice palette menu.

3 Select Preview in the Divide Slice dialog box to preview the changes.

4 In the Divide Slice dialog box, select one or both of the following options:

- Divide Horizontally Into to divide the slice lengthwise.
- Divide Vertically Into to divide the slice widthwise.

5 Define how you want to divide each selected slice:

- Select and enter a value for slices down or slices across to divide each slice evenly into the specified number of slices.
- Select and enter a value for pixels per slice to divide each slice based on the specified number of pixels. Any section of a slice that is left over is made into another slice. For example, if you divide a slice that is 100 pixels wide into three new slices each 30 pixels wide, the remaining 10-pixel-wide area becomes a new slice.

6 Click OK.

Duplicating slices

You can create a duplicate slice with the same dimensions and optimization settings as the original. If the original slice is a linked user slice, the duplicate is linked to the same set of linked slices. For more information, see "Linking slices (ImageReady)" on page 302. Duplicate slices are always user slices, regardless of whether the original is a user slice, a layer-based slice, or an auto slice.

In ImageReady, you can also copy and paste slices within or between documents.

To duplicate a slice:

Do one of the following:

• Select a slice. (In ImageReady, you can select multiple slices.) Then Alt-drag (Windows) or Option-drag (Mac OS) from inside the selection. In ImageReady, you can also choose Slices > Duplicate Slice(s) or Duplicate Slice(s) from the Slice palette menu.

• (ImageReady) Select a slice in the Rollovers palette, and choose Duplicate Slice from the palette menu. (See "Using the Rollovers palette" on page 315.)

The duplicate slice appears on top of the original (offset 10 pixels down and to the right) and can be moved, resized, or otherwise modified.

To copy and paste a slice (ImageReady):

1 Select one or more slices.

2 Choose Copy Slice from the Slice palette menu.

3 If you want to paste into another image, open and display that image.

4 Choose Paste Slice from the Slice palette menu. If you paste the slice into the same image as you copied it from, the pasted slice appears on top of the original.

Combining slices (ImageReady)

In ImageReady, you can combine two or more slices into a single slice. The resulting slice takes its dimensions and position from the rectangle created by joining the outer edges of the combined slices. If the combined slices are not adjacent or are of different proportions or alignments, the newly combined slice may overlap other slices.

Optimization settings for the combined slice are those of the first slice selected before the Combine Slices operation. A combined slice is always a user slice, regardless of whether the original slices include auto slices.

Note: You cannot combine layer-based slices.

To combine slices:

1 Select two or more slices.

2 Choose Slices > Combine Slices.

Arranging user slices and layer-based slices

When slices overlap, the last slice you create is the top slice in the stacking order. You can change the stacking order to gain access to underlying slices. You can specify which slice is on the top and bottom of the stack and move slices up or down in the stacking order.

Note: You cannot arrange the stacking order of auto slices.

To change the stacking order of slices:

1 Select a slice. In ImageReady, you can select multiple slices.

2 Do one of the following:

- With the slice select tool active, click a stacking order option in the options bar: Bring to Front 🖼, Bring Forward 🖼, Send Backward 🖼, Send to Back 🖼.

- (ImageReady) Choose Slices > Arrange, and choose a stacking order command from the submenu; or choose a stacking order command from the Slice palette menu.

- (ImageReady) Drag the slice up or down in the Rollovers palette. (See "Using the Rollovers palette" on page 315.)

Aligning user slices (ImageReady)

In ImageReady, you can align user slices with the top, bottom, left, right, or middle. Aligning user slices can eliminate unneeded auto slices and generate a smaller, more efficient HTML file.

Note: *To align layer-based slices, align the contents of the layers. (See "Repositioning the contents of layers" on page 234.)*

To align user slices:

1 Select the user slices you want to align.

2 Do one of the following:

- With the slice select tool active, click an alignment option in the options bar: Align Top Edges 🖼, Align Vertical Centers 🖼, Align Bottom Edges 🖼, Align Left Edges 🖼, Align Horizontal Centers 🖼, Align Right Edges 🖼.

- Choose Slices > Align, and choose a command from the submenu.

Distributing user slices (ImageReady)

In ImageReady, you can distribute user slices evenly along the vertical or horizontal axis. Distributing user slices can eliminate unneeded auto slices and generate a smaller, more efficient HTML file.

Note: *To distribute layer-based slices, distribute the contents of the layers. (See "Repositioning the contents of layers" on page 234.)*

To distribute user slices:

1 Select three or more user slices you want to distribute.

2 Do one of the following:

- With the slice select tool active, click a distribute option in the options bar: Distribute Top Edges 🖼, Distribute Vertical Centers 🖼, Distribute Bottom Edges 🖼, Distribute Left Edges 🖼, Distribute Horizontal Centers 🖼, Distribute Right Edges 🖼.

- Choose Slices > Distribute, and choose a command from the submenu.

Deleting user slices and layer-based slices

When you delete a user slice or layer-based slice, auto slices are regenerated to fill the document area.

Deleting a layer-based slice does not delete the associated layer; however, deleting the layer associated with a layer-based slice does delete the layer-based slice.

Note: You cannot delete auto slices. If you delete all user slices and layer-based slices in an image, one auto slice layer will remain.

To delete a slice:

1 Select a slice. In ImageReady, you can select multiple slices.

2 Do one of the following:

• Press the Backspace key or the Delete key.

• (ImageReady) Choose Slices > Delete Slice(s), or choose Delete Slice(s) from the Slice palette menu.

To delete all user slices and layer-based slices:

Do one of the following:

• (Photoshop) Choose View > Clear Slices.

• (ImageReady) Choose Slices > Delete All.

Locking slices (Photoshop)

Locking slices prevents you from making changes accidentally, such as resizing or moving slices.

To lock all slices:

Choose View > Lock Slices.

Specifying slice options

Setting slice options lets you specify how the slice data will appear in a Web browser. The available options vary according to the application and the slice type you select. You can only set options for one slice at a time.

Note: Setting options for an auto slice promotes the slice to a user slice.

Viewing slice options

You specify slice options in the Slice Options dialog box (Photoshop) and the Slice palette (ImageReady).

To display the Slice Options dialog box (Photoshop):

Do one of the following:

• Double-click a slice with the slice select tool.

• With the slice select tool active, click the Slice Options button in the options bar. This method is available only in the main Photoshop application, not in the Photoshop Save for Web dialog box.

To display the Slice palette (ImageReady):

Choose Window > Slice, or click the palette button 🖹 on the right side of the options bar for the slice select tool.

Choosing a content type

Formatting and display options for a slice vary according to its content type. There are two types of slice content:

• Image slices contain image data, including rollover states. This is the default content type.

• No Image slices contain solid color or HTML text. Because No Image slices contain no image data, they download more quickly. Photoshop and ImageReady do not display No Image slice content. To view No Image slice content, preview the image in a browser.
(See "Previewing an image in a browser" on page 48.)

To specify a content type:

1 Select a slice. If you are working in Photoshop, double-click the slice with the slice select tool to display the Slice Options dialog box.

2 In the Slice Options dialog box (Photoshop) or the Slice palette (ImageReady), select a slice type from the Type pop-up menu.

Specifying slice names

As you add slices to an image, you may find it helpful to rename slices based on their content. By default, user slices are named according to the settings in the Output Options dialog box. (See "Setting slice output options" on page 361.) Layer-based slices are given the name of the layer from which they are derived.

To change the name of a slice:

Do one of the following:

• Select a slice. If you are working in Photoshop, double-click the slice with the slice select tool to display the Slice Options dialog box. In the Slice Options dialog box (Photoshop) or the Slice palette (ImageReady), type a new name in the Name text box.

Note: The Name text box is not available for No Image slice content.

• Double-click the slice's name in the Rollovers palette, and enter a new name. (See "Using the Rollovers palette" on page 315.)

Specifying slice background colors

The background color option lets you select a color to fill the transparent area (for Image slices) or entire area (for No Image slices) of the slice. In Photoshop, this option is available only if you activate the Slice Options dialog box from within the Save for Web dialog box.

Photoshop and ImageReady do not display the selected background color—you must preview the image in a browser to view the effect of selecting a background color. (See "Previewing an image in a browser" on page 48.)

To choose a background color:

1 Select a slice. If you are working in the Photoshop Save for Web dialog box, double-click the slice with the slice select tool to display the Slice Options dialog box.

2 In the Slice Options dialog box (Photoshop) or the Slice palette (ImageReady), select a background color from the Background/BG pop-up menu:

• (Photoshop) Select None, Matte, Eyedropper (to use the color in the eyedropper sample box), White, Black, or Other (using the color picker).

- (ImageReady) Select None, Matte, Foreground Color, Background Color, or Other (to use the color picker), or select a color from the pop-up palette.

Assigning a URL to an Image slice

Assigning a URL to a slice makes the entire slice area a hotspot in the resulting Web page. When a user clicks in the hotspot, the Web browser links to the specified URL and target frame. This option is only available for Image slices.

To assign link information to an Image slice:

1 Select a slice. If you are working in Photoshop, double-click the slice with the slice select tool to display the Slice Options dialog box.

2 In the Slice Options dialog box (Photoshop) or the Slice palette (ImageReady), enter a URL in the URL text box, or choose a previously created URL from the pop-up menu. You can enter a relative URL or a full URL. If you enter a full URL, be sure to include http:// (for example, enter http://www.adobe.com, not www.adobe.com). For more information on using relative URLs and full URLs, see an HTML reference (either printed or on the Web).

3 If desired, enter the name of a target frame in the Target text box, or choose an option from the pop-up menu. A frame name must match a frame previously defined in the HTML file for the document. When a user clicks the link, the specified file displays in the new frame:

- _blank to display the linked file in a new window, leaving the original browser window open.

- _self to display the linked file in the same frame as the original file.

- _parent to display the linked file in its own original parent frameset. Use this option if the HTML document contains frames and the current frame is a child. The linked file displays in the current parent frame.

- _top to replace the entire browser window with the linked file, removing all current frames.

Note: For more information on frames, see an HTML reference (either printed or on the Web).

Resizing and moving slices using numeric coordinates

You can set the exact position and dimensions for a user slice using the Dimensions options. In ImageReady, you can also set the exact position and dimensions for a layer-based slice using the Layer Apron options.

In ImageReady, if the Dimensions or Layer Apron options aren't showing, choose Show Options from the Slice palette menu, or click the Show Options button ↕ on the palette tab to view them.

To resize and move a user slice using numeric coordinates:

1 Select a slice. If you are working in Photoshop, double-click the slice with the slice select tool to display the Slice Options dialog box.

2 In the Dimensions area of the Slice Options dialog box (Photoshop) or the Slice palette (ImageReady), change one or more of the following options:

• X to specify the distance in pixels between the left edge of the slice and the origin point of the ruler in the document window.

• Y to specify the distance in pixels between the top edge of the slice and the origin point of the ruler in the document window.

Note: The default origin point of the ruler is the upper left corner of the image. (See "Using rulers, columns, the measure tool, guides, and the grid" on page 37.)

• W to specify the width of the slice.

• H to specify the height of the slice.

• Constrain Proportions to preserve the current proportions of the slice.

To resize and move a layer-based slice using numeric coordinates (ImageReady):

1 Select a slice.

2 In the Slice palette, change one or more of the following options:

• L to specify the distance in pixels between the left edge of the slice and the left edge of the layer's content.

• T to specify the distance in pixels between the top edge of the slice and the top edge of the layer's content.

• R to specify the distance in pixels between the right edge of the slice and the right edge of the layer's content.

• B to specify the distance in pixels between the bottom edge of the slice and the bottom edge of the layer's content.

Specifying browser messages

You can specify what messages appear in the browser using the Message and Alt options. These options are only available for Image slices.

Message Lets you change the default message in the browser's status area for a selected slice or slices. By default the slice's URL is displayed.

Alt Lets you specify an Alt tag for a selected slice or slices. The Alt text appears in place of the slice image in nongraphical browsers. It also appears in place of the image while the image is downloading and as a tool tip in some browsers.

In ImageReady, if the Message and Alt options aren't showing, choose Show Options from the Slice palette menu, or click the Show Options button ♦ on the palette tab to view them.

To specify a browser message:

1 Select a slice. If you are working in Photoshop, double-click the slice with the slice select tool to display the Slice Options dialog box.

2 In the Slice Options dialog box (Photoshop) or the Slice palette (ImageReady), type the desired text in the Message text box, Alt text box, or both.

Adding HTML text to a slice

Choosing the No Image type for a slice lets you enter text that will appear in the slice area of the resulting Web page. This text is HTML text—you can format it using standard HTML tags. You can also select vertical and horizontal alignment options. For more information on specific HTML tags, see an HTML reference (either printed or on the Web).

Photoshop and ImageReady do not display HTML text in the document window; you must use a Web browser to preview the text. (See "Previewing an image in a browser" on page 48.) Keep in mind that the appearance of text is affected by the browser settings and operating system it is viewed on. Be sure to preview HTML text in different browsers, with different browser settings, and on different operating systems to see how text will appear on the Web.

Note: Be careful not to enter more text than can be displayed in the slice area. If you enter too much text, it will extend into neighboring slices and affect the layout of your Web page.

To add HTML text to a slice:

1 Select a slice. If you are working in Photoshop, double-click the slice with the slice select tool to display the Slice Options dialog box.

2 In the Slice Options dialog box (Photoshop) or the Slice palette (ImageReady), select No Image from the Type pop-up menu.

3 Type the desired text in the provided text box.

4 (Photoshop Save for Web dialog box and ImageReady) If the text includes HTML formatting tags, select the Text is HTML option. When this option is deselected, all the text you enter (including formatting tags) will be displayed in the resulting Web page.

5 (Photoshop Save for Web dialog box and ImageReady) If desired, select options in the Cell Alignment section of the dialog box.

Horizontal alignment options:

- Default to use the browser's default for horizontal alignment.

- Left to align the text to the left side of the slice area.

- Center to align the text to the center of the slice area.

- Right to align the text to the right side of the slice area.

Vertical alignment options:

- Default to use the browser's default for vertical alignment.

- Top to align the text to the top of the slice area.

- Baseline to set a common baseline for the first line of text in cells in the same row (of the resulting HTML table). Each cell in the row must use the Baseline option.

- Middle to center the text vertically in the slice area.

- Bottom to align the text to the bottom of the slice area.

Optimizing slices

You can optimize Image slices using the Save for Web dialog box (Photoshop) or the Optimize palette (ImageReady).

All Image slices use the optimization settings of the entire image until you apply new settings. If you select multiple slices with different optimization settings, only the controls that are relevant to all of the selected slices are visible. If settings for a control differ among slices, the control is blank. Any settings you choose are applied to all selected slices.

In ImageReady, you can also copy optimization settings from one slice to another within a document, or from a slice in one view to a slice in another view in 2-Up or 4-Up view.

To optimize a slice:

Select one or more Image slices, and specify options in the Optimize panel/palette. (See "Optimizing images" on page 333.)

To copy optimization settings between slices (ImageReady):

1 Select the slice that uses the optimization settings you want to copy.

2 Drag the Droplet icon 🖐 from the Optimize palette onto the slice to which you want to apply the optimization settings.

Linking slices (ImageReady)

Linking slices lets you share optimization settings between slices. When you apply optimization settings to a linked slice, all slices in the set are updated.

Linked slices in GIF and PNG-8 format share a color palette and dither pattern. The dither pattern is applied across adjacent slice boundaries to prevent the appearance of seams between the slices. (See "Optimization options for GIF and PNG-8 formats" on page 338.)

Note: You can also link slices in the Photoshop Save for Web dialog box. (See "Working with slices in the Save for Web dialog box (Photoshop)" on page 335.)

To link slices:

1 Select two or more slices you want to link.

Note: If the first slice you select is a user slice, any auto slices you link to the first slice become user-slices. If the first slice you select is an auto slice, any user slices you select are linked to the auto slice group.

2 Choose Slices > Link Slices.

Each linked set of user slices is assigned a different color for the slice display graphics in the upper left corner of the slice. This helps to identify all the slices in one set.

To unlink user slices:

Do one of the following:

- To unlink a user slice, select the slice, and then choose Slices > Unlink Slices.

- To unlink all user slices in a set, select a slice in the set, and choose Slices > Unlink Set.

- To unlink all user slices in an image, choose Slices > Unlink All.

Creating and viewing image maps (ImageReady)

Image maps enable you to link an area of an image to a URL. You can set up multiple linked areas—called image map areas—in an image, with links to text files; other images; audio, video, or multimedia files; other pages in the Web site; or other Web sites. You can also create rollover effects in image map areas.

The main difference between using image maps and using slices to create links is in how the source image is exported as a Web page. Using image maps keeps the exported image intact as a single file, while using slices causes the image to be exported as a separate file. Another difference between image maps and slices is that image maps enable you to link circular, polygonal, or rectangular areas in an image, while slices enable you to link only rectangular areas. If you need to link only rectangular areas, using slices may be preferable to using an image map.

Note: To avoid unexpected results, do not create image map areas in slices that contain URL links—either the image map links or the slice links may be ignored in some browsers.

Creating image maps

You can create image map areas using an image map tool or a layer.

Tool-based image map areas Are created using an image map tool—you drag in the image to define the image map area. You can view and set options for tool-based image maps in the Image Map palette.

Layer-based image map areas Are created from a layer—the layer's content defines the shape of the image map area and the image map inherits the name of the layer. If you edit the layer's content, the image map area automatically adjusts to encompass the new pixels. You can view and set options for layer-based image map areas in the Image Map palette.

If you plan to add a rollover effect to an image map area, it is often preferable to use a layer-based image map area rather than a tool-based image map area. For example, if you create a rollover button that displays a glow effect in the Over state, a layer-based image map area will automatically adjust to encompass the pixels that are produced by the glow.

Important: If you overlap image map areas, the topmost area is active.

Layer-based rectangle image map compared to polygonal image map

To create an image map area using an image map tool:

1 Select the rectangle image map tool , the circle image map tool , or the polygon image map tool in the toolbox.

2 For the rectangle or circle image map tool, select Fixed Size to specify set values for the image map area's dimensions. Enter pixel values in whole numbers.

3 Do one of the following to define the image map area:

• With the rectangle or circle image map tool, drag over the area you want to define. Shift-drag to constrain the area to a square. Alt-drag (Windows) or Option-drag (Mac OS) to drag an image map area from its center.

• With the polygon image map tool, click in the image to set the starting point. Position the pointer where you want the first straight segment to end, and click. Continue clicking to set endpoints for subsequent segments. Hold

down Shift to constrain the segment to 45° increments. To close the border, double-click, or position the pointer over the starting point (a closed circle appears next to the pointer) and click.

To add points to a polygon image map area, select the image map select tool, and Shift-click where you want to add a point. To remove points from a polygon image map area, select the image map select tool, and Alt-click (Windows) or Option-click (Mac OS) the points you want to remove.

To create an image map area from a layer:

1 In the Layers palette, choose a layer from which to create an image map area. (To use multiple layers in one image map area, first merge the layers.)

2 Choose Layer > New Layer Based Image Map Area.

Converting layer-based image maps to tool-based image maps

Because a layer-based image map area is tied to the pixel content of a layer, the only way to move, resize, or align it is to edit the layer. You can convert a layer-based image map area to a tool-based image map area to unlink it from the layer.

To convert a layer-based image map area to a tool-based image map area:

1 Select a layer-based image map area using the image map select tool . (See "Selecting image maps" on page 306.)

2 Choose Promote Layer Based Image Map Area from the Image Map palette menu. If the layer contains multiple, non-overlapping areas of pixel content, multiple tool-based image map areas are produced.

Viewing image maps

When you select the image map select tool, image map areas show automatically. You can also show or hide image map areas using the Image Map Visibility button.

Image map preferences determine how image map areas appear in the document window. You can set preferences for image map lines, line color, and color adjustments.

To show or hide image map areas:

Do one of the following:

- Click the Image Map Visibility button in the toolbox.
- Choose View > Show > Image Maps.
- Choose View > Show Extras. This command also shows or hides selection edges, slices, text bounds, text baseline, and text selections. (See "Working with Extras" on page 41.)

To set image map display preferences:

1 Do one of the following:

- In Windows and Mac OS 9.x, choose Edit > Preferences > Image Maps.
- In Mac OS X, choose ImageReady > Preferences > Image Maps.

2 To change the color of image map lines, choose a color from the Line Color pop-up menu. Changing the color of image map lines also changes the line color of selected image map areas to a contrasting color.

3 To change the strength of image map color adjustments, enter a value, or choose a value from the Image Map Overlay pop-up slider. The value determines the extent of color adjustments that dim the brightness and contrast of unselected image map areas.

4 To display image map lines only and deselect color adjustment display, select Show Lines Only.

5 To show a bounding box for circular image map areas, select Show Bounding Box.

Selecting and modifying image maps (ImageReady)

You can move, arrange, align, and duplicate tool-based image map areas using the Image Map palette. There are fewer options for modifying layer-based image map areas because they are tied to the pixel content of the associated layer; however, you can select, arrange, and delete layer-based image map areas as you do tool-based image map areas.

Using the Image Map palette (ImageReady)

The Image Map palette displays options for the selected image maps. You can access commands for working with image maps in the Image Map palette menu.

To display the Image Map palette:

Choose Window > Image Map, or click the palette button ▣ on the right side of the options bar for the image map select tool.

Selecting image maps

You select image map areas with the image map select tool.

To select an image map area:

1 Select the image map select tool ✋ .

2 Click on an image map area in the image. Shift-click to add areas to the selection.

You can also select multiple image map areas by clicking outside an image map area and dragging across the image map areas you want to select.

Moving and resizing tool-based image maps

You can move and resize tool-based image map areas by dragging. You can also move and resize rectangular and circular image map areas using numeric coordinates.

Note: To move or resize a layer-based image map area, move or edit the layer.

To move a tool-based image map area:

1 Select one or more image map areas you want to move.

2 Position the pointer inside the image map area, and drag it to a new position. Press Shift to restrict movement to a vertical, horizontal, or 45° diagonal line.

To resize a tool-based image map area:

1 Select an image map area you want to resize.

2 Drag a handle on the image map border to resize the image map area.

To resize and move a tool-based image map area using numeric coordinates:

1 Select a rectangular or circular image map area.

2 In the Dimensions area of the Image Map palette, change one or more of the following options:

- X to specify the distance in pixels between the left edge of a rectangular image map area, or the center point of a circular image map area, and the origin point of the ruler in the document window.

- Y to specify the distance in pixels between the top edge of a rectangular image map area, or the center point of a circular image map area, and the origin point of the ruler in the document window.

Note: The default origin point of the ruler is the upper left corner of the image. (See "Using rulers, columns, the measure tool, guides, and the grid" on page 37.)

- W to specify the width of a rectangular image map area.

- H to specify the height of a rectangular image map area.

- R to specify the radius of a circular image map area.

Changing the shape of layer-based image maps

When you create a layer-based image map area, the default image map area is a rectangle that encompasses all of the layer's pixel data. You can change the shape of the image map area by selecting a Shape option in the Image Map palette.

To change the shape of a layer-based image map area:

1 Select a layer-based image map area.

2 In the Layer Image Map section of the Image Map palette, choose an option from the shape pop-up list: Rectangle, Circle, or Polygon. If you choose Polygon, enter a value or choose a value from the Quality pop-up slider to set the number of segments in the polygon.

Duplicating image maps

You can create a duplicate image map area with the same dimensions and settings as the original image map area.

To duplicate an image map area:

Do one of the following:

- Select one or more image map areas, and choose Duplicate Image Map Area(s) from the Image Map palette menu.

- Select one or more image map areas, and Alt-drag (Windows) or Option-drag (Mac OS) from inside the image map area.

- Select a image map in the Rollovers palette, and choose Duplicate Image Map from the palette menu. (See "Using the Rollovers palette" on page 315.)

The duplicate image map area appears on top of the original (offset 10 pixels down and to the right) and can be moved, resized, or otherwise modified.

Arranging image maps

The Rollovers palette displays the stacking order of image maps. You can specify which image map area is on the top and bottom of the stack and move image map areas up or down in the stacking order.

To change the stacking order of image map areas:

Do one of the following:

- Select one or more image map areas you want to arrange. You can select a combination of tool-based image map areas and layer-based image map areas. Then, with the image map select tool active, click a stacking order option in the options bar: Bring to Front ⬛, Bring Forward ⬛, Send Backward ⬛, Send to Back ⬛. Alternately, choose a stacking order command from the Image Map palette menu.

- Drag an image map up or down in the Rollovers palette. (See "Using the Rollovers palette" on page 315.)

Aligning tool-based image maps

You can align tool-based image map areas to the top, bottom, left, right, and middle.

Note: To align layer-based image map areas, first link the layers, and then choose an alignment option from the Layer > Align Linked submenu.

To align tool-based image map areas:

1 Select the tool-based image map areas you want to align.

2 Do one of the following:

• With the image map select tool active, click an alignment option in the options bar: Align Image Map Top Edges ⊤ , Align Image Map Vertical Centers ╍ , Align Image Map Bottom Edges ⊥ , Align Image Map Left Edges ⊨ , Align Image Map Horizontal Centers ╩ , Align Image Map Right Edges ⊐ .

• Choose an alignment command from the Image Map palette menu.

Distributing tool-based image maps

You can distribute tool-based image map areas evenly along the vertical or horizontal axis.

To distribute tool-based image map areas:

1 Select the tool-based image map areas you want to distribute.

2 Do one of the following:

• With the image map select tool active, click a distribute option in the options bar: Distribute Image Map Top Edges ≡ , Distribute Image Map Vertical Centers ≡ , Distribute Image Map Bottom Edges ≡ , Distribute Image Map Left Edges ╟ , Distribute Image Map Horizontal Centers ╫ , Distribute Image Map Right Edges ╢ .

• Choose a distribute command from the Image Map palette menu.

Deleting image maps

You can delete selected image map areas by pressing the Backspace key or the Delete key, or choosing Delete Image Map Area(s) from the Image Map palette menu.

Specifying image map options (ImageReady)

You can specify a name, a URL, a target frame, and Alt text for an image map area in the Image Map palette.

To change the name of an image map area:

1 Select an image map area.

2 In the Image Map palette, enter a new name in the Name text box.

To specify link options for an image map area:

1 Select an image map area.

2 In the Image Map palette, enter a URL for the link, or choose a previously created URL from the URL pop-up menu. You can enter a relative URL or a full URL. If you enter a full URL, be sure to include http:// (for example, enter http://www.adobe.com, not www.adobe.com). For more information on using relative URLs and full URLs, see an HTML reference (either printed or on the Web).

3 In the Image Map palette, enter the name of a target frame in the Target text box, or choose an option from the pop-up menu. A frame name must match a frame previously defined in the HTML file for the document. When a user clicks the link, the specified file displays in the new frame:

- _blank to display the linked file in a new window, leaving the original browser window open.

- _self to display the linked file in the same frame as the original file.

- _parent to display the linked file in its own original parent frameset. Use this option if the HTML document contains frames and the current frame is a child. The linked file displays in the current parent frame.

- _top to replace the entire browser window with the linked file, removing all current frames.

Note: *For more information on frames, see an HTML reference (either printed or on the Web).*

4 In the Image Map palette, enter text for an Alt tag in the Alt text box. The Alt text appears in place of the image map area in nongraphical browsers. In most browsers, it also appears if the user positions the mouse over the image map area.

Selecting an image map type (ImageReady)

ImageReady can create client-side and server-side image maps. In client-side image maps, the links are interpreted by the browser itself. In server-side image maps, the links are interpreted by the server. Because client-side image maps don't need to contact the server to function, they are often significantly faster to navigate. By default, ImageReady saves image maps as client-side image maps.

Important: *Server-side image maps do not work in images that have multiple slices.*

You select an image map type in the Output Settings dialog box. (See "Setting HTML output options" on page 361.) If you select a server-side image map, ImageReady generates a separate map file based on the server option you select. However, you'll need to update the path to the map file in your HTML file.

Creating Web photo galleries (Photoshop)

You use the Web Photo Gallery command to automatically generate a Web photo gallery from a set of images. A Web photo gallery is a Web site that features a home page with thumbnail images and gallery pages with full-size images. Each page contains links that allow visitors to navigate the site. For example, when a visitor clicks a thumbnail image on the home page, a gallery page with the associated full-size image loads.

Web photo gallery home page and loaded gallery page

Photoshop provides a variety of styles for your gallery, which you can select using the Web Photo Gallery command. If you are an advanced user who has knowledge of HTML, you can also customize a style by editing a set of HTML template files or create a new style.

For more information, see "Customizing and creating Web photo gallery styles" in online Help.

To create a Web photo gallery:

1 Choose File > Automate > Web Photo Gallery.

2 Under Site, do the following:

• Choose a style for the gallery from the Styles pop-up menu. A preview of the home page for the chosen style appears in the dialog box.

• Enter the email address that you want to display as the contact for the gallery.

• Choose an extension for the generated files from the Extension pop-up menu.

3 Under Folders, do the following:

• Click Browse (Windows) or Choose (Mac OS). Then select the folder containing the images that you want to appear in the gallery, and click OK (Windows) or Choose (Mac OS).

• Select Include All Subdirectories to include images inside any subfolders of the selected folder.

• Click Destination, select the destination folder that you want to contain the images and HTML pages for the gallery, and click OK (Windows) or Choose (Mac OS).

4 To set options for the banner that appears on each page in the gallery, choose Banner from the Options pop-up menu. Then do the following:

• For Site Name, enter the title of the gallery.

• For Photographer, enter the name of the person or organization that deserves credit for the photos in the gallery.

• For Contact Info, enter the contact information for the gallery, such as a telephone number or a business address.

• For Date, enter the date that you want to appear on each page of the gallery. By default, Photoshop uses the current date.

• For Font and Font Size, choose options for the banner text.

5 To set options for the gallery pages, choose Large Images from the Options pop-up menu. Then do the following:

• To have Photoshop resize the source images for placement on the gallery pages, select Resize Images. Then choose an option for the image size from the pop-up menu or enter a size in pixels. For Constrain, choose which dimensions of the image you want to constrain during resizing. For JPEG Quality, choose an option from the pop-up menu, enter a value between 0 and 12, or drag the slider. A higher value results in better image quality but larger file size.

• For Border Size, enter the width of the border around the image in pixels.

• For Titles Use, specify options to display caption information under each image. Select Filename to display the filename, or select Caption, Credits, Title, and Copyright to display caption text drawn from the File Info dialog box. For more information, see "Adding file information (Photoshop)" on page 374.

• For Font and Font Size, choose options for the caption text.

6 To set options for the home page, choose Thumbnails from the Options pop-up menu. Then do the following:

• For Size, choose an option for the thumbnail size from the pop-up menu or enter a value in pixels for the width of each thumbnail.

• For Columns and Rows, enter the number of columns and rows that you want to be used to display the thumbnails on the home page. This option doesn't apply to galleries that use the Horizontal Frame Style or Vertical Frame Style.

• For Border Size, enter the width of the border around each thumbnail in pixels.

7 To set options for colors of elements in the gallery, choose Customize Colors from the Options pop-up menu. To change the color of a particular element, click its color swatch, and then select a new color using the Color Picker. The Background option lets you change the background color of each page. The Banner option lets you change the background color of the banner.

8 To set options to display text to appear over each image as an anti-theft deterrent, choose Security from the Options pop-up menu. Then do the following:

• For Use, select Custom Text to enter customized text. Select Filename, Caption, Credits, Title, or Copyright to display text drawn from the File Info dialog box. For more information, see "Adding file information (Photoshop)" on page 374.

• Specify font, color, and text alignment options. To place the text on the image at an angle, choose a rotation option.

Photoshop places the following HTML and JPEG files in your destination folder:

- A home page for your gallery named index.htm or index.html depending on the Extension options. Open this file in any Web browser to preview your gallery.

- JPEG images inside an images subfolder.

- HTML pages inside a pages subfolder.

- JPEG thumbnail images inside a thumbnails subfolder.

Chapter 13: Creating Rollovers and Animations (ImageReady)

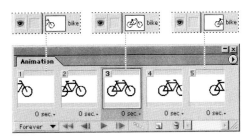

Illustration of an animation. The bicycle image is on its own layer; the position of the layer changes in each frame of the animation.

Adobe ImageReady provides a powerful, easy way to create rollovers and animations in a single document.

About working with layers in rollovers and animations

Working with layers is an essential part of creating rollovers and animations in ImageReady. Placing the image content for a rollover on its own layer allows you to use Layers palette commands and options to create rollover effects. Likewise, placing each element of an animation on its own layer enables you to change the position and appearance of the element across a series of frames.

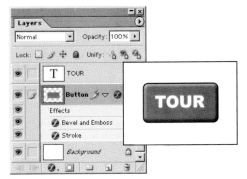

Illustration of a rollover. The button is on its own layer; effects are added to the layer to create a new appearance of the button for the over state.

Editing layers in rollover states and animation frames

Some changes you make to layers affect only the active rollover state or animation frame, while others affect every state and frame in which the layers are included:

State and frame-specific changes Affect only the active animation frame or rollover state. By default, changes you make to layers using Layers palette commands and options—including layer opacity, blending mode, visibility, position, and style—are state and frame-specific. However, you can apply layer changes to all states in a rollover and all frames in an animation using the unify buttons in the Layers palette. (See "Unifying and matching layers rollovers and animations" on page 314.)

Important: *Changes you make to layers in the Normal state or Frame 1—including layer opacity, blending mode, visibility, position, and style—affect all states or frames in which the layers are identical. For example, take a slice that has a Normal state, an Over state, and a Down state. If the layers in the Normal and Over states are identical, and you apply a layer style in the Normal state, the layer style will also be applied in the Over state. However, the Down state will not be affected.*

Inclusive changes Affect every state and frame in which the layers are included. Changes you make to layer pixel values, using painting and editing tools, color and tone adjustment commands, filters, type, and other image-editing commands, are inclusive.

Unifying and matching layers rollovers and animations

By default, changes you make to layers using Layers palette commands and options—including layer visibility, position, and style—apply only to the frame or state (unless you are working with the Normal state or Frame 1). However, you can use the unify buttons in the Layers palette and the Match command to apply changes to all states in a rollover and all frames in an animation:

- The unify buttons determine how the changes you make to a layer in the active state or frame apply to the other states in a rollover or frames in an animation. When a unify button is selected, changes apply to all states and frames; when a button is deselected, changes apply to only the active state or frame.

- The Layer > Match command lets you apply the layer attributes for an existing state or frame to other states in a rollover and frames in an animation.

To unify layers in rollover states and animation frames:

Select one or more unify buttons in the Layers palette:

- Unify Layer Position button ⚓ to apply changes you make to a layer's position to all states in a rollover and all frames in an animation.

- Unify Layer Visibility button ⚓ to apply changes you make to a layer's visibility to all states in a rollover and all frames in an animation.

- Unify Layer Style button ⚓ to apply changes you make to a layer's style to all states in a rollover and all frames in an animation.

To match an existing layer across rollover states and animation frames:

1 In the Rollovers palette, select the state or frame with the layer attributes you want to use.

2 Select the layer you want to match in the Layers palette.

3 Choose Layer > Match, or choose Match from the Layers palette menu.

4 Select one of the following:

- Current Animation to apply layer attributes for the selected frame to all frames in the animation.

- Current Slice/Image Map's States to apply layer attributes for the selected state to all states in the rollover.

- All Rollovers to apply layer attributes for the selected state to all states in all rollovers in the image that include the layer.

5 Select the layer attributes you want to match, and click OK.

Note: Choose Propogate Frame 1 Changes from the Layers palette pop-up menu to dynamically update all rollover states and animation frames, based on a change in the first frame's position, visibility, or layer style.

Using the Rollovers palette

The Rollovers palette lets you create, view, and set options for the rollover states in an image. By default, every image has one state—the Normal state. The Normal state corresponds to the appearance of an image when it is first loaded into a Web browser and no rollover effects have occurred. You can add states to an image that will occur when a viewer performs a mouse action— such as rolling or clicking—over an area of the Web page.

In addition to rollover states, the Rollovers palette can display slices, image maps, and animations frames. Displaying slices and image maps helps you keep track of the elements in an image that contain rollover effects. Displaying animation frames makes it easy to see which states of an image contain animations.

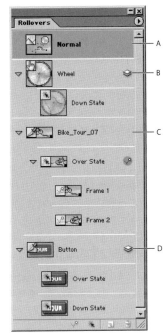

The Rollovers palette with slices, image maps, and animation frames showing:
A. Normal state B. Image map with Down state C. Slice with animation frames in Over state D. Layer-based slice with Over state and Down state

Displaying the Rollovers palette Choose Window > Rollovers. A check mark indicates that the palette is showing.

Using the Rollovers palette menu Click the triangle ⊙ in the upper right corner of the palette to access commands for working with rollovers.

Displaying slices and image maps in the Rollovers palette Choose Palette Options from the Rollovers palette menu. Select or deselect Include Slices and Image Maps, and click OK.

Displaying animation frames in the Rollovers palette Choose Palette Options from the Rollovers palette menu. Select or deselect Include Animation Frames, and click OK.

Changing the size of rollover thumbnails Choose Palette Options from the Rollovers palette menu, and select a thumbnail size. For sizes other than None, select Object Bounds or Entire Document to determine the contents of thumbnails.

Expanding and collapsing states, slices, and image maps Click the triangle to the left of an item in the Rollovers palette.

Creating and editing rollovers

You use the Rollovers palette, in conjunction with the Layers palette, to add rollover effects to an image. When you save the image as a Web page, ImageReady adds JavaScript code to the resulting HTML file to specify rollover states.

About rollovers

A *rollover* is a Web effect in which different states of an image appear when a viewer performs a mouse action—such as rolling or clicking— over an area of the Web page. A *state* is defined by a specific configuration of the Layers palette, including layer location, styles, and other formatting options.

You use a slice or image map area to define the active area for a rollover. When you add a new state to the image, you capture a snapshot of the slice or image map area in the previous state. You can then use the Layers palette to make changes to the image in the new state. When you save an image with rollover states as a Web page, each rollover state is saved as a separate image file.

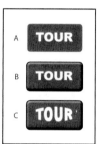 

Illustration of an image with three rollover states:
A. Normal state B. Over state C. Down state

💡 *You can use layer styles to create instant rollover effects. When working with layer-based slices, you can also save the series of states as a rollover style. (See "Applying and creating rollover styles" on page 319.)*

Creating slices for rollovers

You can quickly create layer-based slices for rollovers using the Rollovers palette. Layer-based slices are recommended when creating rollovers because the dimensions of a layer's content may change in the course of creating a rollover, and layer-based slices automatically adjust to encompass the new pixels. For more information on the different types of slices, see "Creating and viewing slices" on page 288.

To create a layer-based slice for a rollover:

1 Select the layer in the Layers palette. The content of the layer will define the active area for the rollover.

2 Click the Create Layer-based Rollover button ✳ in the Rollovers palette.

By default, ImageReady adds an Over state to the new slice.

Creating rollover states

You can add a variety of different states to the slices and image maps in an image.

To add a rollover state to a slice or image map:

1 In the Rollover palette or the image, select the slice or image map you want to add the rollover state to.

Note: If slices are not visible in the Rollovers palette, select Include Slices and Image Maps in the Palette Options dialog box to display them. (See "Using the Rollovers palette" on page 315.)

2 Do one of the following in the Rollovers palette:

• Click the Create Rollover State button ⬛ .

• Choose New Rollover State from the palette menu.

3 Use the default rollover state assigned by ImageReady, or select a different rollover state. (See "Editing rollover states" on page 317.)

4 Modify the layers used in the rollover state. (See "About working with layers in rollovers and animations" on page 313.)

Editing rollover states

When you create a rollover state, ImageReady assigns the type of state by default; however, you can easily change the state. You can also use the Rollovers palette to target the image content of a state for editing.

To edit the image content of a state:

1 Select a state in the Rollovers palette. If necessary, expand the slice or image map to view its states. (See "Using the Rollovers palette" on page 315.)

2 Modify the layers used in the rollover state. (See "About working with layers in rollovers and animations" on page 313.)

To edit the mouse action for a rollover state:

1 Do one of the following:

• Double-click a rollover state in the Rollovers palette.

• Select a rollover state in the Rollovers palette, and choose Rollover State Options from the palette menu.

2 Select a state, and click OK:

Over Activates the image when the user rolls over the slice or image map area with the mouse while the mouse button is not pressed. (Over is automatically selected for the second rollover state.)

Down Activates the image when the user presses the mouse button on the slice or image map area. The state appears as long as the viewer keeps the mouse button pressed down on the area.

Click Activates the image when the user clicks the mouse on the slice or image map area. The state appears until the viewer moves the mouse out of the rollover area.

Note: Different Web browsers, or different versions of a browser, may process clicks and double-clicks differently. For example, some browsers leave the slice in the Click state after a click, and in the Up state after a double-click; other browsers use the Up state only as a transition into the Click state, regardless of single- or double-clicking. To ensure your Web page will function correctly, be sure to preview rollovers in various Web browsers.

Custom Activates the image of the specified name when the user performs the action defined in the corresponding JavaScript code. (You must create JavaScript code and add it to the HTML file for the Web page in order for the Custom rollover option to function. See a JavaScript manual for more information.)

None Preserves the current state of the image for later use, but does not output an image when the file is saved as a Web page.

Selected Activates the rollover state when the user clicks the mouse on the slice or image map area. The state appears until the viewer activates another selected rollover state, and other rollover effects can occur while the selected state is active. For example, a selected state for one button and an over state for another button can occur simultaneously. However, if a layer is used by both states, the layer attributes of the selected state override those of the over state.

Select Use as Default Selected State to activate the state initially when the document is previewed in ImageReady or loaded into a Web browser.

Out Activates the rollover state when the user rolls the mouse out of the slice or image map area. (The Normal state usually serves this purpose.)

Up Activates the rollover state when the user releases the mouse button over the slice or image map area. (The Normal state usually serves this purpose.)

Previewing rollover states

You can preview rollover effects directly in the ImageReady document window by switching to document preview mode. To preview the rollover effect in your computer's default Web browser, click the Preview in Default Browser button in the toolbox. (See "Previewing an image in a browser" on page 48.)

To use rollover preview mode:

1 Do one of the following:

• Click the Preview Document button 🖑 in the toolbox.

• Choose Image > Preview Document.

2 In the document window, perform the action that activates the rollover state. For example, position the mouse over the rollover slice or image map area to preview the Over state. Then click the slice or image map area to preview the Click state.

Note: *If a document contains a Selected state, synthetic states are generated for the other states in the Rollovers palette. The synthetic state represents the appearance of the document when the Selected state is active. Synthetic states are generated automatically and cannot be edited.*

To exit rollover preview mode:

Do one of the following:

• Select any tool in the toolbox.

• Click the Cancel button ⊘ in the options bar.

Adding animation to rollover states

You can add a multiple-frame animation to a state in an image. Adding an animation to the Normal state will cause the animation to play when the image is loaded in a Web browser. Adding an animation to another type of state will cause the animation to play when a user activates the state.

To add animation frames to a rollover state:

1 In the Rollovers palette, select the state in which you want to display an animation. If necessary, expand the slice or image map to view its states. (See "Using the Rollovers palette" on page 315.)

2 Do one of the following to add frames to the animation:

• Click the Create Animation Frame button ⟋° in the Rollovers palette or choose New Animation Frame from the palette menu.

Note: *If the Create Animation Frame button and the New Animation Frame command are not visible, select Include Animation Frames in the Palette Options dialog box. (See "Using the Rollovers palette" on page 315.)*

• Create frames in the Animation palette. (See "Creating and editing animations" on page 321.)

Applying and creating rollover styles

Rollover styles (indicated by a triangle in the upper left corner of the style thumbnail) simplify rollover creation by allowing you to turn a layer into a rollover effect with a single click. A rollover style includes all the attributes of a rollover, including its states and layer effects. When you apply a rollover style to a layer, the layer becomes a layer-based slice.

To apply a roilover style to a layer:

1 Select a layer in the Layers palette.

2 Choose Window > Styles, or click the Styles palette tab, to display the Styles palette.

3 Click the thumbnail for the rollover style you want to apply. Rollover style thumbnails have a triangle in the upper left corner.

To create a rollover style:

1 In the Rollovers palette, create the desired rollover states. (See "Creating rollover states" on page 317.)

Note: *You must use a layer-based slice in order to create a rollover style.*

2 Apply the effects to each state using predefined styles in the Styles palette or by manually setting layer effects in the Layers palette. (See "Using layer effects and styles" on page 246.)

3 In the Styles palette, click the Create New Style button ⬛, or choose New Style from the palette menu.

4 Enter a name for the style, set style options, and click OK. The Include Rollover States option must be selected in order to create a rollover style.

The new rollover style appears in the Styles palette. The thumbnail preview displays the effects in the Normal state.

Copying and pasting rollover states

You can copy a rollover state and paste it into another state in the current rollover or into a state in another rollover. Layers in the source state replace layers in the destination state.

You can also copy frames from the Animation palette and paste them into the Rollovers palette as states, or copy states from the Rollovers palette and paste them into the Animation palette as frames.

Note: Copy commands in the Animation palette and the Rollovers palette use an internal clipboard available to these commands only. Copying frames or rollover states does not overwrite the primary ImageReady clipboard.

To copy and paste rollover states:

1 Select a rollover state, and choose Copy Rollover State from the Rollovers palette menu.

2 Select a rollover state in which to paste the copied state:

- Select a state in the current rollover.

- Open or display another rollover, and select a state.

3 Choose Paste Rollover State from the Rollovers palette menu.

Duplicating rollover states

Duplicating a state is an easy way to add existing animation frames to a new state.

To duplicate a rollover state:

Select a rollover state, and do one of the following:

- Choose Duplicate Rollover State from the Rollovers palette menu.

- Drag the state to the Create Rollover State button ⬛.

The duplicate state and frames appear below the original state in the Rollovers palette.

Rearranging and deleting rollover states

You can move states between slices and image maps by dragging them to a new location in the Rollovers palette. You can also delete individual states or all states in a rollover.

To move states between slices and image maps:

Drag the state up or down in the Rollovers palette. When the highlighted line appears in the desired position, release the mouse button.

To delete rollover states:

• To delete one state, select a rollover state, and either click the Trash button 🗑 on the Rollovers palette or choose Delete Rollover State from the Rollovers palette menu.

• To delete all states in a rollover, choose Delete Rollover from the Rollovers palette menu.

Creating and editing animations

You use the Animation palette, in conjunction with the Layers palette and Rollovers palette, to create animation frames from an original, multi-layer image. You can assign a delay time to each frame, use the Tween command to generate new frames, and specify looping for the animation. The number of frames you can create is limited only by the amount of memory available to ImageReady on your system.

About animation

An animation is a sequence of images, or *frames*, that is displayed over time. Each frame varies slightly from the preceding frame, creating the illusion of movement when the frames are viewed in quick succession.

An image can have multiple animations that are associated with different rollover states. For example, adding an animation to the Normal rollover state causes the animation to play when the Web page is first loaded by a Web browser. Adding an animation to another rollover state causes the animation to play only when the Web user performs the specified action (such as placing the mouse over the rollover or clicking on the rollover).

Using the Animation palette

The Animation palette lets you create, view, and set options for the frames in an animation. You can change the thumbnail view of frames in the Animation palette—using smaller thumbnails reduces the space required by the palette and displays more frames in a given palette width.

Displaying the Animation palette Choose Window > Animation. A check mark indicates that the palette is showing.

Using the Animation palette menu Click the triangle ▶ in the upper right corner of the palette to access commands for working with animations.

Changing the size of animation thumbnails Choose Palette Options from the Animation palette menu, select a thumbnail size, and click OK.

Adding frames

Adding frames is the first step in creating an animation. If you have an image open in ImageReady, the Animation palette displays the image as the first frame in a new animation. Each frame you add starts as a duplicate of the preceding frame. You then make changes to the frame using the Layers palette.

Note: Always create and edit frames in Original view. While you can view frames in an optimized view, the editing options are very limited.

To add a frame to an animation:

1 In the Rollovers palette, select the state in which you want to display an animation. (See "Using the Rollovers palette" on page 315.)

Adding an animation to the Normal state will cause the animation to play when the image is loaded in a Web browser. Adding an animation to another type of state will cause the animation to play when a user activates the state.

2 Do one of the following:

• In the Animation palette, click the Duplicate Current Frame button 🔲 or choose New Frame from the palette menu.

• In the Rollovers palette, click the Create Animation Frame button ⌁ or choose New Animation Frame from the palette menu.

Note: If the Create Animation Frame button and the New Animation Frame command are not visible in the Rollovers palette, select Include Animation Frames in the Palette Options dialog box. (See "Using the Rollovers palette" on page 315.)

3 Modify the image for the frame using the Layers palette. (See "About working with layers in rollovers and animations" on page 313.)

Selecting frames

Before you can work with a frame, you must select it as the current frame. The contents of the current frame appear in the document window.

You can select multiple frames, either contiguous or discontiguous, to edit them or apply commands to them as a group. When multiple frames are selected, only the current frame appears in the document window.

In the Animation palette, the current frame is indicated by a narrow border (inside the shaded selection highlight) around the frame thumbnail. Selected frames are indicated by a shaded highlight around the frame thumbnails.

To select the current frame:

Do one of the following:

• Click a frame in the Animation palette.

• Click a frame in the Rollovers palette. If necessary, expand the state that contains the animation to view its frames. (See "Using the Rollovers palette" on page 315.)

• In the Animation palette or the Layers palette, click the Forward button ▐▶ to select the next frame in the series as the current frame.

• In the Animation palette or the Layers palette, click the Backward button ◀▌ to select the previous frame in the series as the current frame.

- In the Animation palette, click the Select First Frame button ◂◂ to select the first frame in the series as the current frame.

To select multiple frames:

In the Animation palette, do one of the following:

- To select contiguous multiple frames, Shift-click a second frame. The second frame and all frames between the first and second are added to the selection.

- To select discontiguous multiple frames, Ctrl-click (Windows) or Command-click (Mac OS) additional frames to add those frames to the selection.

- To select all frames, choose Select All Frames from the Animation palette menu.

To deselect a frame in a multiframe selection:

Ctrl-click (Windows) or Command-click (Mac OS) a frame to deselect it.

Editing frames

You can use the Animation palette or the Rollovers palette to target the image content of a frame for editing.

To edit the image content of a frame:

1 Select a frame. (See "Selecting frames" on page 322.)

2 Modify the image for the frame using the Layers palette. (See "About working with layers in rollovers and animations" on page 313.)

Rearranging and deleting frames

You can change the position of frames in an animation and reverse the order of selected contiguous frames. You can also delete selected frames or the entire animation.

To change the position of a frame:

1 Select the frame you want to move in the Animation palette or the Rollovers palette.

2 Drag the selection to the new position.

Note: *In the Animation palette, you can select and change the position of multiple frames. (See "Selecting frames" on page 322.) However, if you drag multiple discontiguous frames, the frames are placed contiguously in the new position.*

To reverse the order of contiguous frames:

1 Select the contiguous frames you want to reverse.

2 Choose Reverse Frames from the Animation palette menu.

To delete selected frames:

Do one of the following in the Animation palette or the Rollovers palette:

- Select Delete Frame from the palette menu.

- Click the Trash button 🗑 , and click Yes to confirm the deletion.

- Drag the selected frame onto the Trash button.

To delete an entire animation:

Select Delete Animation from the Animation palette menu or the Rollovers palette menu.

Copying and pasting frames

To understand what happens when you copy and paste a frame, think of a frame as a duplicate version of an image with a given layer configuration. When you copy a frame, you copy the configuration of layers (including each layer's visibility setting, position, and other attributes). When you paste a frame, you apply that layer configuration to the destination frame.

To copy and paste layers between frames:

1 Select the frame you want to copy in the Animation palette or the Rollovers palette.

Note: In the Animation palette, you can select and copy multiple frames. (See "Selecting frames" on page 322.)

2 Choose Copy Frame(s) from the Animation palette menu or the Rollovers palette menu.

3 Select a destination frame or frames in the current animation or another animation.

4 Choose Paste Frame(s) from the Animation palette menu or the Rollovers palette menu.

5 Select a Paste method:

- Replace Frames to replace the selected frames with the copied frames. When you paste frames into the same image, no new layers are added to the image; rather, the attributes of each existing layer in the destination frames are replaced by those of each copied layer. When you paste frames between images, new layers are added to the image; however, only the pasted layers are visible in the destination frames (the existing layers are hidden).

- Paste Over Selection to add the contents of the pasted frames as new layers in the image. When you paste frames into the same image, using this option doubles the number of layers in the image. In the destination frames, the newly pasted layers are visible, and the original layers are hidden. In the nondestination frames, the newly pasted layers are hidden.

- Paste Before Selection or Paste After Selection to add the copied frames before or after the destination frame. When you paste frames between images, new layers are added to the image; however, only the pasted layers are visible in the new frames (the existing layers are hidden).

6 Select Link Added Layers if you want to link pasted layers in the Layers palette. Use this option when you need to reposition the pasted layers as a unit.

7 Click OK.

Tweening frames

You use the Tween command to automatically add or modify a series of frames between two existing frames—varying the layer attributes (position, opacity, or effect parameters) evenly between the new frames to create the appearance of movement. For example, if you want to fade out a layer, set the opacity of the layer in the starting frame to 100%; then set the opacity of the same layer in the ending frame to 0%. When you tween between the two frames, the opacity of the layer is reduced evenly across the new frames.

The term "tweening" is derived from "in betweening," the traditional animation term used to describe this process. Tweening significantly reduces the time required to create animation effects such as fading in or fading out, or moving an element across a frame. You can edit tweened frames individually after you create them.

Example of using tweening to animate warped text

To create frames using tweening:

1 To apply tweening to a specific layer, select it in the Layers palette.

2 Select a single frame or multiple contiguous frames.

If you select a single frame, you choose whether to tween the frame with the previous frame or the next frame. If you select two contiguous frames, new frames are added between the frames. If you select more than two frames, existing frames between the first and last selected frames are altered by the tweening operation. If you select the first and last frames in an animation, these frames are treated as contiguous, and tweened frames are added after the last frame. (This tweening method is useful when the animation is set to loop multiple times.)

Note: *You cannot select discontiguous frames for tweening.*

3 Do one of the following:

• Click the Tween button ⁰⁰₀ in the Animation palette.

• Select Tween from the Animation palette menu.

4 Specify the layer or layers to be varied in the added frames:

• All Layers to vary all layers in the selected frame or frames.

• Selected Layer to vary only the currently selected layer in the selected frame or frames.

5 Specify layer attributes to be varied:

• Position to vary the position of the layer's content in the new frames evenly between the beginning and ending frames.

• Opacity to vary the opacity of the new frames evenly between the beginning and ending frames.

• Effects to vary the parameter settings of layer effects evenly between the beginning and ending frames.

6 If you selected a single frame in step 2, choose where to add frames from the Tween With menu:

• Next Frame to add frames between the selected frame and the following frame. This option is not available when you select the last frame in the Animation palette.

• First Frame to add frames between the last frame and first frame. This option is only available if you select the last frame in the Animation palette.

• Previous Frame to add frames between the selected frame and the preceding frame. This option is not available when you select the first frame in the Animation palette.

• Last Frame to add frames between the first frame and last frame. This option is only available if you select the first frame in the Animation palette.

7 Enter a value, or use the Up or Down Arrow key to choose the number of frames to add. (This option is not available if you selected more than two frames. In this case, the tweening operation alters the existing frames between the first and last frames in the selection.)

8 Click OK.

Specifying looping

You select a looping option to specify how many times the animation sequence repeats when played.

To specify looping:

1 Click the looping option selection box at the lower left corner of the Animation palette.

2 Select a looping option: Once, Forever, or Other.

3 If you selected Other, enter a value in the Set Loop Count dialog box, and click OK.

Specifying delay for frames

You can specify a *delay*—the time that a frame is displayed—for single frames or for multiple frames in an animation. Delay time is displayed in seconds. Fractions of a second are displayed as decimal values. For example, one-quarter second is specified as .25.

To specify a delay time:

1 Select one or more frames.

2 In the Animation palette, click on the Delay value below the selected frame to view the Delay pop-up menu.

3 Specify the delay:

• Choose a value from the pop-up menu. (The last value used appears at the bottom of the menu.)

• Choose Other, enter a value in the Set Frame Delay dialog box, and click OK.

If you selected multiple frames, specifying a delay value for one frame applies the value to all frames.

Note: Delay time may not be accurate during an animation preview in ImageReady. For an accurate preview of delay time, preview animations in a browser.

Adding layers to frames

When you create a new layer, it is visible in all frames of an animation. To hide a layer in a specific frame, select the frame in the Animation palette, and then hide the desired layer in the Layers palette.

You can use the Create Layer for Each New Frame option to automatically add a new layer to the image every time you create a frame. The new layer is visible in the new frame but hidden in other frames. Using this options saves time when you are creating an animation that requires you to add a new visual element to each frame.

To add a new layer every time you create a frame:

Choose Create Layer for Each New Frame from the Animation palette menu. A check mark indicates that the option is turned on.

Setting the frame disposal method

The frame disposal method specifies whether to discard the current frame before displaying the next frame. You select a disposal method when working with animations that include background transparency in order to specify whether the current frame will be visible through the transparent areas of the next frame.

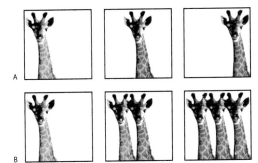

Illustration of frame disposal methods:
A. *Frame with background transparency with Restore to Background option* **B.** *Frame with background transparency with Do Not Dispose option*

The Disposal Method icon indicates whether the frame is set to Do Not Dispose ⚿ or Restore to Background ⟲ . (No icon appears when disposal method is set to Automatic.)

To choose a disposal method:

1 Select a frame or frames for which you want to choose a disposal method.

2 Right-click (Windows) or Ctrl-click (Mac OS) the frame thumbnail to view the Disposal Method context menu.

3 Choose a disposal method:

• Automatic to determine a disposal method for the current frame automatically, discarding the current frame if the next frame contains layer transparency. For most animations, the Automatic option yields the desired results and is, therefore, the default option.

Note: Choose the Automatic disposal option when using the Redundant Pixel Removal optimization option, to enable ImageReady to preserve frames that include transparency.

- Do Not Dispose to preserve the current frame as the next frame is added to the display. The current frame (and preceding frames) may show through transparent areas of the next frame. To accurately preview an animation using the Do Not Dispose option, preview the animation in a browser.

- Restore to Background to discard the current frame from the display before the next frame is displayed. Only a single frame is displayed at any time (and the current frame will not appear through the transparent areas of the next frame).

Flattening frames into layers

You can flatten animation frames into layers. A single, composite layer is created for each frame, containing all of the layers in the frame. The original layers in the frame are hidden but preserved (the original layers will be available if they are needed for another frame).

Note: If you save an animation as a GIF, the animation frames are flattened and the original layers are lost. You should save the original file in Photoshop file format to preserve layers for reediting.

To flatten frames into layers:

In the Animation palette, choose Flatten Frames into Layers from the palette menu.

Viewing animations

Viewing an animation lets you preview the frames in timed sequence. You can preview an animation in ImageReady or in a Web browser.

To view an animation in ImageReady:

1 Click the Play button ▶ in the Animation palette. The animation is displayed in the document window. The animation repeats indefinitely unless you specified another repeat value in the Play Options dialog box. (See "Specifying looping" on page 326.)

2 To stop the animation, click the Stop button ▪.

3 To rewind the animation, click the Select First Frame button ◀◀.

To preview an animation in a browser:

1 Click the Preview in Default Browser tool 🝆, 🝇 in the toolbox, or choose File > Preview In and select a browser from the submenu.

2 Use the browser's Stop and Reload commands to stop or replay the animation.

Optimizing animations

You can apply optimization settings to animated images just as you do to nonanimated images. You should always optimize an animation in GIF format because GIF is the only format in ImageReady that supports the display of animated images on the Web.

Note: While you can optimize an image that includes animation in JPEG or PNG format, these formats do not support animation. The resulting Web page will display only the current frame of the animation.

In addition to the standard optimization options for GIF format, you can optimize frames to include only areas that change from frame to frame. (This greatly reduces the file size of the animated GIF.) ImageReady also applies a special dithering technique to animations to ensure that dither patterns are consistent across all frames and to prevent flickering during playback. Due to these additional optimization functions, ImageReady may require more time to optimize an animated GIF than to optimize a standard GIF.

To optimize an animated image:

1 Choose Optimize Animation from the Animation palette menu.

2 Set the following options:

• Bounding Box to crop each frame to the area that has changed from the preceding frame. Animation files created using this option are smaller but are incompatible with GIF editors that do not support the option. (This option is selected by default and is recommended.)

• Redundant Pixel Removal to make transparent all pixels in a frame that are unchanged from the preceding frame. This option is selected by default and is recommended. The Transparency option in the Optimize palette must be selected for redundant pixel removal to work. (See "Optimization options for GIF and PNG-8 formats" on page 338.)

Important: Set the frame disposal method to Automatic when using the Redundant Pixel Removal option. (See "Setting the frame disposal method" on page 327.)

3 Click OK.

4 Apply optimization settings. (See "Optimizing images" on page 333.)

When optimizing the colors in an animation, use the Adaptive, Perceptual, or Selective palette. This ensures that the colors are consistent across frames. (See "Generating a color table" on page 349.)

Viewing animated images in Photoshop

When you open a file containing an animation in Photoshop, only the frame that was selected when you saved the file in ImageReady is displayed. You cannot edit the animation frames separately, play the animation, or save the animation as an animated GIF.

If you add a new layer to the file while in Photoshop, the layer is added to all frames of the animation. However, the new layer will only appear in the selected frame when you reopen the file in ImageReady. If you change the stacking order of layers while in Photoshop, the stacking order of layers will be changed when you reopen the file in ImageReady.

Saving animations

You can save an animation as a series of GIF files or as a QuickTime™ movie.

Saving animations as animated GIFs

Animations that you view in a Web browser are called *animated GIFs*. When you save an optimized document containing an animation, you can choose to generate an HTML file that contains code for displaying the animated GIF in a Web page. The resulting Web page can contain just the animated GIF or additional Web features, such as links and rollovers, depending on the source document.

To save an animation as an animated GIF:

1 Optimize the animation. (See "Optimizing animations" on page 329.)

2 Save the optimized image. (See "Saving optimized images" on page 359.)

Saving animations as QuickTime movies

You can save an animation as a QuickTime movie. The resulting file is viewable in the QuickTime player and can be opened in other applications that support QuickTime movie format.

To save an animation as a QuickTime movie:

1 Choose File > Export Original.

2 Select QuickTime Movie from the format pop-up menu.

Note: *On Windows, QuickTime Movie format is only available when QuickTime is installed on your computer.*

3 Type a filename, and choose a location for the file.

4 Click Save.

5 If desired, adjust the compression settings, and click OK.

Opening and importing files as animations

You can use the animation features in ImageReady to edit animated GIFs, multilayered Photoshop files, and QuickTime movies.

Opening animated GIFs

You can open an existing animated GIF in ImageReady using the File > Open command. The file is opened as a stack of layers. Each layer corresponds to one frame. In each frame, the layer for that frame is visible, and the layers for the other frames are hidden.

Opening existing animated GIF files in ImageReady is useful primarily for applying optimization settings to the files. The one-layer-per-frame structure of imported animated GIF files may make it impractical to edit animation frames in other ways.

Opening Photoshop files as animations

You can easily create animated GIFs from existing one-layer-per-frame images in Adobe Photoshop file format or from a group of single-layer images.

You can make each layer in a multilayer Photoshop file a separate frame in the Animation palette. The layers are placed in the Animation palette in their stacking order, with the bottom layer becoming the first frame.

You can also import a folder of files and use each file as a frame in ImageReady. Files can be in any format that ImageReady supports. Each file becomes a frame in the Animation palette. The files are placed in the Animation palette in alphabetical order by image filename.

To open a multilayer Photoshop file as frames:

1 Choose File > Open, and select the Photoshop file to open.

2 Choose Make Frames From Layers from the Animation palette menu.

Each layer in the image appears as a frame in the Animation palette. The bottom layer in the Photoshop image is frame 1 in the Animation palette.

 Choose Reverse Frames from the Animation palette menu to reverse the order of frames.

To import a folder of files as frames:

1 Place the files to be used as frames into a folder. Make sure that the folder contains only those images that are to be used as frames. The resulting animation will display more successfully if all files are the same pixel dimensions.

To have frames appear in the correct order in the animation, name the files in alphabetical or numeric order, with the file to be used as frame 1 the first in order. (You can also change the order of the frames in the Animation palette after you import the files.)

2 Choose File > Import > Folder As Frames, and choose the folder to be imported.

The files appear in the Animation palette as frames and in the Layers palette as layers, with each layer assigned to a separate frame. The image that is first alphabetically or numerically by filename is frame 1 in the Animation palette and the bottom layer in the Layers palette.

Opening QuickTime movies as animations

You can open movies in MOV, AVI, and FLIC formats to view and edit in ImageReady.

To open QuickTime-compatible movies:

1 Choose File > Open, and select the movie to open.

2 Select the range of frames to import:

• From Beginning to End to open the full file.

- Selected Range Only to open selected frames. Drag the slider below the movie thumbnail to specify the starting point for the range, then Shift-drag to specify the ending point. (A black bar on the slider indicates the range you select.)

3 Select Limit to Every <number> Frame to specify which frames to include from the selected range. (You can use this option with either Range option.)

4 Click Open.

Chapter 14: Preparing Graphics for the Web

Creating small graphics files is key to distributing images on the World Wide Web. With smaller files, Web servers can store and transmit images more efficiently, and viewers can download images more quickly. Likewise, when preparing images for CD-ROM or other multimedia viewing, it's important to make the image files as small as possible. This conserves file storage space and decreases the amount of RAM needed for image display.

About optimization

Optimization is the process of fine-tuning the display quality and file size of an image for use on the Web or other online media. Adobe Photoshop and Adobe ImageReady give you an effective range of controls for compressing the file size of an image while optimizing its online display quality.

There are two methods of optimizing images:

• For basic optimization, the Photoshop Save As command lets you save an image as a GIF, JPEG, PNG, or WBMP file. Depending on the file format, you can specify image quality, background transparency or matting, color display, and downloading method. However, any Web features—such as slices, links, animations, and rollovers—that you've added to a file are not preserved.

For complete information on using the Save As command to save an image as a GIF, JPEG, or PNG file, see "Saving images" on page 365.

• For precise optimization, you can use the optimization features in Photoshop or ImageReady to preview optimized images in different file formats and with different file attributes. You can view multiple versions of an image simultaneously and modify optimization settings as you preview the image to select the best combination of settings for your needs. You can also specify transparency and matting, select options to control dithering, and resize the image to specified pixel dimensions or a specified percentage of the original size.

When you save an optimized file using the Save for Web (Photoshop) or Save Optimized (ImageReady) command, you can choose to generate an HTML file for the image. This file contains all the necessary code to display your image in a Web browser.

Optimizing images

In Photoshop, you use the Save for Web dialog box to select optimization options and preview optimized artwork. In ImageReady, you can view and work with optimized images at any time in the document window.

Using the Save for Web dialog box (Photoshop)

You use the Save for Web dialog box to select optimization options and preview optimized artwork.

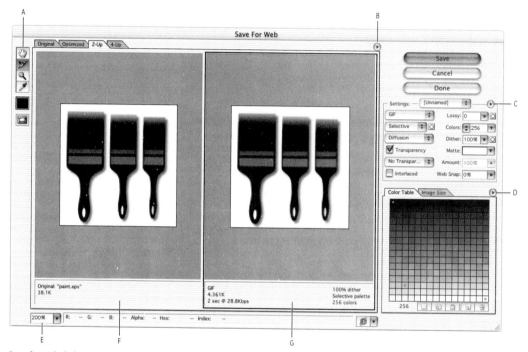

Save for Web dialog box
A. Toolbox B. Preview pop-up menu C. Optimize pop-up menu D. Color Table pop-up menu E. Zoom text box
F. Original image G. Optimized image

Displaying the Save for Web dialog box Choose File > Save for Web.

Previewing images Click a tab at the top of the image area to select a display option: Original to view the image with no optimization, Optimized to view the image with the current optimization settings applied, 2-Up to view two versions of the image side by side, or 4-Up to view four versions of the image side-by-side.

If the entire artwork is not visible in the Save for Web dialog box, you can use the hand tool to bring another area into view. Select the hand tool (or hold down the spacebar), and drag in the view area to pan over the image. You can also use the zoom tool to magnify or reduce the view. Select the zoom tool , and click in a view to zoom in; hold down Alt (Windows) or Option (Mac OS), and click in a view to zoom out. Alternatively, you can specify a magnification level in the Zoom text box at the bottom of the Save for Web dialog box.

Selecting a view Click a different pane in the Save for Web dialog box to select a new view. If you're working in 2-Up or 4-Up view, you must select a view before you apply optimization settings. A black frame indicates which view is selected.

Viewing annotations The annotation area below each image in the Save for Web dialog box provides valuable optimization information. The annotation for the original image shows the filename and file size. The annotation for the optimized image shows the current optimization options, the size of the optimized file, and the estimated download time using the selected modem speed. You can choose a modem speed in the Preview pop-up menu.

Working with slices in the Save for Web dialog box (Photoshop)

If your artwork contains multiple slices, you must specify the slices to be optimized. You can apply optimization settings to additional slices by linking the slices. Linked slices in GIF and PNG-8 format share a color palette and dither pattern to prevent the appearance of seams between the slices.

To show or hide all slices in the Save for Web dialog box:

Click the Toggle Slices Visibility button .

To show or hide auto slices in the Save for Web dialog box:

Choose Hide Auto Slices from the Preview pop-up menu. A check mark indicates that slices are hidden.

To select slices in the Save for Web dialog box:

1 Select the slice select tool .

2 Click a slice to select it. Shift-click or Shift-drag to select multiple slices.

Note: In the Save for Web dialog box, unselected slices are dimmed. This does not affect the color of the final image.

To view slice options in the Save for Web dialog box:

Select the slice select tool, and double-click a slice. (See "Specifying slice options" on page 297.)

To link slices:

1 Select two or more slices that you want to link.

2 Choose Link Slices from the Optimize pop-up menu ⊙ .

The link icon 🔗 appears on the linked slices.

To unlink slices:

Do one of the following:

- To unlink a slice, select the slice, and then choose Unlink Slice from the Optimize pop-up menu.

- To unlink all slices in an image, choose Unlink All Slices from the Optimize pop-up menu.

Using the Optimize palette (ImageReady)

You use the Optimize palette to select optimization options. This palette corresponds to the Optimize panel in the Photoshop Save for Web dialog box.

Displaying the Optimize palette Choose Window > Optimize. To show all the optimization options, click the Show Options control ⬍ on the Optimize palette tab or choose Show Options from the Optimize palette menu.

Using the Optimize palette menu Click the triangle ⊙ in the upper right corner of the palette.

Viewing optimized images (ImageReady)

In ImageReady, you view and work with optimized images directly in the document window. You can view up to four versions of an optimized image simultaneously and easily switch between the optimized and original (non-optimized) versions of an image.

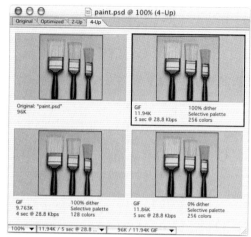

Document window in 4-Up mode

To preview optimized images:

Click a tab at the top of the document window to select a display option:

- Original to view the image with no optimization.

- Optimized to view the image with the current optimization settings applied.

- 2-Up to view two versions of the image side by side.

- 4-Up to view four versions of the image side-by-side.

To select a view:

Click the view you want to select. A black frame indicates which view is selected.

Note: If you're working in 2-Up or 4-Up view, you must select a view before you apply optimization settings.

In 2-Up and 4-Up view, the annotation area below each view provides valuable optimization information. The annotation for the original image shows the filename and file size. The annotation for the optimized image shows the current optimization options, the size of the optimized file, and the estimated download time using the selected modem speed. You can choose a modem speed in the image information box at the bottom of the document window. (See "Displaying file and image information" on page 42.)

To hide or show optimization annotations in 2-Up and 4-Up mode:

Choose View > Hide Optimization Info or View > Show Optimization Info.

Applying optimization settings

You use the Optimize panel in the Save for Web dialog box (Photoshop) and the Optimize palette (ImageReady) to set optimization options. If you're working in 2-Up or 4-Up mode, you can repopulate the views to automatically generate lower-quality versions of the image based on the selected settings.

To apply optimization settings:

1 Select a view to which you want to apply optimization settings.

2 If your artwork contains multiple slices, select one or more slices to which you want to apply the optimization settings. (See "Working with slices in the Save for Web dialog box (Photoshop)" on page 335 and "Selecting slices" on page 293.)

3 Do one of the following:

• Choose a named optimization setting from the Settings menu. For information on creating custom named settings, see "Saving and resetting optimization settings" on page 343.

• Choose a file format from the File Format menu.

4 Set additional optimization options. The file format you chose in Step 3 determines which options are available to you.

For more information on specific optimization options, see "Optimization options for GIF and PNG-8 formats" on page 338, "Optimization options for JPEG format" on page 341, "Optimization options for PNG-24 format" on page 342, and "Optimization options for WBMP format" on page 342.

To apply optimization settings based on file size:

1 Choose Optimize to File Size from the Optimize pop-up menu (Photoshop) or the Optimize palette menu (ImageReady).

2 Choose a Start With option:

• Current Settings to use current optimization settings.

• Auto Select GIF/JPEG to automatically generate a GIF or JPEG file. (Photoshop or ImageReady selects GIF or JPEG format, depending on its analysis of colors in the image.)

3 Enter a value for file size, and click OK.

To repopulate optimization settings:

1 Apply optimization settings to a view in 2-Up or 4-Up mode.

2 Choose Repopulate Views from the Optimize pop-up menu (Photoshop) or the Optimize palette menu (ImageReady).

The the optimization settings for the selected view and the original view are not altered during repopulation.

To restore an optimized version of an image to the original version:

1 Select an optimized version of the image in 2-Up or 4-Up mode.

2 In the Optimize panel/palette, choose Original from the Settings pop-up menu.

Optimization options for GIF and PNG-8 formats

GIF is the standard format for compressing images with flat color and crisp detail, such as line art, logos, or illustrations with type. You can lower the size of GIF images by reducing the number of colors in the file. Like the GIF format, the PNG-8 format efficiently compresses solid areas of color while preserving sharp detail; however, not all Web browsers can display PNG-8 files. PNG-8 settings are very similar to the GIF settings. (See "About file formats" on page 373.)

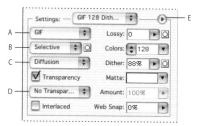

Optimization panel for GIF format
A. *File format menu* **B.** *Color Reduction Algorithm menu*
C. *Dither Algorithm menu* **D.** *Transparency dithering menu* **E.** *Optimize menu*

Note: *In ImageReady, you can control which options show in the Optimize palette by clicking the Show Options control* ◆ *on the Optimize palette tab. To show all options, choose Show Options from the Optimize palette menu.*

Lossy (GIF only) Specify a Lossy value to allow for lossy compression. Lossy compression reduces file size by selectively discarding data—a higher Lossy setting results in more data being discarded. You can often apply a Lossy value of 5–10, and sometimes up to 50, without degrading the image. File size can often be reduced 5%–40% using the Lossy option.

You can use masks from type layers, shape layers, and alpha channels to vary lossy compression across an image. This technique produces higher-quality results in critical image areas without sacrificing file size. (See "Using weighted optimization" on page 345.)

Note: *You cannot use the Lossy option with the Interlaced option or with Noise or Pattern Dither algorithms.*

Color Reduction Algorithm and Colors Choose a algorithm for generating a color table from the Color Reduction Algorithm menu. (See "Generating a color table" on page 349.) Then specify the maximum number of colors in the Colors text box. If you choose Web for the color reduction algorithm, the Auto option becomes active in the Colors pop-up menu. Use the Auto option if you want Photoshop or ImageReady to determine the number of colors in the color table based on the frequency of colors in the image.

You can use masks from type layers, shape layers, and alpha channels to vary color reduction across an image. This technique produces higher-quality results in critical image areas without sacrificing file size. (See "Using weighted optimization" on page 345.)

Dithering Dithering refers to the method of simulating colors not available in the color display system of your computer. Images with primarily solid colors may work well with no dither. Images with continuous-tone color (especially color gradients) may require dithering to prevent color banding.

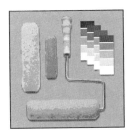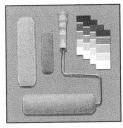

GIF image with 0% dither, and with 100% dither

Choose a option from the Dither Algorithm menu:

- No Dither applies no dither to the image.

- Diffusion applies a random pattern that is usually less noticeable than Pattern dither. The dither effects are extended across adjacent pixels. If you select this algorithm, specify a Dither percentage to control the amount of dithering that is applied to the image. A higher dithering percentage creates the appearance of more colors and more detail in an image, but can also increase the file size. You can use masks from type layers, shape layers, and alpha channels to vary the Dither percentage across an image. This technique produces higher-quality results in critical image areas without sacrificing file size. (See "Using weighted optimization" on page 345.)

Note: Diffusion dither may cause detectable seams to appear across slice boundaries. Linking slices diffuses the dither pattern across all linked slices, and eliminates the seams.

- Pattern applies a halftone-like square pattern to simulate any colors not in the color table.

- Noise applies a random pattern similar to the Diffusion dither algorithm, but without diffusing the pattern across adjacent pixels. No seams appear with the Noise algorithm.

Transparency and Matte Select a combination of Transparency and Matte options to specify how transparent pixels in the image are optimized:

- To make fully transparent pixels transparent and blend partially transparent pixels with a color, select Transparency and select a matte color.

- To make all pixels with greater than 50% transparency fully transparent and all pixels with 50% or less transparency fully opaque, select Transparency and choose None from the Matte menu.

- To fill fully transparent pixels with the selected color and blend partially transparent pixels with the same color, select a matte color and deselect Transparency.

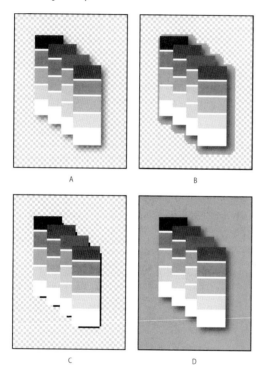

A

B

C

D

Examples of transparency and matting:
A. Original image B. Transparency selected with a matte color C. Transparency selected with no matting D. Transparency deselected with a matte color

To select a matte color, click the Matte color swatch and select a color in the color picker. Alternatively, choose an option from the Matte menu. The matte color should match the background color of the Web page.

Transparency Dithering When the Transparency option is selected, you can choose a method for dithering partially transparent pixels:

- No Transparency Dither applies no dither to partially transparent pixels in the image.

- Diffusion Transparency Dither applies a random pattern that is usually less noticeable than Pattern dither. The dither effects are diffused across adjacent pixels. If you select this algorithm, specify a Dither percentage to control the amount of dithering that is applied to the image.

- Pattern Transparency Dither applies a halftone-like square pattern to partially transparent pixels.

- Noise Transparency Dither applies a random pattern similar to the Diffusion algorithm, but without diffusing the pattern across adjacent pixels. No seams appear with the Noise algorithm.

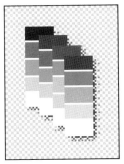

Example of Pattern Transparency
dithering

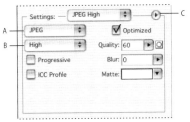

Optimization panel for JPEG format
A. File format menu **B.** Quality Level menu
C. Optimize menu

Interlace Select Interlaced to create an image that displays as a low-resolution version in a browser while the full image file is downloading. Interlacing can make downloading time seem shorter and can assure viewers that downloading is in progress. However, interlacing also increases file size.

Web Snap Specify a tolerance level for shifting colors to the closest Web palette equivalents (and prevent the colors from dithering in a browser). A higher value shifts more colors.

Use Unified Color Table (ImageReady) Select to use the same color table for all rollover states.

Optimization options for JPEG format

JPEG is the standard format for compressing continuous-tone images such as photographs. Optimizing an image as a JPEG format relies on *lossy* compression, which selectively discards data. (See "About file formats" on page 373.)

Note: In ImageReady, you can control which options show in the Optimize palette by clicking the Show Options control ⬍ *on the Optimize palette tab. To show all options, choose Show Options from the Optimize palette menu.*

Quality Choose an option from the Quality Level menu, or specify a value in the Quality text box. The higher the Quality setting, the more detail the compression algorithm preserves. However, using a high Quality setting results in a larger file size than using a low Quality setting. View the optimized image at several quality settings to determine the best balance of quality and file size.

You can use masks from type layers, shape layers, and alpha channels to vary the quality level across an image. This technique produces higher-quality results in critical image areas without sacrificing file size. (See "Using weighted optimization" on page 345.)

Optimized Select Optimized to create an enhanced JPEG with a slightly smaller file size. The Optimized JPEG format is recommended for maximum file compression; however, some older browsers do not support this feature.

Progressive Select Progressive to create an image that displays progressively in a Web browser. The image will display as a series of overlays, enabling viewers to see a low-resolution version of the image before it downloads completely.

Note: Progressive JPEGs require more RAM for viewing, and are not supported by some browsers.

Blur Specify the amount of blur to apply to the image. This option applies an effect identical to that of the Gaussian Blur filter and allows the file to be compressed more, resulting in a smaller file size. A setting of 0.1 to 0.5 is recommended.

ICC Profile Select ICC Profile to preserve the ICC profile of the artwork with the file. ICC profiles are used by some browsers for color correction. (See "Setting up color management" on page 90.)

Matte Specify a fill color for pixels that were transparent in the original image:

• Click the Matte color swatch and select a color in the color picker.

• Choose an option from the Matte menu.

Pixels that were fully transparent in the original image are filled with the selected color, pixels that were partially transparent in the original image are blended with the selected color.

Preserve EXIF Metadata (ImageReady) Select to preserve metadata from a digital camera.

Optimization options for PNG-24 format

PNG-24 is suitable for compressing continuous-tone images; however, it produces much larger files than JPEG format. (See "About file formats" on page 373.)

The advantage of using PNG-24 is that it can preserve up to 256 levels of transparency in an image. To save an image with multilevel transparency, select Transparency. For more information on the Interlaced, Transparency, and Matte options, see "Optimization options for GIF and PNG-8 formats" on page 338.

Optimization options for WBMP format

WBMP format is the standard format for optimizing images for mobile devices, such as cell phones. WBMP supports 1-bit color, which means that WBMP images contain only black and white pixels.

Choose an option from the Dither Algorithm menu to determine the method for converting pixel values to black or white:

• No Dither applies no dither to the image.

• Diffusion applies a random pattern that is usually less noticeable than Pattern dither. The dither effects are diffused across adjacent pixels. If you select this algorithm, specify a Dither percentage to control the amount of dithering that is applied to the image. You can use masks from type layers, shape layers, and alpha channels to vary the Dither percentage across an image. This technique produces higher-quality results in critical image areas without sacrificing file size. (See "Using weighted optimization" on page 345.)

Note: Diffusion dither may cause detectable seams to appear across slice boundaries. Linking slices diffuses the dither pattern across all linked slices, and eliminates the seams.

- Pattern applies a halftone-like square pattern to determine the value of pixels.

- Noise applies a random pattern similar to the Diffusion dithering, but without diffusing the pattern across adjacent pixels. No seams appear with the Noise algorithm.

Saving and resetting optimization settings

You can save optimization settings as a named set and apply the settings to other images. Settings that you save appear in the Settings pop-up menu, together with the predefined named settings. If you edit a named set or a predefined set, the Settings menu displays the term "Unnamed."

In Photoshop, after you optimize an image, you can return to the artboard without losing your settings. When you choose the Save for Web command again, the optimization settings are just as you left them.

To save a named set of optimization settings:

1 Set optimization options as desired, and choose Save Settings from the Optimize pop-up menu (Photoshop) or the Optimize palette menu (ImageReady).

2 Name the settings, and save them in the Presets/Optimized Settings folder inside the Photoshop program folder.

Note: *If you save the settings in a location other than the Presets/Optimized Settings folder, they will not be available from the Settings pop-up menu.*

To edit a named set of optimization settings:

1 Choose the named set from the Settings pop-up menu.

2 Edit the optimization settings as desired. The Settings menu will display the term "Unnamed," since the settings no longer match a named set.

3 Choose Save Settings from the Optimize pop-up menu (Photoshop) or the Optimize palette menu (ImageReady), and save the settings with the name of the original set.

To delete optimization settings:

1 Choose a named set or predefined set of optimization settings from the Settings pop-up menu.

2 Choose Delete Settings from the Settings panel menu.

Note: *You cannot restore deleted settings, so use the Delete Settings command with care.*

To save the current optimization setting (Photoshop):

Do one of the following:

- To save the settings and close the Save for Web dialog box, click Done.

- To save the settings without closing the Save for Web dialog box, press Alt (Windows) or Option (Mac OS), and click Remember.

To reset optimization settings to the last saved version (Photoshop):

Press Alt (Windows) or Option (Mac OS), and click Reset.

Resizing the image during optimization (Photoshop)

When optimizing an image in the Photoshop Save For Web dialog box, you can resize the image to specified pixel dimensions or to a percentage of the original size.

To change the pixel dimensions of an image during optimization:

1 Click the Image Size tab in the Save For Web dialog box.

2 To maintain the current proportions of pixel width to pixel height, select Constrain Proportions.

3 Enter values for Width, Height, or Percent.

4 Choose an interpolation method from the Quality pop-up menu:

- Jagged (Nearest Neighbor) for the faster, but less precise, method. This method is recommended for use with illustrations containing non-anti-aliased edges, to preserve hard edges and produce a smaller file.

- Smooth (Bicubic) for the slower, but more precise, method, resulting in smoother tonal gradations.

For more information on interpolation, see "About resampling" on page 57.

5 Click Apply.

Controlling optimization (ImageReady)

By default, Photoshop and ImageReady automatically regenerate the optimized image when you click the Optimized, 2-Up, or 4-Up tab at the top of the document (if you have modified the image since the last optimization), when you change optimization settings with the optimized image displayed, or when you edit the original image.

In ImageReady, you can turn off auto-regeneration so that the last version of the optimized image remains in the image window until you manually reoptimize the image or reactivate auto-regeneration. This feature is useful if you want to edit the image without pausing for reoptimization with each modification. You can also cancel optimization while it's in progress, and preserve the previous image.

When auto-regeneration is turned off, the Regenerate button ⚠ appears in the lower-right corner of each optimized image view. A regeneration alert symbol also appears in the Color Table palette if the optimized image is in GIF or PNG-8 format, indicating that the color table is out of date.

To turn Auto Regenerate on or off:

In the Optimize palette, choose Auto Regenerate from the palette menu. A check mark indicates that the option is turned on.

To manually optimize an image:

Choose a method for optimizing:

- Click the Regenerate button ⚠ in the lower-right corner of the optimized image (if it appears).

• Choose Regenerate from the Optimize palette menu.

Note: *Manually optimizing an image does not turn auto-regeneration on.*

To cancel optimization:

Click the Stop button next to the progress bar at the bottom of the image window.

Setting optimization preferences (ImageReady)

You can set preferences in ImageReady to determine the default optimization settings and the default configuration of panels in 2-Up and 4-Up views.

To set optimization preferences:

1 Do one of the following:

• In Windows and Mac OS 9.x, choose Edit > Preferences > Optimization.

• In Mac OS X, choose ImageReady > Preferences > Optimization.

2 Choose an option in the Default Optimization section:

• Previous Settings to automatically apply the last used optimization settings.

• Auto Selected GIF or JPEG to automatically optimize the image as a GIF or JPEG. ImageReady selects GIF or JPEG based on an analysis of the image.

• Named Setting and select an option from the Named Settings pop-up menu to apply that setting.

3 Under 2-Up Settings or 4-Up Settings, specify settings for the 1st, 2nd, 3rd, and 4th panes (3rd and 4th panes apply to 4-Up view only):

• Original to display the original image in the specified pane. (This option is available for the first pane only.)

• Current to display the image with current Optimize palette settings in the specified pane. (This option is available for all panes.)

• Auto to display a smaller optimized version of the image generated automatically by ImageReady, based on the current Optimize palette settings. (This option is available for the second, third, and fourth panes.)

• Select one of the named settings to display the optimized image with those settings. (This option is available for the second, third, and fourth panes.)

4 Click OK.

Using weighted optimization

Weighted optimization lets you smoothly vary optimization settings across an image using masks from text layers, shape layers, and alpha channels. This technique produces higher-quality results in critical image areas without sacrificing file size. With weighted optimization, you can produce gradual variations in GIF, PNG-8, and WBMP dithering, lossy GIF settings, and JPEG compression. Weighted optimization also lets you favor colors in selected image areas when you generate a color table.

About masks and weighted optimization

Photoshop and ImageReady automatically generate masks when you create a type layer or a shape layer. You can also manually create masks and store them in alpha channels. When you use a mask to apply optimization settings, the white areas of the mask describe the highest level of image quality, while the black areas for the mask describe the lowest level of image quality. (The level of optimization in gray areas of the mask decreases by a linear scale.)

Weighted optimization is available for specific settings in the Optimize panel/palette, as indicated by the mask button ⬚. To access the weighted optimization dialog box, simply click the mask button.

To create masks for use during optimization:

Do one or more of the following:

- Create a type layer. (See "Creating type" on page 267.)

- Create a shape layer. (See "Creating shape layers" on page 148.)

- (Photoshop) Save a selection as a mask, or create a new alpha channel and use the painting and editing tools to modify it. (See "Storing masks in alpha channels" on page 225.)

- (ImageReady) Use a selection tool to select an area of the image. (See "Making pixel selections" on page 103.) Either save the selection using the Select > Save Selection command, or choose the Save Selection command from the Channel pop-up menu in the weighted optimization dialog box.

Using masks to modify JPEG quality

When you use masks to optimize the range of quality in a JPEG image, white areas of the masks yield the highest quality, and black areas of the masks yield the lowest quality. You can adjust the maximum and minimum level of quality in the Modify Quality Setting dialog box.

To use masks to modify JPEG quality:

1 In the Optimize panel/palette, choose a JPEG setting from the Settings menu, or choose JPEG from the file format menu.

2 Click the mask button ⬚ to the right of the Quality text box.

3 Choose which masks to use:

- All Text Layers to use the masks from all text layers in the image.

- All Vector Shape Layers to use the masks from all shape layers in the image.

- Channel to choose an alpha channel from the menu. In ImageReady, you can choose Save Selection to create a new alpha channel based on the current selection.

4 To preview the results of the weighted optimization, select the Preview option.

5 Define the quality range:

- To set the highest level of quality, drag the right (white) tab on the slider, enter a value in the Maximum text box, or use the arrows to change the current value.

• To set the lowest level of quality, drag the left (black) tab on the slider, enter a value in the Minimum text box, or use the arrows to change the current value.

6 Click OK.

Using masks to modify GIF lossiness

When you use masks to optimize the amount of lossiness (or quality reduction) in a GIF image, white areas of the masks yield the highest quality, and black areas of the masks yield the lowest quality. You can adjust the maximum and minimum level of quality reduction in the Modify Lossiness Setting dialog box.

To use masks to modify GIF lossiness:

1 In the Optimize panel/palette, choose a GIF setting from the Settings menu, or choose GIF from the file format menu.

2 Click the mask button ⊙ to the right of the Lossy text box.

3 Choose which masks to use:

• All Text Layers to use the masks from all text layers in the image.

• All Vector Shape Layers to use the masks from all shape layers in the image.

• Channel to choose an alpha channel from the menu. In ImageReady, you can choose Save Selection to create a new alpha channel based on the current selection.

4 To preview the results of the weighted optimization, select the Preview option.

5 Define the quality range:

• To set the highest level of quality, drag the left (white) tab on the slider, enter a value in the Minimum text box, or use the arrows to change the current value.

• To set the lowest level of quality, drag the right (black) tab on the slider, enter a value in the Maximum text box, or use the arrows to change the current value.

Note: Lossiness is a reduction in quality; therefore, the highest level of image quality is defined by the Minimum value, and the lowest level of image quality is defined by the Maximum value. This is the opposite of the JPEG quality setting.

6 Click OK.

Using masks to modify dithering

When you use masks to optimize the amount of dithering in a GIF, PNG-8, or WBMP image, white areas of the masks yield the most dithering, and black areas of the masks yield the least dithering. You can adjust the maximum and minimum levels of dithering in the Modify Quality Setting dialog box.

To use masks to modify dithering:

1 In the Optimize panel/palette, choose a GIF or PNG-8 setting from the Settings menu, or choose GIF or PNG-8 from the file format menu.

2 Click the mask button ⊙ to the right of the Dither text box.

3 Choose which masks to use:

- All Text Layers to use the masks from all text layers in the image.

- All Vector Shape Layers to use the masks from all shape layers in the image.

- Channel to choose an alpha from the menu. In ImageReady, you can choose Save Selection to create a new alpha channel based on the current selection.

4 To preview the results of the weighted optimization, select the Preview option.

5 Define the dithering range:

- To set the highest percentage of dithering, drag the right (white) tab on the slider, enter a value in the Maximum text box, or use the arrows to change the current percentage.

- To set the lowest percentage of dithering, drag the left (black) tab on the slider, enter a value in the Minimum text box, or use the arrows to change the current percentage.

6 Click OK.

Using masks to modify color reduction

When you use mask to optimize the colors in a GIF or PNG-8 image, the white areas of the masks indicate to the color reduction algorithm which pixels are highly important, whereas black areas of the masks indicate which pixels are less important.

To use masks to modify color reduction:

1 In the Optimize panel/palette, choose a GIF or PNG-8 setting from the Settings menu, or choose GIF or PNG-8 from the file format menu.

2 Choose a color reduction algorithm and specify the maximum number of colors.

3 Click the mask button ▣ to the right of the Color Reduction Algorithm pop-up menu.

4 Choose which masks to use:

- All Text Layers to use the masks from all text layers in the image.

- All Vector Shape Layers to use the masks from all shape layers in the image.

- Channel to choose an alpha channel from the menu. In ImageReady, you can choose Save Selection to create a new alpha channel based on the current selection.

5 To preview the results of the weighted optimization, select the Preview option.

6 Click OK.

Optimizing colors in GIF and PNG-8 images

Decreasing the number of colors in an image is a key factor in optimizing GIF and PNG-8 images. A reduced range of colors will often preserve good image quality while dramatically reducing the file space required to store extra colors.

The color table gives you precise control over the colors in optimized GIF and PNG-8 images (as well as original images in indexed color mode). With a maximum of 256 colors, you can add and delete colors in the color table, shift selected colors to other colors or to transparency, and lock selected colors to prevent them from being dropped from the palette.

Viewing a color table

The color table for a slice appears in the Color Table panel in the Save for Web dialog box (Photoshop) or the Color Table palette (ImageReady).

Note: In ImageReady, be careful not to confuse the Color Table palette with the Color palette or Swatches palette. You use the Color Table palette to optimize colors; you use the Color palette and Swatches palette to select colors.

To view the color table for an optimized slice:

1 (ImageReady) Choose Window > Color Table.

2 Select a slice that is optimized in GIF or PNG-8 format. (See "Selecting slices" on page 293.) The color table for the selected slice appears in the Color Table palette.

Note: In ImageReady, the color table for the selected slice will not appear if Auto Regenerate is off. For more information, see "Controlling optimization (ImageReady)" on page 344.

If an image has multiple slices, the colors in the color table may vary between slices (you can link the slices first to prevent this from happening). If you select multiple slices that use different color tables, the color table is empty and its status bar displays the message "Mixed."

Generating a color table

You can change the palette—or set of colors—in the color table by selecting a color reduction option in the Optimize panel/palette. There are three categories of options:

- Dynamic options use a color reduction algorithm to build a palette based on the colors in the image and the number of colors specified in the optimization setting. The colors in the palette are regenerated every time you change or reoptimize the image. Perceptual, Selective, and Adaptive are dynamic options.

- Fixed options use a set palette of colors. In other words, the set of available colors is constant, but the actual colors in the palette will vary depending on the colors in the image. Web, Mac OS, Windows, Black & White, and Grayscale tables are fixed options.

- The Custom option uses a color palette that is created or modified by the user. If you open an existing GIF or PNG-8 file, it will have a custom color palette.

To select a color reduction algorithm:

Choose an option from the Color Reduction Algorithm pop-up menu (below the file format menu in the Optimize panel/palette):

Perceptual Creates a custom color table by giving priority to colors for which the human eye has greater sensitivity.

Selective Creates a color table similar to the Perceptual color table, but favoring broad areas of color and the preservation of Web colors. This color table usually produces images with the greatest color integrity. Selective is the default option.

Adaptive Creates a custom color table by sampling colors from the spectrum appearing most commonly in the image. For example, an image with only the colors green and blue produces a color table made primarily of greens and blues. Most images concentrate colors in particular areas of the spectrum.

Web Uses the standard 216-color color table common to the Windows and Mac OS 8-bit (256-color) palettes. This option ensures that no browser dither is applied to colors when the image is displayed using 8-bit color. (This palette is also called the Web-safe palette.) If your image has fewer colors than the total number specified in the color palette, unused colors are removed.

Using the Web palette can create larger files, and is recommended only when avoiding browser dither is a high priority.

Custom Preserves the current color table as a fixed palette that does not update with changes to the image.

Mac OS Uses the Mac OS system's default 8-bit (256-color) color table, which is based on a uniform sampling of RGB colors. If your image has fewer colors than the total number specified in the color palette, unused colors are removed.

Windows Uses the Windows system's default 8-bit (256-color) color table, which is based on a uniform sampling of RGB colors. If your image has fewer colors than the total number specified in the color palette, unused colors are removed.

Other color tables appear in the menu if you have saved them previously. (See "Loading and saving color tables" on page 355.)

You can use an alpha channel to influence the generation of color tables. (See "Using masks to modify color reduction" on page 348.)

To regenerate a color table (ImageReady):

Choose Rebuild Color Table from the Color Table palette menu. Use this command to generate a new color table when the Auto Regenerate option is off. (See "Controlling optimization (ImageReady)" on page 344.)

Changing the display of the color table

You can sort colors in the color table by hue, luminance, or popularity, making it easier to see an image's color range and locate particular colors. In ImageReady, you can also change the size of the color swatches in the color table.

To sort a color table:

Choose a sorting order from the Color Table palette menu:

- Unsorted. Restores the original sorting order.

- Sort By Hue, or by the location of the color on the standard color wheel (expressed as a degree between 0 to 360). Neutral colors are assigned a hue of 0, and located with the reds.

- Sort By Luminance, or by the lightness or brightness of a color.

- Sort By Popularity, or by the colors' frequency of occurrence in the image.

To change the size of the color swatches (ImageReady):

Choose Small Swatches or Large Swatches from the Color Table palette menu.

Adding new colors to the color table

You can add colors that were left out in building the color table. Adding a color to a dynamic table shifts the color in the palette closest to the new color. Adding a color to a fixed or Custom table adds an additional color to the palette. (See "Generating a color table" on page 349.)

To add a new color:

1 Deselect all colors in the color table (see "Selecting colors" on page 352).

2 Choose a color:

- Click the color selection box in the Save for Web dialog box (Photoshop) or the toolbox (ImageReady), and choose a color from the color picker.

- Select the eyedropper tool 🖋 in the Save for Web dialog box (Photoshop) or the toolbox (ImageReady) and click in the image.

- Select the eyedropper tool 🖋 , click in the image, hold the mouse down, and drag anywhere on the desktop. You can use this option to select a color displayed in another application, such as a color in a Web page displayed in a browser.

- (ImageReady) Select a color from the Color palette or the Swatches palette.

3 Do one of the following:

- Click the New Color button 🔲 in the Color Table palette.

- Select New Color from the Color Table palette menu.

- (ImageReady) Drag the color from the color selection box, Color palette, or Swatches palette to the Color Table palette.

💡 *To switch the color table to a Custom palette, hold down Ctrl (Windows) or Command (Mac OS) when you add the new color.*

The new color appears in the color table with a small white square in the lower right corner, indicating that the color is locked. (See "Locking colors in the color table" on page 354.) If the color table is dynamic, the original color is displayed in the upper left and the new color is displayed in the lower right.

Including black and white in a color table

You can add black and white to the color table when the image does not include these colors. Including black and white is useful when preparing files for multimedia authoring applications, such as Adobe After Effects®.

To add black or white to the color table for an image:

1 Choose black or white as the foreground color. (See "Choosing foreground and background colors" on page 201.)

2 Add the color to the color table. (See "Adding new colors to the color table" on page 351.)

Selecting colors

You select colors directly in the optimized image or in the color table. In ImageReady, you can select a color from another application, such as a Web page displayed in a browser.

To select a color from the optimized image:

1 Select the eyedropper tool 🖋 in the Save for Web dialog box (Photoshop) or the toolbox (ImageReady).

2 Click a color in the image. A white border 🔲 appears around that color in the color table. Shift-click to select additional colors.

To select a color from another application (ImageReady):

(ImageReady) Select the eyedropper tool, click in the image, hold the mouse down, and drag anywhere on the desktop. You can use this option to select a color displayed in another application, such as a color in a Web page displayed in a browser.

To select a color directly in the color table:

Click the color in the Color Table palette.

To select a contiguous group of colors, press Shift and click another color. All colors in the rows between the first and second selected colors are selected.

To select a discontiguous group of colors, press Ctrl (Windows) or Command (Mac OS) and click each color that you want to select.

To select colors based on a selection in the image (ImageReady):

1 Make a selection in the image using the selection tools or the Select menu commands.

2 Choose Select All From Selection from the Color Table palette menu.

To select all colors:

Choose Select All Colors from the Color Table palette menu.

To select all Web-safe colors:

Choose Select All Web Safe Colors from the Color Table palette menu.

To select all non-Web-safe colors:

Choose Select All Non-Web Safe Colors from the Color Table palette menu.

To view selected colors in an image (ImageReady):

Select the optimized image. Then click and hold a selected color in the Color Table palette to temporarily invert the color in the optimized image, enabling you to see which areas of the image contain the color.

To view a contiguous group of colors, press Shift and click and hold another color. All colors in the rows between the first and second selected colors are inverted.

To view a discontiguous group of colors, press Ctrl (Windows) or Command (Mac OS) and click each color that you want to select, and hold the mouse button down on any color in the group.

To deselect all colors:

Choose Deselect All Colors from the Color Table palette menu.

Shifting colors

You can change a selected color in the color table to any other RGB color value. When you regenerate the optimized image, the selected color changes to the new color wherever it appears in the image.

To shift a color:

1 Double-click the color in the color table to display the default color picker.

2 Select a color.

The original color appears at the upper left of the color swatch and the new color at the lower right. The small square at the lower right of the color swatch indicates that the color is locked. If you shift to a Web-safe color, a small white diamond appears at the center of the swatch.

To revert shifted colors to their original colors:

Do one of the following:

- Double-click the swatch for the shifted color. The original color is selected in the color picker. Click OK to restore the color.

- To revert all shifted colors in a color table (including Web-shifted colors), choose Unshift All Colors from the Color Table palette menu.

Shifting to Web-safe colors

To protect colors from dithering in a browser, you can shift the colors to their closest equivalents in the Web palette. This ensures that the colors won't dither when displayed in browsers on either Windows or Macintosh operating systems capable of displaying only 256 colors.

To shift colors to the closest Web palette equivalent:

1 Select one or more colors in the optimized image or color table. (See "Selecting colors" on page 352.)

2 Do one of the following:

- Click the Web Shift button ⊕ in the Color Table palette.

- Choose Shift Selected Colors to Web Palette from the Color Table palette menu.

The original color appears at the upper left of the color swatch and the new color at the lower right. The small white diamond ◈ in the center of the color swatch indicates that the color is Web-safe; the small square at the lower right of the color swatch indicates that the color is locked.

To revert Web-shifted colors to their original colors:

Do one of the following:

• Select a Web-shifted color in the color table and click the Web Shift button ◉ in the Color Table palette.

• To revert all Web-shifted colors in the color table, choose Unshift All Web Shifted Colors from the Color Table palette menu.

To specify tolerance for shifting colors automatically to the closest Web palette equivalents:

In the Optimize panel/palette, enter a value for Web Snap or drag the pop-up slider. A higher value shifts more colors.

(In ImageReady, click the Show Options control ◆ on the Optimize palette tab or choose Show Options from the Optimize palette menu to view the Web Snap option.)

Mapping colors to transparency

You can add transparency to an optimized image by mapping existing colors to transparency.

To map colors to transparency:

1 Select one or more colors in the optimized image or color table. (See "Selecting colors" on page 352.)

2 Do one of the following:

• Click the Map Transparency button ▢ in the Color Table palette.

• Choose Map Selected Colors to Transparent from the Color Table palette menu.

The transparency grid ▨ appears in half of each mapped color. The small square at the lower right of the color swatch indicates that the color is locked.

To revert transparency to its original colors:

Do one of the following:

• Select the colors you want to revert, click the Map Transparency button ▢ or choose Unmap Selected Colors from Transparent from the Color Table palette menu.

• To revert all transparency-mapped colors, choose Unmap All Transparent Colors.

Locking colors in the color table

You can lock selected colors in the color table to prevent them from being dropped when the number of colors is reduced and to prevent them from dithering in the application.

Note: Locking colors does not prevent them from dithering in a browser.

To lock a color:

1 Select one or more colors in the color table. (See "Selecting colors" on page 352.)

2 Lock the color:

• Click the Lock button 🔒 .

- Choose Lock/Unlock Selected Colors from the Color Table palette menu.

A white square ⊡ appears in the lower right corner of each locked color.

Note: If the selected colors include both locked and unlocked colors, all colors will be locked.

To unlock a color:

1 Click the locked color to select it.

2 Unlock the color:

- Click the Lock button ⊡ .

- Choose Lock/Unlock Selected Colors from the Color Table palette menu.

The white square disappears from the color swatch.

Deleting colors from the color table

You can delete selected colors from the color table to decrease the image file size. When you delete a color, areas of the optimized image that previously included that color are rerendered using the closest color remaining in the palette.

When you delete a color, the color table automatically changes to a Custom palette. This is because the Adaptive, Perceptual, and Selective palettes automatically add the deleted color back into the palette when you reoptimize the image—the Custom palette does not change when you reoptimize the image.

To delete selected colors:

1 Select one or more colors in the color table. (See "Selecting colors" on page 352.)

2 Delete the color:

- Click on the Trash button ⊟ .

- Choose Delete Color from the Color Table palette menu.

Loading and saving color tables

You can save color tables from optimized images to use with other images and to load color tables created in other applications. Once you load a new color table into an image, the colors in the optimized image are changed to reflect the colors in the new color table.

To save a color table:

1 Select Save Color Table from the Color Table palette menu.

2 Name the color table and choose a location where it will be saved. By default, the color table file is given the extension .act (for Adobe Color Table).

If you want to access the color table when selecting Optimization options for a GIF or PNG image, save the color table in the Presets/Optimized Colors folder inside the Photoshop program folder.

3 Click Save.

Important: When you reload the table, all shifted colors will appear as full swatches and they will be unlocked.

To load a color table:

1 Select Load Color Table from the Color Table palette menu.

2 Navigate to a file containing the color table you want to load—either an Adobe Color Table (.act) file, an Adobe Color Swatch (.aco) file, or a GIF file (to load the file's embedded color table).

3 Click Open.

Using master palettes (ImageReady)

You can create a master palette to use with a group of GIF or PNG-8 images that will be placed on a CD-ROM or other multimedia storage medium. When you include the master palette with a batch of images, all images display using the same colors.

To build a master palette, you add colors from a set of images and then build and save the master palette. To create a master palette for a batch of images, you add colors to the palette from other optimized images.

To create and apply a master palette:

1 With an image displayed, choose Image > Master Palette > Clear Master Palette (if available). Clearing the master palette ensures that colors from previous images are not included in the new palette.

2 Open an image whose colors you want to include in a master palette.

3 Choose Image > Master Palette > Add To Master Palette. All color information for the current image is added to the master palette.

4 Repeat steps 2 and 3 for all images whose colors you want to include in the master palette.

5 In the Optimize palette, select optimization settings for the master palette.

6 Choose Image > Master Palette > Build Master Palette to create a new color table from the color information of images used in steps 2, 3, and 4.

7 Choose Image > Master Palette > Save Master Palette.

8 Name the master palette and choose a location where it will be saved. By default, the master palette file is given the extension .act (for Adobe Color Table).

If you want to access the color table when selecting Optimization options for a GIF or PNG image, save the master palette in the Optimized Colors folder, inside the Presets folder in the Adobe Photoshop folder.

9 Click Save.

10 To apply the master palette to the image or images for which it was created, open the image or images and select the master palette:

• If the master palette appears in the Color Reduction Algorithm menu in the Optimize palette, select the master palette from this menu. (The Color Reduction Algorithm menu includes all palettes saved in the Optimized Colors folder, inside the Presets folder in the Adobe Photoshop folder.)

• Load the master palette. (See "Loading and saving color tables" on page 355.)

Working with hexadecimal values for color

You can view colors as hexadecimal values in the Info palette. In addition, you can copy colors as hexadecimal values to the Clipboard and paste them into an HTML document.

Viewing hexadecimal values for colors in the Info palette

In Photoshop, hexadecimal values for colors are displayed in the Info palette when you select Web Color Mode for one or both color readouts. In ImageReady, hexadecimal values for colors are displayed automatically in the right side of the Info palette, next to RGB color values. The Photoshop and ImageReady Info palettes also display other information, depending on the tool being used.

To view hexadecimal color values in the Info palette:

1 Choose Window > Info or click the Info palette tab to view the palette.

2 (Photoshop) Choose Palette Options from the palette menu. Under First Color Readout or Second Color Readout, choose Web Color from the Mode menu and click OK.

3 Position the pointer over the color you want to view hexadecimal values for.

Copying colors as hexadecimal values

You can copy colors as hexadecimal values from files in Photoshop or ImageReady, using the context menu with the eyedropper tool, or using menu commands. In Photoshop, you copy a color as a hexadecimal value while in the main work area (not the Save for Web dialog box).

To copy a color as a hexadecimal value using the eyedropper tool:

1 Select the eyedropper tool 🔎 in the toolbox.

2 Select a color to copy:

- Right-click (Windows) or Control-click (Mac OS) a color in the image to select the color and view the eyedropper tool context menu.

- (ImageReady) Click the color in the image which you want to copy. The color you click becomes the foreground color. With the eyedropper tool still over the image, right-click (Windows) or Control-click (Mac OS) to view the eyedropper tool context menu.

3 Choose Copy Color as HTML (Photoshop) or Copy Foreground Color as HTML (ImageReady) from the eyedropper tool context menu.

The selected color is copied to the Clipboard as a the HTML COLOR attribute with the hexadecimal value (COLOR=#XXYYZZ). To paste the color into an HTML file, choose Edit > Paste with the HTML file displayed in your HTML editing application.

To copy a color as a hexadecimal value using menu commands:

1 Select a color to copy.

2 Copy the color:

• Choose Copy Color As HTML from the Color palette menu.

• (ImageReady) Choose Edit > Copy Foreground Color as HTML.

The foreground color is copied to the Clipboard as the HTML COLOR attribute with the hexadecimal value (COLOR=#XXYYZZ). To paste the color into an HTML file, open a destination application and choose Copy > Paste with the HTML file displayed.

To copy a color as a hexadecimal value by dragging (ImageReady):

Drag the Foreground Color from the toolbox or a selected color from the Color Table palette or the Swatches palette into the HTML file in the destination application.

Note: *This feature is not supported by all text and HTML editing applications.*

Using a droplet to automate optimization settings (ImageReady)

You can save Optimize palette settings for use on individual images or batches of images by creating a *droplet*, a small application that applies the optimization settings to an image or batch of images that you drag over the droplet icon. You can drag a droplet to the desktop or save it to a location on disk. When you create the droplet you can choose where the images will be saved. When you drag an image over it, the droplet launches ImageReady if the program is not currently running.

Note: *You can also drag a droplet onto the ImageReady Actions palette to create an action step, or you can drag a droplet onto a slice to apply the optimization settings to the slice.*

To create a droplet for automating Optimize palette settings:

1 With an image displayed in the image window, choose a compression format and compression options in the Optimize palette.

2 Create a droplet:

• Drag the droplet icon 🐾 from the Optimize palette onto the desktop.

The droplet is named with a brief description of the compression settings, including file format and color palette or quality setting information. You can rename the droplet as you do other desktop icons.

- Click the droplet icon on the Optimize palette. Name the droplet, choose a location where the droplet will be saved, and click Save.

- Choose Create Droplet from the Optimize palette menu. Name the droplet, choose a location where the droplet will be saved, and click Save.

To use a droplet:

1 Drag a single image or a folder of images onto the droplet icon.

As the images are processed, a progress bar appears.

2 Do any of the following to control the processing:

- To temporarily pause the processing, click Pause. You can then click Resume to continue the processing.

- To cancel the processing, click Stop.

- Let the process finish on its own.

For more information on working with droplets, see "Using droplets" on page 410.

Saving optimized images

When you've applied a combination of settings that achieve a balance between quality and file size, you're ready to save the optimized image.

To save an optimized image:

1 Select the view with the desired optimization settings, and do one of the following:

- (Photoshop) Click Save in the Save For Web dialog box.

- (ImageReady) Choose File > Save Optimized to save the file in its current state. If you previously saved the optimized file using the File > Save Optimized command, applying the command again saves the file with the filename and Save options specified in the first save operation. The Save dialog box does not appear.

- (ImageReady) Choose File > Save Optimized As to save an alternate version of the file with a different filename.

2 Type a filename, and choose a location for the resulting file or files.

3 Choose a Format option:

- HTML and Images to generate all files required to use your artwork as a Web page. This includes an HTML file and separate image files for the slices in the artwork. The HTML file includes code for any links, image maps, and other effects in the document.

- Images Only to save your artwork with the specified optimization settings. If the artwork contains multiple slices, each slice is saved as a separate file.

- HTML Only to generate an HTML file but not save any image files.

4 To set preferences for saving image files and HTML files, choose predefined output options from the Settings pop-up menu, or choose Other to set different options. (See "Setting output options" on page 360.)

5 Choose an option for slices from the pop-up menu:

- All Slices to save all slices in the image.

- Selected Slices to save only the selected slices. If you select this option in conjunction with the HTML and Images option, ImageReady or Photoshop generates the HTML code based on the outermost bounds of the selected slices, and generates auto-slices as needed to create a complete HTML table.

Note: You must select the desired slices before starting this procedure.

- (ImageReady) A slice selection to save only the slices in the selection. You must save a slice selection in order for this option to appear in the menu. (See "Selecting slices" on page 293.)

6 Click Save.

Setting output options

When you save an optimized image as a Web page, you can specify how HTML files are formatted, how slices are named, how files are named, and how background images are handled. You set these options in the Output Settings dialog box.

Using the Output Settings dialog box

The Output Settings dialog box displays different sets of options. In ImageReady, you can save your output settings and apply them to other files.

Displaying the Output Settings dialog box Do one of the following:

- When you save an optimized image, choose Other from the Settings pop-up menu in the Save Optimized or Save Optimized As dialog box. The Save and Load options are not available when you use this method to access the Output Settings dialog box.

- (ImageReady) Choose the desired preferences set from the File > Output Settings submenu. Use this method if you want to load and save settings.

- (Photoshop) Choose Edit Output Settings from the Optimize pop-up menu in the Save For Web dialog box. Use this method if you want to load and save settings.

Displaying predefined output options Choose an option from the Settings pop-up menu.

Switching to a different set of options Choose an options set from the pop-up menu below the Settings menu. Alternately, click Next to display the next set in the menu list; click Prev to display the previous set.

Saving output settings Set the options as desired, and click Save. Type a filename, choose a location for the saved file, and click Save.

You can save the output settings anywhere. However, if you place the file in the Presets/Optimized Output Settings folder inside the Photoshop program folder, the file will appear in the Settings pop-up menu in both Photoshop and ImageReady.

Loading output settings Click Load, select a file, and click Open.

Setting HTML output options

You can set the following options in the HTML set:

Tags Case Specifies the capitalization for tags.

Attribute Case Specifies the capitalization for attributes.

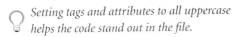 *Setting tags and attributes to all uppercase helps the code stand out in the file.*

Indent Specifies a method for indenting lines of code: using the authoring application's tab settings, using a specified number of spaces, or using no indentation.

Line Endings Specifies a platform for line ending compatibility.

Include Comments Adds explanatory comments to the HTML code. In ImageReady, this option is required when you plan to update the resulting file using the File > Update HTML command.

Always Quote Attributes Places quotation marks around all tag attributes. Placing quotation marks around attributes is required for compatibility with certain early browsers and for strict HTML compliance. However, always quoting attributes is not recommended. Quotation marks are used when necessary to comply with most browsers, even if this option is deselected.

Always Add Alt Tags Adds the ALT attribute to IMG elements to comply with government Web accessibility standards.

Close All Tags Adds close tags for all HTML elements in the file for XHTML compliance.

Include GoLive 5 (or Earlier) Code (ImageReady) Reformats JavaScript code so that rollovers will be fully editable in Adobe GoLive 5.0 and earlier. You do not need to select this option if you plan to edit rollovers in GoLive 6.0.

Note: GoLive does not support the Selected rollover state.

Setting slice output options

You can set the following options in the Slices set:

Generate Table Aligns slices using an HTML table, rather than a Cascading Style Sheet.

Empty Cells Specifies how empty slices are converted to table cells. Select GIF, IMG W&H to use a one-pixel GIF with width and height values specified on the IMG tag. Select GIF, TD W&H to use a one-pixel GIF with width and height values specified on the TD tag. Select NoWrap, TD W&H to place a nonstandard NoWrap attribute on the table data and also place width and height values specified on the TD tags.

TD W&H Specifies when to include width and height attributes for table data: Always, Never, or Auto (the recommended setting).

Spacer Cells Specifies when to add one row and one column of empty spacer cells around the generated table: Always, Never, or Auto (the recommended setting). Adding spacer cells is necessary with table layouts in which slice boundaries do not align, to prevent the table from breaking apart in some browsers.

Generate CSS Generates a Cascading Style Sheet, rather than an HTML table.

Referenced Specifies how slice positions are referenced in the HTML file when using CSS:

- By ID to position each slice using styles that are referenced by a unique ID.

- Inline to include style elements in the declaration of the block element <DIV> tag.

- By Class to position each slice using classes that are referenced by a unique ID.

Default Slice Naming Choose elements from the pop-up menus or enter text into the fields to be combined into the default names for all use slices. Elements include document name, the word *slice*, numbers or letters designating slices or rollover states, slice creation date, punctuation, or *none*.

Setting image map output options (ImageReady)

You can set the following options in the Image Maps set:

Image Map Type Specifies what type of image map is created:

- Client-Side to include all required code for the image map in the image's HTML file.

- NCSA Server-Side to create a separate .map file in addition to the HTML file, using NCSA specifications.

- CERN Server-Side to create a separate .map file in addition to the HTML file, using CERN specifications.

Important: *Photoshop and ImageReady cannot generate server-side image maps for images that contain slices.*

- Client-Side & NCSA Server-Side to create both a client-side and server-side compatible image map, using NCSA specifications.

- Client-Side & CERN Server-Side to create both a client-side and server-side compatible image map, using CERN specifications.

Note: *Contact your Internet service provider to find out whether to use NCSA or CERN specification for server-side image maps.*

Image Map Placement Specifies the location of the image map declaration (the <MAP> tag) in the HTML file:

- Top to place the image map declaration at the top of the HTML body section.

- Body to place the image map declaration above the <IMG SRC> tag for the associated slice.

- Bottom to place the image map declaration at the bottom of the HTML body section.

Setting background options

You can set the following options in the Background set:

View Document As Select Image if you want the Web page to display an image or a solid color as a background behind the current image. Select Background if you want the Web page to display the optimized image as a tiled background.

Background Image Enter the location of an image file, or click Choose and select an image. The file you specify will be tiled behind the optimized image on the Web page.

BG Color Click the Color box, and choose a background color using the color picker, or choose an option from the pop-up menu.

Setting file saving options

You set the following options in the Saving Files set:

File Naming Choose elements from the pop-up menus or enter text into the fields to be combined into the default names for all files. Elements include document name, slice name, rollover state, trigger slice, file creation date, slice number, punctuation, and file extension. Some options are relevant only if the file contains slices or rollover states.

The fields let you change the order and formatting of the filename parts (for example, letting you indicate rollover state by an abbreviation instead of the full word).

File Name Compatibility Select one or multiple options to make the filename compatible with Windows (permits longer filenames), Macintosh, and UNIX operating systems.

Note: Filenames may be truncated after 31 characters.

Copy Background Image When Saving Copies the background image file specified in the Background set into images folder for the Web page.

Put Images In Folder Specifies a folder name where optimized images are saved (available only with documents containing multiple slices).

Include Copyright Includes title and copyright information with the image. (See "Adding title and copyright information to Web pages" on page 364.)

Adding title and copyright information to Web pages

You can add title and copyright information to a Web page by entering information in the File Info dialog box. Title information displays in the Web browser's title bar. Copyright information is not displayed in a browser; however, it is added to the HTML file as a comment and to the image file as metadata.

To enter information about an image:

1 Choose File > File Info.

2 Enter a title that will appear in the Web browser's title bar:

- (Photoshop) In the General section of the File Info dialog box, enter the desired text in the Caption text box.

- (ImageReady) Enter the desired text in the Caption text box.

3 Enter copyright information:

- (Photoshop) In the General section of the File Info dialog box, enter the desired text in the Copyright Notice text box.

- (ImageReady) Enter the desired text in the Copyright text box.

4 Click OK.

Chapter 15: Saving and Exporting Images

Adobe Photoshop and Adobe ImageReady support a variety of file formats to suit a wide range of output needs. You can save or export your image to any of these formats. You can also use special Photoshop features to add information to files, set up multiple page layouts, and place images in other applications.

Saving images

The saving options that are available to you vary between Photoshop and ImageReady. Keep in mind that the primary focus of ImageReady is producing images for the Web. If ImageReady doesn't provide the file format or option you need, you can jump to Photoshop.

You can use the following commands to save images:

- Save to save changes you've made to the current file. In Photoshop, the file is saved in the current format; in ImageReady, the Save command always saves to PSD format.

- Save As to save an image with a different location or filename. In Photoshop, the Save As command lets you save an image in a different format and with different options. In ImageReady, the Save As command always saves to PSD format.

- Export Original (ImageReady) to flatten the layers in a copy of the original image and save the copy in a variety of file formats. Some information (such as slices and optimization settings) is not preserved when an original image is saved to file formats other than Photoshop.

- Save for Web (Photoshop), Save Optimized (ImageReady), and Save Optimized As (ImageReady) to save an optimized image for the Web. (See "Optimizing images" on page 333 and "Saving optimized images" on page 359.)

Saving files

You can save a file with its current filename, location, and format or with a different filename, location, format, and options. You can also save a copy of a file while leaving the current file open on your desktop.

To save changes to the current file:

Choose File > Save.

To save a file with a different name and location:

1 Choose File > Save As.

2 Type a filename, and choose a location for the file.

3 Click Save.

To save a file in a different file format:

1 Do one of the following:

- (Photoshop) Choose File > Save As.

- (ImageReady) Choose File > Export Original.

2 Choose a format from the format pop-up menu.

Note: In Photoshop, if you choose a format that does not support all features of the document, a warning appears at the bottom of the dialog box. If you see this warning, it is recommended that you save a copy of the file in Photoshop format or in another format that supports all of the image data.

3 Specify a filename and location.

4 (Photoshop) Select saving options. For more information, see "Setting file saving options (Photoshop)" on page 366.

5 Click Save.

With some image formats, a dialog box appears. For more information, see one of the following:

- "Saving files in Photoshop EPS format (Photoshop)" on page 367

- "Saving files in GIF format (Photoshop)" on page 369

- "Saving files in JPEG format (Photoshop)" on page 369

- "Saving files in Photoshop PDF format (Photoshop)" on page 370

- "Saving files in PNG format (Photoshop)" on page 371

- "Saving files in TIFF format" on page 371

To copy an image without saving it to your hard disk, use the Duplicate command. (See "Duplicating images" on page 36.) To store a temporary version of the image in memory, use the History palette to create a snapshot. For more information, see "Making a snapshot of an image (Photoshop)" on page 35.

Setting file saving options (Photoshop)

You can set a variety of file saving options in the Save As dialog box. The availability of options depends on the image you are saving and the selected file format. For example, if an image doesn't contain multiple layers, or if the selected file format doesn't support layers, the Layers option is dimmed.

As a Copy Saves a copy of the file while keeping the current file open on your desktop.

Alpha Channels Saves alpha channel information with the image. Disabling this option removes the alpha channels from the saved image.

Layers Preserves all layers in the image. If this option is disabled or unavailable, all visible layers are flattened or merged (depending on the selected format).

Annotations Saves annotations with the image.

Spot Colors Saves spot channel information with the image. Disabling an option removes spot colors from the saved image.

Use Proof Setup, ICC Profile (Windows), or Embed Color Profile (Mac OS) Creates a color-managed document. (See "Embedding profiles in saved documents" on page 100.)

Thumbnail (Windows) Saves thumbnail data for the file. In order to select or deselect this option, you must choose Ask When Saving for the Image Previews option in the Preferences dialog box. For more information, see "Setting preferences for saving files (Photoshop)" on page 374.

Image Previews options (Mac OS) Saves thumbnail data for the file. Thumbnails display in the Open dialog box. You can set these image preview options: Icon to use the preview as a file icon on the desktop, Full Size to save a 72-ppi version for use in applications that can only open low-resolution Photoshop images, Macintosh Thumbnail to display the preview in the Open dialog box, and Windows Thumbnail to save a preview that can display on Windows systems. Keep in mind that Windows thumbnails increase the size of files as delivered by Web servers.

Use Lower Case Extension (Windows) Makes the file extension lowercase.

File Extension options (Mac OS) Specifies the format for file extensions. Select Append to add the format's extension to a filename and Use Lower Case to make the extension lowercase.

Important: To display image preview and file extension options when saving files in Mac OS, select Ask When Saving for the Image Previews option and the Append File Extension option in the Preferences dialog box. For more information, see "Setting preferences for saving files (Photoshop)" on page 374.

Saving files in Photoshop EPS format (Photoshop)

Virtually all page layout, word processing, and graphic applications accept imported or placed EPS (Encapsulated PostScript) files. To print EPS files, you must use a PostScript printer.

To save a file in Photoshop EPS format:

1 Save the artwork, and choose Photoshop EPS from the Format menu. (See "Saving files" on page 365.)

2 In the EPS Options dialog box, select the options you want, and click OK:

Preview Creates a low-resolution image to view in the destination application. Choose TIFF to share an EPS file between Windows and Mac OS systems. An 8-bit preview delivers better display quality but larger file size than a 1-bit preview.

Note: To use the JPEG preview option in Mac OS, you must have QuickTime installed.

Encoding Determines the way image data is delivered to a PostScript output device:

Choose ASCII if you're printing from a Windows system, or if you experience printing errors or other difficulties.

- Binary produces a smaller file and leaves the original data intact. Choose Binary encoding if you're printing from a Mac OS system. However, some page-layout applications and some commercial print spooling and network printing software may not support binary Photoshop EPS files.

- JPEG compresses the file by discarding some image data. Files with JPEG encoding can be printed only on Level 2 (or later) PostScript printers and may not separate into individual plates.

Include Halftone Screen and Include Transfer Function Control print specifications for high-end commercial print jobs. Consult your printer before selecting these options.

Transparent Whites Displays white areas as transparent. This option is available only for images in Bitmap mode.

PostScript Color Management Converts file data to the printer's color space. Do not select this option if you plan to place the image into another color-managed document. Doing so may disrupt the color management.

Note: Only PostScript Level 3 printers support PostScript Color Management for CMYK images. To print a CMYK image using PostScript Color Management on a Level 2 printer, convert the image to Lab mode before saving in EPS format.

Include Vector Data Preserves any vector graphics (such as shapes and type) in the file. However, vector data in EPS and DCS files is only available to other applications; vector data is rasterized if you reopen the file in Photoshop.

Image Interpolation Anti-aliases the printed appearance of a low-resolution image.

Saving files in Photoshop DCS format (Photoshop)

DCS (Desktop Color Separations) format is a version of EPS that lets you save color separations of CMYK or multichannel files.

To save a file in Photoshop DCS format:

1 Save the artwork, and choose Photoshop DCS 1.0, or Photoshop DCS 2.0 from the Format menu. (See "Saving files" on page 365.)

2 In the DCS Format dialog box, select the options you want, and click OK.

The dialog box includes all the options available for Photoshop EPS files. For more information, see "Saving files in Photoshop EPS format (Photoshop)" on page 367. Additionally, the DCS menu gives you the option of creating a 72-ppi composite file that can be placed in a page layout application or used to proof the image:

- DCS 1.0 format creates one file for each color channel in the CMYK image. You can also create a fifth file: a grayscale or color composite. To view the composite file, you must keep all five files in the same folder.

- DCS 2.0 format retains spot-color channels in the image. You can save the color channels as multiple files (as for DCS 1.0) or as a single file. The single-file option saves disk space. You can also include a grayscale or color composite.

Saving files in GIF format (Photoshop)

You can use the Save As command to save RGB, indexed-color, grayscale, or Bitmap-mode images directly in GIF format.

Note: You can also save an image as one or more GIF files using the Save for Web command (Photoshop) or the Save Optimized command (ImageReady). For more information on optimizing images, see "Optimizing images" on page 333.

To save a file in GIF format:

1 Save the artwork, and choose CompuServe GIF from the Format menu. (See "Saving files" on page 365.)

2 For RGB images, the Indexed Color dialog box appears. Specify conversion options and click OK. For more information, see "Conversion options for indexed-color images (Photoshop)" in online Help.

3 Select a row order for the GIF file, and click OK:

- Normal displays the image in a browser only when download is complete.

- Interlaced displays low-resolution versions of the image in a browser as the file downloads. Interlacing makes download time seem shorter, but it also increases file size.

Saving files in JPEG format (Photoshop)

You can use the Save As command to save CMYK, RGB, and grayscale images in JPEG format. JPEG compresses file size by selectively discarding data. (See "About file compression" on page 373.)

Note: You can also save an image as one or more JPEG files using the Save for Web command (Photoshop) or the Save Optimized command (ImageReady). For more information on optimizing images, see "Optimizing images" on page 333.

To save a file in JPEG format:

1 Save the artwork, and choose JPEG from the Format menu. (See "Saving files" on page 365.)

2 In the JPEG Options dialog box, select the options you want, and click OK.

Matte If the image contains transparency, select a Matte color to simulate the appearance of background transparency.

Image Options To specify the image quality, choose an option from the Quality menu, drag the Quality pop-up slider, or enter a value between 0 and 13 in the Quality text box.

Format Options Select Baseline ("Standard") to use a format recognized by most Web browsers, Baseline Optimized for optimized color and a slightly smaller file size, Progressive to display a series of increasingly detailed scans (you specify how many) as the image downloads. Baseline Optimized and Progressive JPEG images are not supported by all Web browsers.

Size To view the estimated download time, select a modem speed. (The Size preview is only available when Preview is selected.)

Note: Some applications may not be able to read a CMYK file saved in JPEG format. In addition, if you find that a Java application cannot read your JPEG file (in any color mode), try saving the file without a thumbnail preview.

Saving files in Photoshop PDF format (Photoshop)

You can use the Save As command to save RGB, indexed-color, CMYK, grayscale, Bitmap-mode, Lab color, and duotone images in Photoshop PDF format.

To save a file in Photoshop PDF format:

1 Save the artwork, and choose Photoshop PDF from the Format menu. (See "Saving files" on page 365.)

2 In the PDF Options dialog box, select the options you want, and click OK.

Encoding Determines the compression method. (See "About file compression" on page 373.)

Note: Bitmap-mode images are automatically encoded using CCITT compression—the PDF Options dialog box does not appear.

Save Transparency Preserves transparency when the file is opened in another application. (Transparency is always preserved when the file is reopened in Photoshop or ImageReady.) This option is not available if the file contains a spot color channel.

Image Interpolation Anti-aliases the printed appearance of a low-resolution image.

Downgrade Color Profile If you selected ICC Profile (Windows) or Embed Color Profile (Mac OS) for a version 4 profile in the Save dialog box, downgrades the profile to version 2. Select this option if you plan to open the file in an application that does not support version 4 profiles.

PDF Security Specifies security options such as password protection and restricted access to a file's content. Choose 40-bit or 128-bit RC4 encryption for a lower or higher level of security. For more information on PDF security, see Acrobat Help.

Include Vector Data Preserves any vector graphics (such as shapes and type) as resolution-independent objects, ensuring smoother output. When it is selected, you can select the following options:

• Embed Fonts ensures that all fonts used in the file are displayed and printed, even on computers that do not have the fonts installed. Bitmap fonts, fonts that don't allow PDF embedding, substitute fonts, type that uses the faux bold style, and warped type cannot be embedded. Selecting Embed Fonts increases the size of the saved file.

• Use Outlines for Text saves text as paths. Select this option if embedding fonts results in a file that is too large, if you plan to open the file in an application that cannot read PDF files with embedded fonts, or if a font fails to display or print correctly. Text saved as outlines is not searchable or selectable in a PDF viewer. You can, however, edit the text when you reopen the file in Photoshop.

Note: The PDF viewer may display a substitute font if both Embed Fonts and Use Outlines for Text are deselected.

Saving files in PNG format (Photoshop)

You can use the Save As command to save RGB, indexed-color, grayscale, and Bitmap-mode images in PNG format.

Note: You can also save an image as one or more PNG files using the Save for Web command (Photoshop) or the Save Optimized command (ImageReady). For more information on optimizing images, see "Optimizing images" on page 333.

To save a file in PNG format:

1 Save the artwork, and choose PNG from the Format menu. (See "Saving files" on page 365.)

2 Select an Interlace option:

• None displays the image in a browser only when download is complete.

• Interlaced displays low-resolution versions of the image in a browser as the file downloads. Interlacing makes download time seem shorter, but it also increases file size.

3 Click OK.

Saving files in TIFF format

TIFF is a flexible bitmap image format supported by virtually all paint, image-editing, and page-layout applications.

To save a file in TIFF format (Photoshop):

1 Save the artwork, and choose TIFF from the Format menu. (See "Saving files" on page 365.)

2 In the TIFF Options dialog box, select the options you want, and click OK.

Image Compression Specifies a method for compressing the composite image data. (See "About file compression" on page 373.)

Byte Order Photoshop and most recent applications can read files using either byte order. However, if you don't know what kind of program the file may be opened in, select the platform on which the file will be read.

Save Image Pyramid Preserves multiresolution information. Photoshop does not provide options for opening multiresolution files; the image opens at the highest resolution within the file. However, Adobe InDesign and some image servers provide support for opening multiresolution formats.

Save Transparency Preserves transparency as an additional alpha channel when the file is opened in another application. (Transparency is always preserved when the file is reopened in Photoshop or ImageReady.)

Layer Compression Specifies a method for compressing data for pixels in layers (as opposed to composite data). Many applications cannot read layer data and will skip over it when opening a TIFF file. Photoshop, however, can read layer data in TIFF files. Although files that include layer data are larger than those that don't, saving layer data alleviates the need to save and manage a separate PSD file to hold the layer data. For more information on RLE and ZIP compression, see "About file compression" on page 373. Choose Discard Layers and Save a Copy to flatten the image.

Note: To have Photoshop prompt you before saving an image with multiple layers, select Ask Before Saving Layered TIFF Files in the File Handling section of the Preferences dialog box.

To save a file in TIFF format (ImageReady):

1 Choose File > Export Original, and choose TIFF from the format list.

2 Specify a filename and location, and click Save.

3 Select a compression method, and click OK. (See "About file compression" on page 373.)

Exporting images in ZoomView format (Photoshop)

ZoomView is a format for delivering high-resolution images over the Web. With the Viewpoint Media Player, users can zoom into or out of an image and pan the image to see its various parts.

When you export an image in ZoomView format, Photoshop creates the following files:

- An MTX file that defines the image to be displayed.
- An HTML file that loads the Viewpoint Media Player and points to the MTX file.
- A folder containing tiles that are used to display the image.
- A folder containing VBS and JavaScript scripts that are used by the HTML file.

To export an image in ZoomView format:

1 Choose File > Export > ZoomView.

2 Set the following options, and click OK:

Template Specify a template for generating the MTX, HTML, and auxiliary files. Choose a preset template from the pop-up menu, or choose Load to choose a different ZoomView Template (ZVT) file. You can download additional templates from the Viewpoint Web site.

Output Location Click Folder to specify an output location. Enter a name in the Base Name text box to specify a common name for the files.

Path to Broadcast License File Specify a URL for the broadcast license file. The Viewpoint Corporation requires that all publishers of ZoomView content acquire a broadcast license. To apply for a key, click Get License.

Image Tile Options ZoomView technology uses image tiling to load only the part of a high-resolution image that a user wants see. Select a Tile Size to control how many pixels are in each tile. A tile size of 128 is recommended for small images; a tile size of 256 is recommended for large images.

To specify an amount of compression for each tile image, choose an option from the Quality menu, drag the Quality pop-up slider, or enter a value between 0 and 13 in the Quality text box. Select Optimize Tables to create enhanced JPEGs with slightly smaller file sizes. This option is recommended for maximum file compression.

Browser Options Specify a width and height for the image in the Viewpoint Media Player. Select Preview in Browser to launch your default Web browser and load the generated HTML file after you click OK.

About file formats

Graphic file formats differ in the way they represent image data (as pixels or as vectors), in compression technique, and in which Photoshop and ImageReady features they support.

For more information on choosing file formats when opening or saving images, see "Opening and importing images" on page 64 and "Saving images" on page 365. For information on choosing a Web optimization format, see "Optimizing images" on page 333.

Note: *If a supported file format does not appear in the appropriate dialog box or submenu, you may need to install the format's plug-in module.*

For more information about specific file formats, see "About file formats" in online Help.

About file compression

Many file formats use compression to reduce the file size of bitmap images. *Lossless* techniques compress the file without removing image detail or color information; *lossy* techniques remove detail. The following are commonly used compression techniques:

RLE (Run Length Encoding)   Lossless compression; supported by some common Windows file formats.

LZW (Lemple-Zif-Welch)   Lossless compression; supported by TIFF, PDF, GIF, and PostScript language file formats. Most useful for images with large areas of single color.

JPEG (Joint Photographic Experts Group)   Lossy compression; supported by JPEG, TIFF, PDF, and PostScript language file formats. Recommended for continuous-tone images, such as photographs. To specify image quality, choose an option from the Quality menu, drag the Quality pop-up slider, or enter a value between 0 and 13 in the Quality text box. For the best printed results, choose maximum-quality compression. JPEG files can be printed only on Level 2 (or later) PostScript printers and may not separate into individual plates.

CCITT   A family of lossless compression techniques for black-and-white images; supported by the PDF and PostScript language file formats. (CCITT is an abbreviation for the French spelling of International Telegraph and Telekeyed Consultive Committee.)

ZIP   Lossless compression; supported by PDF and TIFF file formats. Like LZW, ZIP compression is most effective for images that contain large areas of single color.

PackBits (ImageReady)   Lossless compression that uses a run-length compression scheme; supported by the TIFF file format in ImageReady only.

Adding file information (Photoshop)

File information—also called *metadata*—is increasingly important in all types of publishing. Adobe Photoshop supports the information standard developed by the Newspaper Association of America (NAA) and the International Press Telecommunications Council (IPTC) to identify transmitted text and images. This standard includes entries for captions, keywords, categories, credits, and origins.

In Windows, you can add file information to files saved in Photoshop, TIFF, JPEG, EPS, and PDF formats. In Mac OS, you can add file information to files in any format. The information you add is embedded in the file using XMP (eXtensible Metadata Platform). XMP provides Adobe applications and workflow partners with a common XML framework that standardizes the creation, processing, and interchange of document metadata across publishing workflows.

 For more information, see "Adding file information (Photoshop)" in online Help.

Adding digital copyright information

You can add copyright information to Photoshop images and notify users that an image is copyright-protected via a digital watermark that uses Digimarc PictureMarc technology. The watermark—a digital code added as noise to the image—is generally imperceptible to the human eye. The watermark is durable in both digital and printed forms, surviving typical image edits and file format conversions—and is still detectable when the image is printed and then scanned back into a computer.

Embedding a digital watermark in an image lets viewers obtain complete contact information about the creator of the image. This feature is particularly valuable to image creators who license their work to others. Copying an image with an embedded watermark also copies the watermark and any information associated with it.

 For more information on embedding digital watermarks, see "Adding digital copyright information" in online Help.

Setting preferences for saving files (Photoshop)

In Photoshop, you can set preferences for saving image previews, using file extensions, and maximizing file compatibility.

To set file saving preferences:

1 Do one of the following:

- In Windows and Mac OS 9.x, choose Edit > Preferences > File Handling.

- In Mac OS X, choose Photoshop > Preferences > File Handling.

2 Set the following options:

Image Previews Choose an option for saving image previews: Never Save to save files without previews, Always Save to save files with specified previews, or Ask When Saving to assign previews on a file-by-file basis.

In Mac OS, you can select one or more of the following preview types (to speed the saving of files and minimize file size, select only the previews you need):

- Icon to use the preview as a file icon on the desktop.

- Macintosh Thumbnail to display the preview in the Open dialog box.

- Windows Thumbnail to save a preview that can display on Windows systems.

- Full Size to save a 72-ppi version of the file for use in applications that can only open low-resolution Photoshop images. For non-EPS files, this is a PICT preview.

File Extension (Windows) Choose an option for the three-character file extensions that indicate a file's format: Use Upper Case to append file extensions using uppercase characters or Use Lower Case to append file extensions using lowercase characters.

Append File Extension (Mac OS) File extensions are necessary for files that you want to use on or transfer to a Windows system. Choose an option for appending extensions to filenames: Never to save files without file extensions, Always to append file extensions to filenames, or Ask When Saving to append file extensions on a file-by-file basis. Select Use Lower Case to append file extensions using lowercase characters.

To toggle the Append File Extension option for a single file, hold down Option when you choose a file format in the Save As dialog box.

To display a preview file icon (Windows only):

1 Save the file in Photoshop format with a thumbnail preview.

2 Right-click the file on the desktop (or in any Windows or Photoshop dialog box that displays a file list), and choose Properties from the context menu that appears.

3 Click the Photoshop Image tab.

4 Select an option for generating thumbnails, and click OK.

Preview icons appear on the desktop and in file lists (when the view is set to Large Icons).

Creating multiple-image layouts (Photoshop)

You can export multiple images automatically as contact sheets and picture packages using Automate commands.

Creating contact sheets

By displaying a series of thumbnail previews on a single page, contact sheets let you easily preview and catalog groups of images. You can automatically create and place thumbnails on a page using the Contact Sheet II command.

To create a contact sheet:

1 Choose File > Automate > Contact Sheet II.

2 Under Source Folder, click Choose (Mac OS) or Browse (Windows) to specify the folder containing the images you want to use. Select Include All Subfolders to include images inside any subfolders.

3 Under Document, specify the dimensions, resolution, and color mode for the contact sheet. Select Flatten All Layers to create a contact sheet with all images and text on a single layer. Deselect Flatten All Layers to create a contact sheet where each image is on a separate layer and each caption is on a separate text layer.

4 Under Thumbnails, specify layout options for the thumbnail previews, and click OK.

• For Place, choose whether to arrange thumbnails across first (from left to right, then top to bottom) or down first (from top to bottom, then left to right).

• Enter the number of columns and rows that you want per contact sheet. The maximum dimensions for each thumbnail are displayed to the right, along with a visual preview of the specified layout.

• Select Use Filename As Caption to label the thumbnails using their source image filenames. Use the menu to specify a caption font.

Creating picture packages

With the Picture Package command, you can place multiple copies of a source image on a single page, similar to the photo packages traditionally sold by portrait studios. You can choose from a variety of size and placement options to customize your package layout.

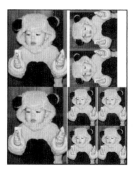

Example of a picture package layout

You can customize and create new layouts for picture packages. For more information, see "Customizing picture package layouts" in online Help.

To create a picture package from a single image:

1 Choose File > Automate > Picture Package.

2 Specify the Source: Frontmost Document to use the currently active image, File to browse to a saved image, or Folder to browse to a folder containing multiple image files. (Select Include All Subfolders to include images inside any subfolders.)

3 Under Document, select page size, layout, resolution, and color mode for the picture package. (A thumbnail of the selected layout is displayed on the right side of the dialog box.)

Select Flatten All Layers to create a picture package with all images and text on a single layer. Deselect Flatten All Layers to create a picture package where each image is on a separate layer and each caption is on a separate text layer.

4 Under Label, select the source for label text from the Content menu (or choose None). Specify font, font attributes, and position for the labels.

5 Click OK.

Placing Photoshop images in other applications (Photoshop)

Photoshop provides a number of features to help you use images in other applications. You can use image clipping paths to define transparent areas in images you place in page-layout applications. In addition, Mac OS users can embed Photoshop images in many word-processor files.

For assistance with image clipping paths, choose Help > Export Transparent Image. This interactive wizard helps you prepare images with transparency for export to a page-layout application.

Using image clipping paths to create transparency

You may want to use only part of a Photoshop image when printing it or placing it in another application. For example, you may want to use a foreground object and exclude the background. An *image clipping path* lets you isolate the foreground object and make everything else transparent when the image is printed or placed in another application.

Image imported into Illustrator without image clipping path, and with image clipping path

To save a path as an image clipping path:

1 Draw a work path that defines the area of the image you want to show. For more information, see "Creating a work path (Photoshop)" on page 148 and "Converting selection borders to paths" on page 165.

Note: *Paths are vector-based; therefore, they have hard edges. You cannot preserve the softness of a feathered edge, such as in a shadow, when creating an image clipping path.*

2 In the Paths palette, save the work path as a path. For more information, see "Managing paths (Photoshop)" on page 163.

3 Choose Clipping Path from the Paths palette menu, set the following options, and click OK:

- For Path, choose the path you want to save.

- For Flatness, leave the flatness value blank to print the image using the printer's default value. If you experience printing errors, enter a flatness value to determine how the PostScript interpreter approximates the curve. The lower the flatness value, the greater is the number of straight lines used to draw the curve and the more accurate the curve.

Values can range from 0.2 to 100. In general, a flatness setting from 8 to 10 is recommended for high-resolution printing (1200 dpi to 2400 dpi), a setting from 1 to 3 for low-resolution printing (300 dpi to 600 dpi).

4 If you plan to print the file using process colors, convert the file to CMYK mode. For more information, see "Converting between color modes (Photoshop)" on page 85.

5 Save the file:

- To print the file using a PostScript printer, save in Photoshop EPS, DCS, or PDF format.

- To print the file using a non-PostScript printer, save in TIFF format and export to Adobe InDesign or to Adobe PageMaker® 5.0 or later.

Note: If you import an EPS or DCS file with a TIFF preview into Adobe Illustrator, the image clipping path transparency may not display properly. This affects the on-screen preview only; it does not affect the printing behavior of the image clipping path on a PostScript printer.

Printing image clipping paths

Sometimes an imagesetter has difficulty interpreting image clipping paths, or a printer finds the image clipping path too complex to print, resulting in a Limitcheck error or a general PostScript error. Sometimes you can print a complex path on a low-resolution printer without difficulty but run into problems when printing the same path on a high-resolution printer. This is because the lower-resolution printer simplifies the path, using fewer line segments to describe curves than does the high-resolution printer.

You can simplify an image clipping path in the following ways:

- Manually reduce the number of anchor points on the path. (See "Adding, deleting, and converting anchor points" on page 162.)

- Increase the tolerance setting used to create the path. To do this, load the existing path as a selection, choose Make Work Path from the Paths palette menu, and increase the tolerance setting (4 to 6 pixels is a good starting value). Then recreate the image clipping path. For more information, see "Converting between paths and selection borders (Photoshop)" on page 164 and "Using image clipping paths to create transparency" on page 377.

Exporting paths to Adobe Illustrator

The Paths to Illustrator command lets you export Photoshop paths as Adobe Illustrator files. This makes it easier to work with combined Photoshop and Illustrator artwork or to use Photoshop features on Illustrator artwork. For example, you may want to export a pen tool path and stroke it to use as a trap with a Photoshop clipping path you are printing in Illustrator. You can also use this feature to align Illustrator text or objects with Photoshop paths.

To use the Paths to Illustrator command:

1 Draw and save a path or convert an existing selection into a path.

2 Choose File > Export > Paths to Illustrator.

3 Choose a location for the exported path, and enter a filename.

4 Click Save.

5 Open the path in Adobe Illustrator as a new file. You can now manipulate the path or use the path to align Illustrator objects.

Note that the crop marks in Adobe Illustrator reflect the dimensions of the Adobe Photoshop image. The position of the path within the Photoshop image is maintained, provided you don't change the crop marks or move the path.

Object linking and embedding (OLE) (Windows only)

Photoshop is an OLE 2.0 server, which means it supports embedding or linking an image in an OLE container application (usually a word-processor or page-layout program). For example, you can insert Photoshop files and selections into other OLE applications such as Adobe PageMaker and Microsoft Word using copy and paste or other methods.

For more information, see "Object linking and embedding (OLE) (Windows only)" in online Help.

Chapter 16: Printing (Photoshop)

Printing is the process of sending your image to an output device. You can print on paper or film (positive or negative), to a printing plate, or directly to a digital printing press.

About printing

Whether you are providing an image to an outside service bureau or just sending a quick proof to a desktop printer, knowing a few basics about printing will make the print job go more smoothly and help ensure that the finished image appears as intended.

Types of printing When you print a file, the Adobe Photoshop application sends your image to a printing device, either to be printed directly onto paper or to be converted to a positive or negative image on film. In the latter case, the film can be used to create a master plate for printing by a mechanical press.

Types of images The simplest types of images, such as line art, use only one color in one level of gray. A more complex image, such as a photograph, has color tones that vary within the image. This type of image is known as a *continuous-tone image*.

Halftoning To create the illusion of continuous tones when printed, images are broken down into a series of dots. This process is called *halftoning*. Varying the sizes of the dots in a halftone screen creates the optical illusion of variations of gray or continuous color in the image.

Color separation Artwork that will be commercially reproduced and that contains more than a single color must be printed on separate master plates, one for each color. This process is called *color separation* and most commonly uses cyan, yellow, magenta, and black (CMYK) inks. In Photoshop, you can adjust how the various plates are generated and create traps.

Quality of detail The detail in a printed image results from a combination of resolution and screen frequency. The higher an output device's resolution, the finer (higher) a screen ruling you can use.

Printing images

Photoshop provides the following printing commands:

- Page Setup and Print display options that are determined by your printer, print drivers, and operating system.

- Print with Preview displays Photoshop's printing, output, and color management options.

- Print One Copy prints one copy of a file without displaying a dialog box.

Note: You cannot print images directly from ImageReady. If you have an image open in ImageReady and need to print it, use the Jump To command to open the image in Photoshop. Keep in mind that ImageReady images open at screen resolution (72 ppi); this resolution may not be high enough to produce a high-quality print.

To print an image with its current options:

Do one of the following:

- Choose File > Print, and click Print or OK.
- To print one copy of a file without displaying a dialog box, choose File > Print One Copy.

Note: By default, Adobe Photoshop prints a composite of all visible layers and channels. To print an individual layer or channel, make it the only visible layer or channel before choosing the Print command.

To set printer and page setup options:

1 Choose File > Page Setup or File > Print.

2 Select an installed printer from the pop-up list at the top of the dialog box.

3 Set additional options, such as paper size and layout, as desired. The available options depend on your printer, print drivers, and operating system.

To set Photoshop print options:

1 Choose File > Print with Preview.

2 Make sure Show More Options is selected. Then do one or more of the following:

- Adjust the position and scale of the image in relation to the selected paper size and orientation. (See "Positioning and scaling images" on page 383.)
- Set output options. (See "Setting output options" on page 384.)
- Click the Screen button then select halftone screen attributes. (See "Selecting halftone screen attributes" on page 386.)
- Set other printing options. (See "Printing part of an image" on page 388, "Choosing a print encoding method" on page 388, and "Printing vector graphics" on page 388.)
- Choose Color Management from the pop-up menu and set color management options. (See "Using color management when printing" on page 388.)

3 Do one of the following:

- Click Print to print the image.
- Click Cancel to close the dialog box without saving the options.
- Click Done to preserve the options and close the dialog box.
- Hold down Alt (Windows) or Option (Mac OS) and click Print One to print one copy of the file.
- Hold down Alt (Windows) or Option (Mac OS) and click Reset to reset the print options.
- Hold down Alt (Windows) or Option (Mac OS) and click Remember to save the print options without closing the dialog box.

To preview the current image position and options:

Position the pointer over the file information box (at the bottom of the application window in Windows or the document window in Mac OS) and hold down the mouse button.

Positioning and scaling images

You can adjust the position and scale of an image and preview how the image will be printed on the selected paper using the Print with Preview command. The shaded border at the edge of the paper represents the margins of the selected paper; the printable area is white.

The base output size of an image is determined by the document size settings in the Image Size dialog box. (See "Changing the print dimensions and resolution of an image (Photoshop)" on page 59.) Scaling an image in the Print with Preview dialog box changes the size and resolution of the printed image only. For example, if you scale a 72 ppi image to 50% in the Print with Preview dialog box, the image will print at 144 ppi; however, the document size settings in the Image Size dialog box will not change.

Many printer drivers, such as AdobePS and LaserWriter, provide a scaling option in the Page Setup dialog box. This scaling affects the size of all page marks, such as crop marks and captions, whereas the scaling percentage provided by the Print with Preview command affect only the size of the printed image (and not the size of page marks).

Important: The Print with Preview command may not reflect accurate values for Scale, Height, and Width if you set a scaling percentage in the Page Setup dialog box. To avoid inaccurate scaling, specify scaling using the Print with Preview command rather than the Page Setup command; do not enter a scaling percentage in both dialog boxes.

To reposition an image on the paper:

Choose File > Print with Preview, and do one of the following:

- Click Center Image to center the image in the printable area.

- Enter values for Top and Left to position the image numerically.

- Deselect the Center Image option then drag the image in the preview area.

To scale the print size of an image:

Choose File > Print with Preview, and do one of the following:

- Click Scale to Fit Media to fit the image within the printable area of the selected paper.

- Enter values for Height and Width to rescale the image numerically.

- Select Show Bounding Box, and drag a bounding box handle in the preview area to achieve the desired scale.

Setting output options

You can select and preview a variety of page marks and other output options using the Print with Preview command.

Page marks
***A.** Gradient tint bar* ***B.** Label* ***C.** Registration marks*
***D.** Progressive color bar* ***E.** Corner crop mark* ***F.** Center
crop mark ***G.** Caption* ***H.** Star target*

To set output options:

1 Choose File > Print with Preview.

2 Select Show More Options, and choose Output from the pop-up menu.

Note: Options not supported by the designated printer are dimmed.

3 Set one or more of the following options:

Background Lets you select a background color to be printed on the page outside the image area. For example, a black or colored background may be desirable for slides printed to a film recorder. To use this option, click Background, and then select a color from the Color Picker dialog box. This is a printing option only; it does not affect the image itself.

Border Lets you print a black border around an image. Type in a number and choose a unit value to specify the width of the border.

Bleed Lets you print crop marks inside rather than outside the image. Use this option when you want to trim the image within the graphic. Type a number and choose a unit value to specify the width of the bleed.

Screen Lets you set the screen frequency and dot shape for each screen used in the printing process. (See "Selecting halftone screen attributes" on page 386.)

Transfer Lets you adjust the transfer functions, traditionally used to compensate for dot gain or dot loss that may occur when an image is transferred to film. This option is recognized only when you print directly from Photoshop, or when you save the file in EPS format and print to a PostScript printer. Generally, it's best to adjust for dot gain using the settings in the CMYK Setup dialog box. Transfer functions are useful, however, when compensating for a poorly calibrated output device.

[?] For more information, see "Compensating for dot gain in film using transfer functions" in online Help.

Interpolation Reduces the jagged appearance of a low-resolution image by automatically resampling up while printing. However, resampling may reduce the sharpness of the image quality. (See "About resampling" on page 57.) Some PostScript Level 2 (or higher) printers have interpolation capability. If your printer doesn't, this option has no effect.

Calibration Bars Prints an 11-step grayscale, a transition in density from 0 to 100% in 10% increments. With a CMYK color separation, a gradient tint bar is printed to the left of each CMY plate, and a progressive color bar to the right.

Note: Calibration bars, registration marks, crop marks, and labels will print only if the paper size is larger than the printed image dimensions.

Registration Marks Prints registration marks on the image (including bull's-eyes and star targets). These marks are used primarily for aligning color separations.

Corner Crop Marks Prints crop marks where the page is to be trimmed. You can print crop marks at the corners.

Center Crop Marks Prints crop marks where the page is to be trimmed. You can print crop marks at the center of each edge.

Caption Prints any caption text entered in the File Info dialog box. (See "Adding file information (Photoshop)" on page 374.) Caption text always prints as 9-point Helvetica plain type.

Labels Prints the filename above the image.

Emulsion Down Makes type readable when the emulsion is down—that is, when the photosensitive layer on a piece of film or photographic paper is facing away from you. Normally, images printed on paper are printed with emulsion up, with type readable when the photosensitive layer faces you. Images printed on film are often printed with emulsion down.

Negative Prints an inverted version of the entire output including all masks and any background color. Unlike the Invert command in the Image menu, the Negative option converts the output, not the on-screen image, to a negative. If you print separations directly to film, you probably want a negative, although in many countries film positives are common. Check with your print shop to determine which is required.

To determine the emulsion side, examine the film under a bright light after it has been developed. The dull side is the emulsion; the shiny side is the base. Check whether your print shop requires film with positive emulsion up, negative emulsion up, positive emulsion down, or negative emulsion down.

Selecting halftone screen attributes

Halftone screen attributes include the screen frequency and dot shape for each screen used in the printing process. For color separations, you must also specify an angle for each of the color screens. Setting the screens at different angles ensures that the dots placed by the four screens blend to look like continuous color and do not produce moiré patterns.

Halftone screens consist of dots that control how much ink is deposited at a specific location on-press. Varying their size and density creates the illusion of variations of gray or continuous color. For a process color image, four halftone screens are used: cyan, magenta, yellow, and black—one for each ink used in the printing process.

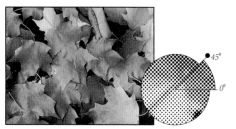

Halftone screen with black ink

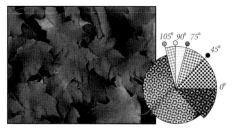

Halftone screens with process ink at different screen angles; correctly registered dots form rosettes

In traditional print production, a halftone is produced by placing a halftone screen between a piece of film and the image and then exposing the film. In Photoshop, you specify the halftone screen attributes just before producing the film or paper output. For best results, your output device (a PostScript imagesetter, for example) should be set to the correct density limit, and your processor should be properly calibrated; otherwise, results can be unpredictable.

Before creating your halftone screens, check with your print shop for preferred frequency, angle, and dot settings. (Use the default angle settings unless your print shop specifies changes.)

To define the screen attributes:

1 Choose File > Print with Preview.

2 Select Show More Options, choose Output from the pop-up menu, and click Screen.

3 In the Halftone Screens dialog box, choose whether to generate your own screen settings:

- Deselect Use Printer's Default Screens to choose your own screen settings.

- Select Use Printer's Default Screens to use the default halftone screen built into the printer. Photoshop then ignores the specifications in the Halftone Screens dialog box when it generates the halftone screens.

4 For a grayscale halftone, enter a screen frequency from 1 to 999.999, and choose a unit of measurement. Enter a screen angle from −180 to +180 degrees.

5 For a color separation, choose from the following options:

- To manually enter the screen frequency and angle, choose a color of the screen for Ink, and enter the frequency and angle; repeat for each color separation.

- To have Adobe Photoshop determine and enter the best frequencies and angles for each screen, click Auto. In the Auto Screens dialog box, enter the resolution of the output device and the screen frequency you intend to use, and click OK. Photoshop enters the values in the Halftone Screens dialog box. Changing these values may result in moiré patterns.

- If you are using a PostScript Level 2 (or higher) printer or an imagesetter equipped with an Emerald controller, make sure that the Use Accurate Screens option is selected in the Auto Screens dialog box (or in the Halftone Screens dialog box if you're entering the values manually). The Use Accurate Screens option lets the program access the correct angles and halftone screen frequencies for high-resolution output. If your output device is not a PostScript Level 2 (or higher) printer or is not equipped with an Emerald controller, this option has no effect.

6 For Shape, choose the dot shape you want. If you want all four screens to have the same dot shape, select Use Same Shape For All Inks.

Choosing Custom from the Shape menu displays the Custom Spot Function dialog box. You can define your own dot shapes by entering PostScript commands—useful for printing with nonstandard halftone algorithms. For information about using PostScript language commands, see the *PostScript Language Reference* published by Addison-Wesley, or consult the imagesetter's manufacturer.

For optimal output on a PostScript printer, the image resolution should be 1.5 to 2 times the halftone screen frequency. If the resolution is more than 2.5 times the screen frequency, an alert message appears. (See "About image size and resolution" on page 54.) If you are printing line art or printing to a non-PostScript printer, see your printer documentation for the appropriate image resolutions to use.

7 Click OK.

To save halftone screen settings:

In the Halftone Screens dialog box, click Save. Choose a location for the saved settings, enter a filename, and click Save.

To save the new settings as the default, hold down Alt (Windows) or Option (Mac OS), and click the —> Default button.

To load halftone screen settings:

In the Halftone Screens dialog box, click Load. Locate and select the settings, and click Load.

To return to the original default settings, hold down Alt (Windows) or Option (Mac OS), and click <—Default.

Printing part of an image

You can use the Print Selected Area option to print a specific part of an image.

To print part of an image:

1 Use the rectangle marquee tool to select the part of an image you want to print.

2 Choose File > Print with Preview, select Print Selected Area, and click Print.

Choosing a print encoding method

By default, the printer driver transfers binary information to PostScript printers; however, you can choose to transfer image data using JPEG or ASCII encoding These options are not available to non-PostScript printers such as many inkjet models.

 For more information, see "Choosing a print encoding method" in online Help.

Printing vector graphics

If an image includes vector graphics, such as shapes and type, Photoshop can send the vector data to a PostScript printer. When you choose to include vector data, Photoshop sends the printer a separate image for each type layer and each vector shape layer. These additional images are printed on top of the base image, and clipped using their vector outline. Consequently, the edges of vector graphics print at the printer's full resolution, even though the content of each layer is limited to the resolution of your image file.

To print vector data:

1 Choose File > Print with Preview.

2 Select Show More Options, and choose Output from the pop-up menu.

3 Select Include Vector Data.

Using color management when printing

Different devices operate within different color spaces—for example, your monitor operates in a different color space than your printer, and different printers have different color spaces. The color management options provided by the Print with Preview command let you change the color space of an image while printing, to get a more accurate color printout. (Depending on the designated printer and print drivers on your computer, these options may also appear in the Print dialog box.)

To use color management when printing, you first specify the source color space containing the colors you want to send to your printer. This space may be the document's current color profile (if you want the printout to match how the document appears on-screen), or it may be the current proof profile (if you want the printout to match your current soft proof). Second, you specify the color space of the printer to which you are sending the document. Specifying the printer space ensures that Photoshop has enough information to interpret and reproduce the source colors accurately on the printer.

For example, suppose your document currently uses an RGB profile, and you want to use your desktop printer to proof the colors as they will appear on an offset press. To do this, set up a proof profile for the press color space. (See "Soft-proofing colors" on page 97.) Then print the document using the proof profile as the source space and the desktop printer profile as the printer space.

To color-manage a document while printing:

1 Choose File > Print with Preview.

2 Select Show More Options and choose Color Management from the pop-up menu.

3 Select an option for Source Space:

• Select Document to reproduce document colors as interpreted by the profile currently assigned to the document.

• Select Proof to reproduce document colors as interpreted by the current proof profile. This option is useful for generating hard proofs of your soft-proof settings. (See "Soft-proofing colors" on page 97.)

4 Under Print Space, choose an option for Profile:

• Choose the profile that matches the color space of your printer to print using that printer space.

• Choose Same As Source to print using the source space profile. No additional conversions will be performed on the colors of the document when it is printed.

• Choose PostScript Color Management to send the document's color data, along with the source space profile, directly to a PostScript Level 2 or higher printer (Level 3 or higher for CMYK images) and have colors managed at the level of the printer. The exact results of the color conversion can vary among printers. Choose this option only if you are printing remotely, if you are printing an RGB EPS file, or if you do not have a profile of the printer's color space. To proof a CMYK image on a PostScript Level 2 printer, choose the Lab Color option.

5 Under Print Space, for Intent, choose a rendering intent to use when converting colors to the destination profile space.

 For more information, see "Specifying a rendering intent" in online Help.

Creating color traps

With CMYK images, you can adjust the *color trap*. A trap is an overlap that prevents tiny gaps from appearing in the printed image, due to a slight misregistration on press. In most cases, your print shop will determine if trapping is needed and tell you what values to enter in the Trap dialog box.

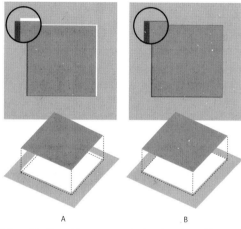

Misregistration with no trap, and misregistration with trap

Trapping is intended to correct the misalignment of solid colors. In general, you don't need traps for continuous-tone images such as photographs. Excessive trapping may produce an outline effect. These problems may not be visible on-screen and might show up only in print. Adobe Photoshop uses standard rules for trapping:

- All colors spread under black.

- Lighter colors spread under darker colors.

- Yellow spreads under cyan, magenta, and black.

- Pure cyan and pure magenta spread under each other equally.

To create trap:

1 Save a version of the file in RGB mode, in case you want to reconvert the image later. Then choose Image > Mode > CMYK Color to convert the image to CMYK mode.

2 Choose Image > Trap.

3 For Width, enter the trapping value provided by your print shop. Then select a unit of measurement, and click OK. Consult your print shop to determine how much misregistration to expect.

Printing duotones

Photoshop lets you create monotones, duotones, tritones, and quadtones. Monotones are grayscale images printed with a single, nonblack ink. Duotones, tritones, and quadtones are grayscale images printed with two, three, and four inks. In these types of images, colored inks are used to reproduce tinted grays rather than different colors. This section uses the term *duotone* to refer to duotones, monotones, tritones, and quadtones.

About duotones

Duotones are used to increase the tonal range of a grayscale image. Although a grayscale reproduction can display up to 256 levels of gray, a printing press can reproduce only about 50 levels of gray per ink. This means that a grayscale image printed with only black ink can look significantly coarser than the same image printed with two, three, or four inks, each individual ink reproducing up to 50 levels of gray.

Sometimes duotones are printed using a black ink and a gray ink—the black for shadows and the gray for midtones and highlights. More frequently, duotones are printed using a colored ink for the highlight color. This technique produces an image with a slight tint to it and significantly increases the image's dynamic range. Duotones are ideal for two-color print jobs with a spot color (such as a PANTONE Color) used for accent.

Because duotones use different color inks to reproduce different gray levels, they are treated in Photoshop as single-channel, 8-bit, grayscale images. In Duotone mode, you do not have direct access to the individual image channels (as in RGB, CMYK, and Lab modes). Instead, you manipulate the channels through the curves in the Duotone Options dialog box.

To convert an image to duotone:

1 Convert the image to grayscale by choosing Image > Mode > Grayscale. Only 8-bit grayscale images can be converted to duotones.

2 Choose Image > Mode > Duotone.

3 In the Duotone Options dialog box, select Preview to view the effects of the duotone settings on the image.

4 Select Monotone, Duotone, Tritone, or Quadtone for Type.

5 To specify ink colors, click the color box (the solid square) for an ink. Then use the color picker or the Custom Colors dialog box to select an ink. (See "Using the Adobe Color Picker" on page 205.)

Note: To produce fully saturated colors, make sure that inks are specified in descending order—darkest at the top, lightest at the bottom.

6 Click the curve box next to the color ink box and adjust the duotone curve for each ink color. (See "Modifying the duotone curve" on page 392.)

7 Set overprint colors, if necessary. (See "Specifying overprint colors" on page 392.)

8 Click OK.

To apply a duotone effect to only part of an image, convert the duotone image to Multi-channel mode—this converts the duotone curves to spot channels. You can then erase part of the spot channel for areas that you want printed as standard grayscale. (See "Adding spot colors (Photoshop)" on page 217.)

Modifying the duotone curve

In a duotone image, each ink has a separate curve that specifies how the color is distributed across the shadows and highlights. This curve maps each grayscale value in the original image to a specific ink percentage.

To modify the duotone curve for a given ink:

1 To preview any adjustments, select the Preview option.

2 Click the curve box next to the ink color box.

The default duotone curve, a straight diagonal line, indicates that the grayscale values in the original image map to an equal percentage of ink. At this setting, a 50% midtone pixel prints with a 50% tint of the ink, a 100% shadow is printed in 100% color, and so on.

3 Adjust the duotone curve for each ink by dragging a point on the graph or by entering values for the different ink percentages.

- In the curve graph, the horizontal axis moves from highlights (at the left) to shadows (at the right). Ink density increases as you move up the vertical axis. You can specify up to 13 points on the curve. When you specify two values along the curve, Adobe Photoshop calculates intermediate values. As you adjust the curve, values are automatically entered in the percentage text boxes.

In the text box, the value you enter indicates the percentage of the ink color that will be used to represent the grayscale value in the original image. For example, if you enter 70 in the 100% text box, a 70% tint of that ink color will be used to print the 100% shadow areas of the image. For more information, see "Using the Curves dialog box" in online Help.

4 Click Save in the Duotone Curve dialog box to save curves created with this dialog box.

5 Click Load to load these curves or curves created in the Curves dialog box, including curves created using the Arbitrary Map option. (See "Saving and loading duotone settings" on page 393.)

You can use the Info palette to display ink percentages when you're working with duotone images. Set the readout mode to Actual Color to see the ink percentages that will be applied when the image is printed. These values reflect any changes you've entered in the Duotone Curve dialog box.

Specifying overprint colors

Overprint colors are two unscreened inks printed on top of each other. For example, when a cyan ink prints over a yellow ink, the resulting overprint is a green color. The order in which inks are printed, as well as variations in the inks and paper, can significantly affect the final results.

To help you predict how colors will look when printed, use a printed sample of the overprinted inks to adjust your screen display. Just remember that this adjustment affects only how the overprint colors appear on-screen, not when printed. Before adjusting these colors, make sure that you have calibrated your monitor following the instructions in "Creating an ICC monitor profile" on page 102.

To adjust the display of overprint colors:

1 Choose Image > Mode > Duotone.

2 Click Overprint Colors. The Overprint Colors dialog box displays the combinations that will result when the inks are printed.

3 Click the color swatch of the ink combination you want to adjust.

4 Select the color you want in the color picker, and click OK.

5 Repeat steps 3 and 4 until the overprint inks appear as you want them. Then click OK.

Saving and loading duotone settings

Use the Save button in the Duotone Options dialog box to save a set of duotone curves, ink settings, and overprint colors. Use the Load button to load a set of duotone curves, ink settings, and overprint colors. You can then apply these settings to other grayscale images.

The Adobe Photoshop application includes several sample sets of duotone, tritone, and quadtone curves. These sets include some of the more commonly used curves and colors and are useful as starting points for creating your own combinations.

Viewing individual printing plates

Because duotones are single-channel images, your adjustments to individual printing inks are displayed as part of the final composite image. In some cases, you may want to view the individual "printing plates" to see how the individual colors will separate when printed (as you can with CMYK images).

To view the individual colors of a duotone image:

1 After specifying your ink colors, choose Image > Mode > Multichannel.

The image is converted to a multichannel image, with each channel represented as a spot-color channel. The contents of each spot channel accurately reflect the duotone settings, but the on-screen composite preview may not be as accurate as the preview in Duotone mode.

Important: *If you make any changes to the image in Multichannel mode, you will be unable to revert to the original duotone state (unless you can access the duotone state in the History palette). To adjust the distribution of ink and view its effect on the individual printing plates, make the adjustments in the Duotone Curves dialog box before converting to Multichannel mode.*

2 Select the channel you want to examine in the Channels palette.

3 Choose Edit > Undo Multichannel to revert to Duotone mode.

Printing duotones

When creating duotones, keep in mind that both the order in which the inks are printed and the screen angles you use dramatically affect the final output.

Click the Auto button in the Halftone Screens dialog box to set the optimal screen angles and frequencies. (See "Selecting halftone screen attributes" on page 386.) Make sure that you select Use Accurate Screens in the Auto Screens dialog box if you're printing to a PostScript Level 2 (or higher) printer or an imagesetter equipped with an Emerald controller.

Note: The recommended screen angles and frequencies for quadtones are based on the assumption that channel 1 is the darkest ink and channel 4 is the lightest ink.

You do not have to convert duotone images to CMYK to print separations—simply choose Separations from the Profile pop-up menu in the Color Management section of the Print dialog box. (See "Printing color separations" on page 394.) Converting to CMYK mode converts any custom colors to their CMYK equivalents.

Exporting duotone images to other applications

To prepare a duotone image for exporting to a page-layout application, save the image in EPS or PDF format (unless the image contains spot channels, in which case you should convert it to Multichannel mode and save it in DCS 2.0 format). Keep in mind that it's important to name custom colors so they'll be recognized by the other application. Otherwise the image won't print correctly—or might not print at all.

Printing color separations

When working with CMYK images or images with spot colors, you can print each color channel as a separate page.

Note: If you are printing an image from another application and want to print spot channels to spot color plates, you must first save the file in DCS 2.0 format. DCS 2.0 preserves spot channels and is supported by applications such as Adobe PageMaker and QuarkXPress®. (See "Saving files in Photoshop EPS format (Photoshop)" on page 367.)

To print separations from Photoshop:

1 Choose File > Print with Preview.

2 Select Show More Options, and choose Color Management from the pop-up menu.

3 Choose Separations from the Profile pop-up menu.

Note: *Depending on the designated printer and print drivers on your computer, these options may also appear in the Print dialog box.*

4 Click Print. Separations are printed for each of the colors in the image.

To prepare an image with spot channels for printing from another application:

1 If the image is a duotone, convert to Multi-channel color mode.

2 Save the image in DCS 2.0 format.

3 In the DCS 2.0 Format dialog box, be sure to deselect the Include Halftone Screen and the Include Transfer Function options. (See "Saving files in Photoshop EPS format (Photoshop)" on page 367.)

4 Open or import the image in the application you will be printing from, and set your screen angles. Make sure that you've communicated to the printer the spot color you want for each of the color plates.

Chapter 17: Automating Tasks

Automating tasks can save you time and ensure consistent results for many types of operations. Adobe Photoshop and Adobe ImageReady provide a variety of ways to automate tasks—using actions, droplets, the Batch command, and task-specific Automate commands.

About actions

An *action* is a series of commands that you play back on a single file or a batch of files. For example, you can create an action that applies an Image Size command to change an image to a specific size in pixels, followed by an Unsharp Mask filter that resharpens the detail, and a Save command that saves the file in the desired format.

Most commands and tool operations are recordable in actions. Actions can include stops that let you perform tasks that cannot be recorded (for example, using a painting tool). Actions can also include modal controls that let you enter values in a dialog box while playing an action. Actions form the basis for droplets, small applications that automatically process all files that are dragged onto their icon.

Action applied to an image

Both Photoshop and ImageReady ship with a number of predefined actions, although Photoshop has significantly more actions than ImageReady. You can use these actions as is, customize them to meet your needs, or create new actions.

Using the Actions palette

You use the Actions palette to record, play, edit, and delete individual actions. This palette also lets you save and load action files.

In Photoshop, actions are grouped into sets—you can create new sets to better organize your actions. (See "Organizing sets of actions (Photoshop)" on page 408.) In ImageReady, you cannot group actions into sets.

To display the Actions palette:

Choose Window > Actions, or click the Actions palette tab if the palette is visible but not active.

By default, the Actions palette displays actions in list mode—you can expand and collapse sets, actions, and commands. In Photoshop, you can also choose to display actions in button mode (as buttons in the Actions palette that play an action with a single mouse click). However, you cannot view individual commands or sets in button mode.

To expand and collapse sets, actions, and commands:

Click the triangle ▷ to the left of the set, action, or command in the Actions palette. Alt-click (Windows) or Option-click (Mac OS) the triangle to expand or collapse all actions in a set or all commands in an action.

To select actions:

Do one of the following:

- Click an action name to select a single action.

- (Photoshop) Shift-click action names to select multiple, discontiguous actions.

- (Photoshop) Ctrl-click (Windows) or Command-click (Mac OS) action names to select multiple, contiguous actions.

To display actions as buttons (Photoshop):

Choose Button Mode from the Actions palette menu. Choose Button Mode again to return to list mode.

Recording actions

Keep in mind the following guidelines when recording actions:

- You can record most—but not all—commands in an action.

- You can record operations that you perform with the marquee, move, polygon, lasso, magic wand, crop, slice, magic eraser, gradient, paint bucket, type, shape, notes, eyedropper, and color sampler tools—as well as those that you perform in the History, Swatches, Color, Paths, Channels, Layers, Styles, and Actions palettes.

In ImageReady, you can drag a command from the History palette to the action in the Actions palette in which you want the command recorded. You cannot drag italicized commands from the History palette to the Actions palette. (Commands in italics are nonactionable.)

- Results depend on file and program setting variables, such as the active layer or the foreground color. For example, a 3-pixel Gaussian blur won't create the same effect on a 72-ppi file as on a 144-ppi file. Nor will Color Balance work on a grayscale file.

- When recording actions that include dialog box and palette settings, keep in mind that only changed settings are recorded. For example, to record an action that sets a particular preference to its current value, you must first change that preference to some other value, and then record the action as you change the preference back to its original value.

- Modal operations and tools—as well as tools that record position—use the units currently specified for the ruler. A modal operation or tool is one that requires you to press Enter or Return to apply its effect, such as the transformation and crop commands. Tools that record position include the marquee, slice, gradient, magic wand, lasso, shape, path, eyedropper, and notes tools.

In Photoshop, when recording an action that will be played on files of different sizes, set the ruler units to percent. As a result, the action will always play back in the same relative position in the image.

- You can record the Play command listed on the Actions palette menu to cause one action to play another.

Creating a new action

When you create a new action, the commands and tools you use are added to the action until you stop recording.

To create a new action:

1 Open a file.

2 In the Actions palette, click the New Action button , or choose New Action from the palette menu.

3 Enter a name for the action.

4 (Photoshop) Choose a set from the pop-up menu.

5 If desired, set one or both of the following options:

- Assign a keyboard shortcut to the action. You can choose any combination of a Function key, the Ctrl key (Windows) or Command key (Mac OS), and the Shift key (for example, Ctrl+Shift+F3).

- (Photoshop) Assign a color for display in Button Mode.

6 Click Record. The Record button in the Actions palette turns red .

Important: *When recording the Save As command, do not change the filename. If you enter a new filename, Photoshop records the filename and uses that filename each time you run the action. Before saving, if you navigate to a different folder, you can specify a different location without having to specify a filename.*

7 Choose the commands, and perform the operations you want to record.

8 To stop recording, click the Stop button, choose Stop Recording from the Actions palette menu, or press the Escape key. To resume recording in the same action, choose Start Recording from the Actions palette menu.

Recording paths (Photoshop)

The Insert Path command lets you include a complex path (a path created with a pen tool or pasted from Adobe Illustrator) as part of an action. When the action is played back, the work path is set to the recorded path. You can insert a path when recording an action or after it has been recorded.

Note: Playing actions that insert complex paths may require significant amounts of memory. If you encounter problems, increase the amount of memory available to Photoshop.

To record a path:

1 Do one of the following:

• Start recording an action.

• Select an action's name to record a path at the end of the action.

• Select a command to record a path after the command.

2 Select an existing path from the Paths palette.

3 Choose Insert Path from the Actions palette menu.

If you record multiple Insert Path commands in a single action, each path will replace the previous one in the target file. To add multiple paths, record a Save Path command using the Paths palette after recording each Insert Path command.

Inserting stops

You can include stops in your action that let you perform a task that cannot be recorded (for example, using a painting tool). Once you've completed the task, click the Play button in the Actions palette to complete the task. You can insert a stop when recording an action or after it has been recorded.

You can also display a short message when the action reaches the stop. For example, you can remind yourself what needs to be done before continuing with the action. A Continue button can be included in the message box. This lets you check for a certain condition in the file (for example, a selection) and continue if nothing needs to be done.

To insert a stop:

1 Choose where to insert the stop:

• Select an action's name to insert a stop at the end of the action.

• Select a command to insert a stop after the command.

2 Choose Insert Stop from the Actions palette menu.

3 Type the message you want to appear.

4 (Photoshop) If you want the option to continue the action without stopping, select Allow Continue.

5 Click OK.

Setting modal controls

A *modal control* pauses an action so that you can specify values in a dialog box or use a modal tool. You can only set modal controls for actions that launch dialog boxes or activate modal tools. If you do not set a modal control, dialog boxes do not appear when you play the action, and you cannot change the recorded values.

A modal control is indicated by a dialog box icon ▣ to the left of a command, action, or set in the Actions palette. Actions and sets in which some, but not all, available commands are modal display a red dialog box icon ▣. In Photoshop, you must be in list mode—not button mode—to set a modal control.

To set a modal control:

Do one of the following:

- Click the box to the left of the command name to display the dialog box icon. Click again to remove the modal control.

- To turn on or disable modal controls for all commands in an action, click the box to the left of the action name.

- (Photoshop) To turn on or disable modal controls for all actions in a set, click the box to the left of the set name.

Excluding commands

You can exclude commands that you don't want to play as part of a recorded action. In Photoshop, you must be in list mode—not button mode—to exclude commands.

To exclude or include a command:

1 To expand the listing of commands in an action, click the triangle to the left of the action you want to work with.

2 Click the check mark to the left of the specific command you wish to exclude; click again to include the command. To exclude or include all commands in an action, click the check mark to the left of the action name.

When you exclude a command, its check mark disappears. In addition, the check mark of the parent action turns red to indicate that some of the commands within the action are excluded.

Inserting nonrecordable commands (Photoshop)

The painting and toning tools, tool options, view commands, and window commands cannot be recorded. However, many commands that cannot be recorded can be inserted into an action using the Insert Menu Item command.

An inserted command is not executed until the action is played, so the file remains unchanged when the command is inserted. No values for the command are recorded in the action. If the command has a dialog box, the dialog box appears during playback, and the action pauses until you click OK or Cancel. You can insert a command when recording an action or after it has been recorded.

Note: When you use the Insert Menu Item command to insert a command that opens a dialog box, you cannot disable the modal control in the Actions palette.

To insert a menu item in an action:

1 Choose where to insert the menu item:

- Select an action's name to insert the item at the end of the action.

- Select a command to insert the item at the end of the command.

2 Choose Insert Menu Item from the Actions palette menu.

3 With the Insert Menu Item dialog box open, choose a command from its menu.

4 Click OK.

Specifying an output folder (ImageReady)

You can specify the folder in which images are placed after actions are performed.

Note: In Photoshop, you can set an output folder when using the Batch command to process files. (See "Using the Batch command (Photoshop)" on page 408.)

To specify an output g:

1 Select the action for which you want to specify an output folder in the Actions palette.

2 Choose Insert Set Output Folder from the Actions palette menu.

3 Select a folder, and click OK.

Recording image size options (ImageReady)

Resizing images is a typical step in preparing irregularly sized images for use on the Web. You can automate this task by creating an action that includes the Image Size command. ImageReady provides several options that give you control over how an action resizes images.

To record Image Size options:

1 Start recording an action.

2 Choose Image > Image Size, and enter the desired image dimensions. (See "Changing the pixel dimensions of an image" on page 59.)

3 Select Action Options.

4 Choose an option from the Fit Image By menu:

- Width to constrain proportions using the new width value.

- Height to constrain proportions using the new height value.

- Width & Height to constrain proportions using either the new width value or the new height value.

- Percent to constrain proportions using the new percent value.

5 Select Do Not Enlarge to prevent images that are smaller than the new dimensions from being sized up.

6 Click OK and continue recording the action.

Inserting optimization settings for selected slices (ImageReady)

When you record a Save Optimized action step, ImageReady includes optimization settings for the entire image. You can insert optimization settings for individual slices using the Insert Set Optimization Settings command.

To insert optimization settings in an action:

1 Select the slice or slices for which you want to record optimization settings. (See "Selecting slices" on page 293.)

2 Select the action in which you want to insert the optimization settings.

3 Do one of the following:

• Choose Insert Set Optimization Settings to *current file format* from the Actions palette menu. (The command indicates the optimization file format currently applied to the selected slice.)

• Drag the droplet icon ![droplet] from the Optimize palette onto the Actions palette.

Playing actions

Playing an action executes the series of commands you recorded in the active document. You can exclude specific commands from an action or play a single command. If the action includes a modal control, you can specify values in a dialog box or use a modal tool when the action pauses.

Note: *In button mode, clicking a button executes the entire action—though commands previously excluded are not executed.*

To play an action on a file:

1 Open the file.

2 Do one of the following:

• To play an entire action, select the action name, and click the Play button ![play] in the Actions palette, or choose Play from the palette menu.

• If you assigned a key combination to the action, press that combination to play the action automatically.

• To play part of an action, select the command from which you want to start playing, and click the Play button in the Actions palette, or choose Play from the palette menu.

To play a single command in an action:

1 Select the command you want to play.

2 Do one of the following:

• Ctrl-click (Windows) or Command-click (Mac OS) the Play button in the Actions palette.

• Press Ctrl (Windows) or Command (Mac OS), and double-click the command.

To undo an entire action:

Do one of the following:

• (Photoshop) Take a snapshot in the History palette before you play an action, and then select the snapshot to undo the action.

• (ImageReady) Choose Edit > Undo *Action Name*.

Setting playback options (Photoshop)

Sometimes a long, complicated action does not play properly, but it is difficult to tell where the problem occurs. The Playback Options command gives you three speeds at which to play actions, so that you can watch each command as it is carried out.

When working with actions that contain audio annotations, you can specify whether or not the action will pause for audio annotations. This ensures that each audio annotation completes playing before the next step in the action is initiated.

To specify how fast actions should play:

1 Choose Playback Options from the Actions palette menu.

2 Specify a speed:

- Accelerated to play the action at normal speed (the default).

- Step by Step to complete each command and redraw the image before going on to the next command in the action.

- Pause For to enter the amount of time Photoshop should pause between carrying out each command in the action.

3 Select Pause For Audio Annotation to ensure that each audio annotation in an action completes playback before the next step in the action is initiated. Deselect this option if you want an action to continue while an audio annotation is playing.

4 Click OK.

Editing actions

After you record an action, you can edit it in a variety of ways. You can rearrange actions and commands in the Actions palette; record additional commands in an action; rerecord, duplicate, and delete commands and actions; and change action options.

Rearranging actions and commands

You can rearrange actions in the Actions palette and rearrange commands within an action to change their order of execution.

To rearrange actions:

In the Actions palette, drag the action to its new location before or after another action. When the highlighted line appears in the desired position, release the mouse button.

To rearrange commands:

In the Actions palette, drag the command to its new location within the same or another action. When the highlighted line appears in the desired position, release the mouse button.

Recording additional commands

You can add commands to an action using the Record button or the Start Recording command in the Actions palette.

To record additional commands:

1 Do one of the following:

- Select the action name to insert a new command at the end of the action.

- Select a command in the action to insert a command after it.

2 Click the Record button, or choose Start Recording from the Actions palette menu.

3 Record the additional commands.

4 Click the Stop button to stop recording.

◯ *In ImageReady, you can drag a command from the History palette to the Actions palette without clicking the Record button or choosing Start Recording from the Actions palette menu.*

Rerecording and duplicating actions and commands

Rerecording an action or command lets you set new values for it. Duplicating an action or command lets you make changes to it without losing the original version.

To record an action again (Photoshop):

1 Select an action, and choose Record Again from the Actions palette menu.

2 For a modal tool, do one of the following:

- Use the tool differently, and Press Enter (Windows) or Return (Mac OS) to change the tool's effect.

- Press Cancel to retain the same settings.

3 For a dialog box, do one of the following:

- Change the values, and click OK to record them.

- Click Cancel to retain the same values.

To record a single command again:

1 In the Actions palette, double-click the command.

2 Enter the new values, and click OK.

To duplicate an action or command:

Do one of the following:

- Alt-drag (Windows) or Option-drag (Mac OS) the action or command to a new location in the Actions palette. When the highlighted line appears in the desired location, release the mouse button.

- Select an action or command. Then choose Duplicate from the Actions palette menu. The copied action or command appears after the original.

- Drag an action or command to the New Action button at the bottom of the Actions palette. The copied action or command appears after the original.

In Photoshop, you can duplicate sets as well as actions and commands.

Deleting actions and commands

If you no longer need an action or command, you can delete it from the Actions palette.

To delete an action or command:

1 In the Actions palette, select the action or command you want to delete.

2 Delete the action or command:

• Click the Trash button 🗑 on the Actions palette. Click OK to delete the action or command.

• Alt-click (Windows) or Option-click (Mac OS) the Trash button to delete the selected action or command without displaying a confirmation dialog box.

• Drag the action or command to the Trash button on the Actions palette to delete the selected action or command without displaying a confirmation dialog box.

• Choose Delete from the Actions palette menu.

To delete all actions in the Actions palette (Photoshop):

Choose Clear All Actions from the Actions palette menu.

Changing action options

You can change the name, keyboard shortcut, and button color (Photoshop) for an action in the Action Options dialog box.

To rename an action:

Double-click the action name in the Actions palette and enter a new name.

To change action options:

1 Do one of the following:

• Select the action, and choose Action Options from the Actions palette menu.

2 Type a new name for the action, or change other options. For more information about action options, see "Recording actions" on page 398.

3 Click OK.

Managing actions in the Actions palette

By default, the Actions palette displays predefined actions (shipped with the application) and any actions you create. You can also load additional actions into the Actions palette.

Note: Photoshop actions are not compatible with ImageReady, and vice versa.

Saving and loading actions (Photoshop)

Actions are automatically saved to the Actions Palette folder in the Adobe Photoshop 7.0 Settings folder. If this file is lost or removed, the actions you created are lost. You can save your actions to a separate actions file so that you can recover them if necessary. You can also load a variety of action sets that are shipped with Photoshop.

Note: The default location of the Adobe Photoshop 7.0 Settings folder varies by operating system. Use your operating system's Find command to locate this folder.

To save a set of actions:

1 Select a set.

2 Choose Save Actions from the Actions palette menu.

3 Type a name for the set, choose a location, and click Save.

You can save the set anywhere. However, if you place the file in the Presets/Photoshop Actions folder inside the Photoshop program folder, the set will appear at the bottom of the Actions palette menu after you restart the application.

Press Ctrl+Alt (Windows) or Command+Option (Mac OS) when you choose the Save Actions command to save the actions in a text file. You can use this file to review or print the contents of an action. However, you can't reload the text file back into Photoshop.

To load a set of actions:

Do one of the following:

• Choose Load Actions from the Actions palette menu. Locate and select the action set file, the click Load. (In Windows, Photoshop action set files have the extension .atn.)

• Select an action set from the bottom of the Actions palette menu.

To restore actions to the default set:

1 Choose Reset Actions from the Actions palette menu.

2 Click OK to replace the current actions in the Actions palette with the default set, or click Append to add the set of default actions to the current actions in the Actions palette.

Saving actions (ImageReady)

All actions you create are saved in the ImageReady Actions folder in the Adobe ImageReady 7.0 Settings folder. ImageReady can only access actions that reside in this folder. You add actions to ImageReady by dragging actions into the ImageReady Actions folder on your computer. Because ImageReady does not include a Load Actions command, you must add files to the ImageReady Actions folder manually.

Note: The default location of the Adobe ImageReady 7.0 Settings folder varies by operating system. Use your operating system's Find command to locate this folder.

You can remove actions from ImageReady by dragging the actions out of the ImageReady Actions folder or by using the Delete Action command in the Actions palette menu. Actions you remove by dragging can be saved in another folder. Actions you remove by deleting are removed permanently.

If you add or remove files from the ImageReady Actions palette, you can direct ImageReady to scan the Actions folder for changes and update the Actions palette. (ImageReady scans the Actions folder and updates the Actions palette whenever you launch the application.)

To update the Actions folder:

1 Drag an action file into or out of the ImageReady Actions folder.

2 Choose Rescan Actions Folder from the Actions palette menu.

Organizing sets of actions (Photoshop)

To help you organize your actions, you can create sets of actions and save the sets to disk. You can organize sets of actions for different types of work—such as print publishing and online publishing—and transfer sets to other computers.

Although ImageReady doesn't allow you to create sets, you can manually organize actions in the ImageReady Actions folder. For example, if the Actions palette contains too many actions, create a new folder inside the ImageReady Actions folder and move less-used actions from the ImageReady Actions folder to this new folder. The relocated actions are removed from the palette until you return them to the ImageReady Actions folder.

To create a new set of actions:

1 In the Actions palette, click the New Set button ⬚ , or choose New Set from the palette menu.

2 Enter the name of the set, and click OK.

To move an action to a different set:

In the Actions palette, drag the action to a different set. When the highlighted line appears in the desired position, release the mouse button.

To rename a set of actions:

1 In the Actions palette, choose Set Options from the pop-up menu.

2 Enter the name of the set, and click OK.

Using the Batch command (Photoshop)

The Batch command lets you play an action on a folder of files and subfolders. If you have a digital camera or a scanner with a document feeder, you can also import and process multiple images with a single action. Your scanner or digital camera may need an acquire plug-in module that supports actions. (If the third-party plug-in wasn't written to import multiple documents at a time, it may not work during batch-processing or if used as part of an action. Contact the plug-in's manufacturer for further information.)

When batch-processing files, you can leave all the files open, close and save the changes to the original files, or save modified versions of the files to a new location (leaving the originals unchanged). If you are saving the processed files to a new location, you may want to create a new folder for the processed files before starting the batch.

💡 *For better batch performance, reduce the number of saved history states and deselect the Automatically Create First Snapshot option in the History palette.*

To batch-process files using the Batch command:

1 Choose File > Automate > Batch.

2 For Play, choose the desired set and action from the Set and Action pop-up menus.

3 For Source, choose a source from the pop-up menu:

- Folder to play the action on files already stored on your computer. Click Choose to locate and select the folder.

- Import to import and play the action on images from a digital camera or scanner.

- Opened Files to play the action on all open files.

- File Browser to play the action on the selected files in the File Browser.

4 Select Override Action "Open" Commands if you want Open commands in the action to refer to the batched files, rather than the filenames specified in the action. If you select this option, the action must contain an Open command because the Batch command will not automatically open the source files.

Deselect Override Action "Open" Commands if the action was recorded to operate on open files or if the action contains Open commands for specific files that are required by the action.

5 Select Include All Subfolders to process files in subfolders.

6 Select Suppress Color Profile Warnings to turn off display of color policy messages.

7 Choose a destination for the processed files from the Destination menu:

- None to leave the files open without saving changes (unless the action includes a Save command).

- Save and Close to save the files in their current location, overwriting the original files.

- Folder to save the processed files to another location. Click Choose to specify the destination folder.

8 Select Override Action "Save As" Commands if you want Save As commands in the action to refer to the batched files, rather than the filenames and locations specified in the action. If you select this option, the action must contain a a Save As command because the Batch command will not automatically save the source files.

Deselect Override Action "Save As" Commands if the action contains Save As commands for specific files that are required by the action.

9 If you chose Folder as the destination, specify a file-naming convention and select file compatibility options for the processed files:

- For File Naming, select elements from the pop-up menus or enter text into the fields to be combined into the default names for all files. The fields let you change the order and formatting of the filename parts. You must include at least one field that is unique for every file (for example, filename, serial number, or serial letter) to prevent files from overwriting each other.

- For File Name Compatibility, choose Windows, Mac OS, and UNIX to make filenames compatible with Windows, Mac OS, and UNIX operating systems.

Saving files using the Batch command options always saves the files in the same format as the original files. To create a batch process that saves files in a new format, record the Save As command followed by the Close command as part of your original action. Then choose Override Action "Save In" Commands for the Destination when setting up the batch process.

10 Select an option for error processing from the Errors pop-up menu:

- Stop for Errors to suspend the process until you confirm the error message.

- Log Errors to File to record each error in a file without stopping the process. If errors are logged to a file, a message appears after processing. To review the error file, click Save As and name the error file.

To batch-process using multiple actions, create a new action and record the Batch command for each action you want to use. This technique also lets you process multiple folders in a single batch. To batch-process multiple folders, create aliases within a folder to the other folders you want to process, and select the Include All Subfolders option.

Using droplets

A *droplet* is a small application that applies an action to one or more images that you drag onto the droplet icon: in Photoshop or in ImageReady. You can save a droplet on the desktop or to a location on disk.

Creating a droplet from an action

Actions are the basis for creating droplets— you must create the desired action in the Actions palette prior to creating a droplet. (See "Recording actions" on page 398.)

In ImageReady, you can also create droplets with the Optimize palette, so that you can apply Optimize palette settings to single images or batches of images.

To create a droplet from an action (Photoshop):

1 Choose File > Automate > Create Droplet.

2 Click Choose in the Save Droplet In section of the dialog box, and select a location to save the droplet.

3 Select the desired set and action from the Set and Action menus.

4 Set Play options for the droplet:

- Select Override Action "Open" Commands if you want Open commands in the action to refer to the batched files, rather than the filenames specified in the action. Deselect Override Action "Open" Commands if the action was recorded to operate on open files or if the action contains Open commands for specific files that are required by the action.

- Select Include All Subfolders to process files in subdirectories.

- Select Suppress Color Profile Warnings to turn off display of color policy messages.

5 Select a destination for the processed files from the Destination menu:

- None to leave the files open without saving changes (unless the action included a Save command).

- Save and Close to save the files in their current location.

- Folder to save the processed files to another location. Click Choose to specify the desti- nation folder. Select Override Action "Save As" Commands if you want Save As commands in the action to refer to the batched files, rather than the filenames and locations specified in the action. Deselect Override Action "Save As" Commands if the action contains Save As commands for specific files that are required by the action.

6 If you chose Folder as the destination, specify a file-naming convention and select file compati- bility options for the processed files:

- For File Naming, select elements from the pop-up menus or enter text into the fields to be combined into the default names for all files. Elements include document name, serial number or letter, file creation date, and file extension.

- For File Name Compatibility, choose Windows, Mac OS, and UNIX to make filenames compatible with Windows, Mac OS, and UNIX operating systems.

7 Select an option for error processing from the Errors pop-up menu:

- Stop for Errors to suspend the process until you confirm the error message.

- Log Errors to File to record each error in a file without stopping the process. If errors are logged to a file, a message appears after processing. To review the error file, click Save As and name the error file.

To create a droplet from an action (ImageReady):

1 For best results, make sure that the action contains at least one Set Optimization command. To add a Set Optimization command, adjust the settings in the Optimize palette, and then drag the droplet icon from the Optimize palette onto the part of the Actions palette where you want to add that command.

If you do not add a Set Optimization command to the droplet, ImageReady will process files using the optimization settings in place at the time the droplet was created.

2 Create the droplet:

- Drag the name of the action from the Actions palette onto the desktop. The droplet has the same name as the action it was created from. You can rename the droplet as you do other desktop icons.

- Select an action, and choose Create Droplet from the Actions palette menu. Name the droplet, choose a location where the droplet will be saved, and click Save.

Creating droplets for use on different operating systems

When creating droplets that may be used in both Windows and Mac OS, keep the following compatibility issues in mind:

- When moving a droplet created in Windows to Mac OS, drag the droplet onto the Photoshop icon. Photoshop will launch and update the droplet for use in Mac OS.

- When creating a droplet in Mac OS, use the .exe extension to make droplets compatible with both Windows and Mac OS.

- References to filenames are not supported between operating systems. Any action step that references a file or folder name (such as an Open command, Save command, or adjustment command that loads its settings from a file) will pause and prompt the user for a filename.

Using droplets to process files

To use a droplet, simply drag a file or folder onto the droplet icon: in Photoshop or in ImageReady. If the application you used to create the droplet is not currently running, the droplet launches it.

In ImageReady, you can control droplet processing in the following ways:

- To temporarily pause processing, click Pause. Click Resume to continue the processing.

- To cancel processing, click Stop.

Editing droplets (ImageReady)

In ImageReady, you can edit the commands in a droplet in the same ways you edit the commands in an action. You can also set batch options for a droplet before or after you create it. For example, you can set the droplet to operate in the background during execution, so that you can work in other applications while ImageReady processes images.

To edit a droplet:

1 Double-click the droplet to open the droplet window in ImageReady. The droplet window looks like a simplified version of the Actions palette.

2 Edit the droplet in the same ways you would edit an action:

- Change the order of commands by dragging them in the droplet list.

- Delete commands by dragging them to the Trash button .

- Add a command by dragging a state from the History palette to the area in which you want the command recorded in the droplet window.

To adjust droplet batch options:

1 Do one of the following:

- Before you create the droplet, select an action and choose Batch Options from the Actions palette menu.

- After you create the droplet, double-click the droplet to open the droplet window, and double-click Batch Options at the top of the droplet list.

2 Select Original (same name and folder) to save the original file with the same name and in the same folder.

3 Select Optimized to save an optimized version of the file. Then do any of the following:

- For In, choose the location in which you want to save the optimized file.

- For If Duplicate File Name, choose how and whether to append numbers or letters to indicate the optimized file in cases of duplicate filenames.

- For Modify File Name For, choose whether ImageReady appends or rewrites the filename using Windows, Mac OS, or UNIX file-naming conventions.

4 Select playback options:

- Run In Background to hide ImageReady during droplet execution, so that you can work in other applications while processing takes place. When you select Run In Background, other playback options requiring user input during processing are turned off. ImageReady appears when the droplet completes execution.

Note: ImageReady is not available for creating and modifying current images while background processing is taking place.

- Display Image to show the images as they are being processed.

- Pause Before Save to stop the processing of each image before saving it.

5 Choose error options from the Errors menu:

- Stop to suspend the process until you confirm the error message.

- Skip Step to not process steps in which errors are encountered.

- Skip File to not process files in which errors are encountered.

Using droplets to automate optimization settings (ImageReady)

You can save Optimize palette settings for use on individual images or batches of images by creating a droplet for the settings. The droplet lets you apply the compression settings to an image or batch of images that you drag onto the droplet icon.

To create a droplet for automating Optimize palette settings:

1 With an image displayed in the image window, choose a compression format and desired compression options in the Optimize palette. (See "Optimizing images" on page 333.)

2 Create a droplet:

- Drag the droplet icon 🖱 from the Optimize palette onto the desktop.

The droplet is named with a brief description of the compression settings, including file format and color palette or quality setting information. You can rename the droplet as you do other desktop icons.

- Click the droplet icon on the Optimize palette. Name the droplet, choose a location where the droplet will be saved, and click Save.

- Choose Create Droplet from the Optimize palette menu. Name the droplet, choose a location where the droplet will be saved, and click Save.

  You can add optimization settings to an action by dragging the droplet icon in the Optimize palette to the Actions palette.

Using the Automate commands (Photoshop)

The Automate commands simplify complex tasks by combining them into one or more dialog boxes. Photoshop includes the following commands (third-party companies may provide additional commands):

- Conditional Mode Change changes the color mode of an image to the mode you specify, based on the original mode of the image. Record this command in an action to ensure that images use the correct color mode and avoid generating unwanted error messages.

- Contact Sheet produces a series of thumbnail previews on a single sheet from the files in the selected folder. (See "Creating contact sheets" on page 376.)

- Fit Image fits the current image to the width and height you specify, without changing its aspect ratio.

Note: *This will resample the image, changing the amount of data in the image.*

- Multi-Page PDF to PSD converts each page of a PDF document you select to a separate Photoshop file. (See "Opening and importing PDF files" on page 65.)

- Picture Package places multiple copies of a source image on a single page, similar to the photo packages traditionally sold by portrait studios. (See "Creating picture packages" on page 376.)

- Web Photo Gallery generates a Web site from a set of images—complete with a thumbnails index page, individual JPEG image pages, and navigable links. (See "Creating Web photo galleries (Photoshop)" on page 309.)

To use an automated command:

Choose File > Automate, and then choose any of the commands listed under it.

External automation

Photoshop supports some external automation using OLE Automation (Windows) or AppleScript (Mac OS). Using either of these methods lets you start Adobe Photoshop and execute actions externally.

Using external automation lets you perform such tasks as:

- Having another scriptable application generate a series of files, and having Photoshop batch-process them.

- Having Photoshop batch-process files and save them to your Web site.

- Writing a script that runs an action and then shuts down your computer late at night after you've gone home.

If you have further questions about OLE, contact Microsoft Corporation. For questions about AppleScript, see your Mac OS documentation or contact Apple Computer.

Creating templates for data-driven graphics (ImageReady)

Templates for data-driven graphics streamline how designers and developers work together in high-volume publishing environments.

About data-driven graphics

Data-driven graphics make it possible to produce multiple versions of an image quickly and accurately. Let's say, for example, that you need to produce 500 different Web banners based on the same template. In the past, you had to manually populate the template with data (images, text, and so on). With data-driven graphics, you can use a script referencing a database to generate the Web banners for you.

You can turn any image into a template for data-driven graphics by defining variables for layers in the image. In addition, you can create different sets of variable data to view what your template will look like when it is rendered.

Using variables

You use variables to define which elements in a template are dynamic (changeable). A variable's type corresponds to the type of data you want to change in a template. Visibility variables let you show or hide the content of a layer. Pixel Replacement variables let you replace the pixels in the layer with pixels from another image file. Text Replacement variables let you replace a string of text in a type layer.

Two versions of a Web image based on the same template:
A. *Visibility variable* ***B.*** *Pixel Replacement variable*
C. *Text Replacement variable*

To define variables:

1 In the Layers palette, select a layer for which you want to define variables.

Note: *You cannot define variables for the Background layer.*

2 Choose Image > Variables > Define, or choose Variables from the Layers palette menu.

3 Select one or more types of variables:

- Visibility to show or hide the content of the layer.

- Pixel Replacement to replace the pixels in the layer with pixels from another image file.

Note: You specify the replacement image when you define a data set. (See "Using data sets" on page 417.)

- Text Replacement to replace a string of text in a type layer.

4 If desired, enter names for the variables. Variable names must begin with a letter, under-score, or colon and cannot contain spaces or special characters (except for periods, hyphens, underscores, and colons).

5 For Pixel Replacement variables, click Pixel Replacement Options, and do the following:

- Choose a method for scaling the replacement image: Fit to scale the image to fit within the bounding box (which may leave parts of the bounding box empty); Fill to scale the image to entirely fill the bounding box (which may cause the image to extend beyond the bounding box); As Is to not scale the image; Conform to scale the image non-proportionally to fit within the bounding box.

- Click a handle on the alignment icon ⬚ to choose an alignment for placing the image inside the bounding box.

- Select Clip to Bounding Box to clip areas of the image that do not fit within the bounding box. This option is only available when the Fill replacement method or As Is replacement method is selected.

6 To define variables for an additional layer, choose a layer from the Layer pop-up menu. Repeat Steps 3 through 5.

7 Click OK.

To rename a variable:

1 Choose Image > Variables > Define, or choose Variables from the Layers palette menu.

2 Choose the layer which contains the variable from the Layer pop-up menu.

3 Enter a name in the Name text box. Variable names must begin with a letter, underscore, or colon and cannot contain spaces or special characters (except for periods, hyphens, under-scores, and colons).

Note: If you are using data sets and want to rename a variable globally (in all layers), change the name in the Data Sets section of the Variable dialog box. (See "Using data sets" on page 417.)

To remove variables:

1 Choose Image > Variables > Define, or choose Variables from the Layers palette menu.

2 Choose a layer from the Layer pop-up menu.

3 Deselect one or more variables.

4 Repeat Steps 2 and 3 to remove variables from additional layers, then click OK.

Using data sets

A *data set* is a collection of variables and associated data. You can switch between data sets to upload different data into your template.

To edit the default data set:

1 Do one of the following:

- Choose Image > Variables > Data Sets.

- If the Variables dialog box is open, choose Data Sets from the pop-up menu at the top of the dialog box, or click Next.

- Choose Variables from the Layers palette menu. Then choose Data Sets from the pop-up menu at the top of the dialog box, or click Next.

Note: You must define at least one variable before you can edit the default data set.

2 Select a variable from the Name pop-up menu or the list at the bottom of the dialog box.

3 Edit the variable data:

- For Visibility variables ⧉ , select Visible to show the layer's content or Invisible to hide the layer's content.

- For Pixel Replacement variables ⧉ , click Browse (Windows) or Choose (Mac OS) and select a replacement image file.

- For Text Replacement variables T , enter a text string in the Value text box.

4 Repeat Steps 2 and 3 for every variable in the template.

5 Do one of the following:

- Click the Save Data Set button 🖫 .

- Click OK.

To create a new data set:

1 Click the New Data Set button ⧉ .

2 Edit the variable data, and click the Save Data Set button.

To rename a data set:

Enter a name in the Data Set text box.

To select a data set:

Do one of the following:

- Choose a data set from the Data Set pop-up menu.

- Click the Previous Data Set button ◄ to select the previous set in the list.

- Click the Next Data Set button ▶ to select the next set in the list.

To change the data in a data set:

Select the data set you want to modify, edit the variable data, and click the Save Data Set button.

To delete a data set:

Select the data set you want to delete, and click the Trash button 🗑 .

Previewing data-driven graphics

Preview Document mode lets you preview how a template will look when it is rendered using different sets of data.

To enable or disable Preview Document mode:

Do one of the following:

- Choose Image > Preview Document. A check mark appears next to the command when Preview Document mode is enabled.

- Click the Preview Document button in the tool box.

To preview data-driven graphics:

1 Enable Preview Document mode.

2 In the options bar, choose a data set from the Data Set pop-up menu, click the Previous Data Set button ◀ , or click the Next Data Set button ▶ .

The data changes in the document window.

Saving templates for use with other Adobe products

You can save a template in PSD format for use with other Adobe products, such as Adobe AlterCast (available only in English) and Adobe GoLive 6.0. For example, a GoLive user can place a PSD template in a page layout, bind its variables to a database using dynamic links, and then use AlterCast to generate iterations of the artwork. Likewise, a developer working with AlterCast can bind the variables in the PSD file directly to a database or another data source.

For more information on using PSD templates to create data-driven graphics, see the *Adobe GoLive User Guide*, GoLive online Help, and the *Adobe AlterCast Developer Guide*.

Index

Production Notes

This book was created electronically using Adobe FrameMaker®. Art was produced using Adobe Illustrator, Adobe ImageReady, and Adobe Photoshop. The Minion® and Myriad® families of typefaces are used throughout this book.

Photography

The following photographers and stock agencies have supplied the photographs and artwork seen throughout this book.

CMCD, Inc.
Bike (page 53)

Definitive Stock
Clock (page 140), Cactus (page 267), Trees (page 397)

Eyewire Photography
Bison (page 121), Horse (page 169)

Mirelez/Ross, Inc.
Leaves (page 78)

PhotoDisc, Inc.
Soccer ball (page 377)

Doug Menuez
Olé No Moiré (page 384)

Julieanne Kost
Grapes (page 82), White flower (page 94), Plate (page 114), Flower Jar (page 108), Flower (page 112), Star (page 115), Door (page 172), Teapot (page 158), Pear (page 174), Lion (page 242), Zebra (page 260), Giraffe (page 327)

Kaoru Hollin
Bicycle illustration (page 54)

Karen Tenenbaum
Clock (page 58), Coins (page 56), Coin (page 123), Shell (page 223)

Lisa Milosevich
Country House (page 172)

Michael Dossev
Chair (page 288)